KING LAUDERD

*"He was truly a man of great spirit …
the honour of our Scots Nation …"*

– Robert Law

*"The Hector of the state is the rascal we hate,
And his plots we will treat with derision."*

– Traditional ballad, 'The Earl of Aboyne'

KING LAUDERDALE

THE CORRUPTION
OF POWER

Raymond Campbell Paterson

BIRLINN

First published in 2003 by
John Donald Publishers
and imprint of
Birlinn Limited
West Newington House
10 Newington Road
Edinburgh
EH9 1QS

www.birlinn.co.uk

This edition published in 2006 by Birlinn Limited

ISBN10: 1 84158 481 9
ISBN13: 978 1 84158 481 2

British Library Cataloguing-in-Publication Data
A catalogue record is available from the British Library

Typeset by Initial Typesetting Services, Edinburgh
Printed and bound by MPG Books Limited, Bodmin

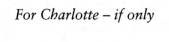

For Charlotte – if only

CONTENTS

LIST OF PLATES

John Maitland, 1st Duke of Lauderdale by John Roettier (1639–1707).

John Maitland, 1st Duke of Lauderdale by Samuel Cooper (1609–72).

John and Elizabeth Maitland, Duke and Duchess of Lauderdale, after Sir Peter Lely.

Edward Hyde, 1st Earl of Clarendon, unknown artist, after Adriaen Hanneman (1601?–1671?).

Anthony Ashley-Cooper, 1st Earl of Shaftesbury, unknown artist (c. 1672–3).

'The Scots Holding their Young King's Nose to the Grindstone', from a pamphlet of 1651.

Ham House from the south, atrrib. Henry Danckerts (late seventeenth century).

Horse Guards' Parade, by Jan Wyck.

John Speed's Kingdom of Scotland, 1662.

Thirlestane Castle.

INTRODUCTION

A MAN FOR ALL SEASONS?

Let us begin by asking a simple question: who was John Maitland? The answer is readily assembled: he was the most significant Scottish politician of the late Stewart age, a man of considerable learning and pronounced ability; he was, in the words of one of his contemporaries 'the greatest Statesman in Europe who is a Schollar, and the greatest Schollar who is a Statesman'.[1] When still in his twenties he was chosen to represent the Church of Scotland as a lay member of the Westminster Assembly, a body set up to consider the question of reform in the English church; he was a leading member of the Committee of both Kingdoms, the prototype for cabinet government in the United Kingdom; he was responsible for negotiating the Treaty of Carisbrooke, sometimes known as the Engagement, an agreement between Charles I and the Scots, designed to save the king and the nation from political extremism. In later life he was Secretary of State for Scotland, one of the most remarkable of all, High Commissioner to the Scottish Parliament, the effective viceroy of Scotland; he was a member of Charles II's 'Cabal', and thus a leading shaper of English foreign policy; and he was the Duke of Lauderdale, the only man who ever enjoyed that title.

The picture is clear, is it not? Who was John Maitland? He was a ruffian, a flatterer and a dissembler, the most dishonest man in the whole 'Cabal', a clown, who danced in petticoats to lift the king out of a depression induced by military defeat; a man to whom it was possible to serve syllabub made out of horse urine, a palace minion rather than a minister of state.[2] He was, in short, a kind of Restoration court jester, the 'king's buffoon and the Caterer of his libidinous pleasures'.[3] He was hated and dreaded in Scotland.[4] No man less honest, Andrew Lang assures us, ever sprang from the House of Lethington, a judgement echoed by W. L. Mathieson, who writes that in him the Maitland tradition was 'blurred and vulgarised almost beyond recognition'.[5] Sir Walter Scott consigns him – 'the crafty Lauderdale' – to his rightful place, carousing with all the other demons of Covenanter

1

mythology at Sir Robert Redgauntlet's hellish banquet.[6] He was an 'uncouth learned savage' with a 'stupid' appearance, though how it is possible to be both learned and savage, and to convey stupidity by appearance alone is, I would imagine, difficult for most people to comprehend.[7]

Any life is bound to convey a number of different, sometimes conflicting impressions; but Lauderdale, perhaps more than any other major figure in British history, has been a victim of assessments that swerve between astonishing extremes, from dark to light and back into dark again. Perhaps there is a certain inevitability to this. He made many enemies during his lifetime, especially in England, where he was largely perceived as an outsider and a threat. He left no party to defend his historical reputation, for he never quite fitted into any political mould: he was a Tory who was at heart a Whig, and a Whig who was in appearance a Tory, if these terms can be used for a man who was neither Whig nor Tory. Above all, he was a Covenanter who was always a royalist, and a royalist who never quite ceased to be a Covenanter. John Graham of Claverhouse, Viscount Dundee, the doyen of the Scottish Cavaliers, saw Lauderdale as the enemy of his party; while on the other extreme Robert Law, a Presbyterian outlaw, and one of the victims of Lauderdale's religious policy, was happy to describe him as 'a man very national, and truly the honour of the Scots nation. . .'[8]

It's unfortunate for Lauderdale's historical reputation that he chose his enemies badly. Although many of his contemporaries, both friends and opponents, were to write positively of his career, the dominant impression of Lauderdale has been left by Edward Hyde, Earl of Clarendon, and, to an even greater extent, by Gilbert Burnet, a Scottish minister who was to become Bishop of Salisbury under William of Orange. Burnet, a self-important busybody, was a one-time protégé of Lauderdale's, who was to be humiliated by him under particularly embarrassing circumstances, and later sought revenge in his 'Memoirs'. The picture he paints of his former patron is among one of his most familiar passages:

> He made a very ill appearance: he was very big; his hair was red, hanging oddly about him: his tongue was too big for his mouth, which made him bedew all that he talked to: and his whole manner was rough and boisterous, and very unfit for a court . . . He was haughty beyond expression; abject to those he saw he must stoop to, but insolent and brutish to all others. He had a violence of passion that carried him often to fits like madness, in which he had no temper. If he took a thing wrong, it was a vain thing to study to convince him: that would rather provoke him to swear that he would never be of another mind: he was to be left

alone, and then perhaps he would have forgot what he had said, and come about of his own accord. He was the coldest friend and the violentest enemy I ever knew: I felt it too much not to know it.[9]

These words, of course, were written many years after Lauderdale's death, at a time when disparagement of the great minister and of Charles II and all his works was a well-established Whig tradition. For a different view one could do no better than consult *A Vindication of the Authority, Constitution and Laws of the Church of Scotland*, published in 1673, with its lavish dedication to Lauderdale, possibly the most unctuous of its kind ever penned, and far too tedious to quote at length. Who was the author? He was the same Gilbert Burnet. He later made a frantic and unsuccessful attempt to suppress all of the extant copies of this work. Public statements and private reflections are, of course, often at variance. The point is that Burnet was under no pressure to write what he did. Lauderdale was to make particularly effective use of this dedication when Burnet was called upon to give evidence against him before the House of Commons, which did much to destroy his credibility as a witness.

The dominant impression left by Burnet and his followers was of an unscrupulous, brutal and arrogant man, which has done much to preclude a proper and balanced assessment of his career. Osmond Airy, the nineteenth-century English historian, mined his way through the endless Lauderdale papers held by the British Museum to produce a three-volume edition of some of the more important documents; but for all his industry he came not one whit closer to understanding the man or his politics. His 1883 paper contained an assessment that does little more than paraphrase Burnet. Lauderdale, he argues, was: 'brutalised ever more and more by the rank excesses of irresponsible power, and lording it over his miserable country for twelve long years, which with senses shattered and reputation gone he sinks into the dreary decadence of his bad and baneful life'.[10]

In considering a portrait of Lauderdale by Sir Peter Lely he adds to this insight by saying that we can see in him: 'the type of all that was coarsest and most brutal among the men of Charles' court; swollen with gluttony, and brutalised by vice, he bears on lip and brow the secure and shameless arrogance which befits the irresponsible proconsul of a distant province, and the privileged comrade in the pleasures of a degraded king'.[11]

This is fairly typical of the Whig view that dominated British historiography for much of the eighteenth and nineteenth centuries, and did so much to obscure a proper understanding of the reign of Charles II. It is perhaps nowhere better represented than in the pages of Lord

Macaulay, who writes of Lauderdale: 'He was . . . the chief instrument employed by the court in the work of forcing episcopacy on his reluctant countrymen; nor did he in that cause shrink from the unsparing use of the sword, the halter and the boot. Yet those who knew him knew that thirty years had made no change in his real sentiments, that he still hated the memory of Charles the First, and that he still preferred the Presbyterian form of church government to every other'.[12]

It would be difficult to parallel such an assessment, so certain and so rich in a deep ignorance of the historical facts. Not content with this, Macaulay tells us elsewhere amongst that endless avalanche of words that once passed for serious historical scholarship that 'The government wanted a ruffian to carry out the most atrocious system of misgovernment with which any nation was ever cursed, to extirpate Presbyterians by fire and sword, by drowning of women, by the frightful torture of the boot. And they found him among the chiefs of the rebellion and the subscribers of the Covenant.'[13]

It's odd that such a monster, contrary to what Burnet alleges, should find solace in the company of relatively modest men, clerics for the most part, who shared his intellectual interests. Apart from Burnet himself, he enjoyed the friendship of Robert Baillie, whom he described with affection as 'the little monk of Kilwinning'; Alexander Henderson, an early associate and a particularly astute judge of character, and Richard Baxter of Kidderminster, whose esteem and respect for Lauderdale was completely misunderstood by Airy. In later life his admirers and defenders included Dr George Hickes, his English chaplain, and Roger North. North was so distressed by the slurs cast on Lauderdale's memory by 'the modern time-serving historians' that he made some small attempt to redress the balance in favour of the 'best and wisest statesman England ever had', without, it has to be said, any lasting success.[14]

For some reason, perhaps associated with the revival of ancient polemics following on from the 1843 schism in the Church of Scotland, the real bile against Lauderdale began to be spooned out in the nineteenth and early twentieth centuries, when many Scottish historians seemingly felt compelled to begin re-fighting old battles in their uniquely partisan way. The renegade Covenanter and perceived suppressor of Presbyterian liberties could expect no mercy from those writing in the Whig tradition. Years after the English historian, S. R. Gardiner, introduced a new spirit of scholarly detachment into his work on the seventeenth century, quite different from that previously practised by Macaulay, J. K. Hewison in his 1913 publication *The Covenanters* was happy to emphasise Lauderdale's 'coarse, negritic features, betokening the brutish forces that lurked beneath', possibly the most tasteless description of a British politician ever written.[15] Losing all grip on reality, another writer was reduced to describing him as 'an emissary of the devil'.[16] However, for an assessment laughable both for its pomposity and shallowness it would be difficult to match John Willcock:

> . . . his personal character was so corrupt and repulsive as to deprive his history of much of the interest which might otherwise have been aroused by his astonishing ability and force of will. To a dispassionate student of human nature, or a theologian in search of illustrations of spiritual degeneracy and depravity, Lauderdale's biography might be one of rare interest and value; but probably the ordinary reader would turn with aversion from a book which announced itself as a record of his career. Perhaps on the whole this is a condition of things which the moralist would not wish to be different.[17]

Having aroused such condescending contempt in the Covenanters, Lauderdale might be expected to have engendered some sympathy amongst the Cavaliers. But for once the two sides seem to have been united. According to Thomas Carlyle, Lauderdale has been pursued through the ages by 'the deep-toned universal sound of curses, not yet become inaudible. . .'[18] Mark Napier, who turned Montrose and Dundee from real historical figures into Scottish versions of Galahad and Parsifal, sees in Lauderdale 'the rankest specimen of that noxious but not unnatural growth of the most zealous and intolerant of covenanters developed into the most bloated and tyrannical royalist'.[19]

The first attempt to create a more balanced assessment of Lauderdale's career came in 1923 with the publication of W. C. Mackenzie's *The Life and Times of John Maitland, Duke of Lauderdale*; but for all his good intentions Mackenzie can hardly be said to have written with much insight or understanding. At some points his assessment descends into the hopelessly pedestrian, and at others he trots out the same kind of specious moral judgements beloved by men like Willcock and Napier. After cutting through some 500 pages one is not that much closer to understanding either the life or the times, and its impact has thus been fairly limited. Writing in the late 1960s K. H. D. Haley, who did so much to rescue the reputation of the first Earl of Shaftesbury, was still able to describe Lauderdale as 'the most repellent politician of his day'.[20] More recently, one of the best assessments of the reign of Charles II persisted in peddling the view of Lauderdale as a zealous Covenanter, which he never was.[21]

Many years ago, when I read Isaac Deutscher's magnificent three-volume account of the life of Leon Trotsky, I remember being struck by a particular image: in attempting to create a true historical picture of his much maligned subject he was obliged, he wrote, to pull him from under a mountain of dead dogs. My own task is different; there are dead dogs piled on Lauderdale's memory, but the materials for an accurate life are freely available: it's simply a question of walking through the door of the mansion without being unduly influenced by the spectres that block the path. What is truly important is not new material but a new way of seeing. But there are dangers that I am only too well aware of. A biographer should have some sympathy with the subject he is investigating, but not to the extent that he compromises his own objectivity. I have no intention of substituting an angel for a devil.

There is indeed a steady process of deterioration in Lauderdale's later career, of action taken in bad temper rather than good judgement. He was fortunate in his choice of friends, and unfortunate in the way he chose to lose them. There is a well-established tendency to date the change in his general outlook to his marriage to Elizabeth Murray, Countess of Dysart, his second wife. She was indeed an important influence, but there were other factors at work, not least of which was the general deterioration in his health, and his growing sense of frustration at his inability to solve the religious problem bequeathed to him at the Restoration. His jealousy of potential rivals underlines a growing sense of personal and political insecurity, which bordered at points on simple paranoia.

The central theme of this book is that there was one Lauderdale, not two, and thus the young idealist was in all essential respects little different from the old conservative. From beginning to end, in the true Machiavellian tradition of his family, he weighed everything politically. He began a search in his early twenties for security; security for Scotland, security for his class and security for Britain, a search that continued for the whole of his career. He began by believing that the best way to achieve this was by limiting the use of royal power; he ended by believing that the only way to achieve it was through its magnification.

The key to Lauderdale's career is thus deceptively simple, although it was beyond the capacity of Airy and all those whose judgement was clouded by the Whiggish tradition to uncover. He was a man true to his times; he was not a democrat, or a crypto-democrat or a populist of any kind. Democracy, for him, was a fearful thing, the bedfellow of anarchy. The forces unleashed by the political crisis of the 1640s, which Lauderdale had unsuccessfully tried to master, could, in the absence of legitimate authority, only be controlled ultimately by military dictatorship, which swept away the liberty of the subject and the rule of law that had always been guaranteed by a tradition of stable royal government. However, it must not be assumed that Lauderdale was a reactionary in the sense that Prince Metternich was at the end of the Napoleonic Wars; he did not try to freeze history, simply to ensure that it travelled down legitimate paths. The royal absolutism with which he is so much associated was, in essence, a device to attempt to introduce some sanity into a religious problem that was spinning out of control.

It is almost impossible to cover all the nuances of Lauderdale's life from the sheer mountain of primary and secondary sources available. This book is not intended as a blow-by-blow account of an enormously varied career; rather it is intended primarily as a political biography, highlighting only those areas most relevant to this central thrust. It might be best to view what follows as an impression, in the manner of a nineteenth-century painting; but impressions can reveal depths of mood and meaning that often escape a more conventional depiction.

This book ends my journey through the seventeenth century that began with the publication of *A Land Afflicted: Scotland and the Covenanter Wars*, and continued through *No Tragic Story: The Fall of the House of Campbell*. It's an endlessly fascinating period in our history, the main currents of which flow through the rich and complex life of John Maitland, second Earl and only Duke of Lauderdale.

RCP
Edinburgh, 2003

1

THE CAMELEON CLAN

Quha does not know the Maitland bluid,
The best in all this land;
In quhalk sumetyme the honour stuid
And worship of Scotland?[1]

In May 1573, under the eyes of a party of English artillerymen, Edinburgh Castle surrendered to the forces of James Douglas, Earl of Morton: the 'lang siege' was over. Among the prisoners were the two most important Scottish politicians of the sixteenth century: William Maitland of Lethington and his younger brother, John Maitland of Thirlestane. The first was the grand-uncle and the second the grandfather of the subject of this book. Lethington's career and life were now drawing to a close; Thirlestane's had yet to begin. Both men were now paying for their exaggerated loyalty to the deposed Queen Mary in the desultory but brutal civil war that had pursued a weary course since the spring of 1570, in opposition to the supporters of her infant son, James VI, now headed by Morton in the post of Regent. The brief noonday glory of the house of Maitland seemed to be over; but in a very real sense it had hardly even begun.

The Maitlands, a family of French descent, first made their appearance on the eastern marches of Scotland in the days of King William the Lion. In 1227 one Thomas Mautelant witnessed a charter in favour of the monks of Melrose.[2] Between 1220 and 1240 the name of another Mautelant or Maitland, William, appears on charters granted to their fellow monks at Kelso. However, the real founder of the family fortunes is generally reckoned to be Sir Richard Maitland – 'Auld Maitland', as he is sometimes known – who acquired lands in Berwickshire by marriage to the daughter and heir of Thomas de Thirlestane, who was killed in 1228.[3] Living so near to England, the family were quickly caught up in the long Border wars, and Sir Richard himself appears as a hero in one of the more minor – and fanciful – of the local poems later collected by Sir Walter Scott.[4] The progress of the family was that of the tortoise rather than the hare, the only significant addition to their territorial power before the Reformation being the lands of Lethington, just to the south of the burgh of Haddington, confirmed in a charter granted by David II in 1345. Two of Lauderdale's ancestors died in battle with the English, at Neville's Cross in 1346 and again at Flodden in 1513.[5] Unlike some of their greater neighbours, who included the Humes, Hepburns and Douglases, the family appear to have been consistently loyal to the crown. In 1621, John Maitland, Lauderdale's father, could look back with justified pride on the conduct of his ancestors 'who, to the fourth generatione, hes had the honour, to be employed in particular service to his Hynes most noble ancestors.'[6]

In many ways the true architect of the later power and prestige enjoyed by the family was Sir Richard Maitland, the father of William and John. He was conservative in outlook and not markedly ambitious. However, unusually for a man of his class, he had a love of books and a marked appreciation of the value of education, which he transmitted to his sons. It was during his time that the family established a definite connection with St Andrews University and possibly also the nearby grammar school at Haddington.[7] Sir Richard was also a poet – not one of any great distinction, it has to be said, although he was well enough thought of by Allan Ramsay, who later commended him in verse.[8] Above all, he appears to have had an air of quiet and unassuming authority, sufficient to earn the respect of many of his contemporaries: Sir Ralph Sadler, an English diplomat, commended his wisdom, and Mary, Queen of Scots thought well enough of him to appoint him keeper of the privy seal for life in December 1562, despite the onset of degenerative blindness.[9]

It was under Sir Richard's guidance that the family, in common with many other lairds, threw off the old Catholic faith and embraced the Protestantism that was sweeping Scotland. Even so, he tended to take a pragmatic and above all a strictly political view of religious questions, which, paradoxically, did nothing to shake the age-old loyalty of the Maitlands to a crown that still adhered to Catholicism, an attitude that he also successfully conveyed to his sons.[10] He remained loyal to Mary of Guise, the Queen-Regent, during the Wars of the Congregation, and was later to greet the arrival of her daughter, Mary, Queen of Scots, in Edinburgh in 1561 with a poem in which he declared himself to be the 'trew servant of thy mother'. Prior to this he tried to preach to the warring factions on the need for some form of political compromise.[11]

The Reformation was to have an impact on the Maitland fortunes far beyond Sir Richard's capacity to understand or to appreciate. He

gave his sons two invaluable things: a good legal education and a distrust
of some of the more exaggerated clerical pretensions now being peddled
by John Knox and his colleagues; but beyond that he would not go.
He was still in outlook very much the minor laird, the country gentleman anxious not to upset the natural order of things, which had long
prescribed a limited political role for men of his class. His own view,
once again committed to poetry, was quite clear – 'To gouerne all and
reull be not our bent.'[12] His sons, for once, spectacularly ignored their
father's advice; they were to ensure that governing all was indeed to be
their bent.

By the late sixteenth century the Scottish state was, by European
standards, still fairly primitive. Problems of government that had been
addressed and settled in England and France during the reigns of
Henry VII and Louis XI were still very much in existence. The Scottish
crown – as opposed to the individuals who wore it – was weak
politically because it was weak economically. Lacking the resources to
pay for a standing army it had always relied on the co-operation of the
senior nobility to enforce its will, a co-operation that could not always
be guaranteed. Moreover, the economic backwardness of the country
had prevented the rise of a politically effective middle class to balance
a dangerously self-interested nobility. The onset of the Reformation,
urged on by the nobility's greed for church land more than its religious
zeal, made the position worse, kicking away the one secure administrative prop of the state. A new type of man was needed, one who
was not motivated by the sectional interests of the great aristocrats,
one who had the patience, the education and the understanding to
work through the complex problems of government, and one who
was able to understand and weigh religious questions in sober political
terms; men, in other words, like the Maitlands.

William Maitland of Lethington, generally known in Scottish history
simply as Lethington, began his political career as a loyal adherent of
his father's teachings. He would weigh and assess all issues in simple
political terms, and follow the course consistent with the interests of
the national community and the state, as he perceived them. Although
a Protestant, his views on religious questions were based on pragmatic
calculation that, unusually for the times, verged at points on simple
cynicism. He was totally dismissive of the theocratic pretensions of
John Knox and his followers. For him the new Presbyterianism was
simply a manifestation of the old Papacy, insofar as both sought to
interfere directly in the affairs of state. Richard Bannatyne, Knox's
secretary, famously described him as the 'Mitchell Wylie' – Machiavelli
– of Scottish politics.[13] This was perhaps a description that Lethington

would not have been too unhappy to accept. Machiavelli's crime, after all, was simply to attempt to describe the real practice of politics free from the ethical and theological fictions in which it had been draped; Lethington's crime was to carry theory into practice. For John Knox, the cynical and worldly-wise Lethington was little better than an atheist.[14] This made little difference to Lethington, who was scathing in his denunciation of Knox's *Book of Discipline* and all attempts at clerical interference in state matters: 'let them bark or blaw alse loude as they list.'[15]

Like his father, Lethington began his political career as an adherent of Mary of Guise, the Catholic Queen Mother, who in 1555 became regent for her daughter Mary, then living in France. There was no surprise in this because the regent, anxious to establish her rule by conciliating all parties, at first pursued a policy of compromise and moderation.[16] Mary, a perceptive and shrewd woman, was soon aware of Lethington's unique political and administrative talents, appointing him to the important post of Secretary. It was a post he made uniquely his own; and as he was once called 'the Great God, the Secretary', it seems appropriate that his is one of those careers in Scottish history where a political office deserves to be written with the initial upper case.

However, in the late 1550s, as Mary turned away from moderation, Lethington, unlike his father, changed allegiance. The Regent's increasingly strident pursuit of orthodox Catholicism was bad enough; but what was far worse was the threat she posed to national freedom. Long survivors of the ancient Border wars, the Maitlands had a deep attachment to the liberty of Scotland. Now the threat came, not from England, but from France. As more and more French troops poured into Scotland to support the Queen Regent, Lethington broke with her and joined the aristocratic confederation known as the Lords of the Congregation in the brief struggle that led up to the victory of the Reformation in 1560. Using his pronounced diplomatic skills, he was able to secure the vital support of Elizabeth of England, who, whatever her commitment to Protestantism, was a deeply conservative and cautious woman.

The Reformation may have been 'necessary business', but it did not alter the Secretary's fundamental allegiance. Soon after Mary, Queen of Scots returned to her native land in the summer of 1561, Lethington attached his star to her train. In doing so he was to make the greatest political miscalculation of his career. Lethington believed that Scotland's future lay in a far closer political union with England, and was thus active in trying to secure Mary's rights as Elizabeth's successor. His well-known contempt for any form of religious enthusiasm was now to blind him to political reality: union, when it came, would not be in the person of the politically inept and emotionally unstable Mary, Queen of Scots, but on the basis of a common Protestant ideology. As Mary stumbled from one self-induced crisis to another the Secretary continued her faithful supporter, only breaking with her briefly over her disastrous marriage to James Hepburn, Earl of Bothwell, generally reckoned to be the murderer of Lord Darnley, her second husband. Even after Mary was deposed and held captive in England, Lethington continued in the belief that Scotland and England could only be united legitimately in her person, an illusion that his younger brother John was induced to share.

John Maitland, though now a generally forgotten figure in Scottish history, was if anything to be even greater than his brother, the Secretary, and far more successful as a politician. Born in about 1545, he too was trained in the law, attending St Salvator's, one of the colleges of St Andrews University.[17] Like his brother, his education was later completed in France.[18] He received his first political appointment when still in his early twenties, when his father resigned the post of keeper of the privy seal in his favour. To the end he remained a loyal follower of the Secretary, learning some important lessons from his eventual political failure.

Almost from the beginning it was reasonably clear that the 'Queen's Men' were on the losing side. Opposed by successive regents, the hopeless cause moved in ever decreasing circles, until only Edinburgh Castle held out for Mary. Both of the Maitland brothers were formally forfeited by Parliament in May 1571, the family estates having already been seized by the Regent Lennox, despite the fact that they still belonged to Sir Richard, who had taken no part in his sons' rebel activities. The 'King's Men' also enjoyed the passive and then the active support of Elizabeth of England, for whom Mary was always a threat. But, true to his convictions, the old Secretary, now seriously ill, continued defiant. John Knox, now himself close to death, launched a last broadside against his old enemy, warning him of the fate that God had in store for him if he continued to adhere to 'that evil cause'. Still dismissive of Knox's assumption of a special relationship with the Almighty, his messenger was instructed to 'go tell Mr Knox that he is but a drytting prophet'.[19]

The walls of Edinburgh Castle were strong enough to defy the curses of Knox, but not Sir William Dury, the provost marshal of Berwick, who came like a modern Joshua in April 1573 with an ample train of English artillery. The surrender followed soon after, and the Secretary, held as a prisoner in Leith, died in early June.

There is something in the career of the Secretary that prefigures that of Lauderdale the following century. Lauderdale, like his grand-uncle, was to come to believe that religious convictions could be made subject of a controlled political calculation. But if the Secretary had to cope with one 'drytting prophet', Lauderdale's prophets were like warriors springing from the dragon's teeth: no sooner had one been dealt with than another dozen appeared. As we shall see, both the Engagement of 1648 and the later attempts at compromise and accommodation were to crash on the reefs of a religious conviction that defied all attempts at political management.

John Maitland's career, as far as could be predicted, was over before it had even begun. Initially a prisoner in Tantallon Castle in Berwickshire he was eventually released into ward, a position which continued for as long as the Regent Morton enjoyed supreme power, which he did for a number of years. But Morton, though an enemy, was also a useful educator: his policy was based on friendship with England abroad and control of the feuding aristocracy and the vociferous and troublesome Kirk at home.[20]

For many years after the Reformation the question of church government had still not been settled with any degree of satisfaction. Whether the church was to be Presbyterian (ruled by church courts), or Episcopal (ruled by bishops), still remained open issues. Morton's solution to this problem was based in one part on political expediency, and in another part on simple greed. A new class of bishops was introduced intended to exercise some degree of discipline and control over the disputatious ministry; but they also provided a useful source of revenue for Morton and his associates.[21] Episcopacy, which had never been an issue of any fundamental importance for Knox and his followers, now declined in popularity under the attacks of the Revd Andrew Melville, a leading reformer of the younger generation, and the most likely author of the *Second Book of Discipline*. Hated by both the nobility and the clergy, Morton, always a grim and rather unapproachable individual, was also hated by the young King James, steadily growing into maturity. Morton's régime shook and then fell. Maitland of Thirlestane's political isolation was now at an end.

From the early 1580s Maitland grew steadily in stature and power. He was never a 'favourite' of a king notorious for a lifelong pursuit of intimate male associates. Favourites came and went; Maitland remained. James was able to recognize talent and political kinship in a man who was determined to elevate the royal prerogative over both church and nobility. His ascent began with his appointment to the Privy Council in August 1583, where his attendance and industry marked him out as a new kind of work horse. His diligence soon made him an essential prop of the new government, and in 1584 he was appointed Secretary of State. Like his brother, he was to make this role uniquely his own, establishing the first fully professional administration in Scottish history, laying the foundations for the kind of royal despotism that had been introduced to England by the Tudors. Although long suspected of harbouring the same political loyalties as Lethington, he had in fact by now outgrown the influence of the old Secretary, and was set to pursue a fairly consistent course, based on the steady magnification of the power of the crown. He was, in the manner of his brother, always to take a pragmatic view of religious questions, but he was careful not to demonstrate the open contempt for clerical pre-tensions that had been such a feature of Lethington's outlook: the ministers would be controlled, though in a far more subtle way.

In 1582 a group of lords, headed by the Earl of Gowrie, worried by Catholic influences at court, seized control of the king at Ruthven Castle, in a kind of Protestant *coup d'état* which came to be known as the Raid of Ruthven. The new administration collapsed within a few months, and the king returned to his rightful place, determined to conclude some unfinished business with the Kirk, suspected of sympathy with the Gowrie faction. Andrew Melville, accused of sedition, took refuge in England, while new clerical statutes, the so-called Black Acts, were brought before Parliament in May 1584. The Black Acts had one simple purpose: to impose the authority of the bishops, and thus that of the king, on a rebel church. One clause, thought to have been drafted by Maitland, announced in clear and unambiguous terms that the king had authority over all persons and causes, which might be said to antici-pate a far grander statement of royal supremacy introduced many years later by his grandson.[22] Anyone who denied the authority of the king and his Privy Council, outlined in the Black Acts, was to be held guilty of treason. These acts, therefore, deserve to be recognised as the first great statement that, while the reformed church might no longer be subordinate to the pope, it was subordinate to the state – a practice that came to be known as Erastianism, after Thomas Erastus, who first defined the concept. Thus begins, it might be said, that long contest between God and Caesar, which was to last for more than a century, and was to have such a profound impact on the life of the future Duke of Lauderdale.

At first many in the Kirk were inclined to resist, but Maitland went to work on the conservative and loyalist leanings of the more moderate among the ministers, separating them off from their more intransigent colleagues, persuading them to accept the authority of the king insofar as it did not conflict with the word of God. Reduced to impotence, the Melville faction raged against Maitland in a libel 'wherein Justice is brought in lamenting, that one of Camelion's clan, one of the disciples of Matchiavell, had so great a place in the commonwealth to the ruin of justice'.[23]

In the years that followed, Maitland continued to perform a valuable service for the king, negotiating a treaty with the English, which survived the execution of Mary, Queen of Scots in February 1587. Bit by bit aristocratic anarchy, which for centuries had done so much to weaken the development of Scottish central government, was brought under control by an efficient and businesslike administration. Under Maitland's guidance, the Parliament of 1587 passed an Act of Annexation, which, amongst other things, allowed for former church lands to be erected into temporal lordships. This created a whole new class – the 'Lords of Erection' – dependent on the goodwill of the government, and thus a valuable political asset. In this fashion was created what might be called a 'nobility of the civil service', men like Maitland himself, hitherto minor lairds or offshoots of the older noble houses, whose fortunes were now tied to the state. One by one these new men began to take the place of the old aristocracy in the government of Scotland. It was obvious to all that a quiet revolution had taken place. In October 1588, William Ashby, the English ambassador, observed that 'the greatest strength of Scotland consisteth in the gentlemen which they here call lairds, and the boroughs which are almost all well affected in religion; therefore the king with these may easily bridle the earls'.[24]

The year 1587 marks the high tide of Maitland's career. He became Chancellor, the first in the century that was not a bishop or a nobleman, with precedence over all other officers of state. As Sir Richard had died the previous year, all of Maitland's property rights were ratified by Parliament: the lordship of Thirlestane, with privileges of regality, the lordship of Musselburgh, the superiority of Leith, his hereditary position as baillie of Lauderdale. In addition to this he was given certain rights over the abbey lands of Kelso, and soon after the barony of Stobo and the lordship of Dunbar.[25]

Inevitably, all of this, as well as his obvious policy of 'belling-the-cat', excited the resentment of the great noble houses, which became especially pronounced after Maitland acquired the chancellorship. Something of the almost unique position Chancellor Maitland had acquired in government can de detected in a public declaration James left behind after setting out for Denmark in October 1589 to meet his future queen, Anne, in a mission that had hitherto been kept as a close secret. It stands as perhaps one of the most remarkable statements ever made by a sovereign about a subject:

> I kepit from the Chancellair as I wes nevir wount to do ony secretis of my wechtyest effearis, twa reasons moving me thairto. First, because I knew that, giff I had maid him on counsail thairoff, he had bene blaimeit of putting it in my heid . . . and thairfor, remembering quhat invyous and injust burding he daile beiris for leading me, be the noyse as it wer, to all his appetitis, as giff I wer ane unreasonable creatur, or a barne [child] that could do nothing of myself.[26]

James took the Chancellor with him to Denmark, supposedly to demonstrate that he approved of this somewhat impetuous journey; in reality it was only the direct presence of the king that guaranteed Maitland's safety from assassination. After he returned to Scotland, James raised Maitland to the peerage as Baron Thirlestane on the occasion of Queen Anne's coronation in May 1590, the only person so honoured; but this did little to mollify the older aristocracy against the intellectually aggressive newcomer, whose whole policy was now so clearly predicated on bringing noble power within the disciplined limits of modern and stable government. Bowes, the English ambassador, was sensitive to the tensions, commenting soon after the coronation on a design 'to draw many noblemen and others into a strong party to provide that the king may govern with his nobility in wonted manner, and not by private persons hated . . . against the ancient rights and privileges of the nobility'.[27]

Despite traditional aristocratic resentment, Maitland was secure for as long as he enjoyed the confidence of the king; nevertheless he was politically isolated, dangerously so. Commanding no party, the relative weakness of his position became evident in early 1592 in the small political earthquake caused by the assassination of the Protestant Earl of Moray by the Catholic Earl of Huntly. James had hitherto shown some favour to Huntly, despite his Catholicism, and, in spite of Maitland's urging, seemed in no particular hurry to avenge the crime. James tended to see Moray not as a victim, but as an ally of the pathologically unstable Francis Stewart, Earl of Bothwell, a man whom the king both feared and hated. Ironically, it was Maitland rather than James who became the object of popular anger. Bothwell launched the onslaught, choosing his target with some care. He clearly could not attack the king, but he undermined the whole drift of royal policy by signalling out Chancellor Maitland, a man he long blamed for his own misfortunes and that of his class. Appealing directly to the ministers of Edinburgh, he accused the Chancellor of being 'the author of all the distress which honest men have sustained within this realm these ten or twelve years bypast'. Case by case Maitland was attacked for his crimes against the Protestant party, with the intention of destroying both the king and his nobility. It was his 'crafty device', Bothwell proceeds, 'to cause . . . every one of us to destroy another; esteeming the destruction . . . of any one of us, should have made him elbow-room, and given the case to a puddock-stool of a night to occupy the place of two ancient cedars'.[28] However, it was James's laxity towards Huntly, rather than Bothwell's attack on Maitland, that weakened the links between church and state, so carefully nurtured by the Chancellor over the years. Nevertheless, no longer secure in his links with the church and under attack by the aristocracy, Maitland did have to leave the court for a time, especially as he had incurred the resentment of Queen Anne, who had long considered him too powerful; but he had not forfeited the confidence of the king.

Anxious to limit the damage caused by the Moray affair, Maitland persuaded the king that the Parliament he intended to summon in late May 1592 should be used to build bridges with the Kirk, best done, he advised, by a partial repeal of the Black Acts of 1584, especially those concerned with the jurisdiction of the bishops, and thus give a limited recognition to Presbyterianism; this was the origin of the so-called Golden Act. The Golden Act was one of history's great conjuring tricks: it promised more by appearance than by substance; it gave unto the church what already belonged to the church, and left with the king what the king already had. The Kirk's Presbyterian structure was recognised, free of the administrative authority of the bishops, with full power of discipline and regulation in those matters having the 'warrant of the word of God'. It did not however abolish Episcopacy: there were still ministers around after 1592 distinguished from their colleagues by the simple fact that they had a vote in Parliament, and thus continued to exercise the traditional political function of the old bishops. Above all, there was no clear line of demarcation between the authority of the church and the authority of the state.

The Golden Act was, in essence, a kind of Trojan Horse: as time would show, the authority of the king was drawn into the Presbyterian citadel. But the gains certainly appeared real enough at the time, and the ministers were grateful to Chancellor Maitland for what they had apparently achieved. It was to be the last great success of his political life.

John, Viscount Maitland, died on 3 October 1595 in Thirlestane Castle. Over the last few years of his life both his health and his political importance had been in steady decline; and in the end, as with another

Chancellor of a different age and time, the king was happy 'to drop the pilot', determined that he should have no successor or equal. Some, the English ambassador included, expected his demise to herald great changes in Scottish government: there were none, which might be said to be the true measure of his success. James wrote a poetic epitaph for Chancellor Maitland; but he voiced the real political epitaph before the English Parliament years later:

> Thus I must say for Scotland and may truly vaunt it: here I sit and govern it with my pen: I write and it is done: and by a Clerk of the Council I govern Scotland now, which others could not do by the sword.[29]

James was by this time also King of England, with the vast increase in power and wealth that this brought. Even so, it was Chancellor Maitland who had provided the means that enabled him 'to govern by pen'. Years later, with no strong guiding hand in Scotland, James's bureaucratic sway over his ancient kingdom began to weaken, all of his English power notwithstanding. The legacy this uncovered was bequeathed to Charles, his son and successor. It would need a new Maitland in quite different circumstances and times to repair the damage caused by Stewart arrogance and complacency, and allow Scotland, once again, to be governed by pen.

Chancellor Maitland has been compared to Thomas Cromwell as one of the great state builders of early modern Europe, and the great moderniser of Scottish administration, which, when he assumed control

> . . . was functioning very feebly indeed; by the time of his death Scotland, for the first time in its history, had an administration that was in some measure professional. By creating this administration, Maitland laid the foundation for that despotism which was to characterize the government of Scotland in the seventeenth century, and which was not finally to be overturned until the revolution of 1688. Many of the political and administrative changes Maitland set in train were not fully visible by the time of his death.[30]

He also worked for the peaceful union of England and Scotland, which came in 1603. By that time the Scotland of James VI was far closer in outward political appearance and administration to the England of Elizabeth I; but by the time James arrived in London England was set to outgrow its absolutist past. James, his head filled with notions of divine right monarchy, failed to grasp one simple fact: later Tudor monarchy had acquired a contractual basis between sovereign and people not evident in the earlier version. Maitland's system had allowed Scotland to catch up with its powerful southern neighbour. Nevertheless, by the time of the Union of the Crowns it was still fifty years or more behind England, politically and constitutionally. There were other problems: the Scottish nobility was quiescent but dangerously under-employed; the church question had lost much of its past bitterness but was still unresolved; the new middle classes, encouraged by Maitland, had been allowed direct access to the levers of power, only to see power evaporate away to the south. All of this was to have a profound impact on the life of Lord John Maitland, the Chancellor's grandson, and the greatest exponent of his political legacy. He was one day to be the new Thomas Cromwell; but a Thomas Cromwell in the court of Henry VIII was one thing; one in the court of Charles II quite another.

2

LORD JOHN MAITLAND

In the summer of 1633 Charles I finally arrived in Edinburgh for his long overdue Scottish coronation. He had succeeded his father James in early 1625, over six years before. On 18 June, the day of the coronation itself, among the six noble youths appointed to carry the pale above the king's head was 17-year-old Lord John Maitland, in what was to be the first recorded act of his long public life.[1]

John, Lord Maitland, the future Duke of Lauderdale, was born on 24 May 1616 just south of the burgh of Haddington in the house of Lethington, later to be renamed Lennoxlove. He was the eldest surviving son of John Maitland, second lord Thirlestane by his marriage to Isobel Seton, second daughter of Alexander Seton, Earl of Dunfermline, who, like the Lord Maitland's grandfather, had been Chancellor of Scotland. Isobel Seton was to die, aged 44, in November 1638, one of the most fateful years in Scottish history, having given birth to some fifteen children in all, of whom four sons and seven daughters predeceased her.[2]

Lord Thirlestane was to be a kind of parenthesis in Maitland family history, sandwiched between a great father and an even greater son, which has inevitably meant that he has been cast somewhat unfairly into the shadow.[3] He was, however, that invaluable asset to any emergent family – a good man of business. During his time the Maitlands continued to accumulate land and wealth, consolidating their position as the first among the gentry of Lauderdale. By the time he was created Earl of Lauderdale in March 1624 the family were a fully established part of the Scottish aristocracy, having long emerged from the role of minor lairds. King James, mindful of the service of Chancellor Maitland, continued to favour his son: in 1612 he was named as one of the commissioners to Parliament; in 1615 he was appointed to the Privy Council, and in 1618 he became a Lord of Session, one of the most senior positions in the Scottish legal system. Although he was removed from this position shortly after the accession of Charles I, he was still a well-respected figure, and was even rumoured as a likely candidate for the post of Lord Chancellor as late as 1630.[4] Years later, with Scotland in the grip of political crisis, James Marquis of Hamilton, Charles' chief agent in Scotland, was to commend his loyalty and integrity to a king in desperate need of friends – 'As for Lauderdale he is a man of no great power; but he is truly honest and most rightly set in all that concerneth your service'.[5]

His reputation for businesslike efficiency was to be of service to his family many years after his death. In 1650, with the English army occupying much of south-east Scotland, Lauderdale's son, the second earl, buried the Maitland charters and deeds for safe-keeping. When these documents were eventually recovered water damage made them all illegible. Establishing a proper legal title to the family estates could have been both costly and time consuming, but for a detailed list of all of the papers prepared by the first earl, which was accepted as a valid record by the Scottish Parliament in 1661, an unusual step which was justified by a reference in the Act to the fact that ' . . . it is notour [well known] that the said Earl . . . was an understanding nobleman of eminent and unquestionable integrity'.[6]

Conservative and cautious in his political leanings, he was always content to follow rather than shape events. His obvious talents could possibly have allowed him to achieve more. However, like so many others, his ambitions, such as they were, are likely to have been frustrated by the relative absence of opportunity for Scottish noblemen after the Union of the Crowns. Lauderdale, moreover, was never the complete yes-man and accomplished courtier that Charles preferred.[7] Besides, Charles tended to favour deracinated Scots like Hamilton and the Duke of Lennox, pleasant in manner but limited in ability. Lauderdale, like his son, was later to become a Covenanter, but it appears to have been a path he took with no great conviction or enthusiasm, unlike some of his fellow nobles. His attitude towards religion, so far as one can tell from the limited sources available, seems to have been firmly within the pragmatic Maitland tradition, which he successfully conveyed to his son and heir.

John Maitland's position in the family hierarchy was confirmed at an early age when he received a royal grant to the lands belonging to the old abbey of Haddington in the Parliament of 1621; the real gift conferred by his father was altogether more significant.[8] True to the Maitland family tradition, considerable care was taken over John's education, which was later to enable him to make use of his ample talents. We cannot be sure about his early schooling, though it is possible that, like other members of his family, he attended Haddington

Grammar School; he was certainly later to attend St Andrews University, his name appearing on the register for 1631.[9] There is no evidence on the course of Lord Maitland's studies, although it is likely to have included some reading in law. But his real talent appears to have been in languages, both classical and modern, so it is reasonable to assume that he must have had some early and extremely thorough tuition. Like most schoolboys and university entrants he would have to have had a good grounding in Latin; but more unusually he also had a knowledge of Greek and, most unusual of all, Hebrew.[10] Of the modern languages we know he was fluent in French, and possibly also had a working knowledge of Spanish and Italian.[11] In later life, when presented with an honorary degree by Cambridge University, he replied to the oration in fluent Latin, perhaps to the astonishment of the assembled dons.[12]

Hand-in-hand with his knowledge of languages came a lifelong love of books and learning. In early 1628 his friend, Alexander Lindsay, made reference in a letter to his father to 'a little kist [chest] with some bonie books, as my Lord Maitland hath'.[13] In 1644, when he was in London as a member of the Committee of Both Kingdoms, at a time of great political tension, he found time to begin a letter to a contact in Scotland with a discussion about books.[14] Later, as a state prisoner of Cromwell's Protectorate, he was to spend time corresponding with the Revd Richard Baxter of Kidderminster, a leading English Presbyterian, on theological and philosophical issues; he was also of some service to Baxter in translating French treatises.[15] According to Gilbert Burnet, he read a great deal of divinity, as well as ancient and modern history; his Hebrew bible, moreover, appears to have been a source of comfort, even at the height of his power in the court of Charles II, in an atmosphere, it has to be said, not marked for its piety.[16] His library, catalogued after his death, included a 1623 edition of the plays of Shakespeare, a 1640 edition of the works of Ben Jonson, an English edition of Montaigne's *Essays*, as well as some of the books of Samuel Rutherford, including *Lex Rex*, a work outlawed as seditious by his own government.[17] Maitland's depth of knowledge was recognised by his contemporaries, including his enemies, if somewhat grudgingly; and he was later described by one nineteenth-century historian as 'one of the most learned ministers who ever lived'.[18]

The great size of Maitland's library was to be a cause of much concern to Anne Home, his first wife. In one of her last letters to him, she was to write in some alarm about the condition of the house they had shared in Highgate for many years – 'I heir the hous of hyghat is laik to fal, that part of it that my mother buelt . . . your bouks has bine the occasion of it . . . I would desire you that you would caus carie your bouk doune to some of the roums below'.[19]

History has very little to say about Anne Home. She was the younger daughter of Alexander, first Earl of Home, a neighbour of the Maitlands, and married Lord John when they were both very young.[20] Marriages of this kind were, of course, matters of profit and calculation; it was an entirely secondary consideration if the people involved had any feelings for one another. This was a good match, though not quite so profitable as the Earl of Lauderdale and his son may have hoped.[21] Over time, Lady Anne and Lord John appear to have acquired some mutual regard, largely born of habit; there is very little evidence of any real depth of affection between them. Marriage to John Maitland was far from being a comfortable or settling experience; owing to the nature of the times and his career they were to spend quite significant periods living apart. She was to be of some use to him, particularly during his long imprisonment in England after 1651, when the whole burden of managing the family's disastrous financial affairs fell on her. However, as far as we can tell, they were far from being intellectual equals. Lord Maitland was eventually to seek solace in the company of more formidable women, who included Lady Margaret Kennedy, the daughter of the staunchly Presbyterian Earl of Cassillis, with whom he carried on a prolonged and intimate correspondence and, above all, Elizabeth Murray, who was eventually to cause a permanent breach between him and his wife. In the end, after he had in effect formally separated from Anne, he was to receive the news of her final illness and death with a detachment bordering on indifference.[22]

Lord and Lady Maitland had three children: a daughter, Isobel, who was born in September 1635 and died shortly afterwards; a son, whose passage through life was so brief that not even his name is recorded, and another daughter, Mary.[23] Lady Mary Maitland was eventually to marry Lord Yester, the eldest son of Lauderdale's close political ally, John Hay, second earl and first marquis of Tweeddale. The marriage was celebrated in London in December 1666, when a witness recorded sourly: 'She is very homely and like a monkey, clothed in gold and silver. He seemeth to deserve such a wife and no more'.[24] Lauderdale's relationship with his daughter, like that with his wife, never seems to have been particularly close. Later, under the influence of Elizabeth Murray, he was effectively to disinherit both her and his own grandchildren.

All of his life, Lauderdale was to have an interest in the occult, inspired at an early age by the case of Margaret Lumsden, an uneducated woman from Duns in Berwickshire, whose apparent spiritual possession in 1630 enabled her to speak in Latin. This caused sufficient sensation at the time for her eventually to be examined with all solemnity before the Privy Council.[25] Young John became aware of the facts from listening to a conversation between his father and the minister of Duns, conveying the details almost thirty years later, when he was a prisoner at Windsor, to Richard Baxter, who later published them in his *Certainty of the World of Spirits*.[26] Even so, unlike many of his contemporaries, he was to maintain a healthy and detached scepticism in such matters, which he demonstrated when, his formal education completed, he set out in 1637 on a mini version of the grand tour, which took him to France and Switzerland. When in Paris in the spring of that year he heard of the possession of the Loudon nuns, and decided to investigate the matter at first-hand. With his formidable intellect and his sense of rational detachment, he quickly became aware that the whole thing was little better than an elaborate hoax: 'Into the chapel I came in the morning of a holy day, and with as little prejudice as any could have, for I believed verily to have seen strange signs; but when I had seen exorcising three or four of them in the chapel, and could hear nothing but wanton wenches singing bawdy songs in French, I began to suspect a fourbe [trick] . . .'

He then spoke to a Jesuit priest who tried to convince him of the truth of the possession. To test this Lord Maitland asked if he could speak to the devils himself, saying that he would use a strange language – possibly the Hebrew that he had mastered. When asked by the priest what language this would be, all Maitland would say was that 'neither he nor all those devils should understand me'. Suspecting a trick, the priest replied disingenuously 'These devils have not travelled.' Maitland laughed.[27]

This experience notwithstanding, he maintained a close interest in the whole question of demonic possession. When temporarily exiled in the Low Countries in 1649 he heard of another case – also a group of women – this time in Antwerp. What he saw was a group of portly Flemish matrons with some audible gastric problems: 'So if these were devils, they were windy devils, but I thought they were only possessed of a morning's draft of too new beer'.[28]

Maitland also used his first trip to the Continent to expand his mental horizons, making the acquaintance of some leading Catholic intellectuals, again demonstrating that his mind had not been enthralled by the narrow Calvinist doctrine of his native land. His contacts included the humanist, Henry Grotius, who served as the ambassador from Sweden, and Cordesius, a fellow bibliophile, whose library was eventually acquired by Cardinal Mazarin.[29] In Geneva he met the Duc de Rohan, a leading French soldier and Huguenot, who had once served Charles I in the La Rochelle campaign, a diplomatic, military and political fiasco that had marked the outset of his reign. Rohan, still smarting from his experience at La Rochelle, apparently told Maitland that Charles was not to be trusted. It was while he was in Geneva that Lord Maitland received news from Gilbert Burnet's father that was to change the course of his life: the fissures that had long been part of the Scottish religious and political scene were splitting wide open.[30] From this point forward politics was to acquire a commanding position in Maitland's life which was never to be lost.

For two men at least the Golden Act of 1592 was little better than unfinished business: Andrew Melville, for whom it left a full Presbyterian polity unrealised; and for King James himself, deprived of a clear Episcopal superstructure, one of the chief props of monarchy. The duelling between the two men, which might be said to echo the much more famous contest between Mary, Queen of Scots and John Knox, came to a head in late 1596, when Melville made an extraordinary assertion in the presence of the king: 'Thair is twa Kings and twa Kingdomes in Scotland. Thair is Christ Jesus the King, and his kingdome, the Kirk, whase subject King James the Saxt is, and of whase kingdome nocht o king, nor a lord, nor a heid, but a member'![31]

The clear implication of this is that if these 'twa kingdomes' did indeed exist they did not do so, in the mind of Melville at least, in a position of perfect equality, which would have been difficult enough for the king to accept; on the contrary, the spiritual kingdom is quite clearly superior to the temporal. Two years later, James published *Basilicon Doron*, a book of kingly advice to his son, Prince Henry, which opens with a sonnet:

> God gives not Kings the stile of Gods in vaine,
> For on his throne his septre doe they sway;
> And as their subjects ought them to obey
> So kings should feare and serve their Gods againe.
> If then ye would enjoy a happie raigne
> Observe the statutes of your heavenlie king,
> And from his house make all your lawes to spring,
> Since his Lieutenant here ye should reacive
> Reward the iust, be steadfast, true and plaine,
> Repress the proude, maintayining aye the right
> Walk always, as euer in his sight.[32]

James went on to define in theory the system of royal government that he and Chancellor Thirlestane had given shape to in Scotland, with a sovereign supreme, by the will of God, over all civil and ecclesiastical matters, in complete freedom from all institutions and subjects; this, in essence, was James' royal declaration of independence – the Divine Right of Kings. Having failed to master the king intellectually, the Melvillians resorted to the more inept tool of political intimidation; but the pro-Presbyterian riots in Edinburgh in 1596 simply played into James' hands. Melville and his faction were politically isolated and, bit by bit, parliamentary and then diocesan Episcopacy put back in place, a design which opened before and continued after the Union of the Crowns in 1603. By 1610 it was as if the Golden Act had never existed.

James had acted with great political skill. Using his prerogative to summon General Assemblies of the church wherever he wished, he chose areas less noted for their radical traditions, and much more amenable to royal authority. But this was only good for as long as his ecclesiastical politics did not impinge on the Calvinist practices of the church; and when they did, even the conservatism of places like St Andrews and Perth was seen to have limits.

James may have succeeded in creating a unified British crown; his ambition to create a unified British state was frustrated, though, at an early stage by the intransigence of both national parliaments. If there was to be no British state, there might at least be a British church: for it was here, in the area of religion, that the royal prerogative was less circumscribed. How was such a model to be defined? For James the answer was immediate and obvious. The Reformation in England had been a partial, state directed process, which allowed the continuation of many older Catholic practices. Above all, the national church was a true mirror to the majesty of the crown. English bishops could, at times, be awkward customers; but nowhere nearly so awkward as Andrew Melville and his adherents, whose preaching frequently became not just impolitic but subversive. Calvinist doctrine was steadily giving way to the softer teachings of the Dutch theologian, Jacob Arminius, which placed a far greater emphasis on free will, so much better suited to circumstances in England than in Scotland, where the struggle between God and man seemed to acquire a harsh immediacy. As if on some kind of missionary work, when James returned to Scotland for a brief visit in 1617, the only one of its kind he ever made after the Union of the Crowns, he brought with him William Laud, then Dean of Gloucester, to demonstrate to the Scots just how seemly the spectacle of religion could be. He also came north with a supplementary task, announced the year before: to introduce a number of innovations which went far beyond those bare issues of church government with which the crown had hitherto concerned itself.

Even against the wishes of John Spottiswoode, Archbishop of St Andrews, who argued that the time for innovation was not yet ripe, James urged on a reluctant northern church five new ceremonies: private baptism, private communion for the sick, kneeling at communion, observance of the principal holy days, and confirmation of children by bishops. A General Assembly held at St Andrews greeted these innovations with so little enthusiasm that the king pointedly urged the ministers to think again, summoning a new Assembly for Perth in 1618. This time he got what he wanted, but with no good grace. The so-called Five Articles of Perth were duly ratified by Parliament in 1621, but only after much arm-twisting. It would not yet be true to say that the monarchy was in a minority of one; but for the first time in years it was dangerously close to this position.

James had one saving feature: frequently drunk on theory, he was always sobered by reality; his divine folly was saved by a little earthly wisdom. When the depth of opposition to the Five Articles, especially kneeling at communion, became known, while refusing to backtrack he made no attempt to ensure that they were uniformly enforced; in other words, established practice became a matter of personal choice. From whatever point of view, the situation was far from satisfactory; and by the time James died in March 1625 the pen no longer governed with its accustomed ease.

James had neither created a unified church nor a unified state; he had simply united disparate political processes in England and Scotland, with the added complication of colonial Ireland. More seriously, there was an undercurrent of opposition to royal policy in both England and Scotland: the English Puritans, silenced within an increasingly Arminian church, but still significant; and the Scottish Presbyterian dissidents given, it might be argued, a new lease by the king himself in the foolish introduction of the Five Articles into a church that gave all the signs of accepting Episcopal government as a permanent state of affairs. James VI and I bequeathed to his successor political and religious problems that would have caused difficulties even for Solomon. Instead of Solomon Britain got Charles I.

So much has been written about this unfortunate and incompetent man that it is difficult to find anything fresh to say. Perhaps the simplest truth is simply stated: he was not bad: he was not even stupid; but he had a bad and stupid conception of monarchy. The job he set out to fill in the spring of 1625 is one of the oddest of all: training, such as it is, was always at the discretion of the incumbent. Charles, of course, up to his twelfth year, had not been expected to be king, a role his older brother Henry was being groomed for, and showed every indication of filling well. Even after the premature death of Henry in 1612 James seems to have made little real attempt to speed up the development of the shy and retiring Charles; amongst other things he was pointedly excluded from the state visit to Scotland in 1617.

Charles, a tiny man, no more than five foot tall, with a life-long stammer, draped himself in majesty as other men drape themselves in armour: to hide the most vulnerable aspects of his personality. For James the Divine Right of Kings had been little more than a theory constantly modified by practice; for Charles the theory was all. The easy informality of the Jacobean court was replaced by a rigid emphasis on protocol. Above all, Charles had almost no skill in handling men or affairs. He had, as Bishop Burnet later expressed it, 'too high a notion of the regal power, and thought that every opposition to it was rebellion'.[33] The irony of Charles' reign is that his opponents in both England and Scotland were almost all conservative, seeking always to re-establish that balance between the crown, church and the common-wealth that had been lost by the arbitrary and ill-advised use of the royal power; Charles turned these men into revolutionaries. In Scotland his reign brought trouble from the very outset, beginning with a wholesale attack on the property rights of every landed family.

In October 1625 Charles introduced an Act of Revocation. Measures of this kind were a fairly common feature of Scottish history, intended to return to the crown all grants of land made during royal minorities. As Charles' own minority was, by seventeenth-century standards, due to run out on 19 November, his twenty-fifth birthday, the measure was introduced with no attempt at consultation. This was bad enough, but far more alarming was the fact that the new revocation was the most sweeping in Scottish history. It was to be backdated to the death of James V in 1542, thus wiping out at a stroke all the lucrative gains in church lands that the nobility had made since the Reformation and before. This would include, of course, Lord John Maitland's grant of the abbey lands at Haddington. It is difficult to overestimate the profound psychological impact the revocation had on the minds of Charles' contemporaries; it was even seriously argued that the right to claw back land grants could extend centuries back into Scottish history, a view that was taken seriously enough for the Court of Session in 1630 to limit its scope to 1455.[34] Charles, of course, intended to do no such thing, and in practice the scope of the revocation was far more limited than its opponents had imagined. Indeed the whole measure had a well-intentioned design: it included, amongst other things, a plan to improve woefully inadequate clerical incomes by establishing them on a sounder fiscal basis. But for the nobility, whose own incomes had been suffering the effects of long-term inflation, the revocation was a matter of serious concern; particularly for the Lords of Erection, the new class that might have been said to have been created by Lord Maitland's grandfather.

In the end the shock of the revocation was far more important than its practical implications. Though no one was forcibly deprived of his lands, few in the Scottish nobility were ever able to trust the king again, and all had been deeply shaken by the proposal. Charles' proposed revolution in property relationships had been, it might be argued, blown in on the cold wind of Continental despotism; if he had had his way title to property would not have been governed by law but subject to royal whim. The alliance between the crown and the nobility that had provided a secure background for James' unpopular ecclesiastical innovations was severely weakened.

Apart from a few Scots courtiers in London, most of the leading men of the realm had never seen the king prior to the coronation of 1633. The occasion was managed with all the splendour that a relatively poor country like Scotland could manage, but even the most enthusiastic royalist could hardly describe it as a great success. The suspicions and fears aroused by the Act of Revocation had been deepened by the time Charles left. He came to Edinburgh, like his father in 1617, accompanied by William Laud, now Bishop of London and soon to be Archbishop of Canterbury. Services were carried out at both Holyrood and St Giles according to the Anglican rite, in the process of being refined, beautified and improved by Laud and his fellow Arminians. The king clearly intended to set an example; for many, it was a simple act of provocation. For Charles the Scottish church offered a poor contrast to its English cousin. He completely failed to understand that it was at least a national church, the one means of self-expression left to a country in danger of being submerged by the Anglo-centric policies that had emerged out of the Union of the Crowns. Having threatened the property rights of the landed classes, and cast doubts on the integrity and teachings of the Scottish Kirk, Charles proceeded to undermine what was left of the political power of the aristocracy.

When the first Parliament of the reign gathered, the bishops were appointed to a prominent position on the Lords of the Articles – a vetting body that screened all legislation to be put before the full assembly. Once legislation was introduced it was not followed by debate in the manner of the English parliament: those in attendance were simply required either to vote for or against. On this occasion a negative vote could easily prove dangerous; for the king himself was present, ostentatiously noting down the names of all those in opposition to his measures. In the course of a single day no fewer than 168 of these were rushed through, including the Revocation, new taxes, and a fresh confirmation of the Five Articles of Perth.

It was quickly made plain that the king would countenance no appeal against any of his measures. Soon after Charles returned to England, William Haig, a prominent Scottish solicitor, drew up a protest against the innovations in ecclesiastical legislation, to be presented as an address to the king. Not only did Charles refuse to hear the petition, but he also ordered the arrest of John Elphinstone, Lord Balmerino, simply for possessing a copy. Haig fled abroad, while Balmerino was charged with treason. The Balmerino trial has been called 'Scotland's ship money case', after the much more famous trial in England of John Hampden for refusing to pay a tax that had no parliamentary authorization.[35] But the Hampden case raised great issues of taxation and representation that were still being fought out over a century later; the Balmerino cast law back to the days prior to *Magna Carta,* when the measure of justice was the will of the king. Balmerino's judges included the Earl of Lauderdale, a position he had been forced into with considerable reluctance. Although a cautious follower of the court party, he acted with considerable integrity, writing to the Marquis of Hamilton of his reluctance to condemn Balmerino, for, as he put it, 'I have not the courage to adventure upon the damnation of my soul'.[36] When the lengthy process finally drew to a close in March 1635 Lauderdale risked royal displeasure by finding Balmerino not guilty on all charges, although he stood condemned by a majority vote.

The whole proceedings aroused such anger that, as a precaution against any attempt to free him, Balmerino was accompanied by a heavy escort each day on his way to the court from his prison in Edinburgh Castle. Public opinion was so violent that John Stewart, Earl of Traquair, a leading member of the Scottish Privy Council, advised strongly against any attempt to have the sentence carried out. Charles reprieved Balmerino, which he no doubt intended to do even without Traquair's advice; but the clumsy attempt to intimidate noble opposition had been a serious error of judgement. Hitherto the king's Scottish policies had created an opposition; the Balmerino trial went beyond this by creating a party. 'My father knew the whole steps of the matter,' Gilbert Burnet later wrote, 'having been the Earl of Lauderdale's most particular friend: he often told me that the ruin of the king's affairs in Scotland was in great measure owing to that prosecution . . . '[37]

During the period of Balmerino's arrest and trial a new threat to the nobles gradually took shape: they were steadily being replaced as the principal power in the land by the bishops, increasingly favoured by the king in filling vacancies on the Privy Council. In 1635 John Spottiswoode, Archbishop of St Andrews, was appointed Chancellor, the highest political office in the land, and the first time a cleric had held the position since well before the Reformation. Many who could normally have expected a position on the Council were left outside in impotent frustration, including James Graham, fifth Earl of Montrose, whose own father had been a member for over twenty years. Charles had in effect created a Privy Council that no longer reflected the true balance of power in the land, and one, moreover, that was deeply divided between secular and clerical interests. Traquair, the Lord Treasurer, was far from pleased by the growing power of the bishops, seeing them as a threat to his own position. Others, most notably Archibald Campbell, Lord Lorne, acting head of one of the most powerful of the Scottish clans, neither liked nor trusted their clerical colleagues. Matters were fine only for as long as the Council was left to deal with routine administrative affairs; the real problem would come when it was forced to face some extraordinary crisis.

James had taken Scotland only part of the way towards a unified British church: Charles decided that it was time to push the matter further. With a self-assurance born of a unique kind of arrogance and political blindness, he made no preparation for this fateful step other than to insist that it should be so. In the worst possible circumstances, having alienated virtually all sections of public opinion in Scotland, beyond the Episcopal party, and not even troubling to consult his own Privy Council, in 1635 he issued a royal warrant authorising a new set of clerical rules – the *Book of Cannons* – to be published the following year. These new rules began by emphasising royal supremacy over the Church of Scotland, and in the most remarkable assertion of this supremacy, required the church to accept a new Liturgy or Service Book – sight unseen – to replace John Knox's *Book of Common Order,* in use since the Reformation.

This Service Book was to be known by contemporaries – and for centuries afterwards – as 'Laud's Liturgy'. In a sense this would appear to be psychologically appropriate, for the simple reason that it expressed a deep sense of national frustration at royal and Anglican arrogance. In reality the book was the work of a panel of Scottish bishops, anxious not to offend the sensibilities of the nation that the straightforward use of the English Prayer Book – Laud's own favoured solution – would have caused. Spottiswoode and at least some of his colleagues were far more sensitive to Scottish opinion than is often supposed. Even so, the circumstances under which the Service Book was conceived and born could not have been worse, leading to all sorts of exaggerated rumours about its contents. In a mood of fearful expectation, the Privy Council managed to delay the first reading of the book to the summer of 1637; but, on the insistence of the king, finally decreed that it would be read on Sunday 23 July, arguably one of the most fateful days in British history.

It would be difficult to exaggerate the mood of fear and excitement that summer. Samuel Rutherford, a Presbyterian dissident exiled to Aberdeen for opposition to the Perth Articles, wrote to his old parishioners in Galloway just ten days before the new book was scheduled to be read, no doubt expressing the feelings of many like-minded people:

> I counsel you to beware of the new and strange leaven of men's inventions, beside and against the word of God, contrary to the oath of this kirk, now coming among you. I instruct you of the superstition of idolatry of kneeling in the instant of receiving the Lord's Supper, and of crossing in baptism, and of obeying of men's days without any warrant for Christ our perfect Lawgiver. Countenance not the surplice, the attire of the mass priest, the garment of Baal's priests. The abominable bowing to alters of tree [wood] is coming upon you. Hate, and keep yourselves from idols. Forbear in any case to hear the reading of the new fatherless Service-Book, full of gross heresie, popish and superstitious errors, without any warrant from Christ, tending to the overthrow of preaching. You owe no obedience to the bastard cannons; they are unlawful, blasphemous and superstitious. All the ceremonies that lie in Antichrist's foul womb, waves of that great mother of fornication, the kirk of Rome, are to be refused.[38]

The truth is that Rutherford and most of his fellow Scots had no idea what the book contained; but that did nothing to stop Dean John Hanna's voice being drowned in curses and catcalls as he attempted a first reading at St Giles, the High Church of Edinburgh, on the Sunday appointed for the purpose. When David Lindsay, the recently appointed bishop of Edinburgh, tried to quieten the unseemly tumult, he was greeted with a variety of epithets, including one accusation that he was the son of the devil and a witch. Like a great wave caused by a rock thrown into a silent pool, the commotion radiated outwards from Edinburgh across the rest of Scotland. James Graham, Earl of Montrose, made the feelings of many of his fellow aristocrats plain when he described the Service Book as emerging from the bowels of the whore of Babylon. Robert Baillie, the minister of Kilwinning in Ayrshire, a future friend and associate of Lord Maitland, expressed the mood of the nation in somewhat more measured terms than Rutherford and Montrose: '. . . there was in our Land never such ane appearance of a sturr; the whole people thinks Poperie at the doores . . . no man may speak for the king's part, except he would have himself marked for a sacrifice to be killed one day. I think our people possessed with a bloody devill, farr above any thing I could ever have imagined . . .'[39]

It was perfectly clear that the Privy Council was well aware of the resentment the reading of the Prayer Book would unleash. In the weeks that followed they were placed in an almost impossible position, caught between the anger of the king and the determination of the opposition; for they were now faced with an opposition, just as determined and just as organised as the Lords of the Congregation had been prior to the Reformation.

Petitions expressing hostility to the king's church policy began to arrive in Edinburgh from many parts of Scotland. Many shared a common theme: the innovations in religion had not been approved by either Parliament or the General Assembly. Faced with this depth of opposition the Council, on its own initiative, suspended the reading of the Liturgy, and made sustained efforts to open the king's mind to the depth of the crisis. True to character, Charles refused to listen. By degrees the political temperature increased. It's almost certain that the whole crisis could have been headed off anytime before the late summer of 1637 by the summoning of an emergency General Assembly, the withdrawal of the Prayer Book, and the cobbling together of some convenient formulae intended to preserve the royal dignity. Charles, however, was not prepared to retreat on any of the issues, choosing to make a stand on his own authority and majesty. This was simply no longer good enough. Before long it was the role of the bishops and the government of the king that were in dispute, not simply the Prayer Book. Charles turned a protest into a rebellion, and then a rebellion into a revolution.

As so often in these situations there appeared to be some kind of fearful dynamic at work that exceeded the motives and expectations of the leading participants. Writing towards the end of 1637 Baillie noted: 'Even if [the king] relent and give way to our supplications, the danger is not passed: We know not where to stand; when the Books of Cannons and Service are burned and away, when the High Commission is down, when the Articles of Perth are made free, when the Bishops' authority is hemmed in with never so many laws; this makes us not secure from their future danger; so whatever the Prince grants, I fear we press more than he can grant'.[40]

By the close of the year government in Scotland was close to paralysis. The bishops, who made up so much of the strength of the Privy Council, were now hunted figures, hardly daring to appear in public. Increasingly the burden of authority fell on Traquair, the Treasurer, a man hardly equal to the terrible task before him. Shortly after the Edinburgh riot he wrote to James, Marquis of Hamilton, Charles' principal Scottish courtier, in a mood of frustration and despair:

> My Lord believe that the delay in taking some certain and resolved courses in this has brought business to such a height and bred such a looseness in this kingdom that I daresay was never since His Majesty's father going into England. The king is not pleased to allow any of us to come to inform him . . . No man stays here to attend or assist the service; and those on whom he lays or seems to entrust his commandments in this business, must turn back upon it whenever any difficulties appear. I am in all things left alone, and God is my witness, never so perplexed what to do. Shall I give way to the people's fury, which without force and the strong hand cannot be opposed? I am calumniated as an underhand conniver. Shall I oppose it with that resolution and power of assistance that such a business requires? It may breed censure and more danger than I dare venture upon, without his majesty's warrant, under his own hand, or from his own mouth.[41]

Like the Soviets in the wings, an alternative authority had already taken shape. That December the various classes of protestors – nobles, ministers, lairds and burgesses – came together to form an executive body known as 'The Tables'. Heading the noble faction were some old opponents of the king, including, amongst others, Balmerino, Montrose, John Leslie, fifth Earl of Rothes, and John Campbell, Lord Loudon. Of all these men, none is perhaps more interesting than Rothes, the last man one would ever expect to head a revolution. His politics were, if anything, narrowly based and reactionary rather than radical and progressive: 'We crave no more but the discharge of the Service-Book, Canons, and High Commission [church court]; that no oath should be taken of Ministers by their ordination but that which is allowed by the Act of Parliament, which gave Bishops the power of ordination . . . and that a General Assembly might be appointed every year . . . and [that] the king would willingly discharge the Acts of Perth'.[42] Loudon is also an interesting case. In years to come he would tend to follow the lead laid down by his kinsman, Lord Lorne, and may on this occasion have been acting as his proxy. Lorne, after all, was still a leading privy councillor, though the role he played throughout the whole crisis was, to say the least, a highly ambiguous one.

The hapless and beleaguered Traquair finally received permission to come to the king early in the new year. He told Charles with com-mendable frankness that he must either abandon the liturgy or come to Scotland with an army of 40,000 men: instead of an army the king gave the Treasurer yet another proclamation. Still believing, after all of the turmoil of the previous year, that a simple assertion of royal authority was enough to dispel the opposition, Charles took the most fateful step of all. He decided to set matters straight: it was he and not Laud or any other bishop who was responsible for the Service Book. There could be no more pretence about 'evil councillors'. Charles was offering a direct challenge to the Tables, fully expecting them to stand down. Sadly for him they did not.

When the new proclamation was read in Edinburgh on 22 February it was greeted with derision, not reverence. In responding to yet another example of royal blindness, the Tables took arguably one of the most important steps in British history. Answer was to be given to the king in the form of an extended address, to be known as the National Covenant. Politics had now moved beyond the private and the limited, beyond areas of compromise and negotiation into the arena of grand historical gestures. The task of drawing up the Covenant, based on biblical precedents and earlier documents of the same kind, was given to Alexander Henderson, the minister of Leuchars in Fife, and a young lawyer by the name of Archibald Johnston of Warriston. Both men went about the task with considerable care. It could not be seen to be too radical, as there were still many ministers, for example, who were not convinced that Episcopacy was contrary to divine law. At its heart lay one simple yet profoundly revolutionary proposition, perhaps not sufficiently recognised at the time: that there should be no innovations in church and state that had not first been tested by free Parliaments and General Assemblies of the church. On 28 February the process of signing the National Covenant began at Greyfriars Church in Edinburgh: it was the death warrant for the divine right of kings. Charles' enemies now acquired a new name – the Covenanters.

Charles had manoeuvred himself into a dangerous dead end. All that could be done by displays of royal displeasure had been done, to little practical effect. From time to time it had been suggested, most recently by Traquair, that the only option left was direct military intervention. However, the prospects for this were not good. Charles had ruled England for eleven years without Parliament, and did not have the resources for a lengthy war with Scotland. Calling a new assembly would uncover serious risks. The early parliaments of the reign had not provided an encouraging or comfortable experience for the king, dominated, as they were, by an able and articulate opposition. These men, insultingly referred to as 'puritans' by their enemies, represented a hard-nosed commercial class that had done very well out of the aggressive and expansionist foreign policy of Elizabeth I, which sought opportunities at the expense of the Spanish Empire. Charles' own early foreign policy had been muddled to the point of almost complete incoherence; even his attempts to intervene on behalf of the French Protestants at La Rochelle had been a disaster, leaving him with a reputation for untrustworthiness, as Rohan told Lord Maitland. Over the years since the last Parliament was dissolved in 1629 the problems had got worse: Catholic influence was strong at court; the growing influence of Laud threatened to upset that balance in the Elizabethan Church of England which had allowed Catholic and Calvinist elements to exist side by side; the various prerogative courts were seen as a threat to the common law of England; and the search for extra parliamentary taxation had caused widespread anxiety, demonstrated in the Ship Money case against John Hampden. Beyond calling Parliament, the only option left for the king was to draw on his existing resources, and to play for time, hoping to divide the opposition in Scotland. He needed a skilful operator, who would be able to draw the various threads of royal policy together. The man chosen for the task of Royal Commissioner was James, Marquis of Hamilton. He was chosen because Charles liked and trusted him; he was chosen because he was the most senior among the Scottish nobility; he was chosen, in the final event, because there was no other. Unfortunately for him, and for his master, he was the worst man possible for the job.

It's difficult to know what to make of James Hamilton. A man of limited abilities, he was often too subtle for his own good. He had an incoherent mind, indulging in elaborate conspiratorial games when only plain words would do. With a strong stake in Scotland, he had too much to lose to be a completely selfless agent of the king. Essentially he was a compromiser, with no strong views on religion, sent to deal with a complex situation already past compromise. He had the capacity to change his mind with bewildering rapidity, turning mountains into molehills and back into mountains again. To make matters worse, he also appeared to suffer from some form of melancholia, bordering at points on outright depression. Robert Baillie, generally well disposed towards Hamilton, said his ways were so ambiguous that no man understood him. It is only fair to add that he genuinely tried to do his best; but he had a reverse Midas touch, turning all to lead. Montrose, in his later royalist phase, was to convince Charles that Hamilton was a traitor, which he never was. By far the most perceptive assessment of this unfortunate and unlucky man was later set down by Clarendon: 'His natural darkness and reservation in his discourse made him thought to be a wise man, and his having been in command under the king of

Sweden, and his continual discourses of battles and fortifications made him thought to be a soldier. And both these mistakes were the cause that made him thought more to be looked upon than in truth he deserved to be'.[43]

When Hamilton arrived in Scotland in the early summer of 1638 the situation for the king was bad; by the time he left that winter it was even worse. None of his schemes and plots had any effect. What is worse, he almost invariably misread the political situation. His attempt to win over Rothes was a dismal failure; and if the king already had far too many enemies, Hamilton succeeded in giving him even more. Chief among these was Archibald Campbell, Lord Lorne.

For centuries, Campbell power had been advancing, largely at the expense of their less fortunate neighbours, headed above all by the Macdonald Lords of the Isles. By the beginning of the seventeenth century Lorne's father, the seventh Earl of Argyll, had driven the Macdonalds from Kintyre and Islay, their last strongholds in south-west Scotland. This was a particularly strong source of resentment among that branch of the clan settled in the north of Ireland, who, under the leadership of the Macdonnell earls of Antrim, had ambitions to recover their lost Scottish inheritance. Aware of this, and of Lorne's political prevarications, Hamilton wrote to Charles urging him to make use of Randal Macdonnell, second Earl of Antrim, against the Campbells. Antrim was a restlessly ambitious figure with about as much political and strategic sense as Hamilton; nevertheless Charles, who shared his lieutenant's taste for cloak-and-dagger intrigue, was quick to act on the suggestion. As a strategy it was both ill-conceived and unnecessary; for Lorne's father, the seventh earl, was still alive. He had converted to Catholicism some years before, and was now living in London, alienated from both his son and his Protestant kin. Even so, it was still open to the king to use the father against the son. Playing with Antrim's ambitions was hardly the way to win over a man of whom Hamilton said 'itt feares me that he will prufe the dangerousest man in this state'.[44] Unable to keep any of their schemes secret for long, the details of Charles' and Hamilton's overtures were soon public knowledge, ensuring that, when the time was right, the most powerful Scot of his generation was one day guaranteed to be the most powerful opponent of the king.

Having exhausted all other options, and still playing for time, Charles finally accepted Hamilton's proposal that a General Assembly, the first since that held in Perth in 1618, be summoned to meet in Glasgow in November, but only on the understanding that the bishops be allowed to attend. This proved to be another of the Commissioner's great miscalculations; not only were the bishops prevented from attending, but the whole affair was so stage-managed that it was packed out with as many lay elders, many of them armed, as ministers. A protest had been prepared in advance on behalf of the truant bishops, which Hamilton, as the king's Commissioner, tried to have read. His interventions were ignominiously ignored as the Assembly proceeded to elect Alexander Henderson as moderator and Archibald Johnston as clerk. Hamilton fought a futile rearguard action against the legitimacy of an assembly that he himself had conjured into being. As a final gesture he declared the gathering illegal, commanding all present to depart on pain of treason. Accompanied by the other royal officials, including the Earl of Lauderdale, Hamilton withdrew, a moment of high drama reduced to low comedy when the doors of Glasgow Cathedral were discovered to be locked and the keys temporarily missing. Hamilton exited with as much dignity as he could muster; ominously Lord Lorne, now the eighth Earl of Argyll, following the recent death of his father, declined to follow.

After the Commissioner's departure, the Assembly, now technically illegal, continued to meet until 20 December. Its proceedings showed how much more radical feeling had become since the Covenant was first signed in February. All that James and Charles had worked for in the church over the past forty years was quickly swept away: the Liturgy, the Canons, the Five Articles of Perth and the Court of High Commission. Even more significant, Episcopacy itself was abolished and the bishops condemned and excommunicated one by one. Presbyterianism was declared to be the one true government of the Church of Scotland, with none of the ambiguity of the Golden Act of 1592. This was a political as well as an ecclesiastical revolution; for the bishops stood condemned not just as church officials but also as officers of state. The historian Leopold von Ranke was later to compare the defiance of the Glasgow Assembly to that moment, a century and a half later, when the French National Assembly resisted the commands of Louis XVI. Among those who witnessed these dramatic events as a silent spectator was Lord John Maitland.

3

COVENANTER AND DIPLOMAT

We cannot be certain exactly when John Maitland returned to Scotland from Geneva, but it is likely to have been soon after he received news of the troubles at home. However, for some considerable time he appears to have played no prominent part in public affairs; it is not until 1642 that he enters into a position of real significance. This raises some interesting questions about his conduct throughout this period. His absence from the records might be easy to explain: it was either because he was still a fairly minor figure politically, or because he was still a relatively young man and the son of a prominent Privy Councillor. There might, however, be a much more subtle process at work, which could possibly reveal something of Lord Maitland's thinking. Hostile sources, such as Clarendon and Bishop Henry Guthry, later tried to make out that he was a leading radical from the outset; but there is simply no contemporary evidence to support such a contention: the earliest surviving copy of the Covenant signed by him is dated 18 October 1638, and he does not feature at all on the lists Rothes compiled of those active in the movement.[1] Writing well after the event Guthry hazards the following speculation: 'About this time [1641] the earl of Lauderdale began to shew himself forward in the cause his son the Lord Maitland had been so from the beginning; but the father withdrew at first, and joined the king; which then made many say, that Lauderdale had chosen the surest way of any; if the covenanters prevailed, his son's zeal would expiate his malignancy; and if the king prevailed, his adhering to him would procure quarter to his son.'[2]

This kind of political insurance policy had been a fairly regular practice among Scottish landed families for centuries, and continued to feature right into the late Jacobite period. Yet there is nothing in the record to support Guthry's cynical and atypical view of the Earl of Lauderdale's conduct; more than this, there is nothing to suggest that there was ever any perceived political difference between the father and the son. Lauderdale remained a loyal adherent of both Hamilton and the king. He was to remain so right up to the time that Charles finally recognised the Covenanters as the legal government of Scotland. This loyalty was to force him to take temporary refuge in England; he appears to have been absent for all of 1640 and most of 1641, not reappearing in the records of the Scottish Parliament until August of that year.[3] Throughout this time Lord Maitland was to do or say nothing that caused any political embarrassment to his father, although he was presumably left to safeguard the family's interests while his father was absent from Scotland. All of the evidence points to the fact that the Maitlands pursued a cautious course, consistent with the traditions of their house, thus avoiding the kind of internecine upheavals that later assailed the Campbells of Argyll and the Gordons of Huntly. Lord Maitland was to cultivate a wide variety of friendships, from the moderate Robert Baillie to the fanatic Archibald Johnston, without in any way compromising his own integrity. Unlike so many of his contemporaries there is nothing to suggest that his views on religion were guided by anything other than pragmatic calculations.

Although Lord Maitland's political interventions would remain fairly muted, at least until the autumn of 1641, he was early noted as a figure of some intellectual weight, despite his lack of experience in public affairs. Early in the course of 1639 the Covenanter leaders decided to write to Louis XIII, the French king, asking him to arbitrate in their dispute with Charles. Under the guidance of Montrose, a letter was drafted, and then circulated for signature by the chief representatives of all the noble houses in Scotland. When Lord Maitland was pressed to sign he refused, pointing out that the document had been written in bad French, presumably to the chagrin of Montrose, a man not noted for his humility. The project was dropped. Of no great importance in itself, this story casts an interesting light on Maitland's character, and his willingness to force his superiors to confront uncomfortable truths. There is, however, more to this than simple intellectual pedantry: an appeal to a foreign king was clearly treasonable, and Maitland had sufficient political skill to recognise it as such, using the bad French as an excuse to have the whole project set aside. Even so, when Charles later acquired a copy of this compromising document he ordered the arrest of Lord Loudon, one of the signatories who happened to be in England at the time, on a charge of treason, and attempted to use it in the English Parliament to incite anger against the Scottish rebels. At another time, and for another king, such a strategy might have worked.[4]

After the failure of the Hamilton mission, emphasised by the fiasco of the Glasgow Assembly, it was patently clear that the issues between

Charles and the Covenanters could not be resolved by any diplomatic means. For Charles war entailed a major risk: he simply did not have the resources to mount a serious military operation; in northern England, for example, the local militia forces – the trained bands – were still exercising with longbows and brown bills, weapons last used at Flodden in 1513. The Scots, moreover, were particularly adept in keeping one step ahead of the king in the propaganda stakes, determined that any military contest with England should not be seen in terms of ancient national rivalries. Even the very title of the conflict was a measure of their success: by the summer of 1639 it was becoming widely known as the *Bellum Episcopalae* – the Bishops' War. King Charles, despite his Scottish birth, was more than ready to resurrect English resentments against the Scots; but while there were many Englishmen who may have been prepared to follow distant trumpets, there were precious few who were prepared to die for Scottish bishops.

The First Bishops' War was one of history's great bluffs; the two sides gave all the appearance of posturing like barnyard cocks, full of sound and fury that signified nothing. Charles' strategy was bold but amateurish: he would advance to the borders at Berwickshire with his main force, while Hamilton sailed to the Firth of Forth with an amphibious expedition, and Antrim sailed from Ireland to attack Argyll in the western Highlands and Islands, supported, it was assumed, by all the anti-Campbell clans. Hamilton was also given the supplementary aim of supporting the loyalist Marquis of Huntly, head of the Gordon family, in Aberdeenshire. But like all such grand armchair strategies, it fell to pieces when faced with the detailed logistical problems that real soldiers always have to face: the men were badly trained and equipped; transport, especially shipping, was a serious problem; there were few secure bases and insufficient stores, and there was no detailed plan of campaign. Thomas Wentworth, Charles' Lord Deputy in Ireland, was particularly contemptuous of the mercurial Antrim, and refused to extend the necessary support for his planned invasion of Scotland. The Covenanters, though little better prepared than the king, at least had the advantage of morale, defending a cause that they believed was just. All internal resistance, most notably that offered by Huntly, was quickly swept aside. There was little to raise the morale of the beleaguered king, who at his camp near Berwick received the following message from Hamilton, anchored impotently in the Forth, on 7 May: 'Your Majestie's affaires ar in ane desperatt condition. The inraged people heir runes to the height of rebellion and walkes with a blind obedience, as by ther tratrous leaders they ar commanded, and resolved they ar rather to obey then to embrace or except of your proffered grace in your last most generous proclamation . . . You will find itt a woorke of great difficultie and of vast expens to curb them by force, ther power being greater, ther combinatione stronger than can be imagined'.[5]

All that remained for the king was the hope that the rebels would eventually back down; that they would blink if he stared at them hard enough. By the early summer it was perfectly clear that this was not going to happen. Unable to continue the war on its present terms, Charles decided to accept what was little better than a truce. Rothes, Henderson and Johnston came to England and agreed the Pacification of Berwick on 18 June. Charles refused to ratify the decisions of the 'pretended' Glasgow Assembly, but agreed to summon a new one to meet in Edinburgh, to be followed shortly afterwards by a Parliament. It was a charade. With no change in the political climate, it was perfectly obvious that the decisions taken in the forthcoming Edinburgh Assembly would simply repeat those taken at Glasgow the previous year. Charles remained for a time at Berwick, more determined than ever to enforce his will; the Covenanters left with equal determination to resist.

Before the Edinburgh Assembly opened in August, Hamilton spent some time rebuilding his political bridges in Scotland. From his contacts with Lord Loudon and the Earl of Lothian, he discovered that the issue had now been pushed far beyond the disputed liturgy; that the Scots intended to abolish Episcopacy as a first step towards limiting the prerogative power of the crown. This would involve a greatly enhanced role for Parliament, which would change from a quasi-feudal court into a genuine national assembly, with powers to make appointments to both the judiciary and the Privy Council.[6] Hamilton, aware of the direction of the wind, declined to accept the dubious honour of the Commissionership for a second time, which fell to the understandably reluctant Traquair. Charles, now obviously playing for time, returned to London, going back on his decision to come to Edinburgh and open the General Assembly in person.

As expected, the Edinburgh Assembly confirmed all the decisions taken at Glasgow the previous winter. But it did even more, uncovering the real causes of the contest with the king. It was no longer a struggle over simple confessional differences, or even over the question of church government: it was over the nature of political power itself. Not only was Episcopacy abolished, but also churchmen were declared incapable of holding civil office. What was worse, from the king's point of view, the appointment of bishops was declared not just to be wrong in practice but contrary to the law of God. Charles had accepted Traquair's argument that Episcopacy might be set aside in the Scottish church as a temporary political expedient. However, to declare it contrary to scripture meant that its rejection could not be limited by space or time. If Episcopacy were universally unlawful how was it to be maintained in England and Ireland? Charles wrote to Traquair telling him to resist: it was too late. Bending to pressure, the Commissioner accepted all of the acts of the Assembly in the name of the king, including a provision to hold annual assemblies from this point forward. The General Assembly of the Church of Scotland, hitherto a temporary and irregular part of the political scene, was set to become one of the most powerful agencies in the land, a development that was shortly to have considerable significance for John Maitland.

Under the guidance of Argyll, now a committed Covenanter, Parliament met soon after the Assembly dissolved and confirmed all of its acts. The abolition of Episcopacy presented the members with an immediate problem: in the absence of the bishops how were the Lords of the Articles to be chosen? For some hours the nobility, reserving the matter to itself, debated the issue. Traquair, supported by Montrose, argued that the king be allowed to appoint an equivalent number of nobles in place of the bishops, which would in effect allow him to maintain overall control of the whole legislative process. Argyll, with the support of Loudon, argued that in future each estate should nominate its own representatives to the Articles, which would effectively end all direct royal control. It also meant a decisive shift in the balance of parliamentary power away from the nobility towards the lesser gentry and the burgesses, far stronger in their Presbyterian convictions. Argyll's motion was passed by a narrow majority.

The Edinburgh Parliament in effect confirmed a revolution: in Scotland royal power, as it was traditionally understood, was dead. It was an impossible situation for Charles to accept, even if he were of a mind to do so: he could not rule as an absolute monarch in one corner of his kingdom and a constitutional monarch in another. For England the situation was particularly invidious because of its more advanced tradition of constitutional law. For Charles to summon a new Westminster Parliament at any time before the outbreak of the First Bishops' War would have been a risky enterprise; after the Edinburgh Assembly and Parliament it was a step wrought with suicidal implications.

The Edinburgh Parliament is important in one other regard: it uncovered a crack within the Covenanter movement later to turn into a chasm. From that point during the Glasgow Assembly when Argyll joined forces with the Covenanters, it was certain that his power, native talents and political prestige would carry him to the forefront of the movement. Up to that time it had been Rothes and Montrose who had tended to determine the agenda. Both were junior to Argyll in the Scottish nobility, and both were highly resentful of his growing influence. Montrose was the first to break ranks, and appears to have reached some understanding with the king while he was at Berwick.[7] His dispute with Argyll over the constitution of the Articles appears to be the first direct evidence of his new political allegiance.

No sooner had Charles returned to London than his mind moved towards a fresh campaign against the Scots. From Ireland he summoned Lord Deputy Wentworth, created Earl of Strafford early in the new year, who along with Laud formed the strongest axis on the royal council. He was just the kind of man the determined but muddle-headed king needed: strong, insightful, competent, and with a clear sense of priorities. He did his formidable best to lift Charles out of his self-imposed difficulties, bringing a new sense of direction to the government. But for all his intelligence and strength of purpose, Wentworth was a disastrous prop for the tottering crown. If Charles understood little of the mood of the Scottish people, Wentworth understood absolutely nothing. More seriously, he misunderstood the mood of England itself. Outraged by the arrogance of the Scots, and almost completely blind to political reality, he convinced himself and the king that all loyal Englishmen would share his attitude. The First Bishops' War had emptied the treasury; therefore, Wentworth reasoned, Parliament would have to be summoned to provide fresh funds, an argument supported by Laud and Hamilton. Now armed with his trump card, the letter to Louis XIII, which Traquair had brought to his attention, Charles summoned his first English Parliament for eleven years in April 1640. To his astonishment, it passed over the letter to Louis in silence. An appeal for funds was ignored as John Pym, a leading Puritan, launched a forensic attack on years of royal mismanagement. Making absolutely no progress, Charles dissolved the Short Parliament within a few weeks. Politically, financially, and militarily, he was worse off than ever.

As the weeks passed, drawing into the summer campaigning season, the king remained in London, gathering all the resources he could. He was not unduly worried, having received assurances from the north that the Scots made no sign of moving; but rather than wait for Charles to take the initiative the Scots launched a pre-emptive strike across the border on 17 August. Under the command of Alexander Leslie, a professional soldier who had served under Gustav Adolphus in what in time was to be known as the Thirty Years War, the Scots advanced on the River Tyne, sweeping aside local forces at the ford at Newburn. From Newburn the advance continued eastwards, through the coalfields of the north-east to the important port of Newcastle. With Newcastle in their hands, the Covenanters had complete control of London's fuel supply; the Second Bishops' War was over almost as soon as it had begun.

Peace negotiations opened at Ripon on 2 October. Charles hoped for a personal treaty like the pacification of Berwick; but the Scots were placing no more trust in royal assurances of good faith, insisting that a final treaty would have to involve the Parliament of England. A provisional treaty was agreed towards the end of the month: the Scots were to be paid £860 a day in expenses and retain control of the northern counties of England, pending conclusion of the final treaty in London. The transfer of the negotiations to London was a particularly dangerous move for the king, allowing close co-operation between the Covenanters and the English opponents of royal power, who assembled in strength for the opening of the Long Parliament on 3 November.

John Pym took up the challenge he laid down during the Short Parliament, almost as if there had been no interruption: item by item he attacked the innovations of Charles' personal rule, from the abuse of the rights of parliament and the advance of unwelcome ecclesiastical innovations to the exaction of illegal taxes. Pym is one of those unfairly neglected figures in English history, whose importance tends to be recognised now only by specialists. He was arguably – along with John Maitland and Oliver Cromwell – one of few genuine political geniuses of the seventeenth century: he was the first great parliamentary manager, whose talents were only ever equalled later that same century by Anthony Ashley Cooper. There is an unfortunate if understandable tendency to see the opponents of King Charles in the Long Parliament as a solid bloc, usually, for the sake of convenience, known as the Puritans. But the Puritans were as divided as much as they were united, particularly over the question of church reform; it was owing to Pym's great skill that a 'party' came into being where there was no party, and held together through some difficult times, not pushing too far to one extreme or the other. He did not wish to destroy the monarchy, and was most certainly not a republican; he simply wished to ensure that the exercise of executive power was balanced by the constant scrutiny of parliament; to ensure, in other words, some degree of harmony between the means and the ends. To attain this he was prepared to use any instrument at his disposal.

For Pym and his allies the presence of the Scots army, and the financial demands this made on the crown, ensured that there would be no early dissolution of Parliament. When the Scots' Commissioners arrived in London on 19 November to continue the discussions begun at Ripon they were well received. However, the peace talks – which continued for some months – did not always go well, despite the initial enthusiasm for the Covenanters. Amongst other things the Scots began to place increasing emphasis on the unity of religion between the two realms. This was not due to any great crusading zeal – important as this was for some – but to a desire to increase the security of the political settlement at home: the Covenanters did not feel safe, in other words, as long as the bishops continued to rule the English church, which might at some future stage lead to the reintroduction of Episcopacy into Scotland.

While there was a growing party in the English Parliament in favour of a wholesale reform of the church, few were prepared to be dictated to on this matter by the Scots. Most Englishmen at this stage were happy to retain Episcopacy, free from some of the high Anglican innovations introduced by Laud. There was also a minority of Puritan radicals, as yet of little political importance, headed by a group known as the Independents, who believed in the autonomy of each congregation, free from the central control of either bishops or Presbyterian courts. Of those who accepted the Scottish confession, none believed in Melville's doctrine of the two states, with a church theoretically free from parliamentary control. When some observations by Alexander Henderson, who came to London with the peace commission, were published in February 1641, urging the immediate abolition of Episcopacy, it was greeted with a wave of national outrage, embracing both King and Parliament. Henderson was forced to issue an apology.[8] This episode, minor enough in itself, demonstrated the need for caution on this delicate issue. Even so, the two sides were never to achieve a complete understanding on the question of church government, a cause of much future trouble.

For the whole period covered by the First and Second Bishops' Wars nothing is recorded of Lord Maitland's activities. It is not until December 1640 that we catch a glimpse of him at the Scottish army headquarters in Newcastle, perhaps on his way to visit his father in London, where he appears just over two months later.[9] In one of his earliest letters on political matters he wrote to Lord Balmerino in early March, commenting on the implications of the Henderson affair and some of the wider issues connected with the ongoing peace talks:

> . . . the violens of that anger I hope is past, as his Majestie was about that paper, which was given on 24 February, and, I believe, the paper which was given in yesterday to clear our intentions will stop all the

violent courses was spoken of, either by proclamation or otherwise. In the meantime, I beleev that paper was not altogether fruitless, for the City was content to lend 160,000 lib. to the Parliament yesterday which they refused befor. This will, I hop, do good to our army, quhen we get our proportion of it.[10]

Although it cannot be proved, it would seem reasonable to suppose that Maitland took the time while in London to witness the impeachment before Parliament of the Earl of Strafford, one of the great political trials of the seventeenth century, which opened on 22 March. Both Strafford and Laud had been arrested the previous year, essentially as scapegoats for years of royal mismanagement, though Strafford himself had only really been of any great significance in the politics of England in the months leading up to the outbreak of the Second Bishops' War. But for Pym and his supporters he was the *bête-noir,* a true representative of everything that was wrong with Charles' government, whose policy in Ireland was to be a model for absolutism in England. Fatally for him, he had also made an ambiguous statement at a meeting of the royal council on the eve of the Second Bishops' War to the effect that the king had an army in Ireland with which 'to reduce this kingdom'. The impeachment failed because of a lack of evidence, but his enemies brought him back before the high court of Parliament on a Bill of Attainder, a terrible device that required only a presumption of guilt. Strafford's words about the Irish army were taken to mean that it should be used in England. Sir Harry Vane, Strafford's enemy, the man who had taken the notes of the meeting, confirmed that this was the case, though this was denied by Hamilton, who had also been present. Strafford was condemned and executed on 12 May. Most Scots, possibly Lord Maitland among them, were happy to see the end of Strafford, an enemy of their nation. In later life, though, this whole process was to acquire a sinister significance for Maitland, when he himself was faced with a similar combination of circumstances.

Once back in Scotland, Maitland continued to cultivate his connections with government circles. Although he still had no official role to perform he was given small commissions, demonstrating that he was an individual held in some trust. Montrose had continued to intrigue and cabal against Argyll, entering into a bond with some of his associates at Cumbernauld House, 'against the particular and indirect practising of a few'. Later still he was to associate himself with an accusation that Argyll aimed at nothing less than to depose the king and set himself up as dictator. Unable to substantiate these charges Montrose was imprisoned for a time in Edinburgh Castle, conducted there in June 1641 by Lord Maitland and the Earl of Lothian, who were given an official commission for the purpose.[11]

The Anglo-Scottish peace negotiations finally reached a satisfactory conclusion, when the Treaty of London was ratified by the king in August 1641. Charles agreed to withdraw all his declarations against the Covenanters and to ratify all the decisions taken by the 1640 Edinburgh Parliament. Reparations of £300,000 were also agreed, the Scots army to begin withdrawal from northern England on receipt of the first instalment. With these formalities out of the way, Charles decided to come to Edinburgh in person, hoping to make a personal peace with the Covenanters as a counterweight to his growing political troubles in England. Although Montrose had failed abysmally in his attempts to create a royalist party in the north, Charles still had some hopes of the Earl of Rothes, a man with a far higher degree of political intelligence. Once again the king's hopes were frustrated when Rothes died in August, ending any immediate prospect of building up a party among the middle-ranking nobility. Hamilton, seriously unsettled by the death of Strafford, and worried for his own future, had entered into a close association with Argyll, which might have brought some political benefits for his master; but this was to be one of those periods when his own acute sense of self-preservation was more important than the interests of the king. In a sense this is quite understandable: Charles had promised to save Strafford; in the end he had allowed his greatest minister to fall victim to parliamentary vengeance.

Rothes' death was a sad preamble to a disastrous trip. Charles, despite his open reputation for untrustworthiness, seems to have convinced himself that a charm offensive, when combined with residual loyalty towards the house of Stewart, would be enough to break up that community of interest that had developed between the Covenanters and the Puritans.

No greater contrast can be imagined between the Scotland of 1633, when Charles had last come, and that of 1641. All hopes of a uniform British church, on a basis once conceived by the king, were gone. Parliament, which had been sitting for a month, had acquired a degree of assertiveness and independence quite unthinkable only a short time before; in the space of a few months it had covered ground that had taken its English counterpart several hundred years. All the radical legislation of 1640, which had placed clear limits on the royal prerogative, was immediately approved by Charles. Keeping his true thoughts to himself he dutifully attended Presbyterian services and even received Lord Balmerino into the royal presence. He even gave tacit approval to the Covenant: though he did not sign the document himself, he allowed his kinsman, the Duke of Lennox, to do so. But it was quickly apparent that he was gaining nothing by his moderate demeanour, and that the axis between Argyll and Hamilton, contrary to expectations, was not working in his favour. Argyll, taking up the challenge laid down by John Pym in England, demanded that no political or judicial office should be filled without parliamentary consent. When Charles attempted to fill the vacant office of Chancellor, long vacated by Archbishop Spottiswoode, with his own nominee – the Earl of Morton – he was faced with a blunt refusal.

Lacking the solid political guidance that would have been provided by Rothes, and apparently abandoned by Hamilton, Charles began to sail in more treacherous seas, seemingly giving his approval to a group of royalist desperados to carry out a *coup d'état,* apparently aimed at Argyll and Hamilton. The lynch pin in this shady business – known in Scottish history as 'The Incident' – was a certain Will Murray, an incompetent aficionado of cloak-and-dagger intrigues. Murray, the son of the former minister of Dysart in Fife, was a gentleman of the royal bedchamber who had served in the function of whipping boy to Charles in his youth. For this service, and others, he was created Earl of Dysart in 1643. Of little importance himself, he was the father of Elizabeth Murray, later to enjoy the title of Countess of Dysart in her own right, who was to become one of the great influences in John Maitland's life.

Details of the projected *coup* were soon widely known, leading to the temporary flight from Edinburgh of Argyll and Hamilton. Charles denied all knowledge, but his political position was now significantly weaker. Instead of Morton, he was obliged to appoint Argyll's kinsman, Lord Loudon, to the Chancellorship, raising him to an earldom in the process. Other appointments followed, confirming the Covenanter grip on all the levers of power. Argyll, now a marquis, was named as principal Commissioner to the Treasury, and Sir Thomas Hope, a leading Covenanter lawyer, was confirmed as Lord Advocate. Lord Balmerino was appointed to the new Privy Council, as was John Kennedy, Earl of Cassillis. The appointments to the Privy Council also included the Earl of Lauderdale, now returned from his self-imposed exile, perhaps in the company of the king.[12]

Ever since the outbreak of the troubles in 1637, Lauderdale had proved to be consistently loyal.[13] Both Charles and Hamilton, with whom Lauderdale had been identified politically, had given their approval to the new regime, so his participation in the Argyll administration was in keeping with the line he had pursued. His attitude of constitutional loyalism precluded taking the hostile attitude later pursued by political mavericks like Montrose and Huntly, allowing him to regain much of the credit lost by his earlier associations. As early as October 1641 he was appointed to a commission set up to investigate 'The Incident'; at the General Assembly the following year he was chosen as one of the assessors to the Moderator, and by 1643 he was acting as President of the Privy Council in the absence of the Chancellor. In 1644 he achieved his most significant appointment as President of Parliament, a position in which he was unanimously confirmed just before his death in early 1645.[14] From the late summer of 1641 onwards there is almost nothing to differentiate the politics of the Earl of Lauderdale from those of his eldest son, which in both cases might be described as moderate Covenanter. Although both men were trusted by the church authorities, neither showed any signs of the kind of intense religiosity increasingly displayed by Archibald Johnston of Warriston, and, to a lesser extent, by Argyll. The observation that Maitland was a 'religious fanatic' in his youth is based on prejudice, not evidence.[15]

By the late summer of 1641 the constitutional and religious revolution initiated with the signing of the Covenant was effectively over: politically, after Charles' visit to Scotland, there was nothing left to achieve: the bishops were gone, the royal prerogative limited, regular parliaments and general assemblies guaranteed by law. But Scotland did not exist in isolation from the rest of the United Kingdom. The Scottish revolution could never be secured until the same constitutional and religious questions were addressed and settled in England. From this point forward the quest for security becomes paramount, a quest made all the more pressing by the outbreak of a major Catholic revolt in Ireland in October 1641. Although Scots troops were to help local British forces retain a hold on eastern Ulster, while loyal Anglo-Irish forces under the Earl of Ormonde prevented Dublin falling into rebel hands, much of the rest of the island came under their control, eventually allowing them to form a confederation based at Kilkenny. For the next few years all serious political initiatives were determined by the complex three-cornered contest in Scotland, England and Ireland.

That same summer, a few days before the king arrived in Edinburgh, Lord Maitland's political career looked as if it was over just as it was about to begin. On 4 August 1641 he and the other eldest sons of noblemen, known in Scottish law as the 'Masters', were forcibly expelled from Parliament, where they had been present as observers, apparently in the middle of a sitting.[16] This was in pursuit of an Act of 1587 passed in favour of the lairds, jealous of the growing power of the nobility, which made it illegal for noble heirs to sit in parliament either as members of the noble estate or as elected members of the commons as long as their fathers were alive, a disability that was not finally removed until the Reform Act of 1832.[17] Seemingly the growing presence of the Masters, some of quite mature years, had been in breach of this act; now with a new assertiveness the lairds and the burgesses combined to have them removed. A petition of the heirs against this public humiliation was simply ignored.[18] Not able to attend parliamentary sittings, the Masters were also effectively prevented from taking part in the deliberations of the Committee of Estates, the executive authority that had succeeded the Tables some time before.

There the matter might have remained, with Lord Maitland and his colleagues forced on to the sidelines; but as compensation for their political isolation some of the Masters were appointed to commissions connected with military affairs, not long after the 1587 Act was confirmed. The most important of these commissions went to Maitland, who on 28 August was delegated to oversee the demobilisation of English forces in accordance with one of the clauses laid down by the Treaty of London. Maitland's appointment indicated that he had some influential friends in Parliament, not willing to allow his perceived abilities to be sacrificed completely. A breach had been made; other more important commissions would follow. For some time, however, in the face of the hostility of the lairds, his position remained uncertain. Fortunately for him there was another avenue for advancement – the Scottish Church – soon to be equal to and in some respects even greater than the organs of government. The 1638 Glasgow General Assembly had established a precedent that lay elders could take a leading part in church affairs, a concession that was soon to be of considerable importance to Maitland, possessed of a level of learning at least equal to the greatest of his clerical colleagues.

After Charles returned to London his political struggle with Parliament intensified. In January 1642, with all the assurance of a sleepwalker, he took a disastrous step, entering the Commons in an attempt to arrest Pym and some of his most prominent colleagues: all were forewarned. Charles left London, chased out by a wave of unpopularity, and for the rest of the year the two sides prepared for the coming Civil War, which finally broke out in October 1642, with the Battle of Edgehill.

At first the Scots were inclined to remain on the sidelines, content to do little more than offer their services to both sides as mediators. It was obvious at that stage, however, that an outright victory for the king was a far greater risk to the security of the political settlement in

Scotland than a victory for Parliament. Hamilton, who had spent much
of the early part of the year in England, arrived in Edinburgh to find
suspicion of Charles at a shockingly high level.[19] Robert Baillie, the
most moderate among the ministers, wrote to Lady Montgomery
expressing the hope that the government would not needlessly yoke
Scotland to the parliamentary cause, but going on to say that he hopes
it:

> . . . will be loath to ingadge us in a new warre with our best friends, for
> no other end bot to put the Isle againe, both for religion and Liberties,
> under the feet and sole pleasure of anie who guides the Court; for we
> believe, that none can be so blind bot they see clearlie, [if] the courtiers,
> for anie cause, can gett this Parliament of England overthrown by forces,
> either at home or abroad, that all either they have done, or our Parliament
> has done already, or whatever anie Parliament should mint to doe
> hereafter is not worth a fig.[20]

Throughout the early part of 1642 the king had made overtures to the
Scots, hoping for support from a government that he after all had put
in power. Hamilton and Will Murray both intervened with Argyll, but
he was far too cautious to make any move. More than this, he shared
much of the country's profound distrust of Charles, a distrust that had
been amplified by the dangerous political situation in Ireland, that
challenged his own security in the west of Scotland, especially as the
king was thought to be secretly in sympathy with the Catholic rebels.
Argyll was also reminded of Charles' past duplicity when Scottish troops
in Ulster captured the histrionic and faintly ludicrous Randal
Macdonnell, Earl of Antrim, who claimed that the king had made him
'general of all the Catholic forces in Ireland'.[21]

Under the guidance of Pym, the English Parliament, playing a much
more clever game, did not ask for an outright military alliance; instead
the Scots were invited to send representatives to England to consider
the question of church reform throughout the British Isles.[22] This
proposal was considered by the General Assembly, meeting at St
Andrews in July 1642. It was now that John Maitland was marked
out as an individual of unusual ability, being appointed by unanimous
decision, on a motion from Argyll, as one of the delegates to be sent to
Westminster.[23] His commission made clear that the ministers and elders
present ' . . . having certain knowledge of the worth and faithfulness
of John Lord Maitland, one of their number, who being witness to all
their intentions and proceedings can best relate their true loyaltie and
respect to their sovereign and brotherly affection to the Kirk and
Kingdom of England therin . . . '[24] In accepting Parliament's invitation

a letter was sent, seemingly written by Henderson, saying that there was no real hope of peace until prelacy was 'plucked up root and branch'.[25]

Maitland's fellow commissioners numbered among them some of the clerical heavyweights, including Henderson, Samuel Rutherford and Robert Douglas; but it was he apparently who carried the real political burden of a mission, in which, Robert Baillie notes, he 'proved both wyse, industrious and happy'.[26] When the delegation returned to Edinburgh on 21 September it was Maitland who reported to the Privy Council, bringing the message that Westminster was determined to destroy prelacy.[27] That same day he appeared before a specially convened meeting of the Kirk Commission, which was told ' . . . of the great things he had done, and then delivered to them the parliament of England's answer to the general assembly's message, shewing their resolution to abolish Episcopacy root and branch, and call an assembly of divines for modelling a new government, whereupon they wished our church to send commissioners'.[28] Years later, and under unimaginably different political circumstances, Baillie reminded him that he was ' . . . the man who procured and brought downe to us the ordinance for the abolition of Episcopacie'.[29]

The success of Maitland's mission opened up the prospect of real security for the future of the church settlement in Scotland; but the real genius behind these opening moves was John Pym, who had placed a virtually insurmountable obstacle between Charles and the Scots. Unless he was prepared to match Parliament's offer, which he would never do, the king could not hope for a military alliance with Argyll; neutrality was now the best he could aim for, but that would depend on a highly volatile set of political circumstances.

By the beginning of 1643 the situation was so finely balanced that any wrong move could prove disastrous for Charles; the best Hamilton and the moderate loyalists in Scotland could hope for was to stop direct intervention by Scotland on behalf of the English Parliament, which made its first direct appeal for military aid shortly after Edgehill. Montrose was now convinced that it was only a matter of time before the Covenanters intervened on behalf of Parliament. In his view it was necessary to launch a pre-emptive military strike. He came to York in February and met Henrietta Maria, Charles' Catholic queen, to discuss his ideas. The queen had already suggested to Charles the necessity of raising a loyal army in Scotland, and was receptive to Montrose. Full of his usual self-confidence, he told the queen that there were thousands of loyal subjects waiting to rise against the Covenanters. His mission was frustrated by Hamilton, newly arrived in York, warning of the acute danger of Montrose's ill-considered proposals. Gilbert Burnet reports as follows:

> The earl of Montrose and a party of high royalists were for entering into an open breach with the country in the beginning of 1643, but offered no probable methods of managing it; nor could they reckon themselves assured of any considerable party. They were full of big words and bold undertakings; but when they were pressed to shew what concurrence might be depended on, nothing was offered but from the Highlanders: and on this wise men could not rely: so duke Hamilton would not expose the king's affairs by such a desperate way of proceeding.[30]

Hamilton was now trying to negotiate his way through a political minefield. His relationship with Argyll was now much cooler than it had been at the time of 'the Incident', and he undoubtedly believed, like Montrose, that it was only a matter of time before the Scots allied themselves with Parliament. The situation required all his political skills. Charles was not trusted by most Scots, who believed that a royal victory in England would be followed by an attempt to reverse the 1641 settlement. Hamilton, as the leading moderate, could only delay Scottish intervention in the English Civil War; they could not be kept out forever. Much depended on the expected royal victory in 1643: beyond that, no promises could be made. If Montrose were given his head at this stage, then disaster would follow. Hamilton did not believe that he would be able to muster the promised support, a prediction that turned out to be true, when Montrose's attempt to invade south-west Scotland in the spring of 1644 turned into a military fiasco. Charles showed his continuing support for Hamilton by awarding him a dukedom; he then proceeded to destroy his political balancing act.

Charles started to fish in Irish waters, with disastrous consequences. Looking for ways to break the military deadlock in England, he began to consider the prospect of a ceasefire with the Irish Confederates. This would release Ormonde's troops for service in England, and, more dangerously, might even lead to an alliance with the Catholic Kilkenny government against Parliament. In late April 1643 the king authorised Ormonde to conclude a truce with the Irish rebels. Negotiations were kept secret for fear of pushing the Scots further into the Parliamentary camp.

A Convention of Estates, a parliament called without royal sanction, was due to assemble in Edinburgh on 22 June to consider the political situation. Hamilton realised that it was fear of the king's future intentions that might conceivably push the Estates into an alliance with

Parliament. On his advice Charles issued a manifesto on 1 June, saying that the rumours that he intended to overturn the Presbyterian settlement in Scotland were groundless. Wide publicity was given to this declaration: any effect it had was destroyed only a few days later, after the discovery of details of a new plot by the Earl of Antrim, a man who continually competed with Montrose for the title of loosest cannon in the royal arsenal.

In late May Antrim was intercepted by Scottish soldiers off the coast of County Down. He was found to be carrying letters from Viscount Aboyne, one of the sons of the Marquis of Huntly, and the Earl of Nithsdale, a leading Catholic nobleman from south-west Scotland. The information obtained from these letters, and from the interrogation of Antrim and his companion, revealed details of an elaborate conspiracy. Arms were to be sent to the north of Scotland for the use of Aboyne and the Gordons; Antrim was to raise a force of his own clansmen in Ireland to join their comrades in Scotland and all the others who hated the Campbells; Alasdair MacColla, a kinsman of Antrim's and a leading representative of the Macdonalds of Kintyre and Islay, was to return from exile in Ireland to lead the attack on Argyll; and Montrose would link up with Nithsdale. The aim was to bring to bear as much force as possible: to destroy the Scots' army in Ireland, and to bring Irish troops to mainland Britain to fight against the Covenanters and Parliament. As details of the Antrim Plot emerged, all Hamilton's manoeuvres were effectively nullified. When the Convention of Estates met it was presented with a paper drawn up by the Commission of the General Assembly, saying that the country was in greater danger from papists now than it had been at the time of the Spanish Armada. Robert Baillie expressed his own feelings of horror:

> . . . a commission was given to Antrim to treat with the Irish rebels, that the English and they might agree . . . the first service of the reconciled Ireland and England should be the disposal of the disaffected Scots; that they should goe by sea to Carlile, wher Nithsdale and the other Southland lords should joyne; that Colekittoch's sones [MacColla and his brother] should waken our Isles; that McClaine and Gorrum [Donald Macdonald of Sleat] and the other clanes disaffected to the Campbells should goe to armes; that Huntly and his son Aboyne, with Bamfe and Airlie, Montrose and Marshall should raise our North . . . that so in a trice we should become a field of blood . . .[31]

John Pym, from the beginning of the Civil War, had realised that Parliament could not prevail against the king without the assistance of the Scots. By the summer of 1643 the military situation for Parliament was bleak: the king's forces had won important victories in the north and the west; Bristol, the second port of the realm, fell; and John Hampden, one of Pym's closest political associates, was killed in battle. Scots participation on the side of Parliament was no longer simply desirable; it was essential. Antrim's bungling plot provided just the right political atmosphere; but Pym, as always, played the game with brilliance. Building on the success of the Maitland mission of the previous year, Pym saw to it that the Scots would come to England as crusaders, not mercenaries.

In early August a Parliamentary delegation arrived in Edinburgh. Sir Harry Vane the Younger, the son of the king's former secretary, came at its head, armed with an invitation to the Scottish Church as well as to the state. Parliament had convened an assembly of leading divines to meet at Westminster to consider the wholesale reform of the English church, to which the Kirk was invited to send its own representatives. Meeting in Edinburgh, the General Assembly had already thanked Lord Maitland for his successful mission to England the previous year; he was now further honoured by being the first elder named to the delegation sent to meet with the English.[32] Negotiations over a military and religious alliance proceeded in tandem: the Kirk was quick to accept the invitation to the Westminster Assembly, appointing a committee of eight to be sent to London – five ministers and three elders. The ministers included Baillie and Henderson, and the elders Maitland and Warriston.[33]

Negotiations over the form of the military alliance proved a little more complex, although they were successfully concluded in a new document to be known as the Solemn League and Covenant. Vane was careful to ensure that England was not committed to a Presbyterian solution to the church question; reformation of the English Church would, rather, be in 'accordance with the word of God and the example of the best reformed churches'. Satisfied with this rather vague formula, and urged on by the necessity of an alliance, the General Assembly quickly gave its approval to the Solemn League and Covenant on 17 August 1643. According to Henry Guthry, Lord Maitland was moved by the occasion to make a short speech, though this was contrary to established procedure:

> It was not the custom in assemblies, for any man, while the roll was calling, to interrupt voicing by discourses; every one was to answer to the question, Yea or Nay, and no more. Yet, the Lord Maitland, was so taken with a thought of his own, that he must needs vent it: so that when his voice came to be asked, he rose up and spoke to the sense,

how upon the seventeenth of August, four years ago, an act passed in that assembly for thrusting episcopacy out of this church, and now upon the seventeenth of August also an act was passed for the extirpation out of the church of England; and that providence having ordained it so, that both happened to be on one day, he thought there much to it, and that men might warrantaly thereupon expect glorious consequences to follow, even further off than England, ere all was done.[34]

The sentiments expressed are typical of any politician, regardless of the age, full of exaggeration and hyperbole. It is not beyond possibility that Maitland did indeed make such a speech; but it is as well to remember that Guthry was generally not well disposed towards him, and the remarks he reports receive no support in any other source, including the official records of the Edinburgh Assembly. For most of his career Maitland was to be fairly cautious as a politician, and is not noted for any tendency to give hostages to fortune. Guthry is anxious to depict him here as a kind of Presbyterian crusader, a role that more strictly belongs to his fellow elder, Archibald Johnston of Warriston.

Two days later Maitland's previous appointment to the Westminster Assembly was confirmed, and he was delegated, along with Alexander Henderson and George Gillespie, another minister, to carry the Solemn League and Covenant to the English Parliament.[35] Maitland, at this stage, was the only lay representative from Scotland to be sent to London; it was to be the most significant appointment of his life to date: for it was clear that he was being sent not just as an elder of the church but as a representative of the state. That same August the Estates passed an ordinance providing for allowances to be paid to Maitland, Henderson and Gillespie 'upon the employment of this Kirk and kingdom'.[36] Maitland was to be paid £3.00 a day, in contrast with the £1.00 to be paid to his clerical colleagues, suggesting that he was expected to play a more enhanced political role.

A fortnight later Maitland, Henderson and Gillespie sailed for London, arriving on 9 September. By the middle of the month all three were formally admitted to the Westminster Assembly. Maitland was to be a regular attender, although he apparently took no part in the theological debate, confining his remarks to political affairs alone, favourably impressing at least one of the English members, who wrote of him speaking 'briefly and sweetly'.[37] However, his importance at the Assembly was far exceeded by the almost ambassadorial function that he began to acquire as the only important civil representative of the Edinburgh government. He carried out his work quickly and efficiently: by 25 September the Solemn League and Covenant was formally sworn by both the Assembly and Parliament, and confirmed as the law of the land on 1 November.[38]

Both Henderson and Baillie, who arrived in London later than their colleagues, quickly acquired a detailed appreciation of Maitland's political and diplomatic skills, which enabled him to acquire a range of contacts within the parliamentary establishment in London, far more significant than those that could ever have been cultivated by the clerics on their own. However, beyond his appointment as an elder to the Westminster Assembly, he still had no official position; his unofficial role as a representative of the Estates was in clear breach of the act of 1587. Before the end of the year there were moves in Edinburgh to have him recalled, presumably initiated by the lairds, as Parliament was about to send its own high-level delegation to London. Baillie and Henderson reacted with alarm. In late December, as the matter was being decided, Henderson wrote to Robert Douglas, a leading fellow minister, and to Argyll:

> We are informed that my Lord Maitland is to be recalled, which troubleth us exceedingly, because his Lordships praecence and paines here have beine more useful then any of us could at first have conceaved, and if we shall want his Lordship heirafter, not onely shall our respect, which we have neid of in this place, be diminished, but we shall not know how or by what meanes to deal with the Houses of Parliament, wpon which the Assembly doth altogether depend . . . My Lord is well acquainted with the chiefest members of both Houses, hath dexterity in dealing with them, and is much honoured by them; but we can nether attend theire times, nor will they be so accessible to ws when we want his Lordship . . .[39]

Baillie added his own appeal, commenting on the damage that would be done to the work of the new commission by the absence of Maitland:

> I think it reasonable and necessarie that come who will, Maitland should be adjoined to them. Forget not this; for this to be neglected, it would be an injurie and a disgrace to a youth, that brings, by his noble carriage, credit to our nation, and help to our cause. The best here makes very much of him, and are oft in our house visiting him; such as Northumberland, [Lord] Sey, Waller, Salisberry, and such like.[40]

These appeals, especially from Henderson, much respected as the architect of the Covenant, clearly had a considerable impact; the opposition from the lairds seems to have evaporated. The new delegation was approved by Parliament in January 1644: it included representatives from each of the estates, with Maitland as an addition.

When the commission was expanded the following July, with all due care given to the balance between the estates, Maitland's appointment was described as 'supernumerary' (the only one), emphasising the unique political status he had acquired.[41] With the Scottish army now poised to invade England the tasks before him were to acquire an even greater significance.

4

UXBRIDGE

The Solemn League and Covenant was a disaster for the royal cause, tipping the balance of forces firmly in favour of Parliament. Hamilton and his brother, William, Earl of Lanark, had done their best to delay its implementation by the Convention of Estates; but the damage done by the Antrim revelations was simply too great. They continued to resist, attempting to persuade their allies and dependants to refuse accession to the Covenant. When this failed, both men fled to England as outlaws. When they reached the king's headquarters at Oxford a surprise awaited them: they were greeted not as friends but as traitors. Montrose and the ultra-royalists had done their work, levelling a series of bogus charges against Hamilton, including a ludicrous allegation that he wanted to make himself King of Scots, in pursuit of an ancient family right. Hamilton, once again, was simply the victim of his own incompetence as a politician; but his incompetence was exceeded by that of his royal master, who built his servants up at one stage, only to pull them down at the next. Lanark escaped, later becoming a Covenanter, more by anger than by conviction, while his brother was hurried away to Cornwall, where he spent the next three years, imprisoned without trial.

Scotland's alliance with Parliament, embodied in the Solemn League and Covenant, was built on a paradox: it was loyal treason. As in 1639 and 1640 the Scots would campaign under a convenient fiction: that they were saving the king from himself. All signatories to the Covenant were pledged to uphold monarchical government. As early as February 1644 the Venetian ambassador in London was aware of the message being spread by Maitland and his fellow commissioners that their forces were coming 'to bring peace, unite the churches and deliver the king from evil councillors'.[1] In the final analysis, despite serious worries about the conduct and outlook of the king, all Scots were royalists, for 'they do not seem disposed to do away with monarchy altogether, lest their kingdom should become a mere province of England'.[2]

The English were anxious to appease the Scots, continuing to encourage, through the Westminster Assembly and elsewhere, their hopes of an early solution to the question of church government; first it was necessary to beat the king. John Pym died in December 1643, his task complete. His work was continued in Parliament by Harry Vane the Younger and Oliver St John, both able men, but without the same spark of genius. It was on their initiative that Parliament set up a new body in February 1644, known as the Committee of Both Kingdoms, which was given full executive authority to co-ordinate the war effort against Charles. England was represented by fourteen MPs and seven peers, Scotland by all the civil commissioners who happened to be in London at any one time. The Committee of Both Kingdoms was a unique body that seemed to allow the Scots to exercise important influence in English public affairs; in practice they were always a minority, with limited influence at best. Scots influence was highest in the early days when they represented the potential of early victory; as the months passed, with victory as far off as ever, they began to lose ground. Lord Maitland was particularly industrious: he attended no less than 205 of the 253 recorded sessions of the Committee, more than any of his colleagues, though his best efforts could not make up for lack of numbers.[3] Sir George Mackenzie was later to claim that Maitland was elected president of the Committee. There is no evidence that such a post ever existed; even if it had, it is unlikely to have gone to a Scot.[4] Maitland was a powerful presence on the Committee. Even so, his English colleagues, no matter how well intentioned, always viewed him and his fellow commissioners as foreigners, whose influence was only as strong as the performance of their army. From the outset only military prowess bought political power, and as the war progressed Scottish credit in London began to run dangerously low.

It's often claimed that the Scots intended to use the Solemn League and Covenant to impose Presbyterianism on England. On the contrary, the Scots had learned some clear lessons from Henderson's experience in 1641: no form of religion could be imposed on so powerful a nation as England against its will. Vane had been careful to ensure in negotiating the Covenant that his country was not committed to any specific model of reformation. The best the Scots could hope for was that once the king was defeated, and prelacy swept away, theirs would indeed be seen as an example of 'one of the best reformed churches'. Yet there were clear signs of a new danger even before the Scots' army crossed the Border. Politically the bishops were a spent force: in the ruins of episcopacy a wide variety of mushrooms appeared, causing the Scots some acute anxiety. The Scots' hopes of the Westminster Assembly were frustrated at an early stage by the religious Independents, as yet insignificant in numbers but prolix in debate.[5] As early as November 1643 Baillie was warning, 'There is no danger for the Assembly from Prelacy, all the danger is from the other syde, which gathereth strenth by delayes both in the Parliament and the miserably distracted City.'[6] The Independents were only part of the problem; the collapse in the authority of the state church was resulting not in a Presbyterian re-naissance but in an alarming fragmentation: 'In the time of this anarchie, the divisions of the people weeklie does much encrease: the Independent partie growes; but the Anabaptists more; and the Antinomians most.'[7] Frustrated by this unexpected opposition, as dangerous politically as it was religiously, Baillie decided that it was best not to meddle with these issues in haste 'till it please God to advance our armie, which we expect will much assist our arguments'.[8]

The Scots finally crossed the Tweed on 19 January, under the command of Alexander Leslie, now Earl of Leven, who had brought them the same way in 1640. Almost from the outset, things did not go well; there would be no repetition of the easy successes of the Second Bishops' War. The weather was atrocious, many of the passes blocked by snow, making progress painfully slow. The army finally made it to the gates of Newcastle, but in contrast to 1640 the city was well defended, and the Scots insufficiently equipped to carry out an assault. As Newcastle settled down to a lengthy siege, all the exaggerated hopes in London, freezing for lack of coal, began to evaporate. Bit by bit, more like a tortoise than a hare, Leven pushed south towards York, delayed by a skilful rearguard action by the Marquis of Newcastle, Charles' commander in the north. But with Leven pressing down, Newcastle was forced to turn his back on Parliamentary forces operating in the north and the eastern Midlands: as summer approached Leven was joined close to York by English forces commanded by Lord Fairfax and his son, Sir Thomas, and by the Parliamentary Eastern Association, commanded by the Earl of Manchester, whose cavalry forces were led by Oliver Cromwell, the MP for Cambridge, a middle-aged man who had proved himself a soldier of natural genius over the past few years. To aid the beleaguered Marquis of Newcastle Charles sent additional forces north under the command of Prince Rupert, his best soldier by far. The two sides finally met at the Battle of Marston Moor in early July, the biggest fight of the war, and a victory for the Parliamentary alliance.

In London the Scots were gratified, having finally made a difference. Yet within an alarmingly short space of time it all came to nothing. Cromwell was not only a great soldier; he was also a great politician with a clear appreciation of the importance of propaganda. What is worse, from the Scots' point of view, he was a supporter of the religious Independents. Within a few days of Marston Moor his agents were active in the City, reporting the victory as the work of their general, giving additional encouragement to Philip Nye and Hugh Peter, leading Independents fighting a prolonged delaying action against the Presbyterians in the Westminster Assembly. Maitland and his colleagues were also aware of some other more serious developments; that the religious toleration espoused by the Independents went hand in hand with a tendency towards a dangerous radicalisation of English politics as a whole. The aims of the Covenant were quite limited: defeat the king and then persuade him to establish a new national church, free of bishops, which would then guarantee the advances made in Scotland. Cromwell and his colleagues seemed to represent a new kind of war party, predicated not simply on the defeat but the complete destruction of the king. For the remainder of the year military considerations gave way to a new political debate, which led to a fundamental realignment in the balance of forces: bit by bit the Scots moved out of the war party into the peace camp.

Newcastle finally fell to the Scots in October 1644, but this made little real difference to the declining status of their army in England, now more often seen as a nuisance rather than an ally. At the end of the month Lord Maitland wrote to the Earl of Lothian giving vent to his fears:

> The church affairs are much hindered by the Independent party, who carry themselves farr otherwise to us then they did when your Lordship was heir; even those who were the activist for us doe turn their cloak quite on the other shoulder. Whither the taking of Newcastle will make them calmer I know not; but, truly, before they undervalued our army strangely.[9]

Contrary to Maitland's hopes, the reputation of the Covenanters was soon to sink even further. In the summer of 1644, about the time of Marston Moor, one of Antrim's schemes finally came to something. The previous year Ormonde, acting on Charles' instructions, concluded a truce with the Irish Confederates known as the Cessation. This embraced all parties to the conflict in Ireland, with the exception of the Scots forces in Ulster, who refused to recognise its validity. It also allowed for some co-operation between loyalist forces and the rebels, determined to remove the Scots altogether from Ireland. With the help of the Confederate authorities, Antrim managed to ship a small army of his own tenants and kinsmen to Scotland, under the command of

Alasdair MacColla, who had featured in his previous plans for an attack on the Covenanters. MacColla, with insufficient forces to mount a prolonged campaign on his own, hoped for support from local anti-Campbell clans, as envisaged in Antrim's previous schemes. All had been cowed by Argyll, showing little sign of joining their Irish brothers until Montrose appeared in central Scotland, armed with the king's commission. With almost all the experienced Scottish troops campaigning in England and Ireland, Montrose quickly swept aside badly trained local levies at Tippermuir near Perth and again at Aberdeen, where his soldiers, in massacring unarmed civilians, committed the first of the war crimes which Maitland was later to say the Scottish people would never forgive.[10]

That same autumn the political debate in England began to proceed in an ever more sinister direction. Ever since Marston Moor, the Earl of Manchester, the commander of the Eastern Association, and a leading English Presbyterian, had been increasingly out of sympathy with Oliver Cromwell, that most political of all soldiers. Cromwell accused Manchester of not wanting to fight the war; Manchester accused Cromwell of wanting to take the conflict in a direction that neither he nor his fellow nobles could support, revealing some unpleasant truths in the process:

> Always my Lord Manchester hes cleared himselfe abundantlie in the House of Lords, and there hes recrimainate Cromwell as one who has avowed his desire to abolishe the nobilitie of England; who hes spoken contumeliouslie of the Scotts intention of coming to England to establish their church government, in which Cromwell said he would draw his sword against them; also against the Assemblie of Divines; and hes threatened to make a partie of sectaries to extort by force, both from king and Parliament what conditions they thought meet. This fire was long under the emmers; now it's broken out, we trust, in good time . . . This matter of Cromwell has been a high and mighty plot of the Independent partie to have gotten an armie for themselves under Cromwell, with the ruine and shamefullie unjust crushing of Manchester's person, of dissolving the union of the nations, of abolishing the House of Lords, of dividing the House of Commons, filling this city, and most of the Commons, with intense warrs, of setting up themselves on the ruine of all . . .[11]

By the autumn of 1644 the Scots, who earlier in the year had been among the most militant opponents of the king, began to make distinct moves towards the peace party in Parliament, headed, amongst others, by the Presbyterian MP, Denzil Holles, and the Earl of Essex, hitherto the chief Parliamentary general.[12] By December there were clear signs that the two groups were beginning to act together, although the Scots' change of alignment was not widely known until the spring of the following year. There were two strands to the new policy: the opening of negotiations with the king coupled with secret discussions for the removal of Oliver Cromwell as a dangerous incendiary.

In November, on the initiative of the House of Lords, where the peace party was strongest, a delegation, Lord Maitland among them, set out for Westminster travelling westwards in search of the king. It was a dangerous journey across a war-torn countryside. The delegates had a safe conduct from Charles, but on at least one occasion Maitland believed that they would all have their throats cut before they reached the royal headquarters.[13] They eventually located Charles at Oxford: the meeting was not encouraging. Royal fortunes had recovered since the defeat at Marston Moor; Charles was encouraged by the growing political divisions at Westminster, and by the continuing success of Montrose against the Covenanters. Charles was frosty, especially after he discovered that the commissioners had no power to negotiate, although he at least agreed that full peace discussions should be opened at Uxbridge early in the new year. It was not a good beginning, though in the circumstances it was probably the best that could be hoped for.

Peace negotiations were clearly going to be difficult, but the moves against Cromwell were to be the most difficult of all. Baillie makes it clear that this was primarily a Scottish initiative: 'It's like for the interest of our nation, we must crave reason of that darling of the Sectaries, and in obtaining his removeall from the armie, which himselfe, by his oure [over] rashness [in attacking Manchester], hes procured to breake the power of that potent faction [the Independents]. This is our present difficill exercise: we have need of your prayers.'[14]

That December, not long after the peace delegation returned from Oxford, a meeting was held in Essex House, attended by the Scots' commissioners and members of the Parliamentary peace party.[15] The Scots were anxious that action should be taken against Cromwell, though their English colleagues, perhaps no less anxious, were much more cautious. Bulstrode Whitelocke, a leading English lawyer, did not believe that there was enough evidence to sustain a charge against Cromwell as an incendiary; but the real reason for the failure to take action against him was that he was well supported in the Commons by Vane and St John. Although it was never discussed, there was perhaps another consideration: Cromwell was Parliament's most successful soldier. He had his own personal following among the cavalrymen of the Eastern Association – now known as the Ironsides – who were unlikely to sit back while their general was indicted. In the end the Essex House conspiracy came to nothing.

While these moves were underway, Cromwell and his friends were pursuing measures for the successful continuation of the war, confident that Charles would reject the peace proposals now under consideration. The first of these was the Self Denying Ordinance, which prevented members of the Lords or Commons from holding a military command. In practice this was directed against lukewarm soldiers like Essex and Manchester, Cromwell himself eventually being exempted from its provisions. This was followed by the New Model Ordinance, which allowed for the creation of a national Parliamentary army, to replace county formations like the Eastern Association, often more defensive than offensive in nature. While the Scots soldiers continued to languish in the north of England, starved of the resources promised by the Solemn League and Covenant, and lacking any real sense of military or political purpose, the New Model Army took to the field in the spring of 1645. Fatally for the king, and for the Scots, a new kind of war was about to begin.

Although not fully understood at the time, the negotiations at Uxbridge, which opened in early 1645, were the last chance, for all of the participants, of a peace based on compromise rather than the utter defeat of one side by the other. It was while the peace talks were underway that Maitland learned of the death of his father: he was now the second Earl of Lauderdale.[16] His own role was too important to allow him to leave Uxbridge; but in Scotland Parliament marked the occasion by suspending business for a few days.

The English historian, Samuel R. Gardiner, once wrote that the peace talks of 1645, known as the Treaty of Uxbridge, were essentially a Scottish initiative, a view that finds some support in Clarendon.[17] Beyond Clarendon, there is little in the way of contemporary evidence to support such a view, which would seem to be based on a fundamental misreading of the political situation; it is a little bit like saying that the Committee of Both Kingdoms was essentially a Scottish institution. Headed by Lauderdale and Loudon, the Scots' commissioners were heavily outnumbered by their English counterparts, who included heavyweights like Sir Harry Vane.[18] There is, however, one sense in which Uxbridge might be justly claimed to belong to the Scots: they now perceived the religious question to be the key to the whole political situation; it was they who made the running on this issue, rather than the English. If Charles could be persuaded to accept Presbytery all else would fall into place; the Independents would be destroyed and Scotland's own constitutional position within the wider political union would be secured. From this point forward the Scots were always willing to make concessions on other issues, particularly over the control of the militia, which the Parliamentarians considered to be vital, if the king would concede this key issue. There is a kind of blindness here, but not that traditionally assumed; the crusading element was far less important than the issue of national security, which only a monarchical and Presbyterian England would guarantee. These issues were made abundantly clear in conversations Lord Balmerino had later that same year with Jean de Montereul, a special agent of the French government:

> . . . if they allowed the Independents to get the advantage of them, one of two things would certainly happen: either the Independents would seek to depose the king, if they thought they were powerful enough to do so, or they would come to terms with him, if they found they were unable to ruin him, and that whichever of these two contingencies happened, the ruin of their kingdom was certain . . .[19]

There is also a sense in which the more Charles clung to Episcopacy in England, the less certain were his past concessions to the Scots, which gave all the appearance of being based on simple expediency, to be set aside at a convenient future opportunity. Before leaving for Uxbridge, Lauderdale told the Marquis de Sabran, the French ambassador in London, that while it might not be necessary to destroy Episcopacy on religious grounds, it was politically essential for the union and peace of England and Scotland.[20] As if to emphasise that there could be no return to the past the almost forgotten figure of Archbishop Laud was executed, with the full approval of the Scots, just prior to the Uxbridge talks. As a political gesture it is more likely to have had a negative impact, though the king's reaction to the death of his old servant appears to have been strangely muted.[21] Charles may have abandoned Laud, but he would never abandon the Anglican Church, a simple truth that was set to wreck not just the Uxbridge talks but most subsequent negotiations.

As expected, Uxbridge opened with a discussion of the question of church government. Although Henderson was present along with Chancellor Loudon, the senior Scottish churchman and the senior Scottish politician, the opening moves were left to Lauderdale, younger but far more experienced on the political issues at stake. Charles' own negotiators included the lawyer, Edward Hyde, the future Earl of Clarendon, who had his first opportunity to assess a man who was set to become a lifelong political enemy. Hyde's assessment of Scots, generally unfavourable, did not relent for Lauderdale, who ' . . . being a young man, not accustomed to an orderly and decent way of speaking, and having no gracious pronunciation, and full of passion, he made everything much more difficult than it was before . . . '[22]

Hyde's 'Memoirs', written years later, rightfully deserve their place among the great documents of English literature; but they were also his way of settling political scores, a curtain of prejudice often falling over people and events. With no other reliable source, all we thus know of Lauderdale's interventions at Uxbridge is that he spoke with a Scottish accent! Nevertheless, Hyde's comments reveal one important fact about Uxbridge: the participants spoke through rather than to each other; there was to be no compromise because there was no basis for compromise. Any successful negotiation, indeed any negotiation, has to set aside areas of disagreement, however large, and concentrate on those areas where some progress may be made, however limited. The problem with Uxbridge was that there were no overlapping areas of agreement whatsoever. Lauderdale appears to have lost faith in the talks at an early stage, an attitude perhaps coloured by his hostile reception at Oxford the previous November.[23] In the end, after twenty pointless days, the discussions were broken off. Lauderdale and his colleagues wrote a gloomy report to Edinburgh on the failure of the initiative: 'The matters of Religion doe most stick with the King and those that are about him; it is the judgement of all that are here of either kingdom upon the Treaty that there is no hope of peace, and that is not to be expected by treaty'.[24]

While the negotiations were underway Montrose continued his war in northern Scotland, decisively beating the Campbells at the Battle of Inverlochy in early February. News of this latest victory is occasionally claimed to have been responsible for a hardening of the royal attitude at Uxbridge; this is not true; the talks were failing well before Charles received Montrose's battle report. All it did was to confirm him in his attitude that he had been right all along to take an attitude that was 'at most ceremonial' to the Parliamentary overtures.[25] Charles, in defiance of all political reality, now increasingly believed, or was led to believe, that outright victory was a distinct possibility.

Montrose's successes did irreparable harm to the Covenanters in England without weakening their determination in Scotland. But there is a deeper irony at work here. The Covenanters had ceased to be the most radical political force in the British Isles, and were now allied with the more conservative elements in the Lords and Commons: any possibility of restoring the king to anything like his ancient dignity would depend on these men, not the ultra royalists.[26] With their power steadily weakening, the Covenanters were less and less able to determine the shape of the peace, or to offer any real hope to their Presbyterian allies in England. Montrose's triumph was, in a way he can hardly have imagined, also the triumph of the Independents, soon to take to the field with the New Model Army. In the months that followed Inverlochy, with the Scots increasingly preoccupied with the crisis at home, and Leven bogged down impotently in northern England, Cromwell and his allies effectively won the war, in the only campaign that really mattered. It would hardly be possible after this to keep them out of the peace, as King Charles was fated to discover. This was the real political cost of Montrose's empty triumphs.

In late May 1645 Lauderdale returned to Scotland after an absence of many months. It was supposed to be a short trip, most probably connected with private legal affairs arising from his father's death; but he was to be away from London for quite some time. His absence was a cause of increasing anxiety to his colleagues in England, who made an early appeal to the Committee of Estates for his return.[27] In his absence the Independents grew steadily in political importance, especially after the first great victory of the New Model Army at the Battle of Naseby in June. By July a note of desperation crept into the pleas for Lauderdale's return, by now one of the greatest political assets the Scots possessed: 'Let it be your care, that Lauderdale be sent back to us with all expedition. No living man is fitter to doe Scottish service against the plotting Independent partie, which, for the time, hes a great hand in the state'.[28] Beyond any personal considerations connected with his family and estates, there would appear to be one good public reason for Lauderdale's truancy: he was now able to enjoy all the political benefits conferred upon him by his title, sitting in Parliament and the Committee of Estates for the first time since his expulsion with the other Masters. It is also possible that he was frustrated by the lack of any real political progress in London, especially after the failure of the Treaty of Uxbridge. In any event, he stayed away for most of the remainder of the year.

This was a bleak time for Lauderdale, both personally and politically. His only son was sick and seems to have died that summer, no further reference to him ever appearing. Edinburgh was beset by plague, the most serious outbreak of the disease that century; and Montrose continued his triumphant career in the north of Scotland, with victories at Auldearn in May and again at Alford in July. By the beginning of August his Irish and Highland army was poised to invade the Lowlands. Events in England, important as they were, seem to have slipped temporarily into the background as the Estates availed themselves of Lauderdale's presence. He was busy sitting on a number of committees and raising fresh forces to counter the danger of Montrose, as well as being appointed to meet some delegates from the English Parliament at Berwick.[29] It is reasonable to assume that the presence of these men at this time must have been a source of some embarrassment to Lauderdale: for he himself was forced to take refuge in the town as a fugitive from his own country; Montrose had invaded the Lowlands and defeated the last effective Covenanter field army at the Battle of Kilsyth in mid-August. Lauderdale now urged a step that should have been taken months before: to deal with the emergency it was essential that at least part of the professional army return from England.[30]

Montrose's final triumph displayed both the strength and the weakness of his whole campaign. His Irish musketeers, the Highland infantry and the Gordon cavalry were far superior to the badly trained part-time soldiers who had repeatedly been sent to intercept him; but they were also, for the most part, irregulars who came and went as the occasion suited them, fully justifying the fears once expressed by Hamilton. Moreover, most of the Highlanders, Alasdair MacColla included, were far more interested in fighting a war against Argyll and the Campbells, rather than for the king; and such a war was not to be fought either in the south of Scotland or in England. After Kilsyth the Highlanders went on to Glasgow; but that was as far from their homes – and the Campbells – as they were prepared to tolerate. All, headed by MacColla, decided to return north, leaving Montrose with only part of the Irish force that had landed the previous summer. Hoping to obtain recruits from southern royalists, especially much-needed cavalry, Montrose advanced towards Selkirk. Lauderdale had by this time returned to his estates near Haddington. It was probably here that he and Argyll joined a large party of cavalry under David Leslie, detached from the army in England. Leslie quickly advanced west, intercepting and overwhelming Montrose at the Battle of Philiphaugh on 13 September, an occasion witnessed by Lauderdale. Montrose escaped, eventually fleeing abroad, but almost all of what was left of his army was destroyed.[31]

With the passing of the emergency there was no more excuse for Lauderdale's continuing absence from London. Finally, in responding to further appeals sent in late October and again in early November, the Estates instructed Lauderdale 'to repair to the assistance' of his fellow commissioners. Even so, further delays followed, and he did not reappear in the English capital until Christmas Day.[32] By this time the military situation for the king was bleak: his last effective field army had been destroyed the previous summer at Langport; the help he daily expected from the Irish Confederates was never to come; the news of Montrose's debacle ended his last great hope. One by one his remaining strongholds were threatened with reduction; victory for the New Model Army and the irrepressible Cromwell was coming ever closer.

Politically the situation was more delicate than ever. Montrose's successes had been bad for the Scots in London; the obvious incapacity of their army in England, which, after the capture of Newcastle, achieved very little militarily, was even worse. Parliament was blind to its neglect of Leven's troops, who had been systematically starved of promised resources, thus forcing them to live off the land, increasing their unpopularity still further. Even for their friends in Parliament the Scots were an embarrassment; so too was the Solemn League and Covenant, which had promised much and delivered little. The rise of the Independents and the New Model Army was a serious threat to the integrity of the alliance and the influence of the Scots. With no fresh initiative, the Scots' commissioners continued to press for a peace based on the Uxbridge propositions; any new conditions would be bound to reduce their influence and weaken the prospect of Anglo–Scottish religious and military union. The prospect that the English might conclude a separate peace, in defiance of the Solemn League, led at least some on the Scots side to consider their own independent initiative: the New Model Army may have won the war; the Scots could still, it was hoped, win the peace.

In the absence of Lauderdale, Lord Balmerino, the leading Scottish layman in London, had opened up secret negotiations with the king, sending Sir Robert Moray to meet with Queen Henrietta Maria in Paris. Lauderdale was initially kept in the dark over these talks, for reasons that are not especially clear. Politically he was not suspected of any disloyalty, so Balmerino's decision not to involve him may simply have been due to an excess of secrecy.[33] Montereul, the French diplomat, was kept advised of the talks, but considered it a mistake not to involve Lauderdale, saying to Balmerino ' . . . did he not consider it necessary to take the Earl of Lauderdale more into our confidence, he being a man of great merit and resolution.'[34] This would appear to be no more than a rather coded way of saying that the deliberate deception of so influential a figure could be a source of future trouble. There is perhaps another dimension to Balmerino's deception: it made Lauderdale's public denials of the rumours of secret negotiations all the more convincing. When the matter came up before the Committee of Both Kingdoms on 17 January 1646 he absolutely denied that any approaches had been made to Charles. He was later to press for all sources of such misleading rumours to be revealed, so that 'all the world may receive satisfaction that these informations are base lyes and calumnyes', a dangerous gamble if this was simply a bluff. This demand was only dropped after some months, by which time he was clearly aware of the full extent of Balmerino's contacts, conducted by Sir Robert Moray, a soldier and diplomat who was to become a close future ally of Lauderdale.[35]

That spring Parliament finally produced a new set of proposals, reflecting a distinct hardening in its attitude towards the king, and its determination, if necessary, to pursue a peace in defiance of its Scots allies. As always, while the main emphasis of the Scots was on the question of religion, the main emphasis of Parliament was control of the armed forces. Once again they demanded that the king surrender control of the militia; this time, in contrast to Uxbridge, control was to be reserved to Parliament alone, with no role for the Scots. Of course this was a matter of English security; but the Scots were confronted by a hostile Parliament, increasingly dominated by the Independents, already in possession of a large army, demanding a complete monopoly of military force. No concern whatsoever was expressed over the Scottish concerns about national security. In April this caused an almost fatal breach in the Solemn League and Covenant: the Scots published a paper denouncing the new proposals, an initiative for which Lauderdale himself may have been responsible.[36] Lords and Commons, for once in agreement, ordered the paper to be burnt by the public hangman. Mutual suspicion, already high, was shortly to get even worse.

For Charles the struggle had always been akin to a game of chess: the one certainty was that he could not be removed from the board. His military options were fast disappearing by the spring of 1646; but he was still the king: there could be no political solution without him. It might be possible to make use of the growing rift between the Scots and Parliament, a strategy encouraged by Montereul, who continually urged the king to try to make terms with the Covenanters. On 5 May a new game began: the king left Oxford in disguise, later riding into the Scots' camp before the royalist stronghold at Newark. It was a complete gamble; although encouraged to treat with the Covenanters by Montereul, he came to Newark with absolutely no political guarantees or even assurances of safety. Lauderdale, previously advised of the king's intentions, tried to persuade him against it, saying that he could be given no guarantees until he was prepared to yield to the Covenanters' religious demands.[37] Charles' unilateral action was clearly a concern to Lauderdale and the commissioners, who issued a statement to cover their embarrassment, saying that his coming was a matter of 'astonishment', and that they would not 'make use of this seeming advantage for promoting any other ends than are expressed in the

Covenants'.[38] Unable to remain in an exposed position in central England with their compromising trophy, the Scots left Newark for the relative security of Newcastle, where they, and the king, were to remain until early the following year.

During the whole of this politically tense time, Lauderdale stayed in London, virtually the only Scot of note who did not pay his respects to the king. At a time when a breach with Parliament was a daily threat, Lauderdale performed a vital diplomatic role preventing the troubled alliance crumbling away altogether; his position was simply too important to allow him to come to Newcastle. His colleagues urged him to remain in post, providing ample testimony to the value of his work.[39] Just how fraught the situation was is illustrated by a memorandum he received at this time:

> That if there be no present settling of religion and peace, whereof there is small hopes to bee in hast of our contentment, it is to be expected they will demand presently the return [to Scotland] of our army, which if refused, it is like the strenth of their armyes will be sent northwards to move yow to go home, against which we know no remedy but the strengthening of your army from Scotland so as yow may be able to pressure your selves, and crave performances of what are obliged by Covenant and Treaty.[40]

Charles himself also came to appreciate the value of Lauderdale's position in London, keeping him advised of developments at Newcastle, with Sir Robert Moray acting on the king's behalf as an unofficial secretary. Lauderdale also kept Charles abreast of the situation in London, where the breach between the Independents and Presbyterians was becoming ever more pronounced, a development not unpleasing to the king, who still believed he could win the game at little personal cost.[41] It is also possible to detect the first signs of a change in Lauderdale's own political outlook, which was to become more pronounced the following year. His correspondence with the king would appear to indicate a growing sympathy for the royal cause, confirmed in September when Charles recommended that he be appointed to the Scottish Privy Council.[42]

Charles needed every friend he could get, for most of the people who surrounded him at Newcastle were far from sympathetic; he was continually badgered to take the Covenant, which he would not do. Parliament finally presented its own peace propositions in June, which, among other things, combined the Scots' demand that the king become a Presbyterian with the English demand that he give up control of the armed forces for a lengthy period of time. Charles hesitated, dissimulated and declined. Frustrated by the failure of his Scottish captors to make concessions, Charles threatened to reach agreement with the Independents, their worst political nightmare.[43] Lauderdale immediately warned him of the dangers:

> This suiting well with the king's inclinations had too good a hearing from him; but my Lord Lauderdale wrote from London very warmly for undeceiving the king, assuring him that he infallibly knew their designs were the ruin of monarchy and the destruction of the king and his posterity . . . But if the king would now consent to the propositions all would go right, and in spite of the devil or the Independents both, he would be quickly on his throne: but delays were full of danger for they that wished well to the king were becoming daily more heartless, and the other party grew more in their insolence.[44]

That same summer Hamilton came to see Charles. Released from his prison in the spring of 1646 by the advance of Sir Thomas Fairfax and the New Model Army into Cornwall, his first reaction had been to retreat from politics altogether in a mood of sadness and depression, which Lanark, his more determined younger brother, had to persuade him against.[45] First contact between the king and his former favourite, imprisoned for so many months by spite alone, was awkward and uncomfortable for both men; but they soon managed to rediscover something of the old warmth. Hamilton, fully aware of the peril of the king's present position, urged him to take the Covenant, an unwelcome message, no more acceptable from him than from any other Scot. Charles was committed to Anglicanism, in defiance of all pragmatic calculation; the very most he was ever prepared to concede was to allow Presbyterianism to be established in England on a three-year trial basis, although he himself would not take the Covenant.[46] Hamilton may have failed to persuade Charles to accept political reality, but he went on to begin the construction of a new royalist party in Scotland, far more broadly based than that of Montrose and the ultras.

Frustrated by the king's intransigence, both on the Covenant and the Newcastle Propositions, in late July the Earl of Loudon threatened to hand him over to the English, the first time this had been raised as a possibility. Charles refused to take the threat seriously, believing it to be just another bluff to make him sign the Covenant; but, in the end, this is exactly what the Scots had to do. It was simply too dangerous to take him across the Border into Scotland with nothing definite decided. Not only would this encourage the extreme royalists, still active in the north, but it was also likely to lead to war with England. Montereul recognised their dilemma in a report to Cardinal Mazarin:

What embarrasses most the Scots is to see themselves burdened with the person of their king, which they can neither deliver up to the English, nor put in prison without perjury and infamy, and are not able to preserve without danger and without drawing down upon themselves all the armies at present in England.[47]

With no other way forward, that October the Scots began to treat with Parliament for the removal of their army from England and the disposal of the king, the task being delegated to Lauderdale, Loudon and Warriston. There were in fact two separate points of negotiation: the payments due to the Scots army for over two years of campaigning in England, and the future location – and circumstances – of the king. The reality is that the two were always going to be considered as dimensions of the same issue, giving the impression that the Scots were prepared to 'sell' their sovereign, which all protests to the contrary did little to mitigate. Time and again, in letters and speeches, the commissioners were to emphasise that their primary function was to finalise arrangements for the removal of their army: 'And so far were they from treating about the disposing of his majesty's person, that in the end of their treaty, when they had finally agreed on all things, it was expressly declared in the first article of the treaty that passed under the great seal, that nothing relating to the king's person was concluded by it; so that after that was ended, the Scottish parliament might still have preserved the king, and brought him with their army to Scotland.'[48]

Lauderdale in particular was to remain vulnerable for the rest of his political life to the repeated charge that he had betrayed Charles.[49] In reality his position was no different from most of his fellow Scots: there were obvious dangers in leaving the king in England; there were even greater dangers in bringing him to Scotland. The charge of betrayal only ever acquires a true piquancy when events are projected forward to the king's execution in January 1649; at the time he was simply being left in the custody of his loyal Parliament, which would have been outraged by any suggestion that they represented a threat to his personal safety. Beyond expressing the rather pious hope that the king would be allowed to settle where he wished 'in honour, freedom and safety' there was little more that the Scots' commissioners, acting on instructions from Edinburgh, could do in the circumstances. Lauderdale, however, more than Loudon or Warriston, was sensitive to the risks of the whole situation, having previously warned Hamilton of the volatile political atmosphere in London.[50] On 13 January 1647, shortly before Charles was scheduled to be handed over to the commissioners of Parliament, Lauderdale left London for Newcastle. Once there, in the company of Traquair, he urged Charles, yet again, to sign the Covenant, promising to take him to Berwick if he agreed.[51] Here we appear to be looking at an alternative political strategy: at Berwick, Charles would still be in England and thus not in breach of any Scottish agreement with Parliament; he would also be close enough to Scotland to harness the support of all of his loyal subjects, secured by his adherence to the Covenant, the only realistic basis for a full restoration. Once again the scheme was wrecked on the rock of Charles' conscience.

Years later Gilbert Burnet was to write of a different conclusion to Lauderdale's meeting with Charles: he was sufficiently won over by the king that he attempted to organize a mutiny in the Scottish army.[52] Lauderdale, in Burnet's version of events, set out to persuade the senior officers to take the king to Scotland, in open defiance of the Estates. The officers agreed, but the scheme came to nothing when the king changed his mind, deciding to stay in England. It's an odd story, wholly at variance with Lauderdale's cautious political approach, to say nothing of his general demeanour at this time. It seems certain that his experience of the radicalisation of English politics was turning him, bit by bit, into a committed royalist; but he had not gone so far down that particular road that he would have risked civil war in Scotland and invasion by England at one and the same time. Dramatic and impulsive gestures were never to be part of Lauderdale's style. It is possible that, as with the Berwick scheme, he was actively working right up to the last minute to prevent the king being handed over to Parliament; but such a risky strategy could only have been pursued if Charles was willing to make concessions. The plot outlined by Burnet is worthy of Montrose or Will Murray rather than a seasoned operator like Lauderdale. It only appears in the first version of the *Memoirs*, and is unsupported by any other documentary evidence; it was almost certainly fed to the author to compensate for the prevalent tales of Lauderdale's alleged treachery towards Charles. Burnet later removed the story from the published version as putting too favourable a light on his former patron.

On 28 January the Scots marched out of Newcastle for the last time. A Parliamentary force under Phillip Skippon moved in. Two days later the first instalment of the agreed expenses was paid, followed by a second soon after: no more was ever received. The Scots came to England in 1644 as allies, who expected to have a say in the final settlement; they left as mercenaries. The ever-perceptive Montereul expressed his own feelings to Mazarin: 'I do not know the result of the bargain that the English have just concluded with the Scots, but it seems to me that they have not separated very satisfied with each other . . . It will be very difficult for the enmity that is between these peoples to remain long without breaking out.'[53]

The surrender of Charles had a sobering effect on Scotland: the intransigence of the clerical party and the more committed Covenanters had left the country far worse off than it had been ten years before. The Westminster Assembly continued its long and weary course, eventually producing a series of standards for worship only ever adopted in Scotland; there was to be no national church and no Presbyterian settlement. In the New Model Army the English possessed the kind of power that Charles could only dream of in 1637; what was worse, this army embraced a religious and political radicalism that was a far greater threat to Scottish security than Archbishop Laud had ever been. The king might be under a form of house arrest in England; but he was still sovereign: there could be no political solution without him. As the year progressed, Lauderdale, sobered by his own experiences, entered into an alliance with Hamilton. Presbyterianism was no longer the most important consideration: the real aim was to save the king.

5

CARISBROOKE

A strange new game was about to be played, perhaps nowhere better characterised than in the pages of Thomas Hobbes, who wrote that while the right of rule was with the king 'the exercise was yet in nobody; but contended for, as in a game of cards, without fighting'.[1] For a time the Scots stood like impotent spectators, concerned by developments in England, but unable to affect the outcome. Their 'allies' were the Presbyterians in Parliament, who continued for the present to insist that Charles took the Covenant as a condition of the final peace; but, as the summer progressed, Parliament began to lose ground to the army, where Cromwell and the Independents were by far the most decisive influence. For a time it looked as if there might be a new political alignment, that Charles might reach an accommodation with the Independents, who had been pleased by his rejection of the Newcastle Propositions, which threatened to place the English Church in a Presbyterian harness. The dispute between Parliament and the army supposedly centred on the payment of arrears of pay; but there were far more fundamental political and religious issues at stake. Any deal between Charles and the Independents was a threat to the security of Scotland; more than that it would usher in a new form of toleration, based on recognition of the sects, which, from the Scottish point of view, was next to complete political anarchy: 'In short, they hated the Independents mortally, and considered their power in England as sure means to the ruin of their religion, and (what they had more at heart) their fortunes.'[2]

As a sign of the new tensions, the Covenanter monolith began to crumble. Two parties began to emerge in the months following the surrender of the king, one headed by Argyll and the other by Hamilton. Argyll had the support of the Kirk, by this time exercising far more independent political authority than it had at any time in the past, but Hamilton had the support of most of the nobility and a strong segment of the middle classes, deeply conservative in outlook and more worried by the direction of political affairs than by the purity of the Covenant.

For a time Lauderdale, still an elder of the church as well as a minister of state, managed to preserve his standing with all parties, although his own sympathies were increasingly with the Hamiltonians. In February he was commended by the Commission of the General Assembly; shortly after this he was rumoured to be on his way south with Argyll to discuss a closer union between the two kingdoms.[3] The following month he received his most significant appointment to date, being named as the sole noble commissioner on a new diplomatic mission to London.[4] His instructions showed the extent to which all leading Scots laymen, Argyll included, were worried by developments in England. He was to insist on the Newcastle Propositions, although once again modified by the position the Scots had previously taken at Uxbridge: if the king was prepared to accept Presbyterianism this would bring some relaxation of the civil clauses. However, the instructions continue, even if Charles remained obdurate Lauderdale was to prevent 'any sudden resolution to his Majesty's disadvantage'. He also came armed with an additional set of instructions, too sensitive to be subject to any form of public scrutiny: in his discussions with the English Presbyterians he was to raise the possibility that in return for granting a three-year-trial of Presbyterianism in England, and parliamentary control of the militia for ten years, Charles would not be pressed to take the Covenant himself and be allowed to return to London to settle all other matters by a 'personal treaty'.[5] The Kirk had not been party to this crucial caveat, which provides the first sign of a split between the religious and civil power in Scotland since the 1638 Glasgow Assembly; it was the beginning of an alignment later to emerge in the Engagement.

No sooner had Lauderdale arrived in London than he was given permission to visit Charles, domiciled at Holmby House in Northamptonshire, in the company of the parliamentary commissioners to persuade him to agree to the Covenant and the Newcastle Propositions.[6] The meeting was not a happy one. Personally, if not politically, the king was far happier at Holmby than he had ever been at Newcastle: he was surrounded by friends and close personal advisors; the parliamentary delegations tended to be more deferential than the Scots had ever been. Once again he was able to comfort himself with the illusion that he was playing a game, the rules of which had always been set in his favour. Lauderdale, with few courtly graces, appears to have been too direct, reminding the king of some uncomfortable political truths. Charles preferred dealing with Lanark, more circumspect but far less intelligent, even though Lauderdale was far better placed to work out an effective scheme for his restoration.[7] Towards the end of April, having made little progress, Lauderdale, in one of his periodically blunt moods, wrote to Hamilton saying that there was little hope of Charles satisfying the desires of the Scots.[8]

In June the temperature increased by several degrees. Cromwell decided to break the deadlock between Parliament and the army: a group of troopers, commanded by Cornet George Joyce, kidnapped Charles, bringing him from Holmby to Newmarket, far closer to army headquarters. Cromwell now controlled the key player; Parliament was angry but impotent. For Lauderdale, whose efforts appeared to be going nowhere, this was a totally unexpected move. It was still not clear what the army intended: at the very least they were likely to present the king with a new set of proposals, which took no account of Presbyterianism or the interests of Scotland. Having no new set of instructions, the government in Edinburgh now seriously divided between the Hamilton and Argyll factions, he decided to act on his own initiative, dropping his political guard in the process. In a mood of deep anger he appeared before a committee of both houses to protest at the army's unilateral action, contrary, he felt sure, to the wishes of Parliament. His statement was unusually frank, a direct challenge to Cromwell and his associates: 'I can also assure you, in the name of the Kingdom of Scotland, that, if there be a need, they will join as one man with this Parliament, to mayntayne with their lives and fortunes the Covenant, the King's Majesty and the just libertyes of both Parliaments according to the Covenant and against whatever violence . . .'[9]

These bold words underestimated the relative powerlessness of Parliament, possessing no military arm of its own; they also overestimated the willingness of the Edinburgh authorities to commit themselves so directly to the royal cause. Hamilton was willing enough to act, but not until he had a military force of his own; the existing Scottish force was largely made up of troops loyal to Argyll. Montereul reported from Edinburgh at the end of June that: 'The Committee of Estates had no action. The offer made by Lauderdale to the English Parliament in the name of the Scottish Parliament was considered to have been done in too great a haste, and it was thought that in making it he had taken as much authority on himself as all the Parliaments [of Scotland] together might possess.'[10]

There was no attempt to recall Lauderdale; he was simply far too important, and enjoyed the support of most of the Committee of Estates. Politically, however, he was more exposed, and clearly more determined than the ever-cautious Hamilton. By October he had lost the support he previously enjoyed from Argyll, if such an interpretation can be placed on Baillie's cryptic warning 'that one verie large man is not now at your back, therefore be verie soft'.[11] Even so, while Lauderdale was beginning to act in almost exclusively political terms, he was careful not to distance himself too far from the clerical party, managing to keep their deepest fears alive, and joining with Samuel Rutherford in a timely warning: 'Wee cannot but with much grief and heaviness of spirit give you an account . . . of the establishing of licentious and pretended liberty of conscience, and of the toleration of all haeresies, sects, abominable wayes and false religions . . . contrare to our Nationall Covenant . . .'[12]

Lauderdale's greatest success that summer was to ensure that there was no deal between the king and the New Model Army. He kept up his contacts with Charles, despite the initial coolness, meeting him at Newmarket in June and again at Latimer's Cross in July, as the king was on his way to a new location at Woburn Abbey. Once again, on what authority is uncertain, Lauderdale held out the prospect of military aid from Scotland. Charles agreed to write a letter to the Committee of Estates, outlining the concessions he was prepared to make in return for such aid.[13] Lauderdale appears to have made satisfactory progress in his negotiations with the ever-stubborn Charles, though he was not beyond resorting to political blackmail to achieve his ends. In private discussions with Montereul he showed him a letter that detailed the desire of the Independents to come to terms with the Scots, provided that they were prepared to abandon the king; and another in which the commander of the Parliamentary naval forces offered to declare for the Scots and the English Presbyterians: 'I am unable to say for what purpose these two letters were shown to me, if it be not that as the Scots believe I correspond with the king of Great Britain, they may have wished to inform me that they can maintain themselves without help from him, whereas he cannot maintain himself without them, so that I, being persuaded of this, might convey it more strongly to their king.'[14]

While these manoeuvres were underway Charles finally rejected the Heads of the Proposals, the peace terms put to him by the army, now believing that the Scots card was his best gambit. It may be at this time that Lauderdale first came to the attention of the army leaders as a potentially dangerous opponent. At the end of July a party of soldiers broke into his lodging near Woburn Abbey while he was still in bed, ordering him to leave without seeing the king.[15] Protests were lodged at Westminster both by Lauderdale in person and by the Committee of Estates in writing; but once again the Lords and Commons were powerless when faced with arbitrary action by the soldiers. It was to be some weeks before he was allowed to see the king again, sufficient time to allow Charles' enthusiasm for the Scots to cool.

Before renewing his approaches Lauderdale appealed for assistance from his fellow nobles, which would have the added benefit of ending his obvious political isolation. In responding to the request the Estates sent Lanark and Loudon to join the commissioner. This may have been part of a deliberate balancing act: Lanark was obviously a leading member of the Hamilton faction, whereas Loudon was an adherent of Argyll's, though perhaps no longer quite as strongly committed as he had been. All three were to act in close collaboration over the next few months in preparing the groundwork for a treaty between Charles and Scotland.

It's worth pausing at this point to consider the relative strengths of the three men, especially in relation to the outcome of their work. In the period leading up to the conclusion of the Treaty of Carisbrooke – also known as 'the Engagement' – in late December 1647 it is impossible to separate their various contributions: all correspondence was signed jointly. However, Lauderdale, in his earlier contacts with Charles, had already laid much of the groundwork for the Engagement: the other two men made no significant original contribution. He had done much to prevent the dangerous conjunction of the army and the king, and was acting as a link between Charles and the English Presbyterians.[16] It seems likely that it was Lauderdale who opened Chancellor Loudon's eyes to the danger of the king's present position, and the necessity of supporting the Engagement.[17] Later, once back in Scotland, and again under the influence of Argyll and the Kirk party, Loudon reverted to his old alignments, openly apologising for his part in the treaty. Lauderdale was also by far the stronger personality, easily dominating the impressionable Lanark.[18] Cornelius Janssen, the Flemish artist, later painted a double portrait in which Lauderdale is seen handing a paper to Lanark. This, it has been argued, may depict a transfer of the Engagement from the former to the latter, which would 'lend additional strength to the supposition founded on the relative strength of the two men'.[19] This cannot be proved one way or the other: it is not, however, an unreasonable conjecture. Lauderdale was at the height of his early political career, enjoying power and influence that was not to be repeated for another twenty years.

In October, the king, since moved to Hampton Court, received the three Scottish ministers for the first time. Meetings were now held on a fairly regular basis, 'no men in so frequent whispers with the king'.[20] Charles was not the easiest man to deal with: he had shifted only slightly from the position he had taken at Uxbridge, and hardly at all from that taken at Newcastle. Clarendon's assertion that Lauderdale was 'passionate for the advancement of the Covenant' is yet another misreading of the aims of a man he constantly underestimated.[21] His whole approach at this time was based on pragmatic calculation, not religious dogma; he knew that if the king were to have any hope of unified Scottish support he would have to make some conciliatory gesture over the question of religion: the Covenant, in other words, would have to be acknowledged in some fashion as a political necessity. Charles was also warned by Lauderdale of the growing threat from radical undercurrents in England, represented by the Leveller movement, which embraced 'principles contrary to all order and government'.[22] No doubt there were genuine fears for the king's safety; but it is also possible that this was just another way of focusing the royal mind. Amongst other things these warnings seem to have included, perhaps for the first time, the suggestion that the king might be put on trial for his life. That same month Charles, clearly in a state of some anxiety, told Ormonde that such a trial could only be prevented by an invasion from Scotland backed up by a diversion in Ireland, ordering him to confer on these matters with Lauderdale and Lanark.[23]

Shortly after this first meeting, according to the account later set down by Bishop Burnet, the king was intercepted by Lauderdale and Lanark while he was out hunting at Nonsuch in Surrey, riding into his presence with some fifty horsemen. He was told they had come to rescue him, but the king refused to accompany them, having given his parole to the army.[24] It's an odd story, hardly in keeping with the men or the times: Charles was never reluctant to go back on his word or to make escape attempts; Lauderdale was not given to impulsive gestures. It would hardly have been possible for a large group of mounted men to come to so sensitive a presence apparently completely unobserved. It gives all the appearance of yet another fiction deliberately fed to the gullible Burnet, intended to depict the stolid politician as a romantic cavalier.

In the course of a further meeting at Hampton Court, Charles, fearful of reported assassination plots by the Levellers, suggested that he might escape to Scotland. This was little better than the action he had taken the previous year at Newark, for, as Lauderdale warned, 'except he resolved to comply with their desires about religion he might expect no better usage from the church party there than he had met with at Newcastle'.[25] It would be better, Charles was told, to go to Berwick, a plan first raised by Lauderdale the previous year. It is quite certain that Charles was now resolved to make an escape attempt; it is equally certain that he resolved not to place himself in the power of the Scots.

Rumours of a planned escape were soon well enough known for the army to place a closer guard on Hampton Court. Despite this Charles managed to get away from his wardens in early November, making not for Berwick or Scotland, but for the Isle of Wight, as the first stage in a projected flight to France. He had hoped for the assistance of Robert Hammond, the governor of Carisbrooke Castle; but Hammond was loyal to Parliament. Charles had in effect fled from house arrest into prison.

Now secured at Carisbrooke, Charles began to play the game anew, with no better intelligence than before. He made conciliatory moves towards Parliament, giving the impression that he would give up all civil power and grant religious toleration if Episcopacy could at least be safeguarded as the national church. This was so far from the Scots' position that the king felt obliged to follow it up with a defensive letter to Lanark, saying that it was only a ploy: nobody was fooled. On 25 November, clearly dissatisfied with royal duplicity, the commissioners sent Charles an unusually blunt message: 'It is no advantage to expostulate about what is past, either the carrying Your Majesty to that sad Place, or the Prejudice Your Service and we suffer by Your Majesty's Message [to Parliament]; for while You study to satisfy all, You satisfy no Interest'.[26] Soon afterwards Parliament presented the king with a new set of proposals, known as the Four Bills, which were concerned exclusively with civil matters, no mention being made of the Covenant. The effect would have been to give virtually unlimited authority to Parliament, allowing it to exercise a monopoly of military force. Lauderdale, Loudon and Lanark immediately warned Charles of the effects of the Four Bills: '. . . you divest yourself and your posterity of the militia for ever; you settle this army . . . over yourself and your Majesty's people perpetually; and by giving leave to adjournment, you and your parliament shall be carried about at the army's pleasure, as their sub-committee'.[27]

With the king isolated on the Isle of Wight, the Scots had real fears that he would come to an agreement with the army, perhaps made all the more real by his continuing unwillingness to act on the proposals they had been putting to him for several months past. Meetings held with Sir John Berkeley, a representative of the king, in early December, made some progress, only for Charles to have them abruptly terminated by recalling him to the Isle of Wight.[28] If this was just another game it was especially dangerous: for time was rapidly running out. Access to Charles was no longer as easy as it had been at Hampton Court, and was likely to become more difficult still. By 8 December Lauderdale and his colleagues were aware of new orders to place Charles under even stricter confinement, 'and from this time began seriously to treat with the king, concluding at last on such terms as they could obtain rather than such as they desired from him'.[29]

Time and again Lauderdale had tried to persuade Charles to take the Covenant, the only real basis for unified Presbyterian support: he failed. Now he was prepared to accept the best terms he could get. Accompanying the parliamentary commissioners to the Isle of Wight, who had come to receive the king's answer to the Four Bills, the Scots were given only a few days to complete their work. Under such inauspicious circumstances the Treaty of Carisbrooke was concluded on 26 December. Charles would reject the Four Bills and was promised the aid of a Scots army; in return he agreed no more than he had been prepared to concede at Newcastle: Presbyterianism to be established in England for a three-year trial period, though neither the king, nor anyone else for that matter, would be obliged to take the Covenant.[30] The Independents and all the other sects would be suppressed. Apart from that the agreement allowed for a kind of free competition between Episcopacy and Presbyterianism, a contest that in England at least was always going to be won by the former. Scotland was also promised a closer political union with England, or, failing that, the establishment of free trade between the two nations. Having secured this agreement Charles rejected the Four Bills out of hand, perhaps a little too hastily, because it gave colour to the rumours that he was attempting to reach agreement with the Scots. The whole business was concluded with as much secrecy as possible. Fearful that they might be searched on their return to London, the commissioners had the treaty encased in lead and buried in the gardens of the castle, a cloak-and-dagger procedure that must have been conducted in a considerable degree of danger.

Clarendon, ever wide of the mark, later wrote that the treaty contained so many monstrous concessions that it could only be performed if the whole of England had been in prison with Charles.[31] One would be hard put to discover what these monstrous concessions were.[32] Charles was to be given an army in return for the vaguest of promises. Sir John Berkeley provides a far more accurate, and sober, assessment: 'At last they came to a conclusion as they could get, not such as they desired from the king, but much short of it: which gave the advantage to the Lord Argyle and the clergy-party in Scotland, to oppose it as not satisfactory.'[33]

It has been written that Carisbrooke was 'an extraordinarily unrealistic treaty' and that 'Not for the last time, Lauderdale underestimated the strength and depth of Scottish opinion when it differed from his own, especially in matters of religion.'[34] This is not an accurate reading.

It's highly likely that all three of the Scots commissioners were only too well aware of the difficulties that lay ahead: Loudon, after all, had been closely associated with Argyll and the Kirk party; Lauderdale was still an elder of the church and a representative in England of the General Assembly as well as the Scottish state. All three may have feared reactions in Scotland; but they feared the power of the English army and the political radicals even more. Charles had been himself responsible for all of the limitations of the treaty: he had procrastinated to a dangerous degree, taking one step forward and two steps back, virtually up to the very last minute. In the end he gave away no more than he felt necessary. Lauderdale, Lanark and Loudon had held out for as long as possible, reaching agreement only the day before Charles' freedom to communicate with them was ended. Even so, there is evidence that the commissioners did not see the treaty as a terminus, but as a stage in an ongoing process of negotiation, which might lead to further concessions on the part of the king.[35]

There is also a regrettable tendency to read backwards from consequences to causes: the Treaty of Carisbrooke was concluded, the second Civil War followed, and the king's head fell after that. There was never any inevitability to this process. Scots armies had helped tip the political balance in England in 1640 and 1644; there is no reason why they could not do so again. There were many in England and Wales rendered deeply unhappy by the drift of events and the increasing arrogance of the New Model Army. This included not just Presbyterians and Royalists but also many former supporters of the Parliamentary party. If this discontent could be co-ordinated and synchronized with an invasion from Scotland there was a strong possibility that the New Model Army would not be strong enough to deal with the combination of forces arranged against it.

The commissioners could also be confident that the Engagement, however imperfect, could expect strong political support at home. Hamilton had done his work well. In the October elections for the Parliament scheduled to meet in March 1648 he had secured overwhelming support: Argyll was left with only eight adherents out of nearly fifty lords and earls. Hamilton had also made good progress among the middle classes: more than half the barons and almost half the burgesses, especially in the larger towns, came out in his support. This was a particularly encouraging development, for these groups had formerly been firm adherents of Argyll.[36] Most of the political talent was now with the Engagers, as Baillie later reported '...that partie, besides the advantage of the number of two at least to one, had likewise the most of the ablest speakers. For us none did speak but

Argyle and Warriston and sometimes Cassillis and Balmerinoch; but they had the Duke, the Treasurer, Lanerick, Lauderdale, Traquair, Glencairne, Cochrane, Lee, all able spokesmen . . .'[37]

The Kirk was the unknown factor; but ever since the Glasgow General Assembly it had tended to follow the lead set by the nobility, and there was no reason why it should not continue to do so. There was still no split between church and state; that would come in the months that followed. Even the most radical of the Presbyterians were outwardly committed royalists, pledged by the Solemn League and Covenant to support the king. All might be expected to share the fears of the commissioners in England, not just about the safety of Charles, but the future prospects of monarchy as an institution.

The Engagement has also been justified when set against the long sweep of history, anticipating agreements made in 1690 and 1707, inasmuch as it was based, however grudgingly, on a recognition by the Scots that the people of England should have the liberty to decide the constitution of their own church.[38] This may be so, but it was not an important consideration at the time for men who were always searching for the minimum conditions for a political agreement. Lauderdale did, however, possess sufficient flexibility of mind to recognise that Scotland and England might exist side by side with different forms of church government.[39]

With the conclusion of the Engagement, and the increasing likelihood of a new war, the commissioners had two tasks before them: to confer with the English opposition, and to convince the Scots of the value and importance of the agreement. Too much time was spent on the first task, with disastrous consequences for the second. It was not until the end of January that the commissioners finally returned to Scotland.[40] In the meantime, several of the lesser members of the London commission, including the earls of Traquair and Callander, returned to Scotland, and though they refused to give details of the Carisbrooke agreement, they let it be known that the king had given 'full satisfaction'.[41] For all who heard this, especially the ministers, it could only mean one thing: Charles had signed the Covenant. For a brief time both the Kirk Commission and the government were united, sharing a mutual pleasure at the news.[42] There were, however, worrying signs: the details were vague, and the Argyll party was quick to distance itself from the early jubilation. Traquair and Callander's reports had 'caused great joy, and a readiness to rise in arms for his [the king's] deliverance. But when I found all bound by oath [not] to reveal any of the particular concessions till the Commissioners returned, I feared the satisfaction should not be found so satisfactory as wes spoken'.[43]

The two men would have been better advised to say nothing, or one of the three principal commissioners should have returned with them; as it was, a considerable amount of political damage was done, raising expectations far above the reality. Lauderdale did his best to make good the damage, speaking before the Committee of Estates on 15 February:

> Lauderdale spoke, undertaking to prove that the Independents had broken the Covenant in all its stipulations and their treaties in each article. Both speakers [Lauderdale followed Loudon] indulged largely in reproaches against the English, the Earl of Lauderdale having remarked somewhat wittily that there were four things that Englishmen could not tolerate, the Covenant, Presbyterianism, monarchical government, and Scotsmen.[44]

It was an interesting approach, an emotional appeal based largely on national prejudice rather than a direct defence of the Engagement, with all its limitations and qualifications, so much less than the 'full satis-faction' that had been anticipated. Opposition from the church was almost immediate, becoming ever more bitter in intensity as the months passed. As early as March, with Parliament assembling in Edinburgh, the clergy were openly declaring that the king had tried to deceive them with the concessions granted at the Isle of Wight. Even the moderate Baillie thought the treaty 'did much blemish' the reputation of the negotiators, apparently blaming Lanark for Lauderdale's apostasy: 'We were malcontent with our commission: their scurvy usage of the Parliament of England, their compassion of the King's condition, Lanerick's power with Lauderdale, and both their workings on the Chancellor, made them to accept lesse, and promise more to the King, than we would stand to.'[45]

The denunciations continued, becoming ever more personal in tone. Hamilton and Lauderdale were likened by the ministers to the biblical figures of Absalom and Achitophel.[46] In July the General Assembly, meeting in Glasgow, thundered against the 'unlawful' Engagement as a union of malignants [a terms of abuse used for cavaliers] to suppress sectaries, 'a joining hands with a black devil to beat a white devil'.[47] In August Lauderdale was dropped from the Commission of the General Assembly, a position he had held for six years.[48]

When Parliament opened in March the divisions became more intense; there were now many in the Hamiltonian party clearly angry at clerical pretensions and their obvious attempts at political interference, openly saying that they would soon have reason to regret the bishops ' . . . that they had driven them away because they wished to have too large a part in civil matters'.[49] The clergy made matters worse by arguing that nothing be agreed without their consent, allowing Hamilton to recall a time when the Kirk had openly denounced the bishops' claim to have a say in secular affairs. Even Argyll was embarrassed by some of the more exaggerated claims made by his clerical allies. It has been wrongly claimed that the Engagement was the first formal recognition that theocracy might be more dangerous than autocracy, and it represented a rebellion of the lairds and nobility against clerical dominance; the issues were not so clearly defined when the agreement was concluded.[50] Rather it was the church's challenge to the authority of Parliament in the spring of 1648 that marks the first serious division within the Covenanter movement between the civil and religious factions.

When Parliament opened, Lauderdale, as Clarendon reports, was among those most concerned for the welfare of the king, though he follows this up with the usual character assassination, hardly consistent with such an attitude; for it was he 'who had been with the forwardest from the beginning of the rebellion, when he was scarce of age, and prosecuted it to the end with most eminent fierceness and animosity'.[51] As the year progressed Lauderdale operated as a political fixer, trying to balance all factions in the interests of the king, largely ignoring the denunciations being heaped on him by his former clerical supporters. In July he was appointed to a parliamentary commission to confer with the representatives of the General Assembly for the 'removall of the unhappie differences betwixt the Church and State, so verie destructive to the ends of the Covenant'.[52] Even after Loudon broke ranks, rejoining the Argyll faction, Lauderdale continued to be friendly, holding frequent private conversations with him, presumably in a search for some kind of political compromise.[53] Political differences did not necessarily mean an end to old friendships: he advised Warriston's wife on how her husband could escape prosecution by the Engager government, and continued to favour Robert Baillie: 'Lauderdaill continues kind to me and regrates much the difference betwixt us; fears it becomes a fountain of great evils, either the overthrow of the designe for Sectarists, or the putting up of the malignant partie so high, that they will hardly be gotten ruled; at best, the making of the government of our church as we exercise it, to be abhorred by all in England and abroad, and intolerable to our own state at home'.[54]

Fully aware of the damage being done by clerical opposition to the Engagement he and Lanark wrote to Charles in March, asking for further concessions, which, true to form, he refused to give.[55] Despite Lauderdale's best efforts, the suspicions of the Kirk party were deep rooted, made all the more so by his contacts with exiled English royalists like Sir Marmaduke Langdale, a Catholic, and Sir Philip Musgrave. These men had no love either for the Covenant or for the Engagement; but their support was vital to secure the success of the Scottish army. Reaching out to one side inevitably meant alienating the other. The task before him was almost impossible, attempting to deal with men wilfully blind to reality. On 5 May Parliament issued a declaration, born of desperate hope rather than serious expectation, saying that all the demands of the Covenant would be met, which only angered the English royalists without winning the support of the Kirk. Soon after, all clergymen were ordered to have nothing to do with the Engagement, an instruction that was largely carried out, uniting extremists like Rutherford with moderates like Baillie. This opposition was fatal for the success of the whole enterprise; the church was the eyes and the ears of the state; without its support the attempt to raise an army was made considerably more difficult.

Hamilton, like Lauderdale, was alarmed by the increasingly bitter dispute with the church. He remained, in most essentials, the same man he had been in 1638, looking for compromise where none was to be found, seeking to satisfy all, only to satisfy none. With the backing of Parliament, political power was his, even more completely than it had been Argyll's in the summer of 1643. Even so, he was anxious not to alienate Argyll or the Kirk any more than was necessary, refusing to intervene on behalf of the imprisoned Marquis of Huntly, despite pleas from the king to do so. In the end it was all in vain, for he was unable to master the forces ranged against him; even before he crossed the Border to save the king the Engagement was close to ruin.

Towards the end of April Hamilton began the task of creating a command structure for his new army. The man he chose to lead the cavalry was John Middleton, a professional soldier who had once helped Montrose defeat the northern royalists during the First Bishops' War. The case of John Middleton is almost as interesting as that of Lauderdale. These two men, destined one day to be the greatest of political enemies, both started their careers as firm supporters of the Covenant. Like Lauderdale, Middleton now realised the importance of compromise. But unlike Lauderdale his political principles went hand in hand with a large measure of personal spite. He now began a journey that, in the end, was to take him as far away as it is possible to imagine from the ideals of the Covenant. He was, above all, a soldier, with a soldier's view of complex problems. Increasingly angered by the Kirk's attempt to interfere in secular affairs, and by the personal humiliation he was to suffer at its hands, he was eventually to tame it by bringing the bishops back to Scotland.

The army had its officers: it now needed soldiers. In early May a proclamation was issued calling the country to arms. It was hoped that 30,000 men would join the colours before the end of the month, even more than had crossed the Border with Leven in January 1644. But the Kirk had done its work well: recruiting officers met with strong resistance, especially in the south-west of Scotland, now emerging as the main heartland of the Covenant, an area where the Presbyterian earls of Cassillis and Eglinton, both supporters of Argyll, had strong influence. Even some 600 of Hamilton's own tenants in Lesmahagow and Avondale rose against him. In Glasgow the burgh magistrates refuse to co-operate with the draft. To avoid being called up, many men from Ayrshire and Galloway took refuge among the Presbyterian communities of Ulster. There was even some resistance in the conservative north-east, though this was probably more to do with the government's treatment of Huntly rather than the influence of the ministers. Hamilton's timetable was now suffering from serious delays. This was particularly bad, for much of England and Wales was rising against the New Model Army: the second Civil War was underway.

Resistance to the Engagement was so strong in the south-west that it eventually took the form of an armed rising, when a large party of armed men gathered at Mauchline Muir, near Kilmarnock, in June. They were easily dispersed by government soldiers, led, among others, by one James Turner, destined to have a close future acquaintance with the area. This small engagement hardly justifies the grand title of the Battle of Mauchline Muir; but it had important repercussions. Hamilton was worried that the country was on the brink of civil war. An attempt to pacify the west would mean yet further delays in the planned invasion of England. Believing that success in England would be a more effective answer to discontent in the west, it was decided not to force the issue. Far fewer recruits were therefore raised in the area than was estimated. For the Covenanters, dispersed but not destroyed, Mauchline Muir was unfinished business, as Robert Baillie prophetically understood, 'so soon as our army be intangled with the English, many of our people will rise on their backs'.

The people of Ayrshire, Lanarkshire and Galloway were to have a particularly far-reaching effect on the course of Lauderdale's life. In 1648 they did much to help ruin the Engagement; twenty years later they were to frustrate all his attempts at religious accommodation. On this occasion he persuaded Hamilton that further action against the rebels would mean unacceptable delays in the invasion of England; thirty years into the future he was to engage in some unfinished business, using a military sledge-hammer in one last desperate attempt to crush all dissent. His reaction to the problems posed by the south-west perhaps provides no better illustration of just how far removed he was intellectually from the more extreme and emotional forms of Presbyterianism; for him the Covenant was always a matter of pragmatic calculation; for the ploughmen of Galloway it was more a matter of life and death. Always a compromiser, the perfect diplomat, he was in 1648 caught between two extremes: an intransigent king and an equally intransigent people, neither of which he ever fully understood.

Having gained the advantage by the action at Mauchline Muir, Lanark was keen to finish business by taking stronger action against the whole Argyll party prior to the invasion of England. Lauderdale argued against this, emphasising that there could be no further delay; some of the English risings were already failing.[56] Hamilton was inclined to accept his brother's argument, but allowed himself to be persuaded by the arguments put forward by Lauderdale, by far the strongest and most determined party in what was in effect a ruling triumvirate. The army was ordered to rendezvous on 4 July at Annan on the western border, to be led south by Hamilton; Lanark and Lauderdale were left to govern Scotland. Soon Lauderdale was given an even more vital task, which turned out to be one of the most significant of his life.

It had always been the intention of the Engagement that the king's eldest son, the 19-year-old Charles, Prince of Wales, should come to Scotland to head their army, and thus give the whole enterprise additional credibility, both at home and in England. He was formally invited on 1 May 1648 to come to Scotland from France, where he had taken refuge with his mother. Nothing more was heard until mid-July, when Sir William Fleming arrived in Scotland with a list of conditions under which the prince would come. Amongst other things, he and his mother insisted that he be allowed to bring his own advisors and to use the Anglican form of worship, to be administered by the royal chaplains.[57] For the Engagers, struggling with acute internal problems, this was disastrous news: the suggestion that the army was to march headed by a prince surrounded by malignants and Laudian priests was simply inconceivable. News of the conditions was widely broadcast, causing David Leslie, a supporter of Argyll, to write ominously that Prince Charles' use of the Service Book is 'licklie to prove dangerous for this kingdom'.[58]

Charles' conditions were particularly galling for Lauderdale, not just because of the additional doubts they cast upon royal sincerity, but also because, of the three men governing Scotland, he was outwardly the most committed, both to the Engagement and to the Covenant. He at once volunteered to go and see the prince, now cruising somewhere in the North Sea with sections of the fleet that had mutinied against Parliament. Lauderdale was by far the best man for the job: he was intimately acquainted with all of the political issues involved and had proved himself to be a skilled diplomat and negotiator. It was also suggested, in a scurrilous pamphlet published at the time, that the Hamilton brothers were anxious to have him out of the way: 'That their intentions of good to this kingdome are so worthy of suspect, as that the Lord Lauderdale, who might be thought (though misguided) to have some honest principles left, is judg'd fit to be packed away to France, as a likely opposer of their bad ends'.[59] The anonymous author goes on to repeat the old libel that Hamilton intended to claim the crown of Scotland for himself, coupled with the even more absurd suggestion that he intended to conquer England. Lauderdale was chosen for this delicate mission because he was trusted. The Maitlands had long been allies of the Hamiltons: Lauderdale's father was a follower of the duke's party through some difficult times, and he himself enjoyed a close partnership with Lanark, right up to the latter's death in 1651.

In the instructions issued to Lauderdale by the Committee of Estates he was to emphasise the importance of Prince Charles' presence in Scotland; to urge him of the necessity of using forms of worship established by law in Scotland, and not to bring with him any against whom 'the kingdom of Scotland hath just cause of exception'.[60] The terms of the mission were widened to include approaches to France and Holland, asking for military support. Just as he was about to sail the Estates wrote to Queen Henrietta Maria commending 'the Earl of Lauderdaill, who hath bein one of the most eminent actors in engaging this kingdome in the present undertakings for his majesties rescue and reestablishment'.[61] Lauderdale sailed from Leith on 4 August.[62] Some royalists were apparently happy to anticipate failure:

> So soon as it came to be noised, that Lauderdale was embarked, the royalists called him a ventrous man, who would hazard to go to the prince, having been so active against the king: For they presumed, that the prince could not be ignorant, how for the space of four years he had resided constantly in London, fomenting the combination betwixt the two parliaments, and never returned until he left the king a close prisoner in Carisbrooke castle . . . And they pleased themselves with conjectures, what the prince's deportment would be to him. But ere long, contrary to expectation, news came, that the prince made him welcome with familiarity and respect enough, which put them to a stand.[63]

Making first for the coast of Holland, Lauderdale's ship anchored at the mouth of the River Maas, asking passing vessels for news of the prince. Charles, he discovered, had left the area some three weeks before, and was somewhere off the south-east coast of England; 'So I resolved to bridle my curiosity, which indeed was great, to see Holland, and to content myself with a sight of the steeples.'[64] He finally caught up with the prince in the Downs, just off the coast of Kent, on 10 August, on board the *Constant Reformation*. There were no doubt many on the English side, including the ever-hostile Edward Hyde, one of the Prince's leading councillors, who joined with the Scots royalists in expecting failure. Lauderdale, now in his early thirties, was hardly the type to appeal to the 19-year-old Charles. We know from Burnet and others he was physically unprepossessing, and was personally blunt to the point of rudeness. His lack of courtly graces had never appealed to the prince's fastidious father. Neither man, so far as we know, had ever met the other; so it seems likely that Charles was primed by hostile briefings from Hyde, who had previously crossed swords with Lauderdale at Uxbridge. Yet, despite all the signs, the meeting was a remarkable success, both on a diplomatic and, more importantly, on a personal level. It succeeded because both men wished it to succeed: whatever the prince, or more likely his mother, had said about religion, he possessed a flexibility of mind, in refreshing contrast to the dogmatic and stubborn Charles I, that allowed him to recognise political reality and dispense quickly with any obstacles that got in the way of his own ambitions. He wanted to come to Scotland, to lead an army, to rescue his father; all other considerations were secondary. Lauderdale spoke with him often, sometimes in private, and assured Lanark that 'I find him as good and as earnest to be with us as is possible . . . The great opinion I have of him I shall leave till meeting, and then I am confident your Lordship will be of my opinion when you see his Highness that we are like to be very happy in him'.[65]

During these crucial days the two men established an understanding – and a mutual affection – that was to last over the years. Charles quickly accepted all the conditions Lauderdale brought: he would worship in Scotland according to the Presbyterian rite and would not bring any to Scotland who were politically unacceptable to the government.[66] This included, amongst others, the Marquis of Montrose, now living in exile on the Continent. Lauderdale also established during these shipboard discussions one of the themes that was to characterise his later administration of Scotland: a deep resentment at any attempt by English ministers or advisors to interfere in purely Scottish affairs, an attitude calculated to provoke Hyde, amongst others.

With these preliminaries out of the way Lauderdale intended to complete his mission by sailing on to France; but Charles would not allow him to go, sending Sir Robert Moray in his place. Instead the two men went to Holland, where further discussions were held in late August. It is almost certain at this point that Prince Charles would have gone immediately to Scotland, landing first at the English port of Berwick, which had been prepared for his reception.[67] Learning of the prince's intention, and anxious not to be abandoned, the sailors seemingly came close to a second mutiny, threatening to throw the Scotsman overboard; but all plans came to nothing when disastrous news came from Scotland: Hamilton had been destroyed, and Argyll and the Kirk party had seized power in a military coup.[68]

After crossing the Border in early July, Hamilton proceeded south with an astonishing lack of urgency. All over England and Wales the resistance to Parliament was collapsing, largely destroyed in a piecemeal fashion, as Lauderdale had predicted. Hamilton was bad as a politician; he was disastrous as a soldier. His army, badly under-strength and short of supplies, had a command structure bedevilled by personal and political rivalries. As always, Hamilton led from behind, content to be directed by others. General John Lambert, commanding the Parliamentary forces in the north, shadowed the Scots on their painfully slow progress south. On 13 August Cromwell joined Lambert, fresh from a successful campaign in south Wales. The combined force then launched an attack on Hamilton's eastern flank, destroying his army in a running battle from Preston south to Warrington in Lancashire. The unlucky duke managed to escape from the debacle, only to be captured by Lambert at Uttoxeter. He was taken to London, later to be put on trial for his life. In his defence he pleaded that he was a Scot, acting on the instructions of the Scottish Parliament; but unluckily for him he also had an English title – the Earl of Cambridge – and was thus condemned to die as a traitor to the people of England. Sentence was carried out in March 1649.

No sooner had news been received in Scotland of the defeat of the Engager army at Preston than the communities of the south-west rose in revolt, as Baillie had previously anticipated, advancing on Edinburgh in what gives all the appearance of a carefully co-ordinated plan. This was the Whiggamore Raid, derived from 'whiggam', a term apparently used by west-country people in urging on their horses.[69] It was later to be shortened to 'Whig', and used as a term of abuse for extreme Presbyterians. Although the rebels had the support of Argyll and some other peers, they were still too ill-armed to overcome Lanark, heading the Engager government, by their own efforts alone. Cromwell crossed the Border on 21 September, reaching agreement with Argyll at Edinburgh. Lanark capitulated and Argyll agreed that all those who had been implicated in the Engagement would be removed from all positions of public trust. A few weeks later Cromwell wrote to the speaker of the House of Commons, announcing that Scotland was 'like to be a better neighbour to you now than when the great pretenders to Covenant, religion and treaties (I mean Duke Hamilton, the Earls of Lauderdale, Traquair, Southesk and their confederates) had the power in their hands'.[70]

It seems certain that Cromwell believed that Argyll and the Kirk party, which now came into its own, would continue to be dependent on English military support, and neglected to conclude a more permanent settlement or peace treaty between the two nations. But this alliance between Covenanter and Independent, both natural enemies, was too unstable to last. The only real fruit it bore was the Act of Classes, passed by a new Parliament summoned by Argyll in January 1649. By this all prominent Engagers, Lauderdale amongst them, were excluded from political or military office. In addition there was a sliding scale of exclusions, ranging from ten years to one, for those guilty of lesser offences.[71] All readmission was subject to the approval of the Kirk, which thus acquired a decisive hold on public life, far beyond the powers held by even the greatest of the bishops. When the showdown came between the Covenanters and the Independents the Act of Classes was to be of major benefit to Cromwell. It's easy to condemn Argyll for this ill-advised measure; at the time, though, it was undoubtedly the minimum condition necessary to prevent a full-scale English invasion, which surely would have followed if Lanark had remained in control. This was a game that had to be played, and Lauderdale was among the losers.

6

THE DARK YEARS

Lauderdale, isolated in Holland, was a minister without a country. Even so, he was not yet ready to give up, in contrast to most of his colleagues. He did not despair at the news of the Battle of Preston; it was certainly bad, but something might be retained from the wreckage. With his deep knowledge of Scottish politics, and all of the leading parties involved, he knew how weak an Argyll government would be, especially as Lanark, even after Preston, continued, for a time, to possess a monopoly of professional military force. He was active in trying to persuade the prince to hold to his resolve to come to Scotland, which would do much to revive the Engager cause.[1] The picture, moreover, was still rather confused: it was to be some weeks before the results of Argyll's discussions with Cromwell became clear. However, Charles' English councillors were undeniably correct in advising against a course of action that could easily have placed him in the power of Argyll or Cromwell. Lauderdale, according to Clarendon, was left to seethe in impotent frustration:

> And within a few days, the earl of Latherdale seemed rather to think of going hither himself, where his own concerments were in great danger, than of pressing the Prince to so hazardous a voyage; and after a few weeks' more stay in the Hague, upon intelligence from his friends in Scotland how affairs went there, he returned thither in a ship that transported him thence, and with much rage and malice against the council about the Prince as against Cromwell himself.[2]

Lauderdale did indeed return to Scotland; but probably unknown to Clarendon, he came on a political as well as a personal mission, armed with secret instructions known only to Prince Charles and his cousin, the Dutch Prince of Orange.[3] We have no firm evidence about the content of these instructions: at the very least they would have involved intelligence gathering, coupled, it also seems clear, with some kind of overture to the new government. It was important to discover where the real source of power lay. Charles had received two messages towards the end of the year, one from Lanark and the other from Argyll. Lanark, no doubt disgusted by the role of the Kirk in the Whiggamore Raid, now disowned the earlier Presbyterian conditions brought to Charles by Lauderdale, and promised to greet the prince with a new army to support the royal cause. Argyll also promised to raise an army for the king, despite his agreement with Cromwell, if only the prince would come to Scotland.[4] Charles sensibly chose to ignore both invitations, sending Lauderdale in his place.

Lauderdale came to Scotland in early January 1649 on a man-of-war supplied by the Prince of Orange, providing further evidence of the public nature of his commission.[5] It was quickly apparent that Lanark was in no position to make good his offer to Prince Charles, and that the Kirk party was in full control:

> As soon as I landed I found that those who after the defeat of the army had usurped the power did proceed with grete violence against all those who ware joined in the engagement and most particularly against my self. I found that William Duke of Hamilton, then Earle of Lanerick, was confined to his house and he and many other persons of quality were turned out of all employments and declared incapable of public trust and that I had been fined and my tenants ruined . . .[6]

It was a dangerous situation for the earl, who, by the newly passed Act of Classes, had effectively been declared an outlaw. He seems to have enjoyed some private assurances of safety from Argyll, powerful but far from supreme, and also came armed with a personal invitation from Lord Balmerino. Argyll's position was hardly a comfortable one, dependent, as he was, on two things: the goodwill of Cromwell and the support of the Kirk party. He was dangerously isolated from his own class, enjoying the support of only a handful of nobles. Despite all he was a royalist, but with no clear sense of how to advance the cause. In England the political situation was extremely worrying: Parliament had been purged of its remaining Presbyterians as a preliminary to the trial of the king. It was probably clear to all by this stage that such a trial could have only one outcome.

Given the circumstances, it seems likely that some kind of discussion took place between Lauderdale and Lanark, on the one hand, and prominent Argyll supporters, possibly Balmerino, on the other. No other explanation would appear to fit the facts: Lauderdale had an official commission, a safe conduct and a formal invitation.[7] Some additional proof is provided by the Countess of Lanark, who later confirmed to the French envoy in Edinburgh that her husband and

Lauderdale were co-operating with the Scottish government.[8] These discussions were most likely concerned with some kind of bridge-building, an attempt to end the disastrous divisions that had rocked Scotland throughout the course of 1648, and had now come close to wrecking the crown. Prince Charles had shown himself willing to make the kind of concessions on the question of religion that his father had always refused. If the king were to be executed by his English Parliament, then some acceptable formula would have to be found for the succession in Scotland. The only alternative to an agreement between the former Engagers and the Presbyterians was the same kind of disastrous civil war that had almost ruined the country in 1644 and 1645, a strategy still favoured by Montrose and the ultra-royalists, with the important difference that England would now be in a position to intervene. Lauderdale was consistent in his defence of a new axis between the Engagers and the Kirk party: even after he was forced into exile he continued to advocate an alliance with Argyll and the established authorities in Edinburgh during debates of the royal council in Holland.[9] Later that year he was to write of the need for 'a happy conjunction between the king and his people in Scotland, which I think the only way for preservation of religion, his Majesty, and the peace and happiness of that poor country'.[10]

Lauderdale's position in Scotland at this time was far from secure, despite the official protection he enjoyed. Balmerino told him that if he sought formal reconciliation with the Kirk he would be expected to make a penitential speech in public, a humiliating procedure to which his old ally Loudon had recently submitted.[11] Even so, Loudon was a special case, having long repented his part in the Engagement; it is unlikely that Lauderdale would have had so simple a passage. There is some evidence to suggest that he did indeed put out some overtures to his opponents, only to have them rejected out of hand, as an English news-sheet of the time reports: 'An Act is past for officers of state to answer, if they appear not they are to be discharged of their trust. E. Loutherdale expresseth a readiness to give obedience to all decrees of Parliament, but was not thought fit, and therefore he was ordered to appear by writ, which was accordingly, a Committee appointed to consider him.'[12]

Besides hostility at home, Lauderdale also had to reckon on the resentment he had engendered in England as one of the chief architects of the Engagement. For many the second Civil War was an act of deep duplicity, and of all men living, as Burnet later relates, Lauderdale was the most odious to the army.[13] In his later memorandum he himself emphasises the risk he was now under: 'I spoke with the Duke Hamilton

[Lanark] and at my return I found quickly that Scotland wold be too hot either for him or for me. For the rebels in London having heard from Holland that I was sent in a man of war to Scotland then presently took jealousie and despatched one Roe to there freands in Scotland to demand the then Earle of Lanerick and me to be delivered unto [them?] . . .'[14]

Ignoring the pleas by Balmerino and the Earl of Cassillis in his favour, Parliament ordered the arrest of both Lauderdale and Lanark on 25 January. Two troops of horse under the command of Robert Hackett were delegated for the purpose, but Balmerino gave Lauderdale sufficient warning to allow him and Lanark to take refuge on board the Dutch ship, anchored at Leith, which presumably enjoyed some extra-territorial status.[15] One John Henderson was allowed on board to order the fugitives to appear before Parliament, on pain of treason, but Lauderdale, not willing 'to trust the Sancts too much', sensibly ignored the summons.[16] On 28 January, having achieved nothing in Scotland, Lauderdale sailed back to Holland: he was thus still at sea when Charles I was beheaded in Whitehall two days later.

While Lauderdale was in Scotland, a tragic drama was closing in England. Angered by the second Civil War, and the perceived faithlessness of the king, Cromwell and a faction in the army decided the time had come to end the constitutional deadlock. The Engagement, 'intended for the king's relief and restoration', James Turner wrote, 'posted him to his grave'. Charles was moved from the Isle of Wight and taken to the more secure prison of Hurst Castle on 1 December. Soon after, the army took control of London, and a party of soldiers, commanded by Colonel Thomas Pride, expelled the Presbyterians from Parliament: all those, in other words, who wished to continue negotiations with the king. The remainder, to be known as the Rump, agreed that a court be appointed to try Charles Stewart 'the man of blood'. All played their allotted parts a little like sleep-walkers, sending the king towards the block at Whitehall; England was now a republic.

The death of the king, carried out in the face of Scottish protests, had a sobering effect on all shades of national opinion. No sooner was news of his execution received in Edinburgh in early February than Chancellor Loudon, dressed in black, immediately proclaimed Charles II, not just as King of Scotland, which he and the government were fully entitled to do, but also as King of England, an obvious provocation to the new Commonwealth authorities in London. Lauderdale, obviously discouraged by the rigidity he had met in Scotland during his recent visit, now detected signs of a change of attitude, as he told Ormonde: '. . . I believe that the horrid murder of the king, and the sense of their own danger, if these bloody villans at London continue still in power, have wrought a change in Edinburgh to the better: and if the right way be taken, I shall not doubt but Scotland may be united and ingaged for the king'.[17]

What was the right way, and how was it to be found? Charles was now by right King of Scotland, but he would never be allowed to exercise this right without making the kind of concessions that his father had always resisted: as a minimum this would mean that he would have to subscribe to the Covenant. This time there was an important difference: in 1643, when the Solemn League and Covenant was devised, Presbyterianism was only held up as a model for the English; now, as far as the Kirk party was concerned, it was the only acceptable form of church government for the whole of the United Kingdom. There was, however, another back door into England, or, so it was thought, one less hedged with conditions than the Scottish route. In Ireland the Earl of Ormonde had at last managed to conclude a working peace with the Confederate authorities in Kilkenny, also sobered by events in England, and happily less insistent on shackling the young king with onerous political obligations. Whether it was best to take a Scottish or an Irish course was to engender serious debate among the royalists well into the early summer of 1649.

In The Hague, temporary headquarters of the royal court, two distinct parties took shape among the exiled Scots: the former Engagers, now under the leadership of Lauderdale, and the extreme royalists, headed by Montrose. Montrose, learning of the arrival in Holland of Lauderdale and Lanark, struck the first blow in what was to become a political war between the two camps, made all the more bitter by deep personal resentment, in a letter to the king: 'I shall not trouble you with much, only let me intreat you take heed to my country-men's cunninge, who upon feare of meddling, doe give out Hamilton's death and that Argyle should be fled from Scotland, and that all the country is the king's. All which is only to abuse the king and withhold, or at least retard, him from taking the courses for his own safety, for they know iff once we ingage, the busyness is halfe-done, and that in a few weeks they must be honest men, or else have no brains left to take their parts'.[18]

Montrose, supported by Hyde, was in favour of the king going to Ireland, for no trust could be given in their view to the Covenanters, who simply wanted him in their power.[19] But if Montrose despised Lauderdale and his cautious counsels, Lauderdale returned the emotion in full measure, realising that the heroic marquis was little better than a dangerous adventurer, devoid of all political sense. Lauderdale was supported by many of his fellow exiles, including, interestingly enough,

the Earl of Callander, a royalist of less extreme views than Montrose.
Alarmed at the prospect of the king seeking restoration at the head of
a Catholic Irish army, all urged him to go to Scotland: 'That if he did
not goe, and that hastily, with a resolution to seal the Covenanters, he
wald alienat the hearts of all the Protestants in all his kingdoms from
him: and this was pressed by the Erls Lauderdail, Calendar, Lanrick
with such evident self denyal of their own interests as being grievously
censured by this present Parliament, that had the king been left to
himself, it was thought he could not but follow their advice.'[20]

It was clearly against the king's interests that his Scottish supporters
should be so bitterly divided. Some attempt was made through Hyde,
perhaps not the most appropriate mediator, to reconcile the two sides,
but Lauderdale in particular was implacable. William, Earl of Lanark,
who became second Duke of Hamilton following the execution of his
brother in early March, should, in theory, have headed the old Engager
party as the most senior of the Scottish nobles; but he was bound,
seemingly in both affection and fear, to Lauderdale. Hyde tells an
interesting story in this regard. As part of his continuing efforts at
mediation he came to see Hamilton one night at the house he shared
with Lauderdale in The Hague. In the course of their interview Hamilton
opened up to Hyde, expressing some contempt for the Covenant and a
desire to be reconciled with Montrose; however, he continued: 'There
is . . . a worthy gentleman who lodges in this house, the earl of
Latherdale, my friend and kinsman, who upon conscience loves me
heartily; and yet I dare say nothing to him, either against the Covenant
or for the marquis of Montrose; and if I should, I believe he would
rather chose to kill me than to join with me; so much is he transported
with prejudice in both these particulars, and incapable to hear reason
upon either of these arguments . . .'[21]

At this point Lauderdale entered in his nightgown, bringing all
discussion to a premature conclusion. No further discussions could be
held, Hamilton later said, 'without giving jealousy to his friend
Latherdale, which he had no mind to do'. As with many of Hyde's
tales, this is another attempt to discredit a man he never fully understood, and is best treated with caution; Lauderdale's attitude towards
the Covenant was always far more pragmatic than Hyde allows.
Hamilton, moreover, was fully aware of the role Montrose had played
in discrediting his brother in the eyes of Charles I and the dangers his
militant counsels represented to a moderate royalist policy in Scotland,
with which he himself was so much associated. Nevertheless,
Lauderdale's personal domination of the impressionable duke during
these days in The Hague finds some confirmation in a letter to

Ormonde: 'I find Duke Hamilton very moderate and certainly he would be much more, were it not for the violence of Lauderdale who haunts him like a fury'.[22]

Following the lead set by Lauderdale, the Engagers refused to meet with Montrose. More than this, if he entered the room, even if the king were present, they immediately withdrew. Hyde angered by this 'absurd' behaviour, tackled Lauderdale directly, asking what offence the marquis had given: 'The earl told him, calmly enough, that he could not imagine or conceive the barbarities and inhumanities that he was guilty of in the time that he made war in Scotland; that he never gave quarter to any man, but pursued all the advantages he ever got with the utmost outrage and cruelty; that he had in one battle killed fifteen hundred of one family, the Campbells, of the blood and name of Argyle and that he had utterly rooted out several names and entire noble families.'[23]

Hyde also reports that, in his passion, Lauderdale was freely telling others that he would rather the king was never restored than that James Graham be allowed to come to court. Lauderdale continued to be held in great favour by Charles at this time, which he surely would have sacrificed if he had ever made such an indiscreet remark. There would appear to be an element of public theatre in this ostentatious display of hostility; this was a game being played out, in other words, for the benefit of other eyes, rather than because it displayed a true measure of real feeling. Lauderdale, unlike Hamilton, had no reason to dislike Montrose personally, having never suffered any direct injury at his hands. Montrose, rather, was a political danger, a serious threat to the integrity of the Engagement, to which Lauderdale was still deeply committed. Hyde and Charles never seem to have fully understood the depth of hostility towards Montrose in Scotland: it would be impossible to conclude any agreement with Argyll and the Kirk party in which he was involved. Moreover, the Irish strategy favoured by sections of the court also entailed a corollary: a fresh military assault on Scotland by Montrose. This whole enterprise could only work in favour of Cromwell and the English sectaries. With commissioners due to arrive in Holland from Scotland to discuss the terms for Charles' accession to the throne, it was clearly vital to put as much distance as possible between moderate royal opinion and the action favoured by Montrose.

The commissioners from Scotland arrived in The Hague on 26 March. They included John Kennedy, Earl of Cassillis, and Robert Baillie, both men with whom Lauderdale had enjoyed good relations in the past. The following day, dressed in mourning as a sign of respect for the late king, they met with his successor. Cassillis spoke for

Parliament and Baillie for the Kirk. Charles was offered the crown of Scotland, but only if certain conditions were observed: he was required to remove from his presence that 'cursed man' James Graham, subscribe to both the Covenants, and submit all ecclesiastical affairs to the General Assembly and all civil affairs to Parliament. These demands reflect a hardening of attitude since the passing of an act of Parliament on 7 February, in which Charles is only required to declare his 'allowance' of the Covenants, suggesting that Argyll was beginning to lose ground to some of his more intransigent colleagues.[24] It was to be some weeks before Charles gave his answer to these unpalatable terms.

Lauderdale, in contrast with the more circumspect Hamilton, was quick to establish good relations with his old colleagues, clearly looking for some chink in the armour. His contacts with them were so close that many of his fellow royalists questioned his loyalty, apparently prepared to believe that he had some secret understanding with Argyll.[25] However, his attempts to obtain some softening in their attitude were frustrated by the rigidity of their instructions. When the matter finally came up in council on 25 May Hamilton refused to give Charles any advice at all, using the somewhat lame excuse that he was 'un-acquainted' with conditions in Scotland, 'but Earle Lauderdale enlarged himself somewhat and was fully for the Covenant'.[26] Unfortunately, this is not very revealing, as the same might have been said of Montrose: in separate discussions he agreed that Charles might accept the National Covenant out of expediency while rejecting the more ambitious Solemn League and Covenant. The difference between the two is that Lauderdale was sincere in his affection for the political aims of the Engagement, and accepted that Charles would have to conciliate a broad range of Presbyterian opinion. He no longer believed, if he ever had, that Presbyterianism could be imposed on England; but that it might be desirable to pay some kind of lip service towards this end, as part of a grander exercise in political expediency. In the end what he aimed at was national unity, or as much unity as could be obtained in the circumstances; Montrose, in contrast, advocated the politics of dissension and division.

Lauderdale's attachment to the Engagement is openly displayed in a letter he wrote in June to Sir Robert Wauchope, a member of the Argyll faction. Scotland, as far as he is concerned, is likely to be wrecked by factionalism, the factionalism of the Kirk party on one side and that of the ultra-royalists on the other: 'I shall strive, God willing, to follow your advice, and to contribute still my best indevours for a happy conjunction betwixt the king and his people in Scotland, which I thinke the onely way for preservation of religion, his Majestie, and the peace and happiness of that poore country. These have been the principles which constantly I have adhered to, to the best of my understanding, how ever I have been misunderstood.'

He continues with a defence of the 'honest, thogh unhappy ingagement', which he describes as being as good an action as he was ever involved in, and for which he refuses to repent, even if it means years of exile. Scotland could only prosper in the pursuit of a policy of national unity: '. . . which is the only way to regaine your reputation, to make you considerable, and to prefer your peace, I should not doubt but by Gods blessing the King and Scotland should quickly agree; for the keeping up of your acts of classis, and those divisions which make you to be lookt upon as a faction, and encourages your enemies to undertake against you . . .'[27]

Robert Baillie, returning in full-measure the friendship Lauderdale had shown to him in 1648, later attempted to defend him – unsuccessfully – before the Glasgow General Assembly in July 1649.[28] Nevertheless, he was clearly disturbed by the latter's stubborn attachment to the beliefs that had guided his actions over the last few years, when so many others were prepared to make terms, ' . . . I wish from my heart,' he wrote in September, 'that Lauderdale may be moved to doe what I find Callendar and Dunfermline ready for . . . which, I hope, may be the means to teach that man for whom alone my love makes me afraid some more wisdome'.[29]

On 29 May Charles, having accepted Montrose's advice, told the commissioners that he would accept the National Covenant and Presbyterian government of Scotland, but that he would give no assurances over church government in England and Ireland until he had consulted the parliaments of those countries. While reasonable enough in itself, it was less than the king's father had promised under the Engagement: the Scots could hardly be expected to fight and die for no better reason than to put Charles on the English throne. In deep disappointment the commissioners left The Hague on 6 June. Charles was still King of Scots, but in name only. Now committed to the Irish road, he drew out the second arrow in his quiver: Montrose was reappointed as commander-in-chief in Scotland with powers to raise foreign forces for a descent on his native land. By September he had sufficient force to take control of the Orkneys, which he proceeded to turn into a base for an invasion of the mainland. Virtually up to the last minute Lauderdale opposed this strategy, even obtaining the support of William of Nassau, Prince of Orange, for an agreement between Charles and the Covenanters. Now, with his advice ignored, he slipped temporarily into the background.

As the summer progressed Charles' favoured scheme began to collapse. In August Cromwell landed in Ireland, cutting a bloody swathe through the island, and ending forever any hope that it might be used as a base for a successful restoration. Scotland alone remained. Too pragmatic to rely exclusively on the advice given by Montrose and others, Charles had maintained contact with Argyll, even after the failure of the talks in The Hague. These had been encouraging enough for the marquis to propose to Parliament in August 1649 that a fresh approach should be made to the king. Although Argyll had chosen his timing with some care, raising the suggestion when some of his more intransigent colleagues were missing, Parliament, in no mood for compromise, only agreed that fresh talks proceed on the basis of the terms rejected by the king in May. With almost no room to manoeuvre, the royal council decided to reopen formal negotiations with the Covenanters at the Dutch town of Breda in March 1650.

Argyll was in a far from comfortable position politically. He was always firm in his support of the Covenant, but he was never a fanatic. He was the nominal head of the government that had been put in place after the Whiggamore Raid. Nevertheless, he appears to have been steadily losing influence to his more intransigent colleagues, men like Archibald Johnston of Warriston, more fully trusted by the saints of the Kirk party. Most of his fellow peers were outlaws or politically quiescent; supporters of the Engagement or uncompromising royalists, which only served to increase his sense of isolation. There was little in the way of republican sentiment in Scotland; but there was an almost total lack of political realism. Cromwell's progress through Ireland, as Argyll must have realised, ended one threat only to substitute another, infinitely more serious in nature. If Scotland were to face a challenge from England it would be crucial to achieve as much national unity as possible, an objective Argyll undoubtedly shared with Lauderdale. In his attempts to persuade Charles to come to Scotland, Argyll continued to maintain contact with Lauderdale and the other leading Engagers, who by January 1650 had reappeared in The Hague in some strength.[30] Lauderdale was particularly useful because he never demonstrated any personal animosity to the men who had effectively disinherited him at home. He had performed a useful bridge-building role in 1649 and could be expected to do so again.

Even before the Breda talks opened Charles had effectively lost the game: his previous preference for the Irish, and the continuing favour he showed towards Montrose, only deepened the suspicions of the uncompromising Scots. The terms he was presented were even less palatable than those of the previous year: he was required to recall

Montrose, confirm all acts of the Scottish Parliament since 1641, sign the Covenants and declare that they applied to all three of his kingdoms, leave behind any of his supporters considered to be malignants, disown Ormonde's treaty with the Irish and introduce new measures against Catholics. Even in his own household Charles was to allow no form of worship other than Presbyterianism, which would mean denying liberty of conscience to his own mother. Lauderdale did his best, and was particularly solicitous towards the commissioners, being 'very studious to doe them all the furtherance and good office that is in his power'.[31] He co-operated closely with the Earl of Lothian, an old associate, and now one of the principal agents of Argyll; he liaised between the king and the commissioners, and successfully persuaded at least some of the Scots of the value of a compromise agreement.[32] Some, following his interventions, were prepared to agree that the king would not be forced to take the Covenants, although whether they had the authority to make such a concession is not at all clear. His efforts, and those of Hamilton, to heal the divisions of 1648 were particularly worthy of note, although at least some thought it was all part of an elaborate deception:

> ... when ever the King goes home, he [Hamilton] and Latherdale and Calander and Dunfermline will be the men that carry all ... these men will ... carry on the design to the same end to which the former Hamiltonian party would have carried it: but to the end they may do it with less opposition, and make the Kirk their instrument, which the late Duke Hamilton disobliged, they are now resolved to omit nothing to perswade Argyle that they perfectly trust him, but their intention is to have him thereby fully in their power and without guard. Believe it, I have it from those who have the rule there, they perfectly hate Argyle and his Kirk, and speak perpetually with indignation, and will destroy them if they prevail ... [33]

There is no evidence for this, either then or later; but it illustrates the intense atmosphere of distrust that surrounded the Breda talks. Charles was no more inclined to accept the new conditions than he had been those of May 1649; he continued to act in bad faith, encouraging Montrose, no longer in the hope that he would enjoy military success, but in the expectation that his efforts might cause the Covenanters to offer a less bitter medicine. In the end his efforts only made the mixture far less palatable.

Montrose crossed to the mainland in April 1650 from his base in the Orkneys, hoping for the successes of 1644; instead his little army, composed of foreign mercenaries and unwarlike Orcadians, was surprised and overwhelmed at Carbisdale in Sutherland. Montrose managed to escape, but was captured soon after and brought to Edinburgh, where he was executed on 21 May. His efforts undid all Lauderdale's work at The Hague. Parliament now insisted on all of the original terms brought to Holland by the commissioners, though a decision was taken, on the suggestion of the moderates, to conceal this from the king on the assumption that, once underway, it would be more difficult for him to refuse. It was an act of calculated hypocrisy.

Lauderdale, throughout the talks in Holland, had been an invaluable asset to both the king and the Covenanters; but this made no difference to his political status: he was still an outlaw from Kirk and nation. On 18 May an act was passed in Edinburgh excluding Lauderdale and others from entering Scotland until they had repented their involvement in the Engagement.[34] Both he and Hamilton were formally forbidden to accompany the king to Scotland, though both men decided to ignore this and risk parliamentary disapproval.[35] All along he had advised the king to make politically necessary concessions, a road he himself was now prepared to take.

When Charles anchored off Garmouth in the Moray Firth on 23 June he learned the full cost expected of him: before landing he would have to sign the Covenants. Charles tried to argue that the laws of England took precedence over them. The commissioners refused to allow this caveat, adding another clause to the Solemn League and Covenant, committing the king to accept all future acts of Parliament embodying the ideals of the text. Charles could either sign or return to Holland: he signed. Scotland now had the pretence of a Covenanted king; for pretence it was. Charles had been deliberately manipulated into a position where he had no choice but to swallow all that was given to him. If the king was cynical in taking an oath that was contrary to his conscience, the Covenanters were equally cynical in forcing him to do so. Even Alexander Jaffray, one of the commissioners, had the sense to recognise this when he noted in his diary: 'We did both sinful entangle and engage the nation, ourselves and that poor young prince to whom we were sent, making him sign and swear a Covenant which we knew from clear and demonstrable reasons that he hated in his heart'.[36]

Soon Charles found himself housed in the splendours of Falkland Palace, with all regal state; but he was still king in name only. The pleasures of his Dutch exile, limited as they were, soon faded into memory as he was confronted by the Spartan realities of Covenanted Scotland. According to Clarendon he was made to observe the Sabbath with more rigour than the Jews. Burnet later described the young king's ordeal:

The king wrought himself into as grave a deportment as he could: he heard many prayers and sermons, some of a great length. I remember on one fast day there were six sermons preached without intermission. I was there my self, and not a little weary of so tedious a service. The king was not allowed so much as to walk abroad on Sundays: and if at any time there had been any gaiety at court, such as dancing or playing at cards, he was severely reproved for it. This was managed with so much rigour and so little discretion that it contributed not a little to beget in him an aversion to all strictness in religion.[37]

Charles was still only twenty-one years old, and there seems little doubt that, as Burnet suggests, what he learned at this time was not piety and nobility of spirit, but the cynicism and calculation with which he was later to measure all religious policy.

Lauderdale, too, was forced to make his own compromises, but these were based on political calculation rather than confessional rigour. Lord Balmerino had told him during his last visit to Scotland that he would be expected to reject the Engagement as part of a humiliating spectacle of public repentance. Despite persuading Charles of the necessity of coming to terms with the Covenanters, and the good relations he had enjoyed with the various commissions sent to Holland, he refused to denounce the Engagement, to the regret of men like his friend Robert Baillie. Now he was faced with a simple choice: repent or accept a new exile, immersed in an even greater isolation than before. No sooner had he landed in Scotland with Charles than he was ordered to leave, because 'he is thought to be an active and a wittye man, and was accessorie to the Engadgement'. Some of his fellow nobles expressed concern about the danger in which he was placed: '. . . Lauderdaill I am sure your Lordship will think, is severly delt with, and now I see no remedye but he must ayther be exposed to the hazard of being catched by the English shippes on his return to Holland, and brought to this place a close prisoner, and be in hazard to be delivered if it should be demanded'.[38]

In Parliament, Alexander Lindsay, Earl of Balcarres, his cousin and boyhood friend, intervened on Lauderdale's behalf, arguing unsuccessfully that he be allowed a temporary reprieve from banishment to allow him to deal with private family business. Lauderdale was to be expelled along with other 'malignants', though he managed to delay execution, presenting his own petition to Parliament in early July, 'humbly showing his impossibility to goe off the countrey and desiring that he may have some short tyme alloued to him for the settling of his affaires, and keeping them from ruine; as also, that they wold be pleased to deall in clemency with him'.[39] There appears to have been some powerful lobbying in his favour: former commissioners supported his petition, and it seems likely that Argyll also lent his support. He was allowed to stay on a temporary basis. A complete reprieve, however, would have to be based on a full confession of his former political sins, which finally came in December 1650, when he appeared before the presbytery of St Andrews to: '. . . expresse and declare his sense of the sinfulness of the Engadgement . . . and . . . humblie acknowledging his accession to that course, and sinful forwarding and activitie above many others in contyrveing and carieing on the same withal testifying his sorrow theirfor, craving pardon of God for it and promiseing in his strenth never againe to owne that or the lyke course'.[40]

Formal public repentance followed in the Kirk at Largo.[41] Soon after he was freed of all public disabilities, although it was to be some time before he appears to have been entirely trusted: for it is about this time that he began to conceal his identity in correspondence, using the pseudonym John Reid or 'Red'.

While the arrival of Charles in Scotland was a clear provocation to the Commonwealth, there is no real evidence, beyond rumour and supposition, that Argyll and the Kirk party were prepared to invade England on his behalf. There were too many internal difficulties for such an attack to be carried out with any degree of unanimity. Few can have looked forward, moreover, to a showdown with the New Model Army. It had been continuously under arms for five years, having proved its superb fighting qualities in two civil wars, and now in the conquest of Ireland. Scotland had only recently suffered a serious defeat and had been largely demilitarised as a consequence. Any new levy of troops was bound to cause problems because of the Act of Classes and the rigour of the Kirk party. David Leslie was the best soldier Scotland had; but he was no Cromwell. All Scotland could do was, in the fashion of ages past, to prepare to defend its liberty against invasion.

Soon after Charles landed Parliament declared war on Scotland. The Covenanters now had to raise a new national army as quickly as possible. Amazingly, even in the midst of this crisis, there was opposition in Parliament to a new levy of troops, because it was felt that many would favour the king, and it would be impossible to ensure that, in a rapid trawl, all men would come up to the required moral standard. The Kirk was also suspicious that malignants, more prepared to fight for King and Country, than Covenant and King, would slip into the ranks. To push the draft through its supporters were obliged to agree that a new commission for the purging of the army be appointed, even before a single soldier was allowed to join the colours.

Lauderdale was able to observe the work of this commission at close hand. It included Archibald Johnston of Warriston, his old friend and colleague, a man with whom he by now had almost nothing in common politically or personally. Cromwell had crossed the Border in late July, advancing up the east coast, so it was a period of acute anxiety. The newly raised Scottish soldiers, assembled at Leith, were gratified by a morale-boosting visit from Charles. This was too much for Warriston, who feared that God would be jealous. Charles was forced to return to Dunfermline, while the commission got to work, virtually under the breath of Cromwell: in a space of three days no fewer than eighty officers and 3,000 men were sent home, although Argyll and Leslie did their best to moderate some of the worst excesses of the purgers. Lauderdale could quite clearly see the damage that was being done in the name of religious purity: 'Had it been thought lawful to have suffered the king and all gentlemen . . . to have stayed, the Isle of Britaine saw not such an army these hundred years. But that was not suffered; and, for all the purges, there are yet men enough, if it please God to blesse them.'[42]

It did not please God. After some skilful manoeuvres and counter-manoeuvres around Leith and Edinburgh Leslie was finally drawn into battle with Cromwell at Dunbar on 3 September, where his army was completely routed. The English now took possession of the whole of the south-east of Scotland, including all of Lauderdale's estates. For Scotland the Battle of Dunbar was to mark the beginning of the end of a period of particularly bleak factionalism: the nation now woke up with a hangover, but in a darkly sober mood, perhaps nowhere better expressed than in John Nicoll's *Diary*: '. . . befoir this airmy wes routtit, thair wes much business maid anent the purging of the Scottis airmy of malignantis be the space of many dayis . . . evin the nycht befoir the feght, our Scottis leaders wer in purging the Scottis airmy, as giff thair haid bene no danger!'[43]

Soon after Dunbar, with what was left of the Scottish army concentrated at Stirling, a new Royalist party, headed by John Middleton, among others, began to take shape in the north-east, while Warriston, as unrepentant as ever, took refuge with the rump of the extreme Covenanter faction in the south-west. Charles, thoroughly tired of his Presbyterian tormentors, and fearful for his safety after Dunbar, decided to escape, intending to join the royalists in the north. Lauderdale was forewarned of his intention and advised against it, presumably well aware that the country could not be seen to fragment at such a critical time, a view supported by George Villers, second Duke of Buckingham, one of the king's leading English companions.[44] The king initially appeared to accept their advice, only to change his mind. In early October he rode out of Perth, accompanied by only a few companions. His absence was soon noted, and he was quickly brought back.

This comic opera incident, known as 'The Start', was trivial enough in itself, but it had important political repercussions, leading directly to the eclipse of the Kirk party. Argyll and some of his more moderate colleagues were seriously alarmed by the implications of a union between the king and the northern royalists. To prevent any repetition, they decided to let Charles to have a taste of real power, inviting him to attend meetings of the Committee of Estates. Arrangements were also made for his coronation, scheduled to take place at Scone on 1 January 1651.

Outwith those areas controlled by the western Whigs a more lenient mood began to descend, confirmed by the rehabilitation of Lauderdale and some of the other members of the old Engager party. But Scotland was faced with the need to raise yet another army, and could not possibly do so while the Act of Classes was still in place, as most of the soldiers would have to be drawn from the Highlands and the north-east, areas strong in royalist sympathies. Even the Kirk was aware of this. On 14 December 1650, the Commission of the General Assembly, under pressure from the government, passed an important resolution: 'We cannot be against the raising of all fensible persons in the land, and permitting them to fight against the enemy for the defence of the Kingdom . . .'[45] This Resolution was the first significant breach in the Act of Classes: it was also the beginning of a major breach in the Church of Scotland itself. Warriston and those sympathetic to his uncompromising views immediately lodged a written protest against any attempt to allow malignants and other ungodly elements into the army. The ministers who accepted the Resolution were in a clear majority; but the protestors, headed by men like James Guthrie and Patrick Gillespie, formed an active and troublesome minority. The ensuing contest between Resolutioners and Protestors cast a long shadow into the future, and was to have an important bearing on Lauderdale's life.

Soon after this first Resolution was passed over twenty former Engagers, one of whom was John Middleton, applied to rejoin the army. His request was granted, only after he submitted to the same degrading public spectacle as Lauderdale: he was dressed in sackcloth and made open repentance of his sins at Dundee. For this humiliation, Middleton was one day to exact his own slow revenge. A second Resolution was passed by the Commission in March; and in June the Act of Classes was finally repealed. Perhaps no one worked more towards this end than Argyll, though it meant the end of his political influence. Ever since The Start he had been distancing himself from Warriston and the Whiggamore extremists. Distrusted by most of his fellow peers, he was now resented by many of his former middle-class allies. By July it was written of him 'he is gone down the wind; nobody takes any notice of him'. After warning against the planned invasion of England, he retired to Inveraray, more hated by the king than he ever realised.

Lauderdale began his steady political ascent at this time, gradually replacing Argyll in the royal council, especially after the coronation in January. Even before the repeal of the Act of Classes he was involved in a number of important commissions, concerned with arranging supplies for the new army.[46] By June he was right at the centre of government, signing a document on behalf of the Committee of Estates, a practice that had in the past been the work of Archibald Johnston.[47]

The new government brought a fresh sense of purpose, turning a factional conflict into a real national contest, as Cromwell himself recognised. Nevertheless, the military situation was still bleak: the English now controlled virtually the whole of southern Scotland. Leslie managed to prevent them pushing past Stirling, but in July his flank was turned when John Lambert forced his way across the Firth of Forth in the face of tough opposition. Charles either had to retreat north in the face of an ever more severe supply problem, or slip south past Cromwell into England, in the hope of raising loyal supporters. He chose the latter, advancing over the same western path that Hamilton had taken in 1648. By early August his army marched into Penrith, where Lauderdale wrote to his wife in a reasonably upbeat mood: 'Never was an army so regular as we have here since we came into England; I dare say we have not taken the worth of sixpence . . . trust me this is the best Scots army that ever I saw and I hope shall prove best. All those who are unwilling to hazard all in this cause with their king, have on specious pretence (most of them) left us. This is a natural purge and will do us much good.'[48]

The reality of their situation was described by Hamilton, who said, in a mood bordering on gallows humour, that Lauderdale and others were: '. . . laughing at the ridiculousness of our condition. We have quit Scotland, being scarce able to maintain it; and yet we grasp at all, and nothing but all will satisfy us, or lose all. I confess I cannot tell you wither our hopes or fears are greater: but we have one stout argument, despair; for we must now either stoutly fight it or die.'[49]

Militarily the situation was indeed desperate. Some Englishmen rallied to the standard, but far fewer than Charles expected; there was a notable lack of enthusiasm for a cause backed up by what was perceived to be a foreign army. In London, *Mercurius Politicus*, the official newsletter, did its best to play up anti-Scottish feeling, detailing the history of their invasions of England right back to that of Malcolm III in 1071. Charles himself was only ever referred to as King of Scots. The only significant English recruit was the Earl of Derby. It was with no high hopes that the army entered the town of Worcester on 22 August, where the exhausted troops were finally allowed some rest. Cromwell had now returned from the north, and, significantly reinforced, began to close in. Like some huge crocodile, the New Model Army, supported by militia units, closed its formidable jaws on Worcester. It was 3 September, the exact anniversary of the Battle of Dunbar. Outnumbered by a factor of two to one, the royal army was destroyed.

In the confusion that followed the Battle of Worcester every man was left to fend for himself. Charles managed to evade his pursuers, eventually escaping back to the Continent and years of frustrating exile. Lauderdale rode north in the company of Buckingham and Derby; but a little beyond the town of Newport they were intercepted and taken prisoner.[50] One Captain Edge was, the month after the battle, awarded £50 by the Council of State for the capture of Lauderdale and Derby.[51] Lauderdale was initially taken to Chester Castle as the news of his capture, and those of the other prisoners, was brought to Cromwell, who wrote to William Lenthall, the Speaker of the House of Commons: 'There are about six or seven thousand prisoners here; and many officers and noblemen of very great quality: Duke Hamilton, the Earl of Rothes, and divers other noblemen – I hear, the Earl of Lauderdale; many officers of great quality; and some that will be fit subjects for your justice.'[52]

Cromwell's reference to 'subjects for your justice' is a clear illustration of the danger that some of the prisoners were in at this time. Parliament was in a vengeful mood. The Earl of Derby was quickly disposed of: he was tried by court-martial and beheaded at Bolton in Lancashire on 15 October. Hamilton was selected for similar treatment, but died of the wounds he received at Worcester.[53] Lauderdale's life was also under threat: for at last the army had in its power a man they had long resented, and probably considered as one of the chief architects of the second Civil War. On 10 September the State Council ordered that he be brought to London as a close prisoner, to be committed to the Tower pending his trial 'to be made an example of justice'; and on 16 October issued further orders that he be proceeded against as 'an enemy of the commonwealth'.[54] Yet about this time the threat to his life started to lift, as he indicates in a letter concerning the terms of his imprisonment.[55]

No details have survived of the reasoning behind this 'reprieve', but in a legal bequest made in 1671 Lauderdale makes it perfectly clear that he owed his salvation to one person: 'I John Earl of Lauderdale being in very good health Doe of those present bequeth to Elizabeth Countess of Dysart the sum of fifteen hundred pounds stirlin in gold which I have left in her possession, to be injoyed and possesst by her as her owne proper goods as soon and whenever it pleases God to call me, and this in token of my gratitude for the paines and charges she was at in preserving my life when I was prisoner in the year 1651.'[56]

Unfortunately, the facts, scarce and difficult to pin down, were later shrouded in a considerable amount of legend. Elizabeth Murray, then the wife of Sir Lionel Tollemache, was a beautiful and intelligent woman, with a keen interest in politics. Royalist in sympathy, and subsequently an agent of the secret society known as the Sealed Knot, she also enjoyed for a time the confidence and friendship of Oliver Cromwell. After the Restoration she was rumoured to have been his one-time mistress, conferring upon her a fashionable notoriety, which she probably did much to encourage. Even those with a passing acquaintance of the character of Cromwell will realise that such a suggestion is absurd; and when she herself was asked directly about him she responded in suitably laconic terms: 'I can only say that I did know him, and I hope I will never know his fellow.'[57]

There is no way of knowing exactly what Elizabeth Murray's feeling was towards Lauderdale at this time. It would appear to have been one of simple gratitude: he had earlier intervened on behalf of Will Murray, her father, when he was threatened with execution in Scotland as a royalist spy.[58] Lauderdale certainly believed, or was led to believe, that her intervention in his favour on this occasion was a crucial factor in his preservation; but there is no real evidence that her influence was in any way decisive. She may indeed have spoken to Cromwell in his favour: even so, it is uncertain what impact this would have had. Cromwell was a powerful figure, the commander of the army and a member of the Council of State. Nevertheless, his influence was not yet decisive; even when it was, he was never a dictator in the modern sense, making decisions on the basis of mood and whim, but rather usually confining his actions within a strict interpretation of the law. There were other considerations weighing against a trial of Lauderdale: the execution of Charles I had effectively dissolved the bonds of common citizenship between the Scots and the English; Lauderdale was the subject of a foreign country, acting on the orders of its parliament; and, most important of all, he had no English title, unlike the Hamilton brothers. All that can really be said is that this is one occasion in which the truth is undeniably less important than the myth: in time Lauderdale's gratitude towards Elizabeth Murray was to become something far more significant.

The Civil Wars were over; the Commonwealth supreme, not just in England but now, by conquest, in Ireland and Scotland. Monarchy had failed, but so too did the experiment in pure parliamentary government; by late 1653 Oliver Cromwell emerged as Lord Protector, king in all but name, having thrown out the Rump, so to speak, on its rear end. Although he continued to search for some parliamentary underpinning to his new regime, his real authority was based on the power of the army. Scotland was united with England, though subject to continuing military occupation, and in such a way as to recall the words of Tacitus, the Roman historian, who wrote 'they make a desolation and call it peace'. Lauderdale, towards the end of his period of imprisonment, was to provide one of the best assessments of the new Union Parliament: 'They were no Parliament – no House of Commons, for there were 60 members of Scotland and Ireland who sure had nothing to doe in one English Parliament, and those from Scotland were as truly as representative of Madagascar as of Scotland.'[59] Most Scots probably shared Lauderdale's assessment, but they also grudgingly accepted the yoke of the Commonwealth: the majority, like Argyll, collaborated passively, while a minority, like Warriston, were to offer their active support.

Under the eyes of the English authorities, the dispute in the Scottish church between the Resolutioners and Protestors continued on its weary way, until their rival General Assemblies were forcibly dissolved by Cromwell's soldiers in 1653: no other was to meet for forty-seven years. The church was divided, the nation ruined, the aristocracy for the most part quiescent but resentful: the monolith of 1638, so impressive at the time, was gone forever. The Scots may have hated the English, either as occupiers or as religious atheists; but they hated each other even more. In the end the Commonwealth and Protectorate was never more than a parenthesis in Scottish history, a period of relative calm between one phase of action and another. It was a period in which a bill was quietly accumulating, and the payment was to be particularly high.

7

RELEASE AND RESTORATION

In April 1657 Lauderdale wrote from his prison in Windsor Castle, one of several places he had been confined ever since his capture after the Battle of Worcester, that 'My dayes of action I think are at an end . . . '[1] His mood appears to have been one of stoic resignation rather than despair, as reported by the Revd James Sharp, the minister of Crail in Fife, a leading resolutioner. Now in his sixth year of imprisonment he was no longer in danger of his life, and the terms of his confinement had long begun to ease. He had exchanged the confines of the Tower for the space of Windsor the year before, and was allowed free access to friends and relatives. On one occasion he was even allowed to spend the day in Eton looking for a book.[2]

Nevertheless, despite the relatively favourable treatment he received, he was still considered as a state prisoner of the first importance, likely to remain in captivity for as long as Cromwell and the Protectorate lasted. He was specifically exempted from the Act of Grace passed in April 1654, which granted pardons to a number of former royalists; even an appeal from the King of Sweden on his behalf the following year was ignored.[3] After all, he was a man, as Clarendon himself admits, against whom Cromwell had always professed 'a more than ordinary animosity'.[4] His circumstances were also liable to change abruptly, depending on external political circumstances: in 1655 he was moved without warning from the Tower to Portland Castle, following an abortive royalist rising in England. Here he remained for two years, before being sent to Windsor.[5] Of necessity he kept his political contacts to a minimum, although he appears to have been able to maintain some communication with the exiled court: there is evidence to suggest that he and the Earl of Crawford-Lindsay, a fellow Scot also captured at Worcester, encouraged Charles to join the Highland clans in May 1654 during the short-lived Glencairn Rising.[6] The following year the king wrote to him to assure him of his continuing affection and esteem, although it is uncertain if he ever received this morale-boosting letter.[7]

In general there would seem to be good grounds for John Thurloe, Cromwell's state secretary, to heed the advice of one of his spies among the royalist exiles on the Continent to 'let an eye be kept on Lather'.[8]

Most of his public contacts were, however, with men like James Sharp, who kept him abreast of the latest religious controversies. Sharp had been sent to London by his fellow ministers in the Resolutioner party to represent their interests with Cromwell, a difficult task, because they were generally regarded as royalists. After Lauderdale was transferred to Windsor, Sharp visited him on a number of occasions, and was favourably impressed by his general deportment. Writing to a fellow minister he says that he finds Lauderdale: '. . . in everie way a changed man to the better, and his close imprisonment under much hardship in that castle [Portland] is mentioned by him as the most blessed dispensation of Providence he did ever meet with'.[9]

Lauderdale confessed himself to Sharp as one who desired to prove himself as a dutiful son of the Church of Scotland. He also asked to be remembered to his old friend and colleague, Robert Baillie, 'the some time little monk of Kilwinning'.[10] The two men had never entirely lost touch, Lauderdale explaining something of his change of mood in a letter to Baillie written in December 1653: 'Although in that I find great prejudice by my long restraint; yet it pleases God to give me some measure of patience and contentedness under the rod; and more then yow wold have looked for, who know my former temper.'[11]

While he was at Portland Lauderdale met the Revd Richard Baxter of Kidderminster, one of the most important contacts he made over these years. Baxter was a kind of English Robert Baillie, a leading Presbyterian, though of moderate views, and a scholar of some note. In the years to follow he and Lauderdale formed a close intellectual partnership: Lauderdale was to find considerable solace in Baxter's theological works and offered him his skills as a linguist in translating some French treatises.[12] Lauderdale also commended Sharp to Baxter as a 'pious and faithful minister'. There is an interesting contrast in Lauderdale's relationship with these two clerics: he quite clearly enjoyed the company of Baxter, who remained friendly in the difficult time to come; Sharp, with whom he was to have a close future political relationship, never seems to have been more than a useful acquaintance; there is nothing to suggest any real warmth or closeness between the two men. In the end Lauderdale was the quintessential politician, whose views of people and their uses tended to change with circumstances. Both Baxter and Sharp were in time to become political tools; but his treatment of the latter was to be far less scrupulous than his treatment of the former.

Lauderdale's prisons became his second university: after so many years in the public arena he had time to reflect, read and generally polish his thinking, a process that was to have clear future benefits. Roger Coke was to describe this, somewhat overstating the case:

> His imprisonment was doubly happy to him; for during the restraint of his body he enlarged the faculties of his mind; being a man of parts, improve them by contemplation and study, wherein he met with more helps than it may be he could have found in Scotland; whereby he became of greater abilities to serve the King, than could be found in any other of his countrymen; and being in England, found better opportunities to have them known to the King, than any of his absent countrymen could.[13]

There is little doubt that his enforced idleness had a less beneficial effect on his character, also to find expression in the time to come. Not only was he facing the prospect of endless imprisonment for as long as Cromwell and his regime were in power, but also his support for the royal cause had left him and his family landless and destitute. Because of his role in the Engagement, all the property he and his wife owned in England was lost; and after the Whiggamore Raid he also lost his Scottish estates. He regained formal possession of the latter on his rehabilitation in 1650, but this was a rather empty technicality; by this time most of the land in question was under English occupation. This notwithstanding, he still pledged his property to provide money for the Scottish army. As the army entered England his personal financial situation was very poor: he was only able to raise £400 for the needs of his wife and daughter, then living abroad.[14] In 1651 the Commonwealth formally confiscated all of his estates, confirmed by the Protectorate in 1654, 'though nothing could be charged against him but the obeying of the laws of Scotland'.[15] By this time these ravaged lands brought very little in the way of financial benefit in any case: it was estimated in 1656 that there were debts of almost £34,000 on estates with an annual rent roll of under £2,200, a burden exceeded only by the Hamilton holdings and those of the Earl Marshal.[16] The lands were gone, among others given away to one John Swinton, an extreme Whiggamore and active collaborator with Cromwell; the debts, however, remained. Anne Maitland was left to manage a desperate situation as best she could, being reduced, on one occasion, to write to her husband 'God help you, you have many enemies'.[17] In financial desperation she was reduced to lodging appeals for assistance to Cromwell and the English authorities, on one occasion asking them to 'Pray consider my deplorable condition'.[18] Lauderdale was also obliged to make appeals for his own maintenance; and although funds were granted, they often slipped into arrears.

By the time he was finally released in March 1660, Lauderdale was close to destitution. It is said that he could not go to the king at an early date because he could not afford to buy boots and had no ready cash for his travel expenses.[19] In the circumstances it is hardly surprising that he would wish to restore his fortunes as quickly as possible. Hand in hand with his intellectual interests went ambition and a desire for wealth, intensified by years of privation. In this he was no different from many of his contemporaries, ruined by the Civil Wars, who in their later scramble for wealth, recognition and pleasure were to take their cue from the king. Lauderdale was later to find in Elizabeth Murray a woman who shared his intellectual interests as well as his more venal tastes. Their joint pursuit of money and wealth was eventually to acquire overtones of corruption, but these were hardly excessive by the standards of the day. Together they later carried out an ambitious and frantic programme of architectural renewal at Thirlestane Castle, Lethington, Brunstane and Ham House in Surrey not just as an exercise in wealth and conspicuous consumption, but arguably as a way of demonstrating that the dark years had passed forever.

Descending ever deeper into a prolonged political hibernation, Lauderdale came back to a rapid consciousness in the autumn of 1658: Cromwell was dead. By some rare historical irony he died on 3 September, the anniversaries of his great triumphs at Dunbar and Worcester. The day before Lauderdale was threatened, for unknown reasons, with a fresh move, this time to Warwick Castle; the day afterwards the order was rescinded. He was later to express his gratitude to his wife, Anne, who was active in attempting to have the proposed transfer rescinded, in a letter to Richard Baxter: 'The day before the Governor [Cromwell] died, it did please the Council to order me forthwith to be removed to Warwick Castle, which would have been grievous to me to be againe hurried into a strange place and nothing is more inconvenient for a long journey than want of money a disease I have long been under, but I bless God my wife prevailed to get the order recalled . . .'[20]

The real reason was almost certainly the reluctance to move so important a prisoner at so sensitive a time. Now, secure at Windsor, he was able to observe developments, in common with many others, both at home and abroad, in a mood of tense expectation.

In place of a giant came a little man: Richard Cromwell succeeded as Lord Protector, for no better reason than he was the son of his father. Few can have had any real expectations of a man Lauderdale was later to describe as 'ane appendix'.[21] However, Richard, contrary to the perceived view, was not entirely without political skill. He was, however, fairly vulnerable, with no real power-base either in the nation or, more importantly, in the army, many of whose senior officers were jealous of his unearned authority. Bit by bit the Protectorate began to unravel. Unable to master either his new parliament or the army, Richard exited the scene in the spring of 1659, a little like a Roman emperor sent packing by barbarian generals. The Protectorate died and the Commonwealth came back to life, only to be torn by an ongoing struggle between civil and military authority.

This was a time that managed to combine expectation and tension in equal measures, some of which managed to slip behind the walls of Windsor Castle. Soon after the death of Oliver Cromwell, the Duke of Buckingham was transferred from the Tower to Windsor. While elsewhere in England royalist conspiracies began to take shape, Buckingham was eager to organize his fellow captives. This apparently involved a plan to seize hold of the castle. Buckingham almost certainly tried to involve Lauderdale in this scheme, though there is no evidence that the latter either encouraged or approved of such a desperate measure. As always he was far more likely to take the cautious approach. Nothing came of the plan because of Buckingham's early release in February 1659.[22] Buckingham was one of those politicians far too theatrical and mercurial for the stolid and cautious Lauderdale, and a man for whom he never expressed any great admiration or respect. He was, however, a useful contact, with a variety of connections across the English political spectrum, and one with whom Lauderdale continued to enjoy a reasonable working relationship.

Although soon after the death of Cromwell Lauderdale was to write that he had no hopes of an early release, this is almost certainly untrue. When Richard Cromwell's new parliament assembled in early 1659 Lauderdale quickly made contact with John Hay, second Earl of Tweeddale, one of the members from Scotland, and a close future associate. Burnet was later to sketch an accurate and fair portrait of Tweeddale, one of the more attractive Restoration politicians:

> The earl of Tweeddale was another of Lauderdale's friends. He was early engaged in business, and continued it to a great age: he understood all the interests and concerns of Scotland well: he had a great stock of knowledge, with a mild and obliging temper. He was of a blameless, or rather exemplary, life in all respects. He had loose thoughts both of civil and ecclesiastical government; and seemed to think that what form soever was uppermost was to be complied with. He had been in Cromwell's parliaments, and had abjured the royal family, which lay heavy on him

. . . though he was in all other respects the ablest and worthiest man of the nobility: only he was too cautious and fearful.[23]

Tweeddale's past associations, and perceived moderation, would almost certainly have ended his political career at the Restoration, had it not been for the support he then enjoyed from Lauderdale. Now he had the chance to be of some service to his future patron and friend, attempting to interest such powerful figures as General John Lambert and Archibald Johnston of Warriston, the most influential Scot in London, in his case.[24] Lambert's involvement, a source of some future political embarrassment to Lauderdale, failed to have the desired effect. As a second best there was a proposal to substitute banishment for imprisonment. Lauderdale expressed his thanks to Tweeddale, though his letter fails to disguise his obvious frustration and disappointment, especially over the suggested banishment:

> Though my thanks be very insignificant yet give me leave to express my true sense to your Lordship's care in my concerns, and specially for indeavouring to engage my Lord Lambert, for there is none to whom I wold so willingly oune ane obligation. His care formally to obtaine my libertie I do most thankfully acknowledge, and though it had not the suces he did desire, yet the favour was every whitt as great. As for that which your Lordship advises in his name, give me leave to offer my thoughts and submit them to his and your discretion. It is true to be banisht is much more desirable then to be put to the severe and ugly want I am in prison, but me thinkes it is somewhat strange for one that hath so faire a plea for the remnant of a poore antient estate to beg the favour to be utterly banisht from it and his country. Nor indeed am I very free to be the carver to my self of a punishment wch in all ages hath been lookt on as nixt to death. To submit to what the Lord shall incline their hearts to do with me is one thing, and to desire it another.[25]

Historical events were soon superseding all personal considerations. George Monck, the Parliamentary commander in Scotland, who enjoyed complete authority over his own section of the New Model Army, watched and waited as the political situation in England became increasingly confused. The Rump was conjured back to life, only to be dismissed once more. For a time John Lambert rose to the top, determined to save the republic, but opinion was moving strongly towards the old constitutional order. Monck, whose loyalty had been to Cromwell rather than the Commonwealth, decided to act. Declaring for a free Parliament, he crossed the Tweed in January 1660. Lambert's forces melted away, and Monck entered London unopposed. As a first step towards a newly elected Parliament all those expelled by Pride's

Purge were restored to the Rump Parliament: for a time England acquired a Presbyterian flavour, at least politically.

James Sharp, now back in London, intervened actively on behalf of his imprisoned countrymen. There was really no need, for Parliament was looking favourably on all those with perceived Presbyterian inclinations, which included Lauderdale. An early review was demanded, as he himself tells in a spirit of ironic good humour: 'Upon the restoring the secluded members they were pleased the very first day to demand ane account to be given of the cause of our restraint. In obedience to which order the warrants for our commitment were sent. I did desire the Governor (in jest) to certifie that my crime was Original Sin, for I told him seriously nothing can be charged against me but I was born in Scotland and obeyed the laws and Supreme authority whence I only owed my alledgance'.[26]

In early March he was finally set at liberty 'after 8 years and just 6 months imprisonment', together with the Earl of Crawford-Lindsay and Lord Sinclair, the only condition imposed being that they all remain in England for the time being.[27] Letters of support and congratulation followed, one of the earliest Lauderdale received coming from Archibald Campbell, Lord Lorne, the eldest son of the Marquis of Argyll, who looked upon it 'as a token for good and this nation. Hoping that as your lordship hath been a remarkable sufferer so the Lord will make you an able instrument in our just settlement'.[28] But the one letter that Lauderdale was surely waiting for arrived from the royal court, now in Brussels, in mid April: '. . . I am very glad that you are at liberty, and in a place where you can do most service, by disposing your frindes to that temper and sobriety, which must be the principal ingredient to that happiness we all pray for. I am confident you had the same opinion and judgement you had when we parted. I am sure I have, and the same kindness for you, and believe you as intirely my owne, as any man and that no other men's passions can work upon you'.[29]

This was a delicate time; a restoration of the monarchy looked likely, but it was by no means inevitable; Monck, a cautious individual, took things one stage at a time, neither pushing too far one way or the other. Presbyterians, for the time being, were strong in the restored Parliament, even ordering that the Solemn League and Covenant be reissued in early March and read in all churches. They were generally regarded as the key to a successful – and moderate – restoration, because they held the middle ground between the republicans and the cavaliers. All were monarchists, but all needed convincing about the sincerity of the young king; there were widespread and damaging rumours that he had converted to Catholicism during his exile, which, if true, would have made his recall virtually impossible.

In the complex game leading up to the Restoration in May Lauderdale was set to play a crucial part, drawing freely on the credit he had previously accumulated with Richard Baxter, an important influence on English Presbyterian opinion. His contacts with the Presbyterians were known at an early stage by the Commonwealth authorities.[30] Even before his release he was offering to visit Baxter in Kidderminster, because he had heard worrying reports 'that you have declared against a Gentleman to whom I wish very well. I doe not believe it; yet friendship compels me to give you this hint.' Lauderdale then proceeds to make the facts plain, as he perceives them:

> The Elder brother [Charles] I know to be a wise and just and excellent person. The second [James, Duke of York] I am confident is not what it seems he is by enemies reported to be . . . For the Lord's sake ingage not in anything wch may hinder you from being a great instrument of union in these churches. If you should smile again at it, I must repeat it, I am confident God will reserv you for that worke . . . Let me but beg that you will not write till I see you. I have nothing else to loose, but I had much rather loose much blood, then you should use ink in such a course . . . Deare Sir ingage not in that wch in my poore judgement may doe so much hurt . . . You shall not be a neuter long, I trust to see you as you have been often, a champion for the good old cause . . . Debate must cleir one of us, we agree in the maine and I trust we shall agree in the means.[31]

These efforts met with an early success, as Baxter later explained in his own memoirs, '. . . but these things were quickly at an end: for many gentlemen who had been with the King in Scotland, especially the Earl of Lauderdale . . . who [was] of a reputation with the people, did speak abroad mighty commendations of the King, both in his temper and piety; whereby the fears of many at that time were much quietened'.[32]

Lauderdale's reference to Baxter as 'an instrument of union in these churches' is also fairly significant: he saw him not just as an important influence in Presbyterian circles, but also as a bridge to moderate Episcopalian opinion, another important factor in the Restoration. At an early stage it was clear that the elections for the new Parliament, scheduled to assemble on 25 April, were likely to produce a strong reaction against the three 'Cs': Covenant, Cromwell and Commonwealth. Even James Sharp, whose first task was supposedly to defend and promote the Solemn League and Covenant, was able to recognise this. The members of the restored Parliament dared not, as he put it, 'press the voting of Presbyterianism government least it prejudice to barr them from being elected against the next parliament, such an aversion there is in the body of the nation from it'.[33] For all but the politically blind, the Scottish Protestor faction in the main, it was obvious that the Solemn League and Covenant was not going to be the basis for a Restoration: Charles did not want it; far more important, neither did England. Lauderdale appears to have been aiming at the best thing possible: a moderate, pre-Laudian, Episcopal establishment, a project with which Sharp appears to have been happy to associate.[34]

For Lauderdale, James Sharp was a useful political adjutant. Though not a figure of the first rank, he held in his hands several important threads, connecting General Monck, the Scottish Resolutioners, the English Presbyterians, and the exiled royalists. He was also by nature and training a conservative man, whose hatred of the fanatical Protestors was probably greater than his love for the Solemn League and Covenant. Lauderdale had an early appreciation of his uses, as he made clear in a letter Sharp delivered to the king in person: 'The honest bearer's activeness and usefulness in your service sets him far above my recommendation; yet I cannot but beare witness what I have seen and knowen for many years, been that God hath made him as happy an instrument in your service all along as any I know of in this country . . . he is above all suspicion of private ends or interests . . .'[35]

James Sharp was now set to become one of the great villains of Covenanter mythology; the reality is he was a very small player in a very big game. He had come to London charged by his Resolutioner colleagues with two tasks: to remind Charles of his commitment to the Covenants, and to blame all the humiliations of 1650 on the Protestors. He was aware, at an early stage, that there was little prospect of the Solemn League and Covenant being imposed throughout the United Kingdom. All that remained was to safeguard Presbyterianism in Scotland, but when he raised this with Charles on a visit to Holland his response was at best ambiguous. For Sharp, the real problem was that the majority of the Scottish nobility, reacting against the politics of the late 1640s and early 1650s, did not want to see the old Kirk party restored in any shape. Sharp was not a knave, as some have alleged, but he was an opportunist: in the end, seeing the drift in the affairs of state, he went with the current. There is no reason to suspect him of dishonesty and treachery; but his plentiful correspondence, with its cramped and fussy style, reveals a shallow, self-centred, rather vain and not particularly likeable individual, easily flattered by the attention of great men. For some he was set to be Judas; in reality he is far closer to the fictitious Uriah Heep, abject and vicious by turns.

Lauderdale continued to play his part with some care. It seems clear that many still suspected him of being a committed Presbyterian, but as he made clear to one of Hyde's agents he was 'of no faction, but will obey the King's command in any thing'.[36] It has been claimed that he emerged from prison as a 'convinced monarchist', a position he had in fact taken many years before.[37] Nevertheless, his experience of revolution and civil war, his loss of personal liberty coupled with the loss of national freedom, had a profound outlook on his thinking. He had once believed that security for Scotland could only be obtained by the abolition of Episcopacy throughout the British Isles:

> He had now learned that the Scottish tail could not wag the English dog. Cromwell's version of uniformity was successful, but only because it was based on military occupation and dictatorship. Only a monarchical framework could preserve order without the use of force, and so the monarchy must be restored and its power enhanced. Within this framework, provided a moderate religious settlement was made, England and Scotland both could be made to fit.[38]

During the spring days leading up to the Restoration, the Solemn League and Covenant played little part in Lauderdale's thinking; interestingly, neither did the Treaty of Carisbrooke, with its promise of a limited Presbyterian experiment in England. It seems clear both in his present attitude and the later position he took over the question of church government in Scotland that Lauderdale envisaged a form of peaceful co-existence between Episcopacy in England and Presbyterianism in Scotland, a position eventually to be attained in 1690. His position, clearly arrived at with some care, was to create confusion in the minds of many of his political enemies, mostly men with less subtle minds, who completely failed to understand his thinking, believing, to their cost, that they were simply dealing with the old Presbyterian Adam.

Lauderdale soon followed Sharp to Breda, having by now acquired both the boots and the travelling expenses. Besides seeking an audience with the king, after a gap of so many years, he came with two additional aims: to make his peace with Hyde, who was clearly the coming man, and to take some political soundings. Hyde describes Lauderdale's eccentric performance when they met: 'He was very polite in all his discourses, called himself and his nation a "thousand rebels and traitors", and in his Discourses frequently said, "when I was a Traitor", or, "when I was in Rebellion", and seemed not equally delighted with any argument, as when He scornfully spake of the Covenant, upon which he brake a hundred Jests.'[39]

If Lauderdale did indeed behave in this clownish fashion the intention was presumably to disarm the suspicious Hyde, a strategy that enjoyed some reasonable success. Although he continued high in the king's affections, it was as well not to have so powerful an advisor as an entrenched opponent. There was also the Scottish cavalier party to consider, now headed by the former General John Middleton, who had become Hyde's protégé. Middleton, starting from the same point as Lauderdale, had travelled much further along the road, becoming both an Episcopalian and an ultra-royalist in the process, a living substitute for the dead Montrose. Also captured at Worcester, he later managed to escape, becoming a favourite of the king in exile. Charles was quick to make use of his professional skills, appointing him to lead the abortive Highland rising against the rule of Cromwell, and later creating him Earl of Middleton. Although far from being a complete fool, Middleton was not a natural politician, tending to take the lead of the more intellectually refined Hyde. Like Lauderdale, he was impoverished and thus ambitious for wealth and office; unlike Lauderdale he had a vicious and spiteful side to his character, which was set to have a major bearing on the nature of the Restoration in Scotland.

It's as well to remember that the Scottish Restoration was a process rather than an event. In England Charles was eventually to come home by invitation of his former enemies, rather than his friends. England had an army, a government and a Parliament, which all helped to ensure that the Restoration was not the complete royalist carnival it would have been if the cavaliers had brought Charles home. Scotland had none of these things: its church was divided, its aristocracy impoverished and its institutions suppressed. In a declaration made at Breda, Charles offered England an indemnity to all former rebels, apart from the regicides, and even held out the prospect of religious toleration; Scotland was given no similar promises or guarantees. For Middleton and his ragged army of cavaliers this ambiguity was ideal: they could both revenge themselves on former Kirk party members and make the nation anew in their own image. At an early stage Lauderdale argued for a greater show of caution and consideration, reminding Charles of the sacrifices Scotland had made in the royal cause since 1648, though in the end he was not prepared to push the point so closely that he would endanger his chance of office.[40] As for Presbyterianism, Lauderdale was told by the king, so he later reported to Burnet, to let that go 'for it was not a religion for gentlemen', a remark that was almost certainly made in jest and repeated in jest.[41] We have no clear evidence to indicate when Middleton first began to perceive Lauderdale as a potential enemy, but the main lines of division seem to have been laid in the weeks before the Restoration. Thus began a political struggle that was to last for almost four years.

Charles finally came home in May, an occasion for wild celebration in both England and Scotland. For both nations this was a return to legitimate God-given and law-sanctioned authority. For Scotland it was something more: a promise of renewed national freedom. There were some, though, chiefly among the Protestors, who viewed the return of the king with considerable apprehension. Despite the general policy of clemency men like Archibald Johnston of Warriston, against whom the king had a particular animus, could expect little mercy. Alarmed by the prospect of his imminent arrest he fled to the Continent, remaining in hiding for a considerable period of time. Argyll, suspecting no design against himself, came to the court, hoping, against all the signs, that he would be favourably received. Instead he was arrested and held in the Tower for some months, before finally being sent back to Scotland to face a variety of charges, including alleged complicity in the murder of the late king. Argyll was hated by Middleton and the cavaliers; he was even more hated by Charles.

Aside from the arrest of Argyll, by now a figure of little real influence, Charles proceeded with caution and moderation. To replace the Commonwealth authorities in Scotland, he called back to life the old Committee of Estates, deposed by Cromwell in 1651, to act as a provisional government until a new Parliament could be assembled. However, there were some provocations that could not be ignored. On 23 August, the same day that the Committee of Estates reassembled, a group of Protestors met in Edinburgh. It might have been more prudent for these men to remain out of the king's sight; instead they did the worst thing possible: they drew up a petition reminding him of his obligation to observe the Covenants. All, including the Revd James Guthrie, were immediately arrested and imprisoned in Edinburgh Castle, soon to be joined by Argyll himself. The fall of the Protestors was almost certainly welcomed by James Sharp, back from London, who wrote to Lauderdale about this time, 'I fear ther can be no remedy against this malady without exercising severity upon the leading imposters Guthiree, Gillespy, Rutherford, which will daunt the rest of the hotheads . . . '[42]

While some slipped into darkness, others emerged into the light. For Lauderdale the sun started to shine once more: his estates were restored, including those lands previously lost to John Swinton.[43] Important as this was, uppermost in his mind at this time was the future shape of the government of Scotland. By the summer the king had started to fill the great offices of state. Most of the posts had probably been pre-allocated, after some extensive jockeying for position before the Restoration. The ultra-royalists expected to be rewarded, and so they were: the most important post went to John Middleton, who was appointed High Commissioner to Parliament, virtually the prime minister of Scotland, while the Earl of Glencairn, a close ally, was named as Lord Chancellor. Lesser posts also went to Middleton's followers, including Sir Archibald Primrose, who received the legal office of Clerk Register, and Sir John Fletcher, who became Lord Advocate. John Leslie, sixth Earl of Rothes, the son of the old Covenanter, was appointed as President of the Council. Rothes, a man with almost no education but plenty of native wit, was still an unknown quantity at this time, though he had a tendency to follow the strongest lead. The cavaliers did not, however, enjoy a complete monopoly of power. As in England, Charles was careful to create a political balance. Glencairn replaced Loudon as Lord Chancellor, but the Earl of Crawford-Lindsay retained the post of Treasurer; even the Kirk party was represented in the shape of the Earl of Cassillis as Justice-General. It seems fairly obvious, though, that the future survival of these men would depend on their ability to adjust to new realities, as Middleton probably realised.

In a sense all of these appointments were technicalities; the future status of the Earl of Lauderdale was by far the most sensitive consideration of all. It was clear that he would be rewarded: Charles liked him as much as he liked Middleton; more importantly, he was the most skilled, the most experienced and by far the most intelligent of all the Scottish politicians. His enemies attempted to head off his appointment to a major post; it is almost certainly at this time that the fiction was invented that he had acted as president of the Committee of Both Kingdoms, to remind Charles of his past misdemeanours. Acting with far greater subtlety, Hyde, now Lord Chancellor of England and soon to be Earl of Clarendon, suggested that Lauderdale be appointed Chancellor of Scotland, a post that would remove him from London and all real political influence.[44] Charles ignored both the bad reports and Hyde's advice, appointing Lauderdale as Secretary of State for Scotland. Hyde had favoured James Livingstone, Earl of Newburgh, for this office. Not only was Newburgh elderly and harmless, but he was also Hyde's favourite kind of Scot: he had been educated in France, married in England and served in Spain; the only Scottish thing about him was his title.[45] Compared with Lauderdale he was a nonentity, and Charles clearly recognised him as such, naming him for the honorific post of Captain of the Scottish Life Guard. Newburgh departed, freshly honoured and deeply resentful.

Hyde was clearly unsettled, though Lauderdale remained outwardly friendly, showing all due deference to the Chancellor and careful to identify himself with the Middleton government. Nevertheless, the Chancellor was obviously unhappy at the degree of Lauderdale's influence with the king, and believed him responsible for the political survival of the Earl of Crawford-Lindsay, still something of an un-regenerate Covenanter. In his memoirs he reveals not only his own resentment, but also the deep divisions behind the facile unity of the new government:

> Whatever appearance there was of unity amongst them, for there is nothing like contradiction, there was a general dislike by them all of the power Lautherdale had with the King, who they knew pressed many things without communication with them, as he had prevailed that the Earl of Crawford Lindsay should continue in the office he formerly held of being High Treasurer of that Kingdom, though he was known to be a man incorrigible in his zeal for Presbytery, and all the madness of the Kirk.[46]

It seems clear that Lauderdale, as a skilled political operator, and a friend of the king, was more or less in the position of naming any post he wanted, with the possible exception of High Commissioner. His choice of Secretary of State is of considerable interest. This post had never commanded any great distinction since the Union of the Crowns. Though an important link between the monarch and the government in Edinburgh, the secretary had often been bypassed when prominent favourites, such as the first Duke of Hamilton, were allowed to manage affairs.[47] Moreover, the post had often been divided, with one man in Edinburgh and another in London. In 1660 the situation was different. Lauderdale had a quick appreciation of new realities: there was no prominent Scottish favourite, and thus no direct danger to the Secretary; more importantly, there could be no return to the lack of certainty and direction that led to the crisis of 1637. Cromwell's union was dissolved physically, but not arguably in spirit: real power would remain in London with the king and with the man who had the ability to translate royal whims into state policy. First from Highgate and then from Ham House, Lauderdale remained thereafter for most of the rest of his life in England, never far from Charles.

He did not, however, have things all his own way. Hyde had lost the contest over the Secretaryship, and also seemingly over Cromwell's enforced union, which he would have preferred to have retained; but he at least ensured that there was a strong English input to the government of Scotland, with a council based in London, which included himself and three other noblemen, as well as any Scots privy councillor who happened to be present. This was to be balanced by allowing two Scots to sit on the English Privy Council. The reality, of course, as Hyde clearly understood, was that the English would have a decisive hold over the government of Scotland. As well as Hyde, the English appointees included his friend Ormonde and George Monck, architect of the Restoration and now Duke of Albemarle, all men who had real weight with the king. The Scots in London were almost invariably men of lesser status. By this Hyde had put a brake for some years on any exercise of undiluted power by Lauderdale; but the real aim was to prevent any return to the personal government of Charles I, which had kept his English councillors out of Scotland until it was too late. Lauderdale lobbied against the move, with no success. His opposition owed less to the nationalist reasons sometimes identified and a lot more to naked self-interest.

For Lauderdale the period of the early Restoration might be likened to creeping through a minefield. Distrusted by Clarendon and resented by Middleton, who together formed an axis that controlled Scotland, he soon found that much of his advice was ignored. He was also suspected of lingering Presbyterian sympathies, which weakened his position still further following the reintroduction of Episcopacy in both England and Scotland. Gilbert Sheldon, the new Bishop of London, a talented individual with Laudian sympathies, had been present during the Uxbridge talks, and would have remembered Lauderdale's advocacy of the Covenant. In 1663 he became Archbishop of Canterbury, a strong friend of Episcopacy in Scotland, alert to any signs of deviation or unorthodoxy on the part of the Secretary. Lauderdale was also the victim of a whispering campaign, clearly aimed at undermining his authority and credibility. James Sharp was among the first to warn him of this: 'By the coming down of other men of late yow are reported to be wholly Presbyterian, and looked upon as a friend to that party in England; upon this account yow have the Episcopal party against yow, and though the King carries fair, yet, knowing yow to be thus affected, yow are not really in favour nor will yow signify much in public affairs.'[48]

A further warning came from his old friend Robert Baillie, who said that it was being rumoured that he was intervening on behalf of Patrick Gillespie, a leading Protestor, soon to be on trial for his life. Lauderdale was alert to the danger: 'But such reports are now no strangers to me. Every week I finde, by letter from Edinburgh, that I am reported to be the great agent for my Lord Argyll, a calumnie fals as the former; but I am so hardened with twentie sorts of lyes, which I heare are vented of me there, that they make little impression on me.'[49]

In the midst of these troubles Lauderdale enjoyed one small political success, all the sweeter because it was against the opposition of Hyde. In debate in the Scottish Council in London in December, the Chancellor, supported by Albemarle, had favoured the retention of English garrisons in Scotland, at least until the final settlement was agreed and in place. Lauderdale, in the presence of the king, summoned up all his debating skills, arguing along national lines against this 'badge of slavery'. It's uncertain if this had any impact on Charles; he was surely moved, though, by the supplementary argument that the forts and soldiers were too great a burden on the royal revenues.[50] The garrisons were ordered to be removed, which, according to Burnet, made Lauderdale very popular in Scotland, as no doubt it did, as the presence of these troops was universally resented. George Mackenzie of Roseheaugh, the future Lord Advocate, says that Middleton took the view advocated by Hyde.[51] However, despite his general tendency to oppose Lauderdale, this was the one occasion on which he happily slipped into the background, unable to appear, as Burnet puts it, 'for so unpopular a thing'.[52]

That same council debated the future form of church government for Scotland; on this more significant question Lauderdale lost. Standing on the sidelines, he was now set to observe as Middleton proceeded to orchestrate a counter-revolution, one that was to have a considerable bearing on his own future. Bit by bit the Commissioner raised the stakes: before long he was aiming at the political destruction of his great rival. Lauderdale, part way over the minefield, now entered its most dangerous section. He came through safely; Middleton did not.

8

REACTION

John Middleton had one task: to make the government of Scotland his own. He began with some strong advantages: the church was divided and weak; the aristocracy, tired of clerical pretensions, in a co-operative and reactionary mood. In contrast with Lauderdale, isolated in London, and not always fully aware of the main currents of political opinion, Middleton had a quick appreciation of the mood of his fellow noblemen. He was soon aware just how deeply unpopular the Covenants were among a class hugely resentful of the loss of influence it had suffered over the past years, a resentment later amusingly expressed in rhyme:

> From Covenanters with uplifted hands,
> From remonstrators with associate bands,
> From such committees as governed this nation,
> From kirk commissions and their protestations,
> Good Lord deliver us.[1]

It's easy to misunderstand John Middleton. He was a soldier with a tendency to favour simple solutions to complex problems; but he was neither a fool nor entirely devoid of ability and charm.[2] While it is true that he tended to take a close lead from Clarendon, he was far from being his 'tool', tending to initiate and pursue policies at a rate far too rapid for the more cautious Chancellor.[3] Ironically, despite their personal rivalry, he was far closer to Lauderdale politically than is often depicted, although there were significant differences between the two men over timing and method. Both were committed royalists, both favoured the elevation and enhancement of the prerogative power, both were determined exponents of the rights and privileges of their class, both were dismissive of clerical interference in government, and both favoured a 'civil' solution to the religious question, The latter point is of particular interest, because of the perceived differences between them. These differences, however, rested on appearance rather than substance;

for both favoured an Erastian solution to the problem of church government. Lauderdale continues to be seen as the architect of royal absolutism in Restoration Scotland; but in a deeper sense he only built on foundations laid by Middleton.

Middleton seems to have concluded at a fairly early stage in the Restoration, even before Charles and Clarendon, that the reintroduction of Episcopacy into Scotland was a distinct possibility. He was confident enough to order the public burning of the Covenant, the kind of gesture politics detested by the more cautious Lauderdale. When the Secretary's displeasure was reported to him he said in his typically provocative and over-the-top manner that 'it mattered not if it were hanged about his neck if he favoured it, and the Book of Common Prayer would soon be settled in Scotland'.[4] He continued to pursue a militantly anti-Presbyterian line when the matter finally came up in the Royal Council in London, meeting in December 1660 to consider the Commissioner's instructions to the forthcoming parliament.

Although the Restoration government continued to favour the moderate Resolutioners over the militant Protestors, by the summer of 1660 it was obvious that no cleric would have any strong input to the final church settlement in Scotland. Sharp was consoled with soothing words by the king, and then sent packing back to Edinburgh with a letter assuring his fellow ministers that the church would be maintained 'as settled by law'.[5] Sharp was thanked for his efforts and the ministers rested content that Presbyterianism was safe in Scotland at least, as the only form of church government that was indeed settled by law. As always, those who tend to read backwards from consequences to causes, view this letter as an exercise in royal duplicity, one in which Sharp was a willing participant; all it really meant was that Charles had not yet made up his mind. Significantly, after Sharp left London, the Resolutioners were ordered to send no replacement. This was a question that would be addressed and settled in secular and political, not clerical and theological terms.

Of the many considerations weighing on the politicians in late 1660 arguably among the more significant is an argument put forward in a memorandum by Thomas Sydserf.[6] Sydserf had once been Bishop of Galloway, and was the last survivor of the great purge of 1638. He had been living in exile for many years, and was no lover of Presbyterianism; but the arguments he put forward in his paper had a convincing logic. Amongst other things, he argued that to allow the continuation of Presbyterianism in Scotland would only encourage the 'discontented party' in England. The nobles would be bound to support the restoration of Episcopacy, for the younger among them were eager

for the king's favour; the others were either so crippled by debt that
they would inevitably depend on the goodwill and indulgence of the
state, or were so conscious of past misdeeds that they would 'never
adventure on new irritations to hasten their owne ruine'. Then, most
crucial of all, Sydserf suggest a drastic remedy, worthy of Hercules and
Alexander the Great: one act by Parliament would serve to wipe out
the actions of all illegally constituted assemblies right back to 1637.
Legally and constitutionally it would then be as if Presbyterianism had
never existed: all opponents could be purged, all incumbent ministers
threatened with disciplinary action if they did not accept the restoration
of Episcopacy, discipline would be maintained by the preservation of a
standing army, and no General Assembly would be permitted to meet.
This indeed was the church militant: the memorandum parallels so
closely the actions taken by Middleton and Charles in 1661–2 that it
is a strong possibility that Sydserf's recommendations may have acted
as a model.[7]

When the royal council met Middleton took the offensive, presumably with the support and encouragement of Clarendon, arguing
with conviction: '. . . that he might for the humiliation of the preachers,
and to prevent any unruly proceedings of their assembly, begin with
rescinding all acts of the Covenant, and all other acts which had invaded
the king's power ecclesiastical, and then proceed to the erecting of
bishops in that kingdom, according to the ancient institution. . . '[8]

Urged on by Glencairn and Rothes, Middleton maintained that such
a move could be very easily accomplished: '. . . because of the tyrannical
proceedings of the assemblies of their several presbyteries had so far
incensed persons of all degrees that not only the nobility, gentry and
common people would be glad to be free from them, but that the most
learned and best part of the ministers desired the same . . .'[9]

Of all those present only the Earl of Crawford-Lindsay came out in
direct opposition.[10] Lauderdale, perhaps suspecting a trap, picked his
way delicately through what was, for him, a particularly dangerous
issue. Presumably to the surprise of Middleton, he immediately
denounced the Covenant, and said there was no one more in favour of
the restoration of Episcopacy than he. But on this politically explosive
issue it was absolutely necessary to proceed with great care, always
conscious of the temper of the people; it was all a question of timing.
This was an area in which it was necessary to move at a snail's pace:
'. . . that if it were undertaken presently, or without due circumstance
in preparing more men than could that short time be done, it would
not only miscarry, but with it his Majesty be disappointed of many
other particulars, which he would otherwise be sure to obtain'.[11]

There were still many, even among the nobility, Lauderdale proceeded, who were infatuated with the Covenant, an argument that presumably received some silent assent from Crawford-Lindsay. Despite his caution this was a dangerous position for a man of his past associations and perceived loyalties to take; the king, likewise a careful politician, appeared convinced, but for Middleton and his allies Lauderdale's whole position was an exercise in subterfuge and duplicity, as Clarendon describes: 'Middleton and most of the Scots lords were mightily offended by the presumption of Lautherdale, in undertaking to know the spirit and disposition of a kingdom which he had not seen in ten years, and easily discerned that his affected raillery and railing against the Covenant, and his magnifying Episcopal government, were but a varnish to cover the rottenness of his intentions . . .'[12]

Lauderdale's position was weak: having conceded Episcopacy he was forced to fall back on the sensitivity of public opinion, which effectively opened the ground to Middleton, who was indeed in a far better position to judge its true temper. Besides, apart from a few eccentrics like Crawford-Lindsay and Cassillis, almost all of the Scots nobility shared Middleton's view. In the instruction issued by the Council the Commissioner was effectively given a free hand to determine the most acceptable solution to the church question. By the spring even Clarendon was beginning to have qualms over the exuberance with which Middleton tackled the issue, even speaking positively of Lauderdale: 'Conscience of the peace prevails more with him than purity of religion.'[13]

This perceptive insight by the normally hostile Clarendon provides the essential key to Lauderdale's thinking at this time. He was more than happy to join with his colleagues in devising a political solution to the church question. It is wrong to assume, as Middleton obviously did, that he was still a zealous Covenanter, a contention that continues to make the occasional appearance.[14] After so many years in the wilderness, political office was far more important to him than any ideological consideration. His 'defence' of Presbyterianism in 1660 was at best muted: it simply offered a less contentious solution to the church question. Like his ancestor, Maitland of Lethington, he was now thinking in purely political terms, all arguments turning on reasons of state.[15] While Middleton, and even some sections of the Presbyterian party in Scotland, continued to think of him as a Covenanter, his real political philosophy was expressed in a letter he wrote to his wife in the autumn of 1663: 'My resolution is to prefer the King's interests [over] all others on earth . . . whatever the King commands shall be punctually done.'[16] Politically Presbyterianism was preferable to Episcopacy; but if the king preferred bishops, then bishops it would be.

Would the Lauderdale solution, it is reasonable to ask, have worked in 1660? The simple answer is, yes, it might. The Resolutioners were desperately eager to please, if only some fragment could be recovered from the wreck of the Covenants. Even the Protestors, broken and leaderless, were not uniformly opposed to a state solution to the church question. Erastian Presbyterianism, after all, was preferable to no Presbyterianism, as James Sharp made clear in a series of letters he wrote to Patrick Drummond, a fellow minister living in London. The following remarks are fairly typical:

> I remembered I sayed to the king whyl my Lord Lauderdaill was by, that now his majesty had the opportunity to secure his interests in the Church of Scotland, and if it were not done I was not to be blamed; the king did then smyle, saying to me you will be counted a malignant when you come home: I have since my return expressed to the brethren with whom I had occasion to speak of these matters that I see no way for the Church of Scotland to redeem themselves and ther doctrine and practices from the imputations which lye upon them, and to secure the order of this church, but to disown whatever hath been preejudiciall to the king's interest; and to make it appear that his authority may be found in this church as in any other of his domains, for I saw evidently that for us ministers in Scotland ther is no reserve but in the king's favor and countenancy of us.[17]

Alarmed by the rumours of an Episcopal restoration, he also wrote to Lauderdale, saying that nothing was more prejudicial to the interests of the king, and that almost all the ministers were loyal to the civil power – 'were the game of the Isle of Wight to be reacted ther would be few of those hairbrain men . . . now found'.[18]

Despite these signs, it has been argued that any policy of Presbyterian moderation was foredoomed; that the failure of the later experiment of concession and compromise, pursued by Lauderdale from 1669 onwards, indicates that such a policy would always have been wrecked by dogmatic intransigence.[19] Such a view underestimates the damage that had been done by eight years of repression, and the effect that this was to have in hardening attitudes. In 1660 there is little evidence of the fanaticism that was to become the natural corollary of Middleton's policy in forcing the church to accept a new form of Episcopacy, and a novel interpretation of the church militant – bishops poised on the barrel of a gun.

When Parliament finally assembled in January 1661 it bore out many of the assumptions Middleton had made in the Royal Council: almost all the nobility and the gentry were eager to put the past behind them and to recover the power and influence they had lost under the successive dictatorships of Kirk and Cromwell. The members were only too willing to collaborate with the Commissioner in resurrecting the 'ancient' royal prerogative. Middleton's first opportunity to gauge the mood of the assembly came with the new oath of allegiance, which recognised Charles as the 'only Supream Governour of this Kingdome over all persons and causes'.[20] This seemed to imply that the king had untrammelled authority over the church as well as the state, and immediately met with objections from a small group of old Kirk party enthusiasts around the Earl of Cassillis. Middleton paused temporarily and took note, even declaring against the 'high church' party in the newly assembled Lords of the Articles. However, the opposition of Cassillis, a man whose dress sense was as old fashioned as his politics, only emphasised just how isolated the Covenanters were. Cassillis wrote to Lauderdale, hoping for support; significantly he never received a reply. His objections were ignored and he left Parliament, vacating all public office soon after.

With Cassillis out of the way, and Crawford quiescent, Middleton proceeded at a breathtaking rate, carried along by a great wave of reaction and loyalty: the king's power to appoint officers of state was restored, as was his right to call and dissolve parliament; an act was passed against renewal of the Solemn League and Covenant; the Convention of Estates of 1643 was annulled, as was the Parliament of 1649.[21] Significantly the last measure had a direct impact on the status of almost all of the ministers; for the Parliament of 1649 had abolished the right of landlords to make appointments to livings under their control. Ministers who had not been presented by a landlord now had effectively no security in law. Further legislation restored to the crown the sole right of declaring war and making peace, the conclusion of treaties and the raising of armies, all of which had been reserved to parliament during the Covenanter revolution. Parliament also repealed the Triennial Act, which previously had allowed it to meet, regardless of royal objections. Middleton also persuaded the members to grant Charles an income of £40,000 a year for life, an extraordinary measure that effectively removed future parliamentary scrutiny over royal expenditure. Parliament was not, however, blind to its own interest: the money was to be raised from duties imposed on beer, and awarded on the understanding that there would be no more 'cess', the burdensome land tax favoured by Cromwell. 'Never,' Sir Archibald Primrose told Lauderdale, 'was there a Parliament so forward for the King . . .'[22]

The centrepiece of Middleton's legislative programme was yet to come. Earlier in the year he had written to Hyde, saying that 'if his Majesty will own and countenance honest ministers it will be no hard work, I hope, to settle the Church upon its old foundations.'[23] Bit by bit he grew in confidence. Cassillis and the Covenanter rump had been routed; Parliament was strongly anti-Presbyterian. Much of the country, moreover, favoured a return to the old ways, confirming a mood that Middleton had probably only guessed at in prior assertions, as Robert Baillie himself regretfully notes: 'Many of our people are hankering after Bishops, having forgot all the evill they have done and the nature of their office. An exceeding great profanitie and contempt both of the ministrie and religion itself, is everywhere prevalent . . .'[24]

The illegal assemblies of 1643 and 1649 had already been declared void; all that remained was to kick away all the remaining props of the Covenanter revolution. This was to be done by means of a new piece of legislation, one of the most sweeping in Scottish history – the Act Recissory. This had the effect of annulling all 'pretended' Parliaments from 1640 onwards, even those approved by the monarch, with the exception of that of 1650–1, wiping out, at a stroke, all public legislation right back to 1633.[25] It was a dramatic measure, supposedly proposed in jest and adopted in haste; but it was quite consistent with the proposal previously laid down in Sydserf's paper.[26]

Middleton and Glencairn wrote to Hyde in early March, requesting royal permission for this risky new step. To consider the proposal the Royal Council was assembled, and the matter debated in the presence of the king. Lauderdale, far too cautious to advocate openly the retention of Presbyterianism, simply said that a return of the bishops would be politically contentious. Charles, too, showed some signs of alarm at Middleton's brinkmanship; only Hyde openly supported the Recissory Act, as a way of wiping out the past, but even he favoured further consultations. Lauderdale expressed his deep misgivings in a letter to Glencairn:

> . . . to swipe away all the acts, even those where his Majestie and his blessed father of glorious memorie were themselves present will be in my opinion of dangerous consequence. For first, that would cut away all the acts of oblivion and if they be repealed, what security can the subject have . . . I see so great a danger and so little advantage that I am far from advising it. Secondly, this would wholly take away the Church government and settle Episcopacie. For you know that the old acts were repealed when King James settled Bishops after coming into England: King Charles did repeal all those and resettle presbyteries. This king hath by his acts, ratified in his late letter, declared his resolution to protect and preserve it. And if you shall now expunge all those acts at one breath, farewell to that unity in Scotland which is so useful to his Majestie.[27]

Middleton and Glencairn were instructed by Hyde to consult with all those who objected to the act, who included James Sharp; it was too late: the Act Recissory was passed on 28 March, before the Chancellor's letter reached Edinburgh. It was immediately followed by an Act Concerning Religion. The first wiped out at a single stroke all the legal underpinnings of the Presbyterian Kirk; the second filled the void with the will of the King – 'as to the Government of the Church his Majestie will make it his care to satle and secure the same in such a frame as shall be most agreeable to the word of God, most suteable to monarchical Government, and most complying with the publict peace and quyet of the Kingdome'.[28]

Middleton's actions had been bold, almost to the point of complete recklessness; even some of his allies advised restraint. He went ahead anyway, determined to seize hold of the political high ground in a true soldierly fashion; he was immediately met with an intense crossfire, both in Parliament and in the church. Baillie wrote to Lauderdale, in blunt and direct terms, for once misdirecting his fire:

> the introducyion of Bishops and Books, and strengthening the King by your advice in these things, I think you a prime transgressor, and liable among the first to answer to God for that great sin, and . . . I tell yow that my heart is broken with grief and that the burden of the publict I find it weightie and hastening me to my grave . . . I think we are very ill-guided . . . what need yow doe that disservice to the King . . . with pulling doune all our laws at once which concerned our church since 1633? Was this good advice, or will this thryve? Is it wisdom to bring back the Canterburian tymes? The same designes, the same prejudices will they not at last bring us the same horrible effects, whatever fools dreame? My Lord, ye are the Nobleman of the world I esteem most and love best. I think I may say and write to you what I like. If you have gone with your heart to forsake our Covenant, to countenance opening a door which I haste will not be closed . . . And if otherwayes your heart be where it was, as I hope indeed it is, and that in your own way yow are doing what yow can for the truth of God (yet daily I have great feares for yow) I think yow stand in a ticklish place . . . if yow and Mr Sharp, whom we trust as our oen soules, have swerved towards Chancellor Hydes principles, as now we see many doe, yow have much to answer for.[29]

Lauderdale was quick to take advantage of Middleton's apparent blunder, saying to Charles that he did not understand the first principles of government.[30] Middleton was quick to react, on the one hand writing to Lauderdale offering friendship, while on the other sending Glencairn and Rothes to London to defend his actions to the king.[31] At the same time a new and more bitter edge entered into the rivalry between the Secretary and the Commissioner: Baillie, now in a more composed frame of mind, warned his old friend of the danger he was in.[32] Sharp, in contrast, was starting to play that two-edged game that was to do much to ruin his historical reputation. Still outwardly professing loyalty to Lauderdale, and to his fellow Resolutioners, he wrote to Middleton in May, once the political temperature had started to cool somewhat, anticipating what was to come: '. . . but now I trust all opposing designs are dashed, and a foundation laid for a superstructure, which will render your name precious to the succeeding generations'.[33]

By the time Sharp wrote this letter Middleton's position had strengthened considerably. He had been proved right: despite the opposition to the Act Recissory, it was clear that the majority of the nation were compliant. Moreover, his combination of the Act Recissory with the Act Concerning Religion had been a brilliant political move: by deferring the matter to the king he had hugely enhanced the prerogative, always of the first importance to Charles. He had played for high stakes, and won. But his victory had been in large measure determined by factors beyond his control. Between the meeting of the Royal Council in March and the adjournment of the Scottish Parliament in July, the first English Parliament of the new reign had gathered in Whitehall. The Presbyterians, whom Clarendon and others had once considered so vital for a successful settlement, had been politically annihilated. The new Parliament was royalist and cavalier; but it was also acutely aware of its own power. Charles had been actively using his prerogative to implement a measure of religious toleration; the Cavalier Parliament at once insisted on the old legitimate order of the Church of England. All dissidents, whether Presbyterian, Quaker or Catholic were politically suspect. With the full backing of the Lords and Commons, the bishops returned, triumphant and arrogant. A party had been created in church and state ready to give Middleton its full support for his efforts in Scotland.

When Sharp arrived in London that spring he found the wave in favour of Episcopacy practically irresistible: he himself was soon to be carried along on its crest. Lauderdale, for once, was on the defensive. Middleton returned from Scotland with all the accolades of a victorious Roman general. Another meeting of the Royal Council was summoned in July, once again attended by Charles in person. Lauderdale again placed the greatest emphasis on the need for moderation, a position that began to look alarmingly like cowardice. Middleton, supported by Glencairn and Rothes, urged the immediate adoption of Episcopacy.

Lauderdale, in an attempt to apply the brakes, suggested that a new General Assembly be summoned or, as an alternative, some soundings be taken among the provincial synods of the church. These schemes, Middleton countered, would only serve to perpetuate Presbyterianism. The Secretary was predictably backed up by Crawford-Lindsay, a man who enjoyed no great credit with Charles, and James Douglas, formerly the Earl of Selkirk and now the third Duke of Hamilton.[34] Hamilton, despite his prestigious title, was never to be a figure of any real political weight. Hyde, now Earl of Clarendon, threw his formidable bulk behind the Middeltonians: 'God preserve me from living in a country where the church is separate from the state, and may subsist by their own acts; for there all churchmen may be kings.'[35] This was political theatre of a high degree, with an audience of one – the king.

Charles, clearly remembering the arguments of the previous December, decided that the Commissioner had a better understanding of public opinion than the Secretary. On 14 August a proclamation was issued, delivered to the Privy Council in Scotland a few weeks later, in which the king declared that Presbyterianism was not compatible with the dignity of the monarchical estate, and announcing the restoration of government by bishops.[36] It was received at first in complete silence, finally broken by Tweeddale, who suggested that the king be urged to summon provincial assemblies. Against the opposition of the majority, he immediately backed down; but his boldness had marked him out to Middleton as a potential enemy. A few days later Tweeddale was arrested and imprisoned in Edinburgh Castle, supposedly because he had objected to the execution of James Guthrie: in reality he was being singled out as the kinsman and friend of Lauderdale.[37]

Lauderdale, not so committed to Presbyterianism that he would risk his career, quickly accepted the new realities; so, too, did James Sharp. Sharp, never more than a spectator when it came to the real decision-making, had long since given up on even the moderate Presbyterianism desired by his Resolutioner colleagues. Now the game was clearly lost, so he allowed himself to be carried along by the prevailing wind, all to his greater glory and personal profit. In December he was consecrated at Westminster as Archbishop of St Andrews, the first man to occupy this office since the death of John Spottiswood in 1639. Perhaps in anticipation of this final outcome he had written some time before that 'in spyte of malice I shall be found faythfull to the king and my countrey and to my Lord Lauderdaill. I will not give two pence of what others say of me'.

Charles, Lauderdale and Sharp had all hoped that other prominent Resolutioners would accept the remaining vacant bishoprics: all declined. Besides calling on old royalists like Thomas Sydserf, long-term expatriates like Alexander Burnet, and eccentrics like Robert Leighton, the government was forced to dig deep into the second division of the Scottish clergy to fill all the available places, homing in on mediocrities like Andrew Fairfoul and James Hamilton. For the most part they were a fairly pathetic crew, always subject to the state, with little of the prestige and power of the English bishops, soon to be headed by Gilbert Sheldon. From beginning to end the restoration of the Scottish Episcopate had been a purely political affair; more than this, as Middleton clearly intended, it was also profoundly anti-clerical.[38] Sharp was never more than a marionette, contrary to the picture that Gilbert Burnet paints of him. As attitudes are, however, often determined by outward impressions, Sharp found himself uniquely hated as a renegade and a Judas, often denounced in the most intemperate terms: '. . . that limb of Antichrist and infernal locust, the Apostate Arch-Bishop *Sharp*, being a Revolter and consequently profound to make Slaughter, with the Malice like his Father the Devil . . . '[39]

Almost up to the last minute Sharp's old colleagues, including Robert Douglas, had attempted to stand against the tide, hoping to enlist the support of Lauderdale in asking for a General Assembly. The Secretary finally wrote back demolishing all hope of such a prospect, in a letter that offers conciliation and threat in equal measure:

And to deal freely with you. The great miscarriages in the exercise of our Church government these 20 years, the constant opposing the Royal favour, yea and the politics of 1643 and the setting up an authoritie so point blank against the supreme authoritie of King and Parliament, the disuniting the people from obedience to them, the rigide actings of the Commission of the Kirk both before and specially after his Majestie was first in Scotland, the grievous schisms which hath been in the Church since. These things I say seemed to have great weight with his Majestie to incline him to the resolution he hath now taken and wch he hath commanded his Privie Councell to intimate and see execute. And although his Majestie is fully resolved to imploy his authority to settle the Church as it was before the troubles yet he commanded me to let you know, He will use all tenderness and moderation to be used towards such of a contrarie judgement who shall not wilfully oppose his Majesties and the parliaments resolution: and that he expects from you such compliance and submission, at least to the law and to his declared pleasure as not to oppose this same but both by yourselves and your interest with yr friends endeavour that peace may be preserved and no opposition made to what is enjoined. Give me leave to tell you, any opposition will be construed to have a worse designe at bottome. And if

I have any skill in the constitution of affairs the resolution of settling
Episcopacie is unalterable and there is no way to produce peace . . . but
by complying with the resolution now taken and wch the King will
certainly carry on.[40]

Lauderdale and Middleton now agreed on the outward forms of
religion; their mutual hostility, however, was bitterer than ever. Earlier,
making use of his opposition to the Act Recissory, Middleton had hoped
to open his rival to a charge of 'leasing-making' – misrepresenting the
intentions of Parliament, with the intention of sowing deliberate
dissension between the king and his subjects.[41] Lauderdale was far too
clever to be caught in so simple a trap, denying that it had ever been
his intention to create any form of misrepresentation. Glencairn and
Rothes, acting for Middleton, asked Clarendon for his advice on how
to proceed. Clarendon immediately warned the Scots of any attempt
to use any form of procedure that effectively undermined the authority
of the king, advice that was subsequently ignored, with ruinous
consequences for Middleton.[42]

Still the attacks continued, one following hard upon the other. In
August Lauderdale, it was rumoured, had been a correspondent of the
long dead Henry Ireton, Cromwell's son-in-law and one of the leading
regicides.[43] The following month, Middleton tried to have him bypassed,
suggesting, through the Privy Council, that the king's letters be sent
directly to Edinburgh, without reference to the Secretary.[44] It seems
certain that Middleton had hoped for Lauderdale's ruin over his defence
of Presbyterianism; and when this failed to work, proceeded to embrace
ever more dangerous strategies. By the autumn their mutual hatred
was public knowledge, giving substance to the warning Lauderdale
had received earlier in the year from Sir William Bellenden, the Treasurer
Depute: '. . . yow have many enemies heir, who do entertayne themselves
with a full expectation of your fall . . . now or never your part is to be
acted, which I hope will be in such a way as may best confirme people
in the former high esteem held of yow, and give occasion to your enemies
to blush and repent themselves for their attempts against yow'.[45]

Lauderdale's consciousness of danger did not deter him from accepting additional challenges: one of the most serious came over Middleton's
attempt to destroy the house of Campbell. Argyll's trial finally opened
in the spring of 1661. The indictment, prepared with great care,
effectively loaded all the troubles of the revolution and civil wars on
his shoulders, with the additional burden that he had collaborated
with Cromwell in securing the death of Charles I. Of this Gilbert Burnet
wrote, 'The Earl of Middleton resolved, if possible, to have the king's

death fastened on him. By this means, as he would die with the more infamy, since nobody durst move in favour of the son of one judged guilty of that crime. And he, as he believed, hoped to obtain a grant of his estate.'[46] Argyll answered all the charges against him with great skill, so much so that the whole prosecution looked likely to fail; there was simply insufficient evidence to prove that he had played any part in the murder of Charles. In the end he was effectively condemned for no other reason than that he had collaborated with the Cromwellian occupation, a crime that would have taken virtually the whole of the Scottish nobility to the block.[47] He was beheaded on Monday, 27 May 1661. Middleton had achieved part of his aim: Archibald, Lord Lorne, as the son of a forfeited traitor, was not allowed to succeed to his father's title or estates.

Lauderdale is not particularly revealing in his attitude towards Argyll; the two men, despite past collaboration, never seem to have been particularly close. Besides, Argyll was a dangerous friend, hated by Charles almost as much as he hated Johnston of Warriston. There was the additional consideration that any intervention on the Secretary's part on behalf of the condemned man was bound to be misconstrued, suggesting lingering sympathies with the Kirk party.[48] Lorne was another matter; not only was he related to Lauderdale, but he also had a record of proven loyalty.[49] Even so, Lauderdale was clearly losing out to Middleton politically, and this was yet another area where he had to tread with a considerable amount of care.

Middleton's ambitions were personal, as well as political. He had no territorial power in his own right, so he aimed at the lucrative Campbell inheritance. According to James Kirkton, a Presbyterian dissident and later historian of the church, Middleton hoped, in time, to become Duke of Argyll.[50] To achieve this Lorne would first have to be destroyed. The opportunity came in a deceptively simple manner. After his father's death, Lorne continued to lobby for the restoration of the Argyll estates, spending much time in London. Knowing of Clarendon's hostility to the Campbells, he attempted to influence the Chancellor indirectly by enlisting the support of one of his friends. Confident of the success of his efforts, he wrote to Alexander Sutherland, Lord Duffus, his brother-in-law, saying of his enemies in the Scottish Parliament that the king will 'soon see their tricks'. On its way to Scotland this letter was intercepted and brought to the attention of Middleton. Acting at once, the Commissioner submitted the document to Parliament in June 1662, saying that Lorne's observations were a gross reflection on its conduct. It was agreed that he should be charged with leasing-making, the same accusation that the Middeltonians had attempted to level against Lauderdale. Parliament asked the king to send Lorne back to Edinburgh to stand trial, a request conveyed to him by George Mackenzie of Tarbet, a supporter of Middleton then in London. Charles was initially sceptical, but agreed to the request rather than give offence to an assembly that had given so many proofs of its loyalty.

Lorne was in considerable danger, for leasing-making was a capital crime. Lauderdale now exerted himself to mitigate the terms of his arrest. Tarbet wanted him sent down as a prisoner. The Secretary argued against this 'knowing how great a disadvantage it is for a pannel to appear before the bar as a prisoner'.[51] Lauderdale was well aware that if Lorne stood before Parliament as a prisoner, as his father had done, it would imply that the extraordinary measures taken against him had royal approval; better if he came of his own volition. Tarbet countered by saying the offence was treason and therefore not bailable. Lauderdale took the bold step of offering to stand caution for his kinsman, life for life, a safely theatrical gesture that Charles clearly would never accept. Tarbet, perhaps concerned that this would give Lorne additional political insurance, initially argued against it, but was persuaded to change his mind by Clarendon, 'by which the Chancellor designed to render Lauderdale odious to the Parliament of Scotland in becoming surety for one who had abused them; and to engage likewise all Lauderdale's enemies against Lord Lorne, whose person he hated passionately'.[52] Lorne was duly despatched to Edinburgh, put through the formality of a trial and sentenced to death in August 1662, though the king gave instructions that execution was not to be carried out. Even so he was held prisoner in Edinburgh Castle for almost a year, while the struggle between Middleton and Lauderdale moved towards a turbulent climax.

Middleton was angry that his moves against Lorne had only enjoyed partial success: in characteristic fashion he and his supporters followed up the trial by introducing a measure in Parliament making it a criminal offence to petition the king on behalf of those attainted by Parliament, a measure clearly aimed at the Secretary.[53] This was politically danger-ous because it was a direct challenge to the royal prerogative of mercy. Once again the Commissioner was exceeding his instructions; this time, though, he was diminishing rather than enhancing the power of the king. Boldness was a sword with two edges: the total lack of caution demonstrated over the Act Recissory was shortly to lead to Middleton's political extinction.

The second session of Scotland's 'Cavalier' Parliament opened in May 1662. Once again Middleton combined the political and the personal, one seemingly carrying as much weight as the other. One of the first measures was an act formally re-establishing the 'antient government of the Church by Archbishops and Bishops'.[54] Both Covenants were declared unlawful, as was the General Assembly of 1638. It was made treasonable to preach against the king's prerogative and supremacy in church questions, or against Episcopacy. All ministers appointed since the abolition of lay patronage in 1649 were to be presented by a lawful sponsor before they were allowed to collect their stipends; and they were to seek collation – confirmation of their office – from the bishop of their diocese. All who did not obtain presentation and collation by 20 September 1662 were to be deprived of their livings. Synods, kirk sessions and presbyteries were not allowed to meet without the authority of a bishop. All of this was important, but of particular significance for the future was one of the lesser measures, the Act Against Conventicles, which declared: '. . . his Majestie considering that vnder the pretext of religious exercises, divers unlawful meetings and conventicles (the nurseries of sedition) have been kept in private families . . . do doth heirby discharge all private meetings or conventicles in houses whivh vnder the pretence, or for religious exercises may tend to the prejudice of the publict worship of God in the Church, or to the alienating of the people from their lawful pastors, and that duetie and obedience they ow the Church and State'.[55]

This steady process of reaction had a demoralising effect on Robert Baillie, who saw much of his life's work reversed. Lauderdale, his old and valued friend, had been corrupted by Clarendon; Middleton and the bishops were now supreme. All the past suffering had been pointless, as he concludes in a final note: 'Our Kirk, all the English tymes, had been very faithful to our King, and so instrumental as we could for his restoration. We had lost much blood at Dunbar, Worcester and elsewhere, and at last our libertie in his cause. We did firmly expect, at his Restitution, a comfortable subsistence to ourselves, and all our Presbyterian brethren, in his dominions; and believed the King's intention was no other; but by divine permission, other counsels thereafter prevailed, and now carry all.'[56]

The 'little monk of Kilwinning' died in August 1662, so it was later claimed of a 'broken heart', a condition no longer medically or historically fashionable; the simple truth is that he had, as his biographer puts it, 'lived beyond his time'.[57]

After the Revolution of 1688, Sir George Mackenzie of Roseheaugh, the former Lord Advocate, wrote an apologia, justifying his past actions and the part he had played in the government of Charles II. His comments on religion are clearly addressed more to future generations than to his contemporaries: 'The Reader will be astonished, when we inform him; that the way of worship in our Church, differed nothing from what the Presbyterians themselves practiced (except only, that we used the Doxologie, the Lord's Prayer, and in Baptism, the Creed, all which they rejected). We had no Ceremonies, Surplice, Alters, Cross in Baptisms, nor the meanest of those things which would be allowed in England by the Dissenters, in way of accommodation . . .'[58]

Mackenzie was absolutely right. While diocesan Episcopacy had been restored in the form it had before 1638, this was purely an organisational change. The innovations in worship and the liturgy that led to the riots of 1637 were all absent. The general mood of anti-clericalism at the Restoration, most clearly expressed by Middleton, was to ensure that both bishops and ministers would be firmly subordinated to the state. Sharp and his colleagues were, for the most part, not figures of any great spiritual authority – this was no Laudian settlement – but little more than glorified civil servants. It was a clear and obvious Erastian solution to the question of church government, and thus all the more repugnant to committed Protestors; but even so much might have been achieved with a little careful handling; by any man, that is, other than John Middleton.

Middleton seems to have expected no real resistance to the acts of presentation and collation; but as the due date approached it was clear that he had a major problem on his hands. Far from their being only a few irreconcilables, most of the ministers in the western Whig heartlands either walked out or simply ignored the order. Middleton was shocked by the unexpected reaction of 'these mad fellows'. His precipitate actions, moreover, had had the effect of uniting the whole of the old Protestor party with the anti-Erastian wing of the Resolutioners, men who were far from being natural allies. Faced with the political embarrassment of having so many parishes vacant at one time, the deadline was extended to 1 February 1663. It made little difference: in the end some 300 ministers, one-third of the Scottish establishment, either resigned or were ejected. If this had been evenly spread across the whole ministry it would have been bad. What made it far worse was the geographical concentration of the resignations. In the synod of Galloway only 3 out of 37 ministers were left; in the synod of Glasgow and Ayr, the largest in the church, only 35 of 130 ministers remained in post. Deprivations in Lothian and Fife were also high, but it was clear that those areas that had effectively ruined the Engagement in 1648 were now set to cause the most trouble.

Middleton's rush to impose Episcopacy was the cause of almost three decades of unrest and upheaval in south-west Scotland. The church question, dormant for much of the Cromwell period, was thus destined to remain at the centre of national politics, just as it had been in the 1630s. Men barely adequate for the task replaced the ousted ministers. Gilbert Burnet, himself in Episcopal orders, called them the 'dregs and refuse of the northern parts'; in other words, men drawn from the conservative north who, for one reason or another, had been unable to obtain livings close to home. Local people simply dismissed them as the 'curates'. It was one thing to get these men into their new churches, quite another to get people to come and hear them. Soon a new problem emerged, not even anticipated in the Act Against Conventicles, which only mentioned illegal house assemblies. People now took to listening to their old ministers in the fields. From small beginnings these field conventicles were to turn into huge problems of public order, with as many as 10,000 men, women and children turning up to hear a particularly popular preacher. What is worse, as the years passed many of the men who attended came with arms. Middleton had sown the wind; it was Lauderdale, his great rival, who was eventually to reap the whirlwind.

Because Middleton's career was to end so spectacularly, and because his reintroduction of Episcopacy was so inept, there is a tendency to overlook his success in implementing in Scotland what might be referred to as the 'Clarendon programme'. The Chancellor had envisaged a new form of royal government designed to replace the disorders and anarchy of the past. Rule by council would replace rule by Parliament, and church and state in both England and Scotland would be subject to the will of the king. This ideal was never to be achieved in England because Parliament took a firmly empirical approach to royal finance, and remained suspicious of some of the perceived deviations in government policy, especially over the question of dissenters and their relation to the national church. For Charles absolutism in England was a goal, constantly reached for and never attained. Middleton, with the co-operation of the Scottish Parliament, which he always managed with great skill, had gone a large part of the way to amplifying the prerogative power in Scotland, creating a political divergence that was to grow wider over the years. This was to be another legacy he bequeathed to Lauderdale.

By the summer of 1662 Middleton had achieved the public part of his programme; the time had now come to complete the private. Lauderdale, who so far had survived both intrigue and direct attack, would be destroyed. One by one his allies and friends were being knocked away: Cassillis was gone, Tweeddale eclipsed and Lorne imprisoned. Early in 1662 there were rumours that moves were being

made against the Earl of Crawford-Lindsay, the last substantial associate
of Lauderdale still enjoying political office in Scotland.[59] Crawford-
Lindsay, isolated and vulnerable, entered the line of fire; the real target
was the Secretary, who received a clear warning from Lady Balcarres,
the sister of the Earl of Rothes: '. . . they profess yr invie agenst Craford,
but truly (he says) its agenst Lauderdaill, for they think if you war out
our Samson, whose hear is cot, wold doe what they ples'.[60] It is not
clear from this if Rothes, hitherto a close associate of Middleton, is
simply speaking too freely to his sister, or if he is deliberately passing
the hint to Lauderdale to be on his guard. It is possible to detect in this
the beginnings of a new alignment: Rothes not only survived the
eventual collapse of the Middleton faction, but also moved up the
ministerial ladder, which he is unlikely to have done without the active
support of the Secretary.

Middleton finally made his move in September. He was a man in a
hurry: Clarendon controlled England, and Ormonde, his close friend
and ally, had returned to Ireland as Lord-Lieutenant; Middleton was
determined to complete the Cavalier triumvirate. To smoke out all the
remaining Presbyterian foxes an act was passed obliging all office
holders to denounce the Covenants. This was too much for Crawford-
Lindsay, who now departed the scene, to be replaced as Treasurer by
Rothes. Lauderdale was a different matter. Middleton was clearly
convinced that the new oath would force the Secretary to end his
dissimulation, and reveal his true political sympathies; he completely
misread his man. With Lauderdale ideology always took second place
to pragmatic calculation. When he heard of Middleton's actions he is
said to have laughed and declared that he could cope with a cartload
of such oaths rather than lose office.[61] Some more desperate proceeding
was clearly necessary, and Middleton once again demonstrated the
total lack of caution he had shown over the Act Recissory. Boldness
and surprise were soldierly tactics that had served him well in the past;
this time they led him into oblivion.

John Maitland,
1st Duke of Lauderdale
by John Roettier (1639–1707).

———

John Maitland, 1st Duke of Lauderdale
by Samuel Cooper (1609–72).

———

John and Elizabeth Maitland,
Duke and Duchess of Lauderdale,
after Sir Peter Lely.

———

NATIONAL PORTRAIT GALLERY,
LONDON

Edward Hyde, 1st Earl of Clarendon,
unknown artist, after Adriaen Hanneman
(1601?–1671?).

———

Anthony Ashley-Cooper,
1st Earl of Shaftesbury,
unknown artist (c. 1672–3).

———

'The Scots Holding
their Young King's Nose
to the Grindstone',
from a pamphlet of 1651.

Ham House from the south,
atrrib. Henry Danckerts (late seventeenth century).

———

Horse Guards' Parade (detail), by Jan Wyck.

———

John Speed's Kingdom of Scotland, 1662.

———

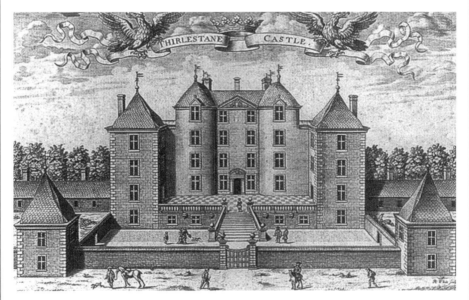

Thirlestane Castle.

———

9

THE FALL OF MIDDLETON

On 9 September 1662, a few days after the oath against the Covenants, Parliament passed the Act of Indemnity, something Lauderdale had long pressed for.[1] This was a reasonable measure that was intended to extend to Scotland the same guarantees of a similar English act, ending the uncertainty of former perceived enemies of the crown. Although rehabilitation would be offered at a price, a formal scale of fines at least ended the threat of intimidation and blackmail, freely employed by the less scrupulous royalists against their former opponents. Middleton had seen to it that he and all the other threadbare cavaliers would not lose out by this, persuading the king that his most loyal adherents should be fully compensated for past suffering from the fines thus gathered; he also saw to it that he would benefit politically. Some months before the act was passed he decided that some former Covenanters and collaborators with Cromwell should be exempted, and declared incapable of public trust. There was nothing inherently sinister in this; the English act contained similar disabilities. In the end the whole procedure acquired extraordinary overtones because of the use Middleton made of it: he manipulated both Parliament and the king in his determination to destroy Lauderdale.

When the measure was being debated in Parliament earlier in the year, Middleton persuaded the members, with no authority whatsoever, that it was the will of the king that up to twelve, as yet unspecified, individuals should be exempted from the general offer of indemnity. The king was then persuaded that it was the will of Parliament. A meeting was held in Glencairn's house, attended by Middleton, Primrose and Fletcher, the chief legal officers. It was obvious, even at this early stage, that Lauderdale had been selected as the chief target of the Indemnity Act. To calm any suspicions he may have had, two copies of the bill were prepared, one with the exemptions clause, and one without. Much would depend on how this matter was handled in London. The man chosen for the task was Sir George Mackenzie of Tarbet, who was immediately sent for.[2] After some hesitation, Tarbet agreed to present the matter to the king, having first negotiated his way around the Lauderdale wall. Thus began one of the oddest political crises in Scottish history, in time to be known as the Billeting Affair.

Tarbet was a good choice; he was a clever and able lawyer and a skilled diplomat, by far the most intelligent of Middleton's adherents; most important of all, he hated Lauderdale. He was an ultra-royalist, an admirer of Montrose, who had opposed the recalling of the old Committee of Estates in 1660, because of the Covenanter associations of some of its members, and blamed Lauderdale when it was brought back into being.[3] As soon as he arrived he had a meeting with Clarendon, who arranged for him to have an audience with Charles. Lauderdale, always suspicious when any of his fellow countrymen sought direct access to the king, was particularly angry that the request had not come through him. But, judging by his subsequent actions, Charles was clearly impressed by Mackenzie, falling under the spell of his obvious charm. A meeting of the Royal Council was duly summoned to consider the Indemnity Bill. Before this Tarbet soothed the outraged feelings of the bristling Secretary, disarming him with a copy of the Bill, minus the exemption clause. But when the full measure was subsequently presented in council Lauderdale, furious at the deception, immediately denounced Tarbet, who was obviously prepared for this fallout: 'To which it was calmly answered by Tarbet, that the Secretary was not to know his instructions; a main article whereof was founded upon a humble desire to his Majesty, to exempt some persons from publick trust; and that the Secretary desir'd only a copy of the Act of Indemnity, which he had deliver'd to his Lordship as a private person.'[4]

In the presence of the king, his brother James, Duke of York, Clarendon and Ormonde, Lauderdale, unbriefed and unprepared, attacked the exemption clause, using his formidable intellect to identify the very thing that was eventually to destroy Middleton's strategy: it was unfair and unjust; a form of forfeiture that had not received royal approval. No one ought to be subject to such a penalty whose case had not first been considered by the king: 'they ought to be pursued legally, and not punish'd without hearing, in an arbitrary manner.'[5] The argument was a good one; but the Secretary was fighting against established practice: if the Scottish exemptions were illegal so too were those applying under the English Act. None of those present, with the possible exception of Tarbet, suspected that the Scottish bill might be used against the Secretary himself.[6] Lauderdale, in a minority of one, was overruled.

This was the low point of Lauderdale's political career. He had lost out, not just over the Indemnity Act, but also on almost all the other major questions of the day. His advice was ignored, his authority undermined and his friends threatened. Even Charles seems to have lost some of his old affection for a man with little in the way of personal charm, so abundantly displayed by Tarbet. He was now brought so low that the king would ostentatiously close the door on him when he called Tarbet to his presence: 'he was undervalued by his enemies, and deserted by his friends . . .'[7] At no other time in his life did it look so certain that his political career was coming to a premature conclusion. But Lauderdale was a fox, at his most cunning when under threat. He had taken care to ensure that he had agents in Scotland, chief amongst whom was William Sharp, the brother of the archbishop, well placed to observe the manoeuvres of his enemies.

Middleton had won the first round with commendable speed; with equal speed he proceeded to lose the game. His first serious mistake was his failure to maintain an effective presence at court. No sooner had the Royal Council dissolved than Tarbet returned to Scotland, in the company of the Earl of Newburgh and Charles Stuart, Duke of Richmond and Lennox, the king's distant cousin. Richmond was a political nonentity, of no significance whatsoever; but once in Scotland he was sufficiently flattered by Middleton to take an active part in his intrigues. Middleton also seriously misread the situation, apparently seeing Richmond as a surrogate for the king, an error the duke was probably eager to encourage.

As soon as Tarbet and his party arrived in Edinburgh Middleton summoned them to a meeting at Holyrood Abbey to decide on future action. On a suggestion by Tarbet, supported by Richmond and Newburgh, it was decided that the exemptions be chosen by a ballot, or billet, in the Scottish Parliament.[8] Each member would be asked to compile a secret billet with the names of up to twelve people they wished to see excluded, the most frequently named appearing on the final list. This was a dangerous procedure, as presumably Tarbet and any of the other conspirators with classical education must have known: they had effectively revived the process of ostracism, last used in the democracy of ancient Athens, a procedure hardly likely to appeal to a man like Charles. It was even more dangerous because they also decided that Parliament would be pressurised into producing the 'right kind' of list, with Lauderdale, of course, appearing right at the top. With Richmond approving each stage of this shady process, Middleton was obviously convinced that he would have the approval of the king. Middleton was so confident of success that he even planned to replace Lauderdale as Secretary of State for Scotland with Mackenzie of Tarbet, yet another astonishing piece of political arrogance.[9]

The billeting was aimed not just at the Secretary himself but also at what remained of his party, including Tweeddale, rehabilitated since the Guthrie episode, though still vulnerable, and Sir Robert Moray, another close ally, who had first become acquainted with Lauderdale when Charles I was at Newcastle. Perhaps no other example shows the sheer spite behind the whole billeting conspiracy than the inclusion of Moray among those selected for the purge. Lauderdale and Tweeddale had suspect political pasts, unlike Moray, whose views had always been highly moderate. He had Presbyterian sympathies, and had opposed the reintroduction of Episcopacy, but his royalism had always come first. He had been a soldier who, following a long Scots tradition, had entered the French military service during the reign of Louis XIII, later becoming a diplomat. He was well known to both Middleton and Glencairn, serving under them during the abortive Highland rising against Cromwell. Soldier and diplomat, he was also a scientist of some distinction, going on to become one of the founders of the Royal Society after the Restoration. For a long time he and Lauderdale were not just allies but close personal friends. Above all, he was the most intelligent of Lauderdale's associates and a possible successor as Secretary of State. Middleton and Tarbet clearly saw him as just another head of the hydra, which had to be cut off before they could be secure.

Lauderdale was made aware at an early stage that there was a sinister intention behind the exemption clause. William Sharp kept him informed, using secret messages, in which Lauderdale is referred to as 'John Red', the pseudonym he had adopted some years before. On 6 September, just after the passing of the oath against the Covenants, the Secretary received an alarming report: 'A spat [?] is at present running highlie here, and to damm it here I see [?] not the possibilitie . . . When the Act that past yesterday was moved in the articles, it wes amongst some talked of that Mr Hastie [Crawford-Lindsay] and Mr Red were meant . . .'[10]

Another message followed a few days later, by which time billeting was underway in Parliament: 'When I wrot by the last that Mr Red wes to be concerned in the exception of the 12, but it seems viceroy [Middleton] hes taken pains to be roy in his word, that he would make Mr Red know it'.[11]

William had access to privileged information, being kept advised by his brother James, present in Parliament as part of the new Episcopal order, but taking no part himself in Middleton's manoeuvres. Lauderdale was urged to be on his guard, 'For the paper filled with the names of the 12 exempted persons is to be divulged to M [Charles] sealed and not to be divulged till he declare his pleasure'.[12] He was subsequently told that Middleton and his allies had used their power to influence the selection in Parliament, and that he, Tweeddale, Moray and Crawford-Lindsay had all been billeted, in a process that also appears to have entailed a degree of intimidation. No sooner had the measure been adopted, than Middleton, on his own authority, gave the seal of royal approval. Tarbet and Richmond were delegated to carry the act to Charles, and persuade him that it was the will and desire of his loyal subjects. At the same time Newburgh was sent to Ireland to enlist the support of Ormonde. At no time, though, was Clarendon advised, an error of fatal dimensions.

Tarbet made his way south, confident in his persuasive abilities, and with no idea that anything was wrong. Lauderdale, in the course of an interview with the king, asked in a disarmingly casual fashion what would happen if he himself had been billeted. Charles replied that no one would dare attack his servants. The Secretary then threw a rock into the silent pond: not only had he been billeted, but Middleton had also touched the act with the sceptre.[13] The reports we have of this probably underestimate the degree of royal surprise and anger: the king had been duped. He was to lose one of his most faithful servants by will of Parliament, a deeply uncomfortable echo of the past. News spread quickly through the court. No sooner did Tarbet and Richmond arrive in London than they received a highly unpleasant surprise. Summoned to Clarendon's presence they were asked: '. . . if they were mad, and plainly told that by that they had changed the scene now, and that instead of attacking Lauderdale they must now betake themselves to the defensive; for all that could now be done was to set out Middleton's zeal and services so advantageously as to obtain a pardon for his last error; but they had now established Lauderdale; so with this melancholy prospect of ill success they came to wait on the king'.[14]

The billeting affair was so laughably incompetent that Clarendon was even moved to remark in jest that it might have been planned by Lauderdale's own friends, so much did it rebound in his favour. All the political and personal advantages that Tarbet had gained during his last visit had been thrown away on a turn of the cards. Charles threw the act into his cabinet unopened and ordered Tarbet back to Scotland, telling him that he and his colleagues must have been either drunk or insane.[15] Tarbet was packed off to Scotland and Middleton told to remain there, while Rothes, who had been careful to keep his hands clean, was summoned to court to give an account of the affair. Lauderdale, like Clarendon, was quick to see just how much Middleton's political incompetence had worked to his advantage; before the end of

September he was even able to find some humour in the whole affair, remarking to a correspondent that 'I am not yet knokt on the head nor feld with a billet'.[16] He was afterwards to refer to the occasion as 'Saint Billeting's Day', the king himself happily sharing the joke, as a letter by Moray written the following summer makes plain: 'The first thing the king said upon his opening your relation of what past in parliament was (and I promised to let you know it) that, if you write not upon better paper and with better pens, wee will have yow billeted again'.[17]

The immediate political consequences were far from funny: Clarendon had exerted all his skills to ensure that Middleton, at least temporarily, was kept in place. In Council he defended his success in the restoration of Episcopacy, implying that his demise would only give heart to the Presbyterian dissidents, who looked for favours from Lauderdale.[18] While the Secretary and the Chancellor were far from being natural allies, their relationship had been a little less frosty over the past few years; now it was set to return to its natural state, spilling over from dislike into outright hatred. For Lauderdale the longer Middleton survived the more dangerous he became. In January 1663 Lord Bellenden informed him of a new intrigue. The Middeltonians, as a last ditch defence, were resurrecting an ancient libel: '. . . I think it fitt to let yow know that the papers of all transactions betwixt the Scottish commissioners and parliament of England, are now in the custodie of some who are very confident that use may be made of them in pursuance of the act of Billeting. I am told that it is intended to draw something from the papers to your prejudice, and that at next session of Parliament it is resolved to bring the busieness to a publique hearing'.[19]

This confirms an earlier suggestion by William Sharp that if Lauderdale refused to accept his exclusion from office under the Act of Indemnity then his enemies were prepared to resort to blackmail, accusing him of complicity in the surrender of Charles I in 1647.[20] This was a charge to which Lauderdale was always vulnerable, forcing him later to commit a defence to paper; but the evidence is very thin. In his memoirs, Sir George Mackenzie of Roseheaugh, a kinsman of Tarbet, says that Sir John Chieslie, a former clerk of the Committee of Both Kingdoms, gave certain incriminating papers to Middleton, clearly implicating Lauderdale in the decision to hand over the late king to Parliament.[21] Years later, when the heat had gone out of the Billeting Affair, and old hatreds forgotten, Middleton is said to have handed over these papers to Lauderdale, who promptly had them destroyed – so other than Mackenzie's account no proof of this exists. The story makes no sense. Why would Middleton, pushed into a corner, and fighting for his political life, have failed to use the one weapon that would have justified all of his actions? There appears to be little doubt that such papers were actively sought; there is equally little doubt that none were found.

Middleton was finally summoned to London in February 1663 to defend his actions as Commissioner before the king. As he crossed the border at Coldstream an old woman is said to have shouted that he would never lord it over Scotland again. Once in the capital he found that the Secretary had prepared a formidable indictment, delivered on 5 February before Charles and a gathering of the ministers of both nations, calling to mind the very arguments that he had first made in Council the year before, when Tarbet had introduced the exclusion clause:

> . . . by Billeting any man's honour, his life, his posterity may be destroyed without the trouble of calling him. Billeting hath the wonderful power to destroy any man, and yet the collective body of that judiciary, who use it, shall never be troubled with his name till it comes to be executed. This is a stranger engine than white gunpowder, which some fancy, for sure this shoots without any noise at all. But, blessed be God, this dreadful engine was never known as a punishment amongst any people, heathen or christian, who had the blessing to live under monarchy. Some republics use the billet or the ballot in giving places, but I never so much as read anything like it as to punishment, except by ostracism among the Athenians, who were governed by that cursed sovereign lord the People . . .[22]

Lauderdale's speech was one of the greatest he ever made. Item by item he examined and dismantled the whole system of government constructed by Middleton: he had exceeded his authority, deceived both king and Parliament, and, worst of all, he had shown contempt for the royal prerogative. Turning to the king himself, Lauderdale introduced a personal note: 'Six times I have been excepted: twice for life, twice for my estate, and twice thus. Yet I bless God that five of the times was during rebellion, and by usurpers, by serving your royal father and yourself, and this last I hope shall be found to be done neither by your Majesty nor by your Parliament.' Middleton's response to Lauderdale's act of demolition was evasive and unconvincing; he was reduced to excusing himself by saying that he had only consented to and not devised billeting.

Despite Lauderdale's formidable accusations, and the anger of the king, it was no easy task to replace the Commissioner; he had powerful friends among the cavalier establishment in England, amongst the bishops and in Parliament. In the end, he effectively finished himself by giving new substance to Lauderdale's charge of arrogance. Towards the end of January the king, almost certainly acting on the advice of the Secretary, had instructed the Privy Council to suspend collection of the fines due under the Indemnity Act. Middleton complained to Clarendon, who raised the matter with Charles and had the decision reversed. Shortly after the Council meeting of 5 February the Commissioner wrote to Edinburgh in the name of the king demanding the fines be paid. Lauderdale told Charles, who immediately denied that he had given any such authority, and immediately reissued his original order.[23] It seems that Charles may not have properly understood Clarendon when he mentioned Middleton's objection to the January decree, with the result that government temporarily descended into farce. Middleton had now done something even worse than billeting: he had embarrassed the king.

From this point forward Middleton was politically doomed. In a clear mood of despair he disappeared into his chamber for four days on end, as Lauderdale reported triumphantly.[24] It was a slow and lingering death, which did not fully run its course until May. By then it was being reported to Ormonde that Lauderdale had the upper hand and that Middleton was likely to be dismissed as Commissioner: 'These reports are very dissatisfying to most of the House of Commons, who not without some passion extol all the late good services of Middleton, and with some warmth exaggerate the past disservice of the other, who nevertheless loses no ground in our master's good opinion, though for all I see he stands single in our English court, whatsoever party he hath among his own countrymen.'[25]

Lauderdale had to be careful; his political standing in England was weak, perhaps never more so now that he was on the point of defeating one of his greatest enemies. Parliament had rejected the king's attempt to introduce a measure of religious toleration, and thus end the monopoly of Anglican uniformity. Lauderdale was still suspected of harbouring Presbyterian sympathies, which would require some careful political handling. He also had enough personal skill to avoid the kind of political trap that had seduced Middleton. By the spring of 1663 his great enemy, Clarendon, was looking vulnerable, having lost some of the confidence of the king. Sensing an opportunity, the ambitious George Digby, Earl of Bristol, sought to finish him off; but the attempt was so badly managed that the Chancellor recovered some of his former favour. Lauderdale had avoided committing himself to Bristol's onslaught, demonstrating that any personal ambitions took second place to his loyalty to the crown.[26]

Skill was also required in dealing with the demise of Middleton, finally deprived of the Commissionership at the end of May.[27] According to Mackenzie, Lauderdale declined the appointment for himself, since the first task of the new Commissioner was to investigate the Billeting Affair, and it would therefore be wrong for him to be both judge and jury.[28] Rothes was chosen instead. It was a good move: Rothes was free of the kind of suspicions attached to Lauderdale; he had also been a close associate of Middleton, though he had managed to avoid being compromised by the billeting fiasco. Middleton's ship may have sunk, taking with it Tarbet and Sir John Fletcher, the Lord Advocate, but there were no other major casualties. Headed by Glencairn, most of the Middeltonians remained in place. Lauderdale was under close scrutiny, by bishops and cavaliers, both in England and Scotland; he was soon to surprise them all.

In June 1663, in his first official visit to his country, the Secretary accompanied Rothes to Scotland for the opening of the new session of Parliament. Moray was left in London to attend to business in his absence as Deputy Secretary. Middleton had earlier tried to frighten the bishops by warning of the dangers of a change of government; Lauderdale and Rothes came with an invitation to the archbishops of St Andrews and Glasgow to join the Privy Council, giving them an enhanced political role. It was an inspired move; all the rumours that the Episcopal party was to be destroyed were at once shown to be false.[29] An act was passed in Parliament confirming Episcopal authority, and a further act passed against conventicles, modelled on the recent English measure. All those who wilfully exempted themselves from their local parish church – presumably to attend conventicles – were to be subject to heavy fines. Lauderdale followed all of this up by a speech expressing his full satisfaction with the present church settlement, ending any lingering hope that he was about to lead a Presbyterian revival. Sharp and his colleagues were delighted, as Lauderdale informed Moray, allowing a slight note of personal pleasure to creep in to his report: 'The bishops in a body gave me a solemn visit about it and one of them said aloud that what I had said would get the more authority than the Act. This I had not the vanity to tell the King nor do I desire you should.'[30] Moray disobeyed, as the Secretary clearly intended he should: 'The King had made me read the Act and yours [letter to the king] to him both and when I had done I read him also yours [letter to Moray] and my self not refraining even that which you did not desire that I should impart of the compliment one of the Bishops put upon you. He laughed at it and [said] if he's not mistaken, thinks the Bishop was not much in the wrong.'[31]

Charles was so pleased that he ordered the speech to be published, telling Moray that all those fearful of Lauderdale's attitude were now openly admitting that they had been wrong.[32] Confirmation of this came from none other than Gilbert Sheldon, Archbishop of Canterbury, who said that Lauderdale had been as good as his promise.

Charles was to receive further reassurance that his position in Scotland had not been damaged by the fall of Middleton. In accordance with his instructions, and with the support of Parliament, the Lords of the Articles were reconstituted on the same basis that had been established in 1633: the bishops chose first, in turn determining the composition of the next estate, and so on, thus ensuring that all other nominees to this guiding committee reflected the will of the king. The work of enhancing the prerogative, begun by Middleton, had been deepened and extended, as Moray explained on Lauderdale's behalf: 'I told him that by what was done he might see that the very first thing done in this session of parliament improved his service more than anything done heretofore. In regard that it was evident that this constitution of parliament, differing somewhat from former practices, is so much to his Majesties advantages that he and his successors must forever hereafter be absolute in all Scottish parliaments . . .'[33]

Lauderdale now went even further down this road. Charles was sent proposals for a new Scottish militia, to be made up of 22,000 men, to be used in enforcing the royal will anywhere in the United Kingdom.[34] This was to be the ultimate test of a new and certain loyalty:

> . . . whatever hath been suggested concerning the appearance of troubles from this kingdome. Yet his Majestie may now rest assured of the loyaltie and affection of the much greater part of Scotland, and that there is little reason to apprehend the least disturbance to his affaires from hence that if his Majesties service in any of his dominions doe require the assistance of this kingdom he may confidently promise to himself a more universal concurrence of the body of this Kingdom for maintenance of his authority either within Scotland or in any other of his dominions . . .[35]

This was the origin of a proposal, renewed six years later, that was destined to cause Lauderdale a considerable amount of future trouble. Considering that only twenty years before the English Parliament had executed the Earl of Strafford for a far less concrete proposal than this, it seems odd that he should surrender himself so willingly as a hostage to fortune. There are two points to be made: first, this was, in large part, a phantom army, only ever existing on paper; and second, the Secretary was playing the game of gesture politics on a grand scale: what other subject could offer his sovereign such an impressive force?

It was a statement, nothing more. Lauderdale was attempting to turn history on its head, reversing the politics of 1638 and 1643: Scotland, the former nursery of rebellion, was now so secure that it could send thousands of armed men anywhere the king wished in defence of his interests. There was no suggestion that this might involve subverting the constitution of England, though it did not prevent some, notably Gilbert Burnet, from making such a claim: 'Nobody dreamt that any use was ever to be made of this; yet the earl of Lauderdale had this end in it, to let the King see what use the king might make of Scotland, if he should intend to set up arbitrary government in England.'[36] The simple reality is that Scotland was never to be in a position politically, financially or temperamentally to assist in such a project. As Lauderdale was soon to discover, there were parts of the country where it would have been suicidal to put the ordinary citizens in arms.

Rothes may have been Commissioner; but the whole programme was clearly Lauderdale's, with an eye on English as well as Scottish politics. Some resistance was mounted by sections of the old Middleton party, which faded almost to nothing as the summer progressed. The Billeting Affair was duly investigated and just as duly condemned; all mention of it was ordered be expunged from the records of Parliament: 'Of this nature wes that strange act incapacitating tuelve transmitted to his Maiestie sealed (and which he hes so ordered it shall never more come to light) and the way of voting by Billets, a way never befor practised vnder Monarchie nornever heard of vnder any government as to punishment in such a maner as this wher the persons concerned wer so far from being accused, heard or upon evidence condemned . . .'[37]

A formal report on the whole billeting affair was sent to the king, together with a recommendation that Middleton should be removed from his remaining public employments.[38] In early 1664 he lost his place as the Captain of Edinburgh Castle and General of the royal forces in Scotland, and was reduced to spending his time 'in back lanes among persons obscure and malcontents'.[39] He was eventually to creep back into a kind of favour, being packed off to Africa as governor to the outpost of Tangier, a possession England acquired by the marriage of Charles to Catherine of Braganza, a Portuguese princess.

One other matter of business was brought before Parliament: the fate of Archibald Johnston of Warriston, the conscience of the Covenant. He had fled to the Continent at the Restoration, but had finally been tracked down in France and brought home for trial. Lauderdale was not without sympathy for his old comrade, even though he was a man with whom he now had almost nothing in common, either in religion or philosophy. He is reported to have told Lady

Warriston that he would do his best to aid her husband when his differences with Middleton were over.[40] But in the end he was up against the sheer hatred of the king for a man who reminded him of all the humiliations of 1650. When he finally stood before the bar of Parliament, Lauderdale was clearly shocked by the appearance of a man once so certain of God's grace, and now broken in both mind and spirit: '. . . I must confess I never saw so miserable a spectacle. I have often heard of a man feared out of his wits, but never saw it before; yet, what he said was good sense enough, but he roared and cryed and expresst more fear than ever I saw'.[41]

Gilbert Burnet, Warriston's nephew, claims that, though Lauderdale had once lived in great friendship with his uncle, he would do nothing for the condemned man, seeing that the king was set against him.[42] This is true, up to a point. Having won a considerable political victory over Clarendon and Middleton it would have made little sense for Lauderdale to endanger his career for the wreckage of the past. Even so, it is clear that he made some effort on Warriston's behalf, though probably more for a delay of execution than an outright reprieve, judging by remarks Moray makes in his correspondence: 'As to the matter of that wretched creature I finde no disposition at all in the king to set any kind of limit to the course of justice theirin', followed not long after by another letter in which he tells the Secretary that there is nothing to be done in the matter.[43] Warriston was duly hanged as a traitor, though he managed to recover some of his composure prior to death.

Nothing was to be done for Warriston, unlike Lord Lorne, who was finally released from prison in June 1663. Soon after, he was created ninth Earl of Argyll, the title of marquis remaining permanently forfeit. Lauderdale had been an invaluable friend to the house of Campbell at a particularly critical time, and played a leading part in having at least some of the Argyll titles restored.[44] Argyll's mother, the widow of the Marquis, conveyed her gratitude to the king, but made it effusively plain to whom the real thanks were due:

> I do esteem my self bound to express my humble thankfulness for the King's singular favour and benevolence extended to my eldest son and other children in that he hath been pleased to restore this poor family out of the ashes . . . The many favours yr Lordship hath done to my children and the great pains yr Lordship has been at for them and me . . . in this time of our sad affliction which under God and next to the King's Majestie we owe the thanks to your Lordship. It doth engage me to using what power I have of them as a mother to be devoted to your Lordship with that serviceable obedience with so tender respects as your

Lordship has merited at our hands doth deserve. I know that they are very sensible to your Lordship's constant favours and what I can say or express in so great things would but cloud that which is indeed due to be acknowledged from all of us to your Lordship . . .[45]

Over the years the new Earl of Argyll was to become a close ally of Lauderdale, and an important part of his system, though never a figure of the front rank. Intellectually and politically he was not the equal of such men as Moray, Tweeddale and Alexander Bruce, Earl of Kincardine, another of Lauderdale's protégés, which probably explains why he survived so long in the Secretary's uncertain affections; he was also more dependent on him for his personal security than any other leading man. It has been argued that in favouring him Lauderdale showed 'total indifference' for justice and peace in the Highlands.[46] There is little to suggest that the rule of Middleton and the cavaliers had been noted for its beneficial effects among the clans. In supporting Argyll, and returning him to his traditional role of peacekeeper and lawman in the western Highlands, Lauderdale was indeed reaching for old solutions; it is difficult to see what the alternative could have been, other than a return to the ruinously expensive peacekeeping of the Protectorate. Besides, not all the terms of Argyll's restoration were beneficial: he had been left burdened by all of the debts accumulated by his father, but only part of his territory, with the result that he was forced to be particularly attentive when it came to collecting his own debts, especially from his close neighbours, the Macleans of Duart. His activities, good or bad, were always subject to malicious interpretation, as he later complained to Lauderdale in a tone of injured innocence: 'It hath of late beene told to me by some, betwixt jest and earnest, that in endeavouring the peace of the Highlands, I secure my owne interest.'[47]

Lauderdale had had a full and active summer, as he complained in one of his notes to 'Deare Robin': 'No dogg leads so busie a life. Torment of visitors in crowds not companies; and incessant meetings. No sleep or time to write and nothing like recreation makes me a very slave'.[48] It had also been a summer of triumph: the man of the moment was Lauderdale; he had undermined all damaging preconceptions and disarmed the opposition; even Glencairn was anxious to make peace.[49] Rothes was clearly under his thumb. Even so, the new Commissioner was far from simply being the drunkard and sensualist depicted in Gilbert Burnet's memoirs. He was a shrewd political operator whose lack of education was more than made up by an abundance of cunning and well developed skills in the management of men: 'The subtlety of his wit', Mackenzie of Roseheaugh writes, 'obliged all to court his friendship'.[50] Potentially he was as dangerous an opponent as Middleton: perhaps even more so, as his credit with the king was almost as great as Lauderdale's. The Secretary was soon to return to London, so it was important that Rothes and the other Scottish politicians were given as little opportunity for mischief-making as possible. Parliament had to be dissolved. Lauderdale at once set to work, urging Moray to tell the king that long parliaments were more unfit for Scotland than for any other place, for once the formal business was out of the way they only served as a cradle for intrigue: 'Most knowing men were much alarmed with a designe in some to have perpetuated this Parliament, and under that colour to have altered our forme of government and settle the last Commissioner as a Viceroy over us: and, thogh his Majesties grace and goodness broke that designe by changing the Commissioner, yet nothing will so perfectly cure feares of it as the ending this parliament.'[51]

To reassure Charles that any future assembly would prove itself as loyal, Moray was to remind him of the recent changes to the Articles, which gave him an absolute control over all legislative business. Charles probably required little real persuasion; his problems in England provided sufficient illustration, if any were needed, of the dangers of long parliaments. Lauderdale got his way: Middleton's cavaliers were all sent home; it was to be another six years before they and their successors returned to Edinburgh.

When Lauderdale left Scotland the main lines of future policy had been set: Episcopacy was confirmed and magnified; dissenters were to be fined. Rothes, in his capacity as Treasurer rather than Commissioner, a role in temporary abeyance, was left to manage affairs, seemingly with no clear idea of how to proceed. In the summer of 1663 active dissent was still on a fairly small scale; but it seems clear that Lauderdale underestimated the potential problems posed by the intransigents of the south-west, just as he had in 1648. He did not approve of, nor did he sanction, a policy of active repression; the threat of heavy fines was clearly conceived of as a sufficient deterrent. What if it was not? The church establishment was now in a much more militant mood: James Sharp, the reluctant convert of 1661, was now a convinced advocate of Episcopacy. Alexander Burnet, recently appointed Archbishop of Glasgow, supported his view. Over the next few years a new axis developed between church and state in Scotland, in the person of Sharp and Rothes, anxious to take Lauderdale's commitment to orthodoxy at his word. They were to be actively supported by an impoverished nobility and gentry, hungry for military commissions, and eager for the collection of fines. Scotland was now poised on the threshold of a period of serious disorder, the very thing that had the potential to wreck Lauderdale's credibility at court.

These spectres had little bearing on the Secretary's present standing; he returned to London in the full glow of political success. Even former opponents like Sir Henry Bennet, a rising figure in the government, were completely won over, as he wrote to Ormonde: 'My Lord Lauderdale came last night. The great things that are done in Scotland in the vindication of his Majesties authority in all points have made him very welcome to those that cared not for him before. I confesse ingeniously for my own part hee hath cozened me and I am glad to be soe to his Majesties advantage.'[52]

Lauderdale's power was still not complete; he had soundly defeated Middleton, but Clarendon was still a threat to his future ascendancy. A new bitterness now entered into the relations between the two men. Although the Chancellor was innocent of the Billeting Affair his support of Middleton was a source of deep resentment. Lauderdale, no longer behaving with the same degree of circumspection towards the English politician, was soon openly boasting that the fall of Middleton had removed one of the mainstays of the Chancellor. Their enmity was now public knowledge, even reported as far away as The Hague, where there was talk of a 'scuffle' between them in January 1664, though it is not clear if this meant a verbal exchange or if it was thought that the two senior statesmen descended into a punch-up![53] Samuel Pepys records his own impressions in his dairy entry for 22 February 1664: 'That my Lord Lodderdale, being Middleton's great enemy and one that scores [scorns?] the Chancellor, even to open affronts before the King, hath got the whole; whereas the other day he was in a fair way to have had his whole estate and honour and life voted away from him.'[54]

Earlier that month Pepys noted that Lauderdale was caballing against Clarendon with Sir Anthony Ashley Cooper, who had been raised to the peerage as Baron Ashley soon after the Restoration.[55] This is the first notification we have of one of the more unusual friendships in British political history. Anthony Ashley Cooper was, like Lauderdale, a man of singular ability. Also, like Lauderdale, he had had a varied political career: he had started the Civil War as a royalist, later switching to the parliamentary side; he had served in the parliaments of both the Commonwealth and Protectorate, turning against Cromwell just as he had turned against the king. In 1660 he had been a leading member of the Convention Parliament, chosen as one of the delegates to invite Charles to England. He is one of those men who is almost impossible to pin down politically or philosophically; he was a conservative with

an almost intuitive understanding of the popular mood, which he had
the capacity to manipulate to his own advantage; he was of no fixed
view in religious matters, which led him to favour a general toleration
for all who did not represent a danger, in his view, to the liberty of the
nation. He and Lauderdale seem to have been attracted to each other
for no other reason than a simple dislike of Clarendon. They were an
odd pair, as Ashley Cooper was as small as Lauderdale was large. Many
were to be amused by the sight of the 'mickell man and the lickell
man', and they were seen often enough in each other's company to be
referred to as Saint Paul and Titus.[56]

In their hostility towards Clarendon they were even willing to associate
with the politically incompetent Earl of Bristol, as de Ruvigny, the French
ambassador, noted in early 1664. The Chancellor was worried enough
by the new association against him to invite his friend Ormonde to return
from Ireland for his advice against 'the cabal of Lord Lauderdale which
has swindled him out of knowledge of the affairs of the kingdom'.[57] De
Ruvigny goes on to confirm the observation made by Pepys, saying that
Lauderdale was 'united with Ashley, Lord Roberts, and some others,
who spare no pains to ruin Clarendon in the free convivial entertainments
which are of daily occurrence. They do not scruple to speak of him with
freedom in the presence of the King'.[58]

Charles may have been tiring of the censorious Chancellor, but he
was still the lynch pin of the royal government, whose importance
increased with the outbreak of the Anglo-Dutch war, the second that
century, in 1664. That same war increased the vulnerability of Lauderdale;
for it dragged a reluctant Scotland on the coat-tails of England into a
struggle with her main trading partner: no Scottish interest was
threatened and none served. Economic distress added to a seething
undercurrent of religious discontent, made all the worse by the fact
that the Dutch were fellow Calvinists, who gave refuge to Scottish
dissidents. Full-scale rebellion could not be discounted. By late 1664
the peace and security that Lauderdale had promised Charles in the
summer of 1663 was now looking very remote. By December Rothes
was warning the Secretary ' . . . our phanaticks as becum much boulder
then they have bin this twealmunthe past'.[59] Sharp and Burnet were
also active in sending alarmist reports to England about the condition
of the Scottish church, some of which reached Clarendon, a clear threat
to Lauderdale's political and personal integrity. With Clarendon's help
Burnet even managed to secure an interview with Charles, who agreed
on the need for a policy of continuing firmness against religious
dissidents. There was really no need for the meeting; it was simply an
ideal opportunity to embarrass Lauderdale.

In 1663 Lauderdale had offered the king a grand army to defend his interests anywhere in Britain; in truth the forces available in Scotland were hardly adequate to deal with the problem of domestic disorder let alone a foreign threat. Moreover, the legislation against conventicles had no effect on the growth of field assemblies. In Galloway the position was particularly bad because many Presbyterian ministers from Ulster had taken refuge there, following the reimposition of episcopacy in Ireland. Sir James Turner, commanding the available forces in the south-west, was ordered to hunt them down, as well as taking continuing action against conventicles. Military intervention was growing from a temporary expedient into a permanent feature of government policy. Nothing seemed to work, neither the intervention of soldiers, the declarations of the Privy Council nor the anger of the Archbishops; the problem was intractable. In clear frustration Rothes wrote to Lauderdale in November 1665, blaming the field preachers, especially for the effect they were having upon the women. As always, the Commissioner's spelling was atrocious, even by the lax standards of the age:

> . . . the caus of most of this trubell uie reseffe in this caynd is occasioned by some outed ministers against uhom both counsill and commission hes prosided against . . . thes roges stirs up the uimin [women] so as they are uors than deivils, yay I dare say if it uear not for the uimin uie should have litill trubell uith conventickils or such caynd of stuff, bot ther ar such a ffuilth jenerasione of pipill in this cuntrie uho ar so inflensied uith ther fanatick uayffs [wives] as I thinck uill bring ruin upon them.[60]

There was another problem that the Secretary had to deal with at this time: a new political assertiveness on the part of the church, perhaps not previously anticipated. Burnet's contacts with the English establishment was one sign of this; another was the growing confidence of James Sharp, who put himself forward, with the support of Rothes, as a likely candidate for the vacant Chancellorship after the death of Glencairn in March 1664. Sharp continued to grow in political stature, even presiding over the convention summoned in 1665 to provide funds for the Dutch war.[61] Earlier that same year Lauderdale had received a plea from Lady Margaret Kennedy, the daughter of the Earl of Cassillis, and a close personal friend: 'for God's sake, endevour to persuade the King to part with the bishops, for I much feare we will all be lost. They are now hated, and hated by all as much as by Presbyterians'.[62]

By the time he received this letter, the earlier alliance Lauderdale had enjoyed with Rothes and Sharp had broken down, leaving him politically isolated, almost as much as he had been during Middleton's time. Once again Lauderdale showed himself at his best during adversity. There was little he could do to follow Lady Margaret's advice; bishops were an established and permanent part of the political scene; but they could overstep themselves, as indeed could the Commissioner. A new church–military party was in control of Scotland, wedded to a policy of repression.[63] Lauderdale, now closely associated with Tweeddale and Kincardine, the leading Scottish moderates, was convinced that that the policy followed by Sharp and Rothes would create rebellion, the very thing it was supposedly attempting to prevent.[64] Careful as always, he waited for an opportunity, confiding in Gilbert Burnet that he believed Sharp to be heading for destruction: '. . . he was persuaded that he [Sharp] would ruin all: but he said he was resolved to give him enough line, for he had not credit enough to stop him; nor would he oppose anything he proposed unless it were very extravagant . . .'[65]

Sharp was flying too close to the sun. Even Rothes, initially an enthusiastic ally of the primate, was beginning to cool off, wary of involving himself in the kind of intrigues that had destroyed Middleton. He knew he himself was vulnerable: Lauderdale had told him that the king was concerned about his excessive drinking, a pointed warning indeed in a time noted for its loose moral standards.[66] He took the hint: in September he warned Lauderdale that Sharp was trying to interest him in an alliance with the disgraced Middleton, now living in England.[67] It was a dangerous game, and one that the archbishop was not really equipped to play, temperamentally or politically. He had few allies among the Scottish nobility, more resentful than ever of clerical interference in secular affairs. Clarendon was very soon to be a serious liability rather than a significant friend. Lauderdale was now looking for a major change in direction; the opportunity came in November 1666. Pushed beyond endurance the Covenanters of the south-west rose in revolt.

10

KING LAUDERDALE

Rothes was in London when the rebellion began, ingratiating himself with Lauderdale and assuring the king that all was well in Scotland, leaving Sharp in charge of the government. In the west Sir James Turner had enough troops to cause a serious nuisance, and not enough to deal with the results. In early November 1666 a small act of provocation got out of hand; Turner was taken prisoner; the news spread and several hundred men gathered in arms. The Covenants were renewed and, in a tragic repetition of the Whiggamore Raid, the little army marched on Edinburgh. Some time before this the States-General, the Dutch parliament, had passed a secret resolution to help Scots rebels with arms and money; but the present rising was an outburst of spontaneous anger by desperate men, not a well-organised conspiracy. Outside the capital the little tidal wave finally broke: the rebels were intercepted by government forces under Tam Dalyell of the Binns and defeated at the Battle of Rullion Green in the Pentland Hills, a location which gave a name to the whole tragic and pathetic business.

It has been said that the Pentland Rising rendered void the whole of Lauderdale's policies, both political and ecclesiastical, 'for the peace had not been kept, and the basic requirement of security had not been met'.[1] This is not an accurate reading. The settlement of 1663 had been destroyed; but for some time Lauderdale had not identified himself with the violent interpretation of this settlement; this had been the work of Rothes, the church militants, and posturing soldiers, both professional and amateur. During the whole period of the early Restoration the politics of personal survival were far more significant for Lauderdale than the details of good administration. He may have underestimated the difficulties he left behind in 1663, but he was always sensitive to the way in which the actions of others affected him personally. Now he was faced with an additional problem: the likely beneficiary of the Pentland Rising was James Sharp.

Sharp had always been consistent. In defending the 1661 church settlement he had, in a sense, been carrying on an old struggle: most of the dissenters were Protestors and most of the conformists Resolutioners. He also had an early appreciation that religious dissent was all too often a cover for political sedition. He may not have been a great churchman, but he was an able administrator, far better certainly than the dissolute Rothes. But Rothes had a native political cunning, unlike Sharp. While Sharp understood that he and his fellow churchmen were not popular with the nobility, he had no real appreciation of just how isolated he was politically. Lauderdale had probably started to see him as a potential political rival some time before: the two men had previously clashed over the nomination of candidates to vacant bishoprics, demonstrating a lingering hostility on Sharp's part to any suggestion of Erastianism. He was also too ambitious for his own good, his desire for the chancellorship being a source of particular resentment. Lord Bellenden, close to the centre of government, had a particular loathing for his clerical colleague, and did his best to undermine him with Lauderdale: '. . . he is too well known-heir to be trusted, what esteem he hath at court I know not, but doe conceive it fit that his Majestie may be tymelie informed how unacceptable a person he will be to fill the roume [place] of Chancellor, besydes his incapacitie for it . . .'[2]

He had in fact behaved well in the crisis, too well for his own good. The rebellion caused a minor panic in Whitehall, no doubt conjuring up memories of 1638, quickly becoming a source of some discomfort to Lauderdale, who did his best to minimise its impact, as Pepys noted: 'My Lord Lauderdale doth make nothing of it, it seems; and people do censure him for it, whereas it doth appear to be a pure rebellion'.[3] The Secretary's refusal to panic was fully justified by the rapid end of the affair; but it was clear that the political beneficiaries were likely to be Sharp and Rothes, now busy dealing with the aftermath. This was easy enough to counter. Sharp could not be blamed for suppressing rebellion; he could be blamed for provoking it in the first place. He could also be depicted to the king as an unscrupulous intriguer, planning to bring back the disgraced Middleton, though just how he was to accomplish this is not at all clear. Rothes, always the survivor, stood to one side, while his colleague was cut to pieces. By the end of the year Sharp's political disgrace was complete; he was to remain an outcast for months afterwards. Compared with the Middleton contest this battle had been all too easy. Lauderdale, with acute insight into the character of the primate, had no desire to get rid of him altogether; best if he was made totally dependent on the Secretary's favour. By July of the following year Sharp was attempting to creep back, writing a fawning letter to Lauderdale.[4] He was to become a useful tool, attempting to sell Lauderdale's policies to his sceptical colleagues.

Lauderdale had been as anxious as any other man to ensure that the Whig rebellion was stamped out in violence and terror. Once the initial shock was over, his attitude began to change, especially as it became clear that many of the men involved were not hardened dissidents. A few days after the Battle of Rullion Green Lord Bellenden informed him of the true character of the rebels: ' . . . some of them [are] the most obdurate villains that ever I did see or heard of, the rest simple mislead people . . .'[5] Moderation and conciliation might in the end prove more productive than the repression being advocated by the soldiers, a suggestion taken up in January by Argyll:

> Generall Lieutenant Drummond is coming up to you. I thinke he hath to greate a jealousie of all the West. Let all be done can be done to secure the peace; but I thinke ther is a greate odds betwixt those rose in armes and those that did not. As farr as I can learne none but the old remonstrators [Protestors] were upon the late rebellion, and of these only such as went not to church. Enstead of many tys I thinke it would contribute most to his Majesties service that strike [strict] engadgments were taken of all persons in the West to live peaceably and never to rise in armes against his Majestie or his commission, and, if you will, to compeare when called. If those who refused this were without hesitation transplanted, as I think they ought, and those that did it had hopes given them of protection as other subjects, I think it would much alay the humour of that people who are all of them in agast, as if it were resolved to take all they have and cut their throats; and if some proclamation wer enacted shewing his Majesties purpose towards those in the West that lived peaceably and did duty I think it were to good purpose.[6]

Argyll's moderation contrasted sharply with the advice of General Dalyell, who appears to have recommended what in present-day terms might be referred to as ethnic cleansing: '. . . the forsis ar to marth [march] to the vaist the morou for satlen that country vhitch I am confedent is not possible vithout the inhabetens be remouet or destroit . . .'[7] It was a monstrous suggestion that could never appeal to Lauderdale, who, his past associations and sympathies apart, was a man of humane temperament. It seems evident that fairly early in the new year the Secretary was beginning to consider a major change in direction, soon to be reflected in some important political changes. Sharp was confined in anxious retirement at St Andrews, though the church–military party were still something of a nuisance. Rothes, moreover, was still playing something of a double game, as Lauderdale learned from Lady Margaret Kennedy in February: 'The discontents are universal, and tho many are not so unjust as to father them all upon your friend [Rothes], yet, not to lie, all conclude he might do more to hinder them nor he does . . . but never man was more hated . . . and he studies all he can to make *Lauderdale so* [section encoded].'[8]

Rothes was threatening a new and potentially dangerous combination, which included such diverse interests as Dalyell and the military reactionaries, the militant bishops, represented most particularly by Alexander Burnet of Glasgow, and the impecunious aristocrats, represented paradoxically by the Duke of Hamilton.[9] Hamilton and Rothes were boozing buddies, and could therefore be expected to share a similar outlook on life. Insofar as he had any politics at all Hamilton was sympathetic to the Presbyterians; he was even more sympathetic to his purse, and financially dependent on the pickings from his military commission. Rothes and his party had little intellectual weight, in contrast with that being built up by Lauderdale. Apart from Tweeddale and the multi-talented Moray, the Secretary was increasingly to call on the services of Alexander Bruce, Earl of Kincardine, the nearest thing Scotland possessed at the time to an industrial entrepreneur. Kincardine was an old friend of Moray's who shared many of his scientific interests, detailed in a lengthy correspondence. None of these men were religiously orthodox in the accepted sense; Kincardine had openly opposed the act punishing non-conformity passed by the Parliament of 1663, and had publicly clashed with Sharp. For an ally among the clerics they were soon to look to Robert Leighton, appointed Bishop of Dunblane in 1661, and one of the great oddballs of Scottish church history. Sir Robert Moray was sent to Scotland to look into the background of the Pentland Rising and the suggestions of military extortion. Lauderdale quickly won yet another round in a game where he had few equals: '. . . with these friends, and the power he had with the king, he was able enough to overthrow all their designes against him . . .'[10]

Rothes was too important to be set aside like Sharp; best if he was simply made harmless. The easiest way to do this was a 'promotion' that would take away both his posts of Treasurer and High Commissioner. What better way than by offering him the vacant position of Chancellor, the very appointment that Clarendon had been anxious to thrust on Lauderdale at the Restoration. The Chancellor was the nation's chief legal officer, a burdensome task without the same degree of political clout as Treasurer or Commissioner. With the approval of Charles, Moray told Rothes of the proposed change. News of his 'good fortune' came as an unwelcome shock. For a post that supposedly required knowledge of Law and Latin, Rothes, who struggled painfully even with written English, was singularly ill-equipped. It's possible to sympathise across the centuries with the heartfelt appeal he sent to Lauderdale: '. . . banishment could not have bin more unuelcom . . . for I teack the great God to be my witness I knou no mor hou to dischearg that pleas then I had bin bred in an other kingdoum, and to leat my ignorans apier, the thoughts of it is layck to breck my heart'.[11]

He also wrote to the king expressing his concern, again asking for Lauderdale's aid in the matter, saying 'iff you do not assist me to be ffrie of it you ar not so much my ffriend as I beliff'.[12] In the end, persuaded by Moray, and bowing to the will of the king, he duly submitted. Now only Lauderdale had the direct authority to represent the king in Scotland, though it was to be another two years before he formally appeared in the role of High Commissioner. Some time before, in anticipation of this move, Tweeddale had told him, 'The news pleas me ueall that the keys shall hing at the right belt.'[13] He was to make sure that they continued to hang there. Rather than appoint a powerful new treasurer, the office was put in commission; but Lauderdale made sure that the membership of this body was firmly weighted in his favour: Tweeddale and Moray were in the first wave of appointments, later supplemented by Kincardine, Argyll and Charles Maitland of Hatton, the Secretary's younger brother.

Lauderdale, fully advised by Moray and Tweeddale, now had an accurate picture of political conditions in Scotland, and the excesses of the previous administration. Rothes, who liked 'sogeris above all the other wayes of living', had given military men like Drummond and Dalyell virtually a free hand, and terrified the bishops with the dangers that a change of direction might bring. On reporting on conditions in the west Moray told Lauderdale, 'The more I enquire the less appearance I finde that there was a formed designe of rebellion, and it might have been more easily quasht than it was.'[14] The standing forces, so valued by Hamilton and others, aside from being a cause of oppression, were an intolerable burden on a weakened economy. They could only be maintained at a ruinous cost, so much so that it was even rumoured that a captain's commission would shortly be worth more than a Scottish barony.[15] The situation required some delicate handling: the military had to be disbanded and the bishops reassured. What better way to calm an anxious church establishment, Moray told Lauderdale, than by enlisting the support of the disgraced Sharp, humbled and eager to please? 'You told me formerly . . . you knew how to make use of a knave as well as another . . . '[16] Lauderdale took the hint: Sharp was rehabilitated by degrees. By October the Secretary was confident enough to tell him that not just a change of government but also a whole change of policy was intended. The king was determined to maintain the church as it was established by law: 'But in my humble opinion it will not be unfit for your Lordships of the clergie to endeavour to moderate severities as much as may consist with the peace and order of the church. That as wilful opposers and contemners must be severlie punished, so peaceable dissenters may be endeavoured to be reclaimed and that they may have just cause to thank the bishops for any indulgence they meet with, to the end the people may be more and more gained to your order and persons.'[17]

The day before this letter was written Charles had signed a pardon for all those involved in the Pentland Rising, less than a year after its outbreak. Ironically the failed rebellion had by now received a partial justification: the military regime was crumbling, the bishops humbled, and the government prepared to recognise the necessity of giving some relief to peaceable religious dissent. It was a clear signal that Lauderdale had achieved a complete ascendancy over all opposition, both in the church and the state, a position made even more secure by important changes within the English political establishment: Clarendon was gone.

For England the war with Holland, which began with such promise, was one of diminishing returns; by the spring of 1667 the returns had diminished to virtually nothing. In June the Dutch fleet had even managed to penetrate the Medway, attacking the Royal Navy anchored at Chatham, in a seventeenth-century version of Pearl Harbor.[18] Popular anger was directed against the government, particularly the unpopular Clarendon, rather than the Dutch. This was unfair, but Clarendon, arrogant and opinionated, was one of those men who made enemies far more easily than he made friends. What was worse, Charles was tiring of a man who had for long been the main support of his administration. At the end of August he was forced to resign as Chancellor; in October, threatened with parliamentary impeachment, he left England, never to return. Clarendon's tragedy was Lauderdale's triumph: the last significant brake on his personal power had now been removed. We have no evidence that he played any direct part in the political demise of the Chancellor, but it may be significant that he was closely associated with the Duke of Buckingham, one of those most eager for the impeachment. Clarendon's downfall was believed to have removed one of the main exponents of the policy of repression in Scotland.[19] Rothes, ever the opportunist, was quick to express a favourable view:

'there is non here that I have spock with but rejouaysis at it and conclouds it uill meack a great chang in the gufferment of affears'.[20] The end of the Chancellor also meant the end of the Scottish Council at Whitehall; from now on the Secretary would decide policy in consultation with the king, free from the interference of other English politicians. Writing from Scotland Moray had an acute insight into the true importance of the change:

> These 7 years past you have constantly walkt with singular tenderness in all matters, both as to the state and the church . . . let me now mind yow of two things . . . if yow look back yow will certainly finde the following of courses yow would never have advised and wisely forebore to curb [re-establish episcopacy, Church Commission, the application of money for the maintenance of troops] hath been far from succeeding well; the errors thereof are now conspicuous enough to the authors. And next observe that as either other courses must be followed, or things abandoned, these people being unfit, or indeed unable, to manage matters aright, so whatever be the success of any courses that shall hereafter be resolved it will certainly be mainly attributed to yow and in some measure to your friends. It is therefore my clear judgement that yow stick no more at the considerations have formerly prevailed with yow, but frankly without hesitation propose, advise carry on, whatsoever you judge fittest for the good of the King's service, please or displease whom it will below him. All mists are now cleared up. Nobody can make the King suspect your loyalty, your integrity, your affection to him, nor the candour of your professions as to the things ecclesiastical as well as civil.[21]

Lauderdale, who had learned to guard his feelings over the years, allowed his enthusiasm to spill over in a letter to Tweeddale: 'Oh, it would do your heart good to see what a new world is here and how bravely the kings' business goes on . . . now the king is the king himself.'[22] Caution and good judgement probably prevented him adding that he himself was increasingly being referred to as 'King of Scotland'.[23] Nevertheless, despite the changed realities, he was too canny a politician to introduce any sudden departure in the main lines of policy. Still suspected by many as a Presbyterian he proceeded all the more cautiously. In October he wrote to Moray, urging him to be careful: 'I am well pleased with the measures in your counsels, but for the Lord's sake be vigilant over that perverse incorrigible fanatick partie . . . let them rather go to America than plot the troubles of Scotland.'[24]

Lauderdale, like a colossus, stood astride two worlds. Clarendon's departure brought a new ministry to power. It included Buckingham and Anthony Ashley Cooper – two of the Secretary's close political associates – Henry Bennet, now Lord Arlington, Lord Thomas Clifford, and Lauderdale himself. Before long it was noticed that the word 'Cabal' could be made out of the initial letters of the names of the five members: Clifford, Arlington, Buckingham, Ashley and Lauderdale. The term had always had a slightly sinister and conspiratorial note, destined to acquire an added significance as the activities of the ministry came under increasing parliamentary scrutiny. In reality the Cabal was always more – and less – than it seemed: membership was not exclusively confined to the five men identified, and, unlike the Clarendonians, it did not have a recognised leader or parliamentary following.[25] Arlington, the State Secretary, enjoyed as much power in England as Lauderdale did in Scotland, though he was never to have the same kind of coercive influence formerly possessed by Clarendon. There was also a major fault line in the ministry, virtually from the beginning, with Arlington and Clifford falling on one side and Buckingham, Ashley and Lauderdale on the other.

The Cabal reversed the position prevailing under the old Chancellor: Lauderdale now had some input into the affairs of England, rather than Englishmen having an input into the affairs of Scotland. He was a member of the powerful Foreign Affairs Committee, with a say over English policy in Europe, which he continued to exercise even after the ministry collapsed. The Cabal had one other important bearing on Lauderdale's future conduct. Clarendon's ministry had been Anglican and orthodox; the Cabal was anything but. Lauderdale's own background was well known; Arlington and Clifford had Catholic sympathies, while Buckingham and Ashley had strong links with the Protestant dissenters.[26] Any religious innovations that Lauderdale brought to Scotland, it seemed reasonably certain, were not going to be subject to the same scrutiny exercised by Clarendon.

The end of the Dutch war brought new opportunities and challenges for Lauderdale. Security was no longer an overriding consideration; the time had come to let the military stand down, to introduce some sanity into the church question and to consider the issues the war had raised about Scotland's place in the Union.

Shortly after the Restoration the Cavalier Parliament passed a Navigation Act, which had the effect of treating Scotland as a foreign country for the purposes of trade. Scotland was prevented from enjoying the benefits of the English colonial markets; even her trade with Holland was hampered. A bad situation was made even worse because Scottish foreign policy, a matter reserved to the king, was inevitably tied to that of England, to the detriment of domestic economic considerations, so fully illustrated by the Dutch war. It was clearly of some importance that Scotland was not again involved in a war without being able to draw some commercial or political benefit. No sooner was Clarendon out of the way than Lauderdale called for a joint Anglo-Scottish commission to consider the whole question of trade and the operation of the Navigation Act.[27] The problem was that this was an issue on which Charles, though sympathetic, was unwilling to take a decisive lead, perhaps fearing the reaction of Parliament, still seething over the incompetent handling of the recent war, and dominated by commercial interests hostile to major concessions to the Scots.

Under the direction of Westminster the English commissioners met their Scottish counterparts, headed by Lauderdale, in January 1668; but the prospects were far from good.[28] The problem was quite simple: this was not a meeting of equals; England had much to offer, Scotland little to give. When it came to the decisive issue of mutual benefit Scotland was too poor to offer the English the kind of concession that it would have made it worthwhile for them to set aside the Navigation Act and sacrifice their own commercial interests. Before long the talks were caught up in an impossible log-jam, which could only have been released by an exercise in prerogative power – an intervention Lauderdale seems to have expected. Charles, for obvious reasons, refused to oblige. However, it seems possible that Lauderdale may have expected the negotiations to fail all along as a preliminary to persuading his countrymen of the necessity of increasing the stakes by giving consideration to a full political union. In his address to the Scottish Parliament in October 1669, his first appearance as High Commissioner, he said that the discussions on the commercial union had 'produced no effect, unless it were conviction of the difficulty, if not impossibility, of settling it in any other way, than by a nearer and more complete union of the two kingdoms'.[29] For Lauderdale this was not new: it had been raised as long ago as the Treaty of Carisbrooke. Most of his fellow Scots, in contrast, now viewed the prospect with distaste, coming so soon after the dissolution of Cromwell's imposed union, which continued to be perceived as a national humiliation. There were other considerations of a deeper, more personal nature, destined to make the first serious talks on a voluntary political union for over sixty years the one great area of Lauderdale's career where we have few real clues to his innermost thinking.

For most of 1668 the government was working slowly towards an accommodation with the Presbyterian dissidents. Rothes was resentful, but compliant. Hamilton was still posturing, upset by the sudden end of his military career; but he was more of a nuisance than a serious political threat, anxious for his prestige and his purse in roughly equal measures. Moray had little time for the ambitious nobleman, destined to be a source of much future trouble, describing his conduct to Lauderdale in a tone of ironic contempt, 'And if nothing be done for itt hee may use such free language to John Red [Lauderdale] as may make them less friends hereafter; but John Red is wiser than to be moved by this prediction, or his performance, if he be such a fool to do what he says.'[30]

It's as well to remember these remarks when considering Hamilton's later political career. Though by title and precedence he was the most senior of the Scottish nobility, he was never to be a figure of any great intellectual or moral authority. His horizons were always very narrow; he tended to measure the great questions of the day in terms of his own sectional interests; he was by turns a defender of dissidents and an oppressor, changing to suit the occasion. His lands, mostly in the west, were specifically excluded as a recruiting ground for the militia that Lauderdale planned to replace the standing army, for obvious reasons of national security; but that did not stop him complaining that he had been deprived of his legitimate right to a military position.[31] He was in many ways the kind of man better to have in the tent than out; but he had little in the way of natural ability, and all the potential to be a dangerous maverick. Gilbert Burnet, who spent some time at Hamilton Palace researching the lives of the first two dukes, had a unique opportunity to observe the third at close hand, allowing him to sketch arguably the best of his pen portraits:

> He wanted all sorts of polishing: he was rough and sullen, but candid and sincere. His temper was boisterous, neither fit to submit nor to govern. He was mutinous when out of power, and imperious in it. He wrote well, but spoke ill: for his judgement when calm was better than his imagination. He made himself a great master in the knowledge of the laws, of the history, and of the families of Scotland, and seemed always to have a great regard to justice and the good of his country: but a narrow and a selfish temper brought such an habitual meanness on him, that he was not capable of designing or undertaking great things.[32]

Alexander Burnet was another serious nuisance along the path to change. Created Bishop of Aberdeen in 1663, he was elevated to the archbishopric of Glasgow shortly after on the death of Andrew Fairfoul. He was conceivably the worst man for the job, possessing none of the personal or diplomatic skills necessary to manage the most sensitive posting in the church. Unlike James Sharp he had no Covenanting background, his royalist and Episcopalian sympathies forcing him to spend a large part of his life in exile. Interestingly he seems to have had little in the way of personal political ambition, and could not be bullied and intimidated like Sharp. He had the integrity of the stupid, believing that people in power genuinely wanted to hear what he said, and that he only had to shout loud enough to attract their attention. He was the church's equivalent of Tam Dalyell, anxious to bring salvation on the barrel of a gun. In the correspondence of Moray and Lauderdale he appears as a kind of comic turn, acquiring the nickname of 'Longifacies' or 'Nez Long' – big nose – though it's uncertain if this is a reference to his physical appearance or his marked tendency to interfere in business that was not his.[33] His Cassandra-like pleading to Clarendon and Gilbert Sheldon was a source of considerable annoyance to Lauderdale, who by 1667 was actively looking for ways to get rid of a man who simply refused to be silenced.

Hamilton and Burnet may have been awkward, but Sharp at least was compliant. As the new policy took shape it was important to ensure his co-operation. His fragile ego had been salved by a letter from the king, a cynical move suggested by Moray to wed him more firmly to the Lauderdale interest. His gratitude was effusively expressed to the Secretary early in the year:

> . . . his Majesties hand with the diamond seal, was to me a resurrection from the dead, whose obligation swell so high, as to overflowe all returnes of gratitude, the expressions must fall short of the sense . . . your Lordship has not dealt with me by halves; by yow I am restored to the good opinion of my most gracious master, which is dearer to me than my lyfe. I believe I am reintegrated in your Lordship's favour, the eclipsing of which has been more bitter to me than death; what more can be done to give me title to call myself to all the world wholly your lordship's . . .[34]

Middleton's great error in 1661–2 was to unite the two wings of a warring church, thrusting Protestors and Resolutioners together in opposition to the state; the task was to separate them again. How was this to be done? There were two possible ways forward – accommodation or indulgence. Accommodation was based on an attempt to reconcile the dissidents to the episcopacy by the introduction of major modifications, a strategy that was to be particularly associated with Bishop Robert Leighton of Dunblane. Though sincere, the early experiments in his own diocese were far from encouraging. Lauderdale first raised the possibility of indulgence in his letter of October 1667 to Sharp; in May 1668 Tweeddale gave some more precise indication what form it was likely to take: 'The dangers of uhat I urot in my last concerning the outid ministers is not soe great bot that it may be preuentid if any of the soberest uer settled somuher in chirches uher ther uer no danger from them . . .'[35]

Matters were likely to proceed to a quick conclusion but for one sudden and unexpected shock: an attempt was made on the life of Archbishop Sharp. On 11 July, as he was travelling by coach up the High Street of Edinburgh in the company of Bishop Andrew Honeyman of Orkney he was fired on from the crowd; the assassin missed his immediate target, wounding Honeyman in the arm. In the confusion the gunman managed to escape, eventually fleeing abroad, but by the end of the month he was discovered to be one James Mitchell – 'a lean and hollow cheek'd man, of a truculent countenance'.[36] Mitchell was a fanatic, forfeited for his part in the Pentland Rising. It may have given him added comfort – if he had known – that his murderous intention put a temporary halt to the moves towards an Erastian Indulgence. In deep frustration Tweeddale wrote to the Secretary, trying to salvage something from his proposal: 'I must tell yow, I was never so putt to it to know what is best for nether lenity will work with these peopel nor severity be suffered by them; and without they be divided there is no ordering them, for god sake therefore think of all ways to doo it . . .'[37]

For the time being Lauderdale's mind was on other things. Mitchell's attack had been a shock, a challenge to the whole political establishment, and he was quick to express his earnest sympathies to the badly frightened archbishop: 'No friend you have is more concerned in God's mercie in preserving your Grace from that murdering villaine who shot at you, nor more troubled for so infamous ane action to have been attempted in Edinburgh, and for the wounds of my Lord Bishop of Orkney.'[38]

Once the shock died down, however, matters continued much as before, urged on by the logic of the whole political situation. Mitchell was hardly typical of dissident opinion, hardly even typical of the hard core of irreconcilables with which he was associated, not yet willing to condone the murder of the 'ungodly'. There would be some form of indulgence, but Lauderdale was determined to ensure that it would be very much on his terms; proposals to indulge all of the outed ministers was the kind of Trojan Horse that the Secretary was not prepared to contemplate. Toleration would be extended to peaceable dissenters only.

Throughout this whole period, up to the granting of the First Indulgence in July 1669, policy was made with a considerable amount of caution, two steps forward and one step back. It is yet another misreading of Lauderdale's career to assume there are distinct phases of activity, subject to a clear separation: indulgence and repression were always to proceed hand in hand. The Secretary was continually mindful of the effect of the political situation in Scotland on his standing and credibility in England; he could not be seen to go too far down a particular road or deviate overmuch from orthodox practice. Early on there were alarming signs that the more relaxed atmosphere was giving rise to the very problems anticipated by Alexander Burnet. By the spring of 1669 conventicles, as Kincardine reported, were beginning to grow at a worrying rate:

> . . . it is groune to that height that those who were lookt upon formerly as sober persons have now broke out into those disorders and not only on Sundayes, but all the dayes of the weeke, they avowed conventicles through most of the disaffected part of the countrie. This puts us quit from thinkeing of any thing els, and when we have thought our best wee know not what remedie to use, for that which wee resolve upon one day, new emergents make us change our opinions of it the nixt. Yet ere we part I doubt not wee shall put things in that order that no hurt shall arise from that hand to any but that foolish crew who can never be satisfied or quiet.[39]

Toleration should be given, not taken, a view very much in accordance with that of Lauderdale. However, confronted by continual shows of defiance, and the blurring of the lines between religious dissent and political sedition, a new cynicism crept into his attitude by July; it's almost as if he was beginning to anticipate failure: ' . . . I am desperate as to the other partie. They are unsatisfiable; what they wold have begd before they will reject when offered. Oh, they are a terrible insolent generation'.[40] Tweeddale did his best to reassure him that they were on the right course, though he seems to have been only partially convinced: 'The grounds for your hope are I confess rationall, and I trust as much the gentlemen who give yow the hope as any man can do; yet when I consider the insufferable humour of these unsatisfiable cattle I confess I can not hope, but a little time now will cleir us and let us see what is to trust to'.[41]

In July the king's letter was read in the Scottish Privy Council, announcing his intention to offer an Indulgence to peaceable ministers.[42] It was not an exercise in toleration for its own sake: it was intended, rather, as a way of separating the moderates from the extremists, with a view to destroying the latter. Some of the ministers ejected in 1662 and 1663 were to be allowed to return to their old parishes, or another vacant charge, provided they restricted their activities to their own churches. Although required to attend church courts, and pay lip service to the Episcopal authorities, they did not have to seek collation from a bishop. A number of the old Resolutioners, including Robert Douglas, accepted this meek Presbyterianism. By March 1670 some forty-three men had taken the Indulgence, seventeen of them being restored to their old parishes.

The Indulgence immediately came under a heavy crossfire from unusual allies: the Whig extremists on the one hand, and the Episcopal establishment on the other. James Renwick, one of the most obdurate of the field preachers, was to say that it was 'very visible and palpable to increase differences, divisions and animosities' based on the old Machiavellian principle of divide and rule. Alexander Shields conveyed the same message: it was 'a crafty device, not only to overthrow the Gospels, but to break the faithful and to *divide, between the mad-cap and moderate Fanaticks* (as they phrased it) that they might the more easily destroy both'.[43] Men like these could be safely ignored; the bishops could not. Both Sharp and Burnet pointed out that the Indulgence was contrary to the law, undermining the authority of the established church.[44] This was a direct and unanswerable challenge that would have to be taken up at the earliest opportunity. Sharp, as always, argued with a rapier-like caution, advancing and retreating as the occasion demanded; Burnet, in contrast, fired off his old blunderbuss, delivering himself directly into the hands of Lauderdale.

Alexander Burnet is one of those historical figures difficult to understand and almost impossible to like; but he had a simple-minded integrity far in excess of most of his contemporaries. According to James Kirkton he is said to have remarked that the 'gospel was banished out of his diocese the day the army was disbanded'. He was especially angered by the Indulgence, which allowed 'rebels' to be supported from church funds. Showing a singular lack of judgement he decided to protest in the worst possible way, allowing a Remonstrance to be drawn up, the first for many years. For Charles the Glasgow Remonstrance awakened unpleasant memories – 'this damned papers shews Bishops and Episcopal people are as bad in this chapter as the most arrant Presbyter or Remonstrator [Protestor].' Moray sent news of Burnet's political bomb-shell to Lauderdale, with a considerable show of personal anger: '. . . the nature of the paper to be such as deserves the uttermost severity. Insomuch as I incline to think the Archbishop and his whole synod, at least all that command in it, ought to be deposed and banished, if not worse . . . I take this to be the greatest ignominy that ever Episcopal government fell under since the Reformation, and shews that it must be better managed to be a support to monarchy or a pillar of religion.'[45]

Lauderdale gave orders that the document was to be burned, as the hapless Burnet was forced on to the defensive. Soon the Secretary was on his way to Scotland to set matters right. In September he was formally appointed as High Commissioner to the forthcoming Scottish Parliament.[46] This was the high water mark of Lauderdale's career; as Secretary of State and High Commissioner his power was unparalleled, a Viceroy in all but name. But there were still obvious dangers, much as there had been in 1663, when he was far less secure politically. The Indulgence, coupled with the attack on the Episcopal establishment, was giving new colour to the old rumours about Lauderdale's true inclinations. He was under close scrutiny, both in England and Scotland: 'There was great fear and great hopes among persons of different persuasions before this parliament sat down; fears among the prelatick partie that they should be cashired; hopes amongst the presbyterian partie that their government should again be restored.'[47] As always, Lauderdale never behaved quite as expected. Soon he was to repeat the trick of 1663, with one important difference: all men, Presbyterian or Episcopal, minister or bishop were to be subject to the absolute will of the king. This was to be the new centrepiece of the Lauderdale system.

Lauderdale's progress towards Scotland was as splendid as that of any king: 'he has been more numerously received than any other Commissioner, the crowds of people being very great and expressing much satisfaction'.[48] As Commissioner he had two tasks before him: once again to attend to the church question, and to develop the new proposals for a complete political and parliamentary union between England and Scotland. When Parliament opened in October, he was quick to demolish the expectations of the Presbyterians, just as he had in 1663: the king was determined to maintain the Episcopal establishment and take further action against illegal field assemblies.[49] But the bishops, apparently magnified, were at once diminished; for a new Act of Supremacy subjected them, and the church, to the royal will. Charles was to be supreme over all persons and all ecclesiastical causes, an amplification of the prerogative first outlined by Middleton, but now patently clear to all. Tweeddale had first put the necessity of this move to Lauderdale earlier in the summer, owing to the objections raised by Sharp and others to the Indulgence:

> The primate was yisternight as far out of tune as ever and the grudge is still that thes matters have been transacted without him, implying that whatsoever the King does order in Church matters without the concurrence of the clergy is illegal; and I have heird he says that the King's Commission in ane assembly hes not the lik authority as in a Parliament, for the supremacy is personal and can not be delegat, bot in the King's personal absence understands the primate to be his vicar.

> This I tell yow that yow may see what nesescity ther is of explaining acts of Parliament and asserting the King's autority mor fully . . .[50]

Politically and personally this was a God-sent opportunity for Lauderdale. Few of his fellow noblemen had any regard for clerical supremacy, and were ever ready to give fulsome demonstrations of their loyalty to the king, so there was little real danger in setting the royal supremacy on a new basis. It was also a way of showing Charles just how far the loyalty of the Scottish Parliament contrasted with its English counterpart, often hostile and suspicious in its dealings with the government. The implication was to be perfectly clear: Charles spoke and Lauderdale delivered. In November Parliament passed the Act of Supremacy. An odd historical irony was at work. In 1534, during the Reformation, Henry VIII had been made Supreme Head of the Church in England; now Lauderdale had made Charles II Supreme Head of the Church in Scotland, with the kind of authority that his own English Parliament would never have conceded. Soon afterwards a new Militia Act was passed, which did little more than renew and restate the act of 1663; but Lauderdale was quick to exploit his twin successes, giving the measure a new explanatory gloss. Unwittingly he had created what was to be a source of much future political trouble. Now he simply seized the moment, reporting his actions to the king in a mood close to jubilation:

> I received your instruction concerning your supremacie dated the 9th instant and immediately went about obeying of it. On Sunday before noon I shew it to my Lord St Andrews, he said he acquiesced, but I found the old spirit of presbeterie did remaine with some of the Bishops, and that a most impertinent paper was drawen, even against the act (so unwillingly are churchmen, by what name or title soever they are dignified to part with power), and that they wold forsooth desire a conference with me about it, which I easily laid aside by declaring I wold not alter a sillable in the Act. Then I discovered a designe in some others to have harangued against it, but I found wayes to fright them out the current of their conceit. So this morning early I went to the articles and resolved to bring it in the first business; I brought it into parliament before eleven, and had it past without so much as a contrarie vote before noone. As soon as it was voted, I called for your sceptre and solemnly touched it and the Act of Militia to be forthwith printed and solemnly publisht; the first makes you Sovereign in the Church. You may dispose of Bishops and ministers, remove and transplant them as you please (wch I doubt you cannot do in England). In a word this Church, nor no enacting nor ecclesiastical person in it can never trouble you more unless you please;

and the other Act settles you twentie thousand men to make good that power. But by the way they say the Militia Act gives jealousie in England, because it is declared you may command to any of your dominions; about that is no new clause in this act; it was verbatim in the act six yeares ago. This only ascertains and regulates the Militia, and if any shall talke to you of such a jealousie, you may easily tell them they cannot move unless you command them; and if you shall command them you may tell them from me better news. That if you command it not only the militia but all the fencible men in Scotland shall march when and where you shall please to command, for never King was so absolute as you are in poor old Scotland.[51]

All of this was simply a master politician's exaggeration, a kind of personal manifesto, turning the commonplace into a fictitious grand design. The Act of Supremacy had been conceived to achieve two things: to give retrospective justification to the Indulgence and to get rid of the troublesome Alexander Burnet. The Militia Act simply restated the earlier intention to replace a professional fighting force with a cheaper alternative. It created a Falstaff army, barely competent to deal with emergencies at home, let alone march into England or Ireland. The only time it was assembled in any strength was in 1678, when it reached only a fraction of its anticipated strength, and had to be supplemented by Highland clansmen. The simple truth is that Lauderdale's actions in 1669 have been made to bear far too much weight, both by contemporaries and by some historians: he was certainly magnifying the prerogative, but the absolutism he supposedly created in the process was a sickly creature. For Gilbert Burnet and the later Whigs Lauderdale's actions were part of a sinister plot to subvert the constitution of England; he had the money, the men and the arms and was ready to act on the command of the king.[52] In practice he had no money, few men and insufficient arms. If Scotland was a 'citadel' for the king's service, as some have supposed, it was one where the walls were heavily fractured.[53] Although Lauderdale was always careful to disguise reality in magnifying his successes, Scotland was the weakest of the king's three realms, both economically and politically, continually torn by religious conflict in the Lowlands and civil strife in the Highlands.

Soon after the Act of Supremacy was passed Alexander Burnet was dismissed from his post in Glasgow, like a disgraced civil servant rather than a mighty prince of the church. To replace him Lauderdale selected Robert Leighton of Dunblane. The reasons for this are not hard to detect: Leighton was a refreshing contrast to the bellicose Burnet; he was a man whose espousal of a more primitive form of episcopacy, free from the corruptions of prelacy, might be expected to appeal to the more reasonable sections of dissident opinion. He was to be an agent of reconciliation, intended to bridge the gap between the indulged and the established church. Unfortunately Lauderdale seems not to have taken the trouble to sound him out beforehand. Leighton, more shocked than pleased by his good fortune, held out for some months; not until the early summer of 1670 did he finally give in, and only then on the understanding that he would not accept the title of archbishop, but simply administer the diocese *in commendam*, continuing in his role of Bishop of Dunblane. He was also promised official support for a new accommodation scheme, though similar attempts had made little progress in the past.

Leighton, as it turned out, was not a good choice. Though refreshingly spiritual in contrast with the worldly Alexander Burnet, he was as much out of touch with the main currents of Scottish opinion as his predecessor. There is a modern tendency to see Leighton as the lost saviour of the Scottish church, as a 'saintly' and moderate man. Most of his contemporaries would have seen him as a man remarkably lacking in personal consistency, who had successively accepted the Covenant, the favours of Cromwell and a bishopric without any conflict of conscience.[54] Those he drew in to the accommodation talks were among the most reasonable of the dissidents, not the wild men of the hillsides; but it seems certain that few trusted a man who appeared to have no real insight into the feelings and motives of his opponents. He was a man who was 'never fixed in the point of Kirk government, counting it a thing indifferent; whether it was Independency, Presbytery or Episcopacy'.[55] His apparent lack of principle and his ability to change his commitments as if he were changing coats, were ultimately to destroy any prospect of reconciliation within the church.

The dismissal of Burnet, followed by the long vacancy in the Glasgow diocese, created additional problems for Lauderdale: the official church had been humiliated and weakened, giving rise to new fears – and hopes – that it would fall away altogether. Indulgence, moreover, had created more problems than it solved; it had only been intended to operate in the disaffected west, causing anger in other locations, less politically troublesome, but equally hostile to the episcopate. Conventicles, hitherto mostly confined to the west, began to spread across the Lowlands, a particularly worrying one being held at the Hill of Beath in Fife in June 1670. Ever mindful of his standing in England, particularly among the bishops, Lauderdale began to consider a new strategy. His problem was that all of his actions hitherto had had a contrary effect, fuelling the old stories of his latent sympathy for the Presbyterian cause, highlighted years later by Sir James Dalrymple: 'I shall not load the memory of the Duke of Lauderdale, who was most zealous for the honour of his countrey, but was over-ruled by measures, laid before he came to his greatness and by difficultie he came to be in, upon the account of his favouring the phanaticks.'[56]

If Lauderdale gave, even more was expected. The time had clearly come to immerse these feverish expectations in an icy bath of reality. In the parliamentary session of 1670 he introduced the most ferocious measure yet against conventicles, the so-called Clanking Act.[57] Those attending field conventicles were to be heavily fined; those who preached at them were threatened with death.[58] It certainly had the sobering effect intended – 'Never was there in such a law made in Scotland since the dayes of King Fergus, that a preacher of the true gospel of Jesus Christ should be condemned to die for his labour'.[59] This new measure did not indicate a retreat from moderation, but a renewed confirmation that severity was never that far removed from leniency. It was also in line with policy in England, where the Second Conventicle Act announced a further wave of persecution. Even so the Clanking Act was a naked threat rather than a working policy, and no minister ever suffered the full penalty of the law. When the two men who preached at the Beath conventicle were captured, Lauderdale was quick to urge that no extraordinary measures be taken against them, and to allow 'bygones to be bygones'.[60] There may have been no real violent intent behind his actions on this occasion; but this is perhaps the first indication of the impatience that was to become a defining characteristic of Lauderdale's attitude towards the more dangerous forms of dissent. Up to this time he was probably a figure unknown to most Englishmen; now with the Act of Supremacy, the Militia Act and the Clanking Act behind him he could be depicted by some as an exponent of a ruthless autocracy, a sort of Scottish Thomas Cromwell, no matter if the substance was far weaker than the appearance.

Parliamentary union was the other great matter that preoccupied the Secretary in the sessions of 1669 and 1670. For some, most notably Tweeddale, full political union was the only way forward for a backward and impoverished Scotland. The new discussions, announced by Lauderdale in 1669, were a natural corollary of the failed commercial negotiations. Now we have to raise one of the most intriguing questions of Lauderdale's whole career: was he in favour of union or not? His contemporaries were clearly not sure: Sir George Mackenzie says he was not, Gilbert Burnet says he was.[61] Though he had embraced union as far back as 1647, and was acutely aware of the economic benefits that would accrue, for once he was not prepared to give a definite lead, playing instead a very close game. There were important emotional considerations here, issues of national pride that could not be completely disregarded, as he tells Moray as early as November 1669, only a month after his announcement in Parliament:

> Yow cannot imagine what aversion there is generally in this kingdome to the Union. The indeavour to have made us slaves by garrisons and to ruine of our trade by severe laws in England frights all ranks of men from having to doe with England. What is done is purely in obedience to his Majestie, and it may be the worke was more difficult then is imagined. Indeed it was. But to press more before England take notice of the matter wold render the proposer most odious as the betrayer of his countrey. For God's sake let his Majestie lay another punishment on me, no command could be more grevious. This I must say, yet if he doe command it I shall not dispute but obey come what can come. Yet I must assure yow it does quite overthrow the service and render the union hier impossible.[62]

It's difficult to reconcile this with Burnet's assertion that he pushed for union 'vehemently'; but a joint commission was duly set up in both Scotland and England, discussions continuing on a weary and inconclusive course until the summer of 1670. How would union have affected Lauderdale personally? One modern historian has challenged the commonly accepted belief, arising from Mackenzie, that it would have undermined his personal power: 'This is manifestly mistaken; Lauderdale's authority rested solely on the king's favour, not upon the constitutional relationship between England and Scotland.'[63] Royal favour did nothing to save Thomas Wentworth from the block, or to prevent the later fall from power of Thomas Osborne, Earl of Danby. Westminster was a powerful and unpredictable animal, as Lauderdale understood, more than capable of destroying even the most promising political career or the most powerful of the king's advisors. Lauderdale was the longest lasting of Charles II's ministers precisely because he was not subject to the scrutiny, or at least the control, of the English Parliament; all later attempts to destroy him were wrecked by this simple truth. Moreover, the argument that Charles intended to use Scotland to force absolutism on England is extremely weak; Scotland may have been bent to the prerogative power but it was hardly in a position economically or militarily to force its model of government on its powerful southern neighbour, even with the support of the king. It is of course possible to argue that full political union would have given Lauderdale a powerful block of supporters at Westminster, which he so obviously lacked, allowing him to operate as a powerful party manager, as Archibald, Earl of Islay, and Henry Dundas were to do in times to come. Such support could not, however, be absolutely guaranteed; Hamilton could hardly have been kept out, and to allow Sharp and his colleagues to sit alongside Gilbert Sheldon and the English bishops would surely have brought an unwelcome increase in the independence of the Scottish episcopate.[64] The alternative argument that Charles simply used Lauderdale and the union talks to disguise his secret negotiations for a French treaty, though intriguing, is without foundation in evidence.[65] In the end the union proposal failed because opinion in both England and Scotland was not yet ready for such a move, not because Lauderdale believed that his interests and the interests of Charles were best served by keeping the two nations separate.[66] Unlike 1706 there were no pressing political or constitutional issues that made it a necessity. In the end it was Lauderdale himself who brought the discussions to a full stop by insisting that union had to involve nothing less than the merger of the whole of the Scottish Parliament with that of England, a quite unacceptable suggestion. He may have been acting on the instructions of the king, though we cannot be sure of this. The *dénouement* is detailed in a letter he wrote in late October 1670 to Lord Yester, his son-in-law:

> The King thought fit to call some of us and of them together to debate it fairly and freely. We met on Wednesday, of us the King called [the] Lord Chancellor, your father, Earl of Kincardine, my brother, Lord Stair and myself. And we (according as we had been resolved among us) did declare our willingness that both Parliaments might unite into one, [but] we showed the unreasonableness and impossibility of taking any less than all our Parliament, for what reason was it that part of our Parliament should join with all of their Parliament and how is it to be imagined that our Parliament would consent to extinguish itself forever and leave only part to be joined to the whole parliament of England? How could we, who act by the authority of Parliament, consent to incapacitate any nobleman, any shire any burgh? This we did enlarge sufficiently. They offered not a word against it, but they argued the impossibility of posing that in either house. The King offered fair expedients, but they did not take with them so the King commanded an adjournment of the treaty till next week at which time I think the difficulties will appear so great that no further progress can be made at this time. Now it appears to our commissioners that for zeal to unite I am as [far] from betraying the rights of Scotland as any of them.[67]

Lauderdale's appearance as Commissioner had been a great personal success; he won renewed praises from Charles and was openly commended at Westminster by Arlington. In London Moray continued to perform good service: 'I told them there were so many good lawes made now that there is no room left to deceive any more.'[68] But in Edinburgh, perhaps aware how unassailable he was, he was demonstrating a new imperiousness, destined to cause a considerable amount of resentment. In late December 1669, the last day of the current parliamentary session, the formal restitution of Argyll came up for consideration.[69] This should have been a technicality, merely ratifying a decision made six years before; but Argyll's creditors could not let such an opportunity slip past, objections at once being raised by the Earl of Errol amongst others. Lauderdale overruled this, in an undiplomatic show of anger, causing needless offence in the process. Arguably it was to be one of his great weaknesses as Commissioner that he was never to be as skilful a manager of Parliament as Middleton had been:

> In this Parliament, the members were rather overawed than gained to a compliance; for Lauderdale was become so lazy, and was naturally so violent, and by his Majesty's favour and his own prosperity so far raised above all thought of fear, that he never consulted what was to be done; nor were the members of parliament solicited by him, or his friends, upon any occasion; whereas, on the contrary, he would ofttimes vent at his table, that such Acts should be past in spite of all opposition.[70]

It is perhaps sensible to treat Mackenzie, as hostile a source as Burnet, with some caution. Nevertheless, there was a new kind of assurance in Lauderdale's attitude, unconstrained by parliamentary considerations, demonstrating, it might be thought, a lingering contempt for a body that had been seduced by billeting. This was to be a source of much future trouble: for Lauderdale's high noon was soon to slip into the shadows of evening.

11

HAMILTON AND THE PARTY

We have no firm evidence of exactly when Lauderdale renewed his relationship with Elizabeth Murray, Countess of Dysart. It would appear to have been some time after the death of Sir Lionel Tollemache, her first husband, in 1669; thereafter he was a fairly regular visitor to her home at Ham House in Surrey, where she established herself as a political hostess, one of the most brilliant of the age. The status of Lauderdale's relationship with Anne Home, his wife, is also uncertain at this time: it is said to have remained good until about two years before her death, though this did nothing to stop a rumoured association between him and Lady Margaret Kennedy, known even to the Covenanter underground.[1] In March 1670 the Countess of Lauderdale obtained a pass to go to France, sailing the following month for Calais, later settling in Paris; she and her husband almost certainly never met again.[2] Intellectually Lauderdale was far more compatible with Dysart than he ever had been with the under-educated Anne. In all respects she appears to have been a remarkable women, with all the tastes of the age, both admirable and not so admirable:

> She was a woman of great beauty, but of far greater parts. She had a wonderful quickness of apprehension and an amazing vivacity in conversation. She had studied not only divinity and history, but mathematics and philosophy. She was violent in everything she set about, a violent friend, but a much more violent enemy. She had a restless ambition, lived at a vast expense, and was ravenously covetous; and would have stuck at nothing by which she might encompass her ends.[3]

She was to have a great influence over Lauderdale, though perhaps not as considerable as Burnet and others have suggested. Her relationship with him, though chaste by the standards of the time, or at least by the standards set by the king, was subject to rumour and gossip, especially among the friends of the Countess of Lauderdale, as she complained to the Countess of Tweeddale:

I assure you I am beholding to that Pack: they have spread fine reports of me. So they do so much defame ye best of men [Lauderdale]: our Good Friend: that att present hee is made guilty of all his Ladyes faults. She is commended highly, hir trials under his Tirany pitied, and her going to France said to be against her will forced upon her by her lord's anger who they report took from her all hir jewels . . . and does not alow hir to live withal, itt is further added that this Lady was passionately ernest to have on of ye children with her but itt was refused: as all other things were purposely to make hir breake hir hart.[4]

Her liaison, and subsequent marriage, with Lauderdale comes just at the time when he is moving steadily away from the policies of moderation with which his government was formerly associated, suggesting some kind of causal relationship. The real picture is far more complex. By 1671 it was increasingly clear that both indulgence and accommodation were failing, ushering in a new kind of severity based largely on disillusionment. Although the Clanking Act would appear, at least superficially, to have had some effect on stopping the spread of conventicles, these were soon becoming as widespread and as dangerous as ever. Leighton did his best to persuade the moderate dissenters, now the indulged, of the merits of a primitive episcopacy, but he simply was not trusted, either by the Presbyterians or by his fellow bishops. This was a man who, after all, had offered no resistance to the Act of Supremacy, which in theory allowed the king to dictate any religion he pleased. Leighton's talks, which took place in Paisley from December 1670 to January 1671, made little headway, finally failing altogether. Lauderdale, who had never been that enthusiastic for Leighton's scheme, openly expressed his growing sense of impatience to James Sharp: 'By letters from Edinburgh I finde that the unsatisfied preachers are unsatisfied still, and it is no news. I expect no peace or unity from them. They are peevish and unsatisfyable; and I written to my Lord Chancellor, E. Tweeddale and E. Kincardine, that I meane to trouble my head no more with them. And if we all do our duties, they shall repent it. By God's grace nothing shalbe wanting on my part for the good of the church as it is by the law established . . .'[5]

For Sharp this was good hearing. He had never been persuaded that accommodation was a good idea, believing it would leave nothing to the bishops other than 'the insignificant title'.[6] Tweeddale was also left in little doubt about the Secretary's feelings on the matter:

. . . nor am I surprised with the little success of the conferences that have been kept with the dissenters; I know them to be a peevish, wilful and unsatisfiable generation. And although I acknowledge it was rational to try those wayes first, yet I never expected good of it, because I think that partie desires no peace. I wish sober men's eyes may be opened to see at last what those people drive at, when they refuse so reasonable offers, and that some may solide course way be layd doune to prevent the mischief that certainly they would do if they could . . .[7]

Indulgence had at least separated some of the moderates from the extremists, but not enough to make any real difference; accommodation seemed to be the only way to bridge what had become an entrenched schism within the church. If that failed only repression was left. Despite this Lauderdale was not yet committed to a major change of course, even trying to rescue the sickly accommodation scheme by insisting that Leighton accept the full title of archbishop of Glasgow, which he was finally induced to do in October 1671. That some hope still existed came with an assurance from Kincardine that the failure of the accommodation talks had upset many ministers, who were hoping for churches.[8] Even Sharp, who acquired additional hope from Lauderdale's letter, was soon forced back into his box. 'Yow need not be directed how to use him,' Kincardine wrote to Lauderdale in July, 'yow know cajoling looseth him; and that he is never right but when he is kept under.'[9] Sharp had no choice but to accept Leighton's elevation, though he continued to cast as much gloom as he could on accommodation.

That same year Lauderdale started to break with some of his oldest friends and allies, beginning with Sir Robert Moray. Burnet says that Lady Dysart, jealous of Moray's influence and power, was the cause of the break, in part confirmed by Mackenzie, who claims that Moray raised objections against her marriage to Lauderdale, thereby incurring the enmity of both.[10] But Lauderdale's relationship with Moray had been cooling as far back as 1668, for reasons that are not entirely clear, the final breach coming in early 1671, over a year before the Secretary's second marriage.[11] Moray wrote to Lauderdale in January offering to let 'bygones be bygones', though unfortunately not detailing the cause of their quarrel.[12] There seems to have been no further exchange of letters after this. We may perhaps obtain a small clue to Lauderdale's altered attitude in a letter Moray wrote to the Duchess of Hamilton in October 1671. In this he says that Lauderdale, if properly humoured, will apply himself to serve, though 'he must be cannily handled, els a very small provocation will make him fly quite off the hindges'.[13] Others were to remark on the Secretary's excessive bad temper, notably Sir John Lauder of Fountainhall, a senior Scottish lawyer.[14] There are many references to his 'taking the waters' from this time forward, a sure indication of an onset of health problems, which might provide a partial explanation for his rising anger. The problem for Moray, and others, was that Lauderdale was simply no longer as manageable as he had once been. Moray died suddenly on 4 July 1673, the same year as John Middleton, still languishing in distant Tangier. A year or two before his death Moray is said to have accused Lauderdale of betraying his country, though what the basis of such an accusation could have been is difficult to say, since both men had essentially pursued the same policies.[15] It was recorded by John Aubrey at a time when Lauderdale was a very unpopular figure in England, and is probably typical of a number of similar stories without real basis in fact.

   Tweeddale's fall can be attributed much more directly to the influence of Lady Dysart, who clearly saw not just him but his whole family as an obstacle in the way of her own ambitions. He had long enjoyed a close personal relationship with Lauderdale, cemented in the marriage in 1666 between John Hay, Lord Yester, his eldest son, and Mary Maitland. Both men were proud of their grandchildren, whose exploits often feature in their correspondence. Besides the political benefits of an alliance with the Maitland family, the Hays could also expect enormous territorial gains. In 1665 a charter was issued granting Mary Maitland and her heirs all of the Lauderdale titles and dignities. This was confirmed in 1667 after her marriage to Lord Yester, though Lauderdale reserved the right to change his mind and alter the will. If there were no children by the marriage the title and estates were to revert to his brother, Charles Maitland of Hatton.[16] Now, according to Burnet, Hatton and Dysart entered into an alliance aimed at displacing both the Hays and Mary Maitland.[17] Dysart's intention was to marry her eldest daughter to Hatton's eldest son, and thus graft a Murray–Tollemache connection on to the Maitland tree, the best way of passing the inheritance into her own bloodline, as she and Lauderdale, both well into middle age, were unlikely ever to have children of their own. Sir George Mackenzie details the background to Lauderdale's breach with Tweeddale:

> The Earl of Lauderdale did now begin to shift Tweeddale and professed that he was ashamed to have it believed, that he was yet under tutory; which was instilled in him by my Lady Dysart and the Earl of Rothes: nor was Lauderdale himself unwilling to be freed of a person, who was an enemy to his amours with her, for whom he now professed an open gallantry. The first appearance of a breach was when Sir John Baird went to ask Lauderdale if he would write for Tweeddale to come up from Scotland, (where he had stayed to manage the affairs of that nation in Lauderdale's absence) to which Lauderdale, in a huff, answered that if he pleased he might come, but he would write for no man: and when Tweeddale came, and was received near London by his own friends,

Lauderdale did publicly rally their journey; and two days after, when Tweeddale was to go out to Ham, where my Lady Dysart lived upon design to complement her, Lauderdale told publicly at table, that he could not go without his governor.[18]

Some effort was made to patch up relations with Lauderdale, Gilbert Burnet acting as an intermediary; but by the close of 1671 the relationship had degenerated beyond recall. In one of his last letters to Tweeddale, Lauderdale retreats into an icy formality:

> You tell me that Mr Gilbert Burnet when he called at Yester [the family home] said that I Commanded him so to doe; indeed I did not suspect he wold faile in that duety, he told me he intended it and I did approve it, not dreaming it needed a command from me. But I do more wonder he should pretend a commission from me to say that it should be your fault if it was not as well betwixt us as ever. Surely I never employed him in such a message; I know no business he had heir . . . but I should never have dreamed he wold have created such ane errand for his returne . . . And I am as farre to seek for understanding your discourse of mistakes and of your having taken so many wayes to remove them; but my greatest admiration is at what you adde, that you have suffered all you can by them, for I am wholly ignorant of those sufferings till you shall be pleased to informe me. Certainly I have neither been the occasion nor cause of them, nor doe I comprehend what those jealousies are which you take to be coup du ciel of which you commit the removal to God.[19]

Of Lauderdale's old allies only Kincardine was left. The practically worthless Charles Maitland was elevated in the place of Tweeddale, eventually becoming Treasurer-Depute and Master of the Mint, taking the post into new depths of corruption. James Kirkton describes him as 'the man of all that ever I knew in power in Scotland who believed most perfectly his own pleasure to be righteousness'.[20] During the course of 1673 Lauderdale altered his will in favour of his brother, now one day to succeed to the earldom. Lady Dysart did less well than expected: Hatton's son resisted all pressure to marry her daughter. In a sad postscript to the whole affair it is uncertain if Mary Maitland ever saw or spoke to her father again.

Lauderdale also came close to a breach with Argyll, a man he always seems to have viewed more as a protégé than a leading political ally. Much of their correspondence is concerned with domestic and family matters, rather than the great issues of the day. Ever mindful of the role Lauderdale had played in saving his house, Argyll named one of his younger sons after him: 'I hope your godson [John Campbell of Mamore] shall make his fortune by having your name, for at least he gets many sure promises for your sake but I know not if my lady would like to have them name you, for I deny not they are as bold with your name as Lilly [Peter Lely, the artist] was with your face, pronouncing it in several hundred ways.'[21]

Argyll was also to offer the older man, the greatest Scottish politician of the day, some avuncular advice, warning him against over-absorption in the affairs of the world: 'Your Lordship's temptations of this kinde, are farre greater then mine; I pray God you may never have cause to repent which I have.'[22] Lauderdale took this conceit in good part; he was less pleased by Argyll's second marriage to Lady Anna Mackenzie in June 1670. Lady Anna was the widow of Alexander Lindsay, Earl of Balcarres, a childhood friend of Lauderdale's, who took a close personal interest in the welfare of his children, believing them to be compromised by an Argyll connection. To try and repair the damage Lady Anna wrote a personal appeal:

> Some say your Grace is also displeased with my Lord, who, I can say, deserves [it] not from you. It's hard, for his affection to so near a relation of your own, it should be so, he being ignorant of it. I shall beg of your Grace, whatever you are pleased to allow me, that you may be to my Lord friendly. You have experience of his love, and [may] believe you are not capable almost to do that he will take ill from the Earl of Lauderdale. If you do not so, your Grace will but please your enemies and displease those wishes you as well as any upon earth does. My Lord is so faithful and excellent a person that I think all should covet his love and friendship. I am sure I could justify this by the testimony of his greatest enemies, would they be so good themselves as to speak the truth; but the sincerity of his love and respect will, I know, hardly allow him to say to your Grace that which may be looked upon as a compliment. It's almost certain that person lives not that honours, loves, and will be more concerned for you, and industrious to serve you.[23]

It's not known if Lady Anna ever received a reply, but the Argyll connection was too important to be dropped altogether. Two things probably saved Argyll from the permanent personal banishment suffered by Moray and Tweeddale: he was never a serious political rival for Lauderdale, almost certainly the most important consideration, and he would not have been easy to replace as the chief policeman of the western Highlands. Besides, for Lady Dysart, always on the lookout for an opportunity, a Campbell connection was far too good to be overlooked. In 1678 Elizabeth Tollemache, her daughter, was married to Archibald, Lord Lorne, Argyll's eldest son, the future first duke. It was not to be a happy association.

The long-neglected Anne Home died in Paris in December 1671, and was buried with all honour by the French authorities, so says Mackenzie, as the 'Vice-Queen' of Scotland.[24] Argyll reported her death to his cousin Glenorchy 'which may make many changes'.[25] The biggest change came sooner than perhaps most expected: on 17 February 1672 Lauderdale married Elizabeth Murray in St Peter's Church in the parish of Petersham, Surrey. Most of the Cabal were present, including Anthony Ashley Cooper, who acted as a witness. Some people had been bold enough to advise against such a hasty match: 'But she had such an ascendancy over his affections, that neither her age, nor his affairs, nor yet the clamour of his friends and the people, more urgent than both these, could divert him from marrying her within six weeks after his lady's decease; which confirmed much the former suspicions that the world entertained of their deportment . . .'[26]

Lauderdale, for most of the remainder of his career, based himself at Ham House. He was now a considerable figure in British politics. In November 1671, Viscount Conway, a leading Anglo-Irish politician, was told that 'we want a Lauderdale at court for watching for Ireland as they do for Scotland'.[27] His importance had taken him right to the heart of foreign policy; it also allowed him to be one of the victims of an act of royal duplicity, arguably among the greatest in British diplomatic history.

There were two issues that concerned Charles at the end of the 1660s: the restrictions Westminster was placing on the exercise of prerogative power, and a far from satisfactory pursuit of English aims in Europe, so fully demonstrated in the lamentable conclusion of the Dutch war in 1667. Any attempt to renew the ongoing struggle with the Dutch entailed a huge risk: the expense involved required a further approach to Parliament, already profoundly suspicious of the general direction of royal policy. In 1670 Charles looked as if he had found a way out of his dilemma: Louis XIV, King of France, held out the prospect of an alliance, specifically directed against the Netherlands. In return for embracing Catholicism Charles would receive a large cash subsidy from his cousin, thus freeing him from the tutelage of Parliament. On this general basis the secret Treaty of Dover was concluded on 22 May, Clifford and Arlington among the signatories.

There is perhaps more confusion and muddle-headed thinking over this one treaty than any other act in English diplomatic history: Charles was bound to make a personal declaration of faith, though the nineteenth-century Whig view still persists that he intended to deliver the entire realm to Catholicism. The whole process was also deeply cynical, in true Carolinian style. Charles was sympathetic to

Catholicism, but he was never to make the promised declaration, or to take any practical steps towards it; it was simply a way of deriving maximum benefit for minimum expense. But the Catholic clause was politically explosive, which meant that all three of the Protestant members of the Cabal were kept in the dark about the whole treaty. However, it would hardly be possible to implement the military clauses of the agreement without their direct involvement. The dilemma was solved when Buckingham, supported by Lauderdale and Ashley Cooper, offered to negotiate a second treaty with France, in complete ignorance of the first. Charles agreed, entering happily into the deception. On 21 December another secret agreement was concluded, this time in London, basically trotting out the same terms as the first, with the obvious omission of the Catholic clause. This treaty was renewed at Whitehall in February 1672, shortly before the declaration of war against the Netherlands.

Lauderdale was far from being one of the big players in this game. The renewal of the Dutch war, moreover, entailed clear risks for him at home, raising the same problems of security that had been prevalent during the earlier war at a time when a solution to the question of religious dissent was as far off as ever. However, to oppose a war that Charles was clearly intent on, though it may not have ended his political career, would have entailed a serious loss of influence right at the heart of power, a fate suffered by Ormonde. Lauderdale, it seems certain, was determined to present himself as the most reliable of Charles' ministers; even after he became aware of the Dover treaty he expressed no anger at the deception, unlike his colleague, Ashley Cooper. For his immediate co-operation he was amply rewarded, along with the other members of the Cabal. He became Duke of Lauderdale and Marquis of March, titles conferred upon his immediate male heirs only; he also received the Order of the Garter.[28] His friend Ashley Cooper received the title by which he is known to history – the Earl of Shaftesbury. Both men gave their support, along with the rest of the Cabal, to a new Declaration of Indulgence, offering a measure of relief to English recusants, issued just before the declaration of war in March.

Lauderdale now stood at what is perhaps the great crossroads of his life. Charles knew him and trusted him as much as he was capable of trusting anybody, saying that he would venture him with any man in Europe for prudence and courage.[29] Yet he was in a difficult position politically, distrusted by the old cavalier party and out of favour with the dissenters, both in England and Scotland, who clearly had expected much more from him.[30] From the early 1670s he was to be subject to an increasing campaign of propaganda, at first directed against the Cabal in general, and subsequently more specific and highly personalised in nature. The ending of the alliance with Moray and Tweeddale had deprived him of the advice of two talented individuals, who provided him with an honest insight into the daily realities of Scottish and British politics. This was to do much to increase his sense of isolation and a growing tactlessness, soon to be amply demonstrated in the new session of the Scottish Parliament.

War with the Netherlands required a new sitting of Parliament in Edinburgh, to vote fresh subsidies for the government and to address the continuing issues of national security. Lauderdale came north for the occasion in great state, accompanied by his new wife. Matters did not begin well; Parliament was adjourned for a fortnight while the duke took his wife on a kind of royal progress around Scotland, at least according to Burnet, not always a reliable source.[31] Burnet also claims that many of the nobility were so angered by this, and the additional tax demands to be raised in Parliament, that Hamilton was approached with a view to heading an opposition. It is possible that Hamilton may have been involved in some preliminary talks at this time, but the party he was eventually to head did not make an appearance until the following year. Having caused needless offence Lauderdale made matters worse by allowing Lady Dysart to attend the opening session of Parliament, seats being provided to allow her and her ladies to observe proceedings, though this was contrary to all precedent: '. . . a practice so new and extraordinary that it raised to indignation of the people very much against her; they hating to find that aspired to by her, which none of our Queens had ever attempted'.[32]

Both Burnet and Mackenzie are hostile sources, best treated with caution; but what is reasonably certain is that Lauderdale was investing heavily in future political trouble. The Dysart incident simply demonstrates the kind of insensitivity to parliamentary feeling first illustrated by the Argyll business in 1669. Lauderdale always seems to have viewed parliament at best as a temporary necessity, not bothering overmuch to ensure that he had the kind of personal backing that would allow him to carry policy forward from one session to the next. If the nobility were restive it was best to ensure that the other estates were kept onside. However, one of the first acts of the new session reduced the privileges of the royal burghs by allowing trading concessions to the burghs of regality and barony.[33] This was a matter in which the Commissioner had a direct interest, having a close business association with Musselburgh, one of the burghs of regality. Lauderdale had long since relied on the support of Sir Andrew Ramsay, the Provost of Edinburgh, to manage the burgh estate; now his desertion of their interests had made Ramsay vulnerable and the burghs angry. This was the one estate that had long been behind Lauderdale; now its support could no longer be automatically assumed.[34]

Lauderdale, in his general approach to Parliament, and the general coalition of interest that it represented, seems to have behaved as if nothing had changed politically; as if the Act Recissory had not only wiped out all the legislation of the Revolution but also returned the legislature to an ancient and subservient state. But not all the gains of the past had been wiped out at the Restoration. It had once been the procedure for the Scottish Parliament to pass legislation in a block, without debate, right at the end of the session. Although the Lords of the Articles had a decisive control of business, members now met every other day and openly debated measures under consideration. Material interests were now given much greater consideration than they had been in the past, often surpassing the religious problems that so preoccupied the government.[35] The Scottish assembly may have been far more primitive than its self-assured English cousin, but it was not without teeth. The real parliamentary challenge to the Lauderdale regime was, significantly enough, to open with an attack on its economic basis, not over its record on religious persecution.

In the 1672 session one member, William Moor from Inverurie, took the status of Parliament seriously enough to make a novel proposal: that time be allowed for members to advise their constituents of matters under consideration, in imitation of the practice in England. Lauderdale did not react well to this proposal: '. . . whereupon the Commissioner, chaffed by the former speeches, resolved to vent his passion on the weakest, and hoping here to terrify others, desired that he might be sent to the bar, for offering to impose the customs of England upon the parliament of Scotland: which discourse was delivered with so much passion, that all kept silence'.[36]

After a brief period of imprisonment Moor apologised before the Commissioner; but if the intention had been to reduce the house to a state of compliant torpor it was to have only a limited effect, probably achieving little more than adding to a general sense of discontent.

In dealing with the continuing problem of religious dissent, Charles had left the Commissioner with a free hand. The problem of vacant churches in the west had now become so severe that Leighton had complained that 'ye people in most of ye parishes would not receive angels, if they commit the horrid crime of going to presbyteries and synods'.[37] Though increasingly disillusioned with the whole policy of concession Lauderdale gave his backing to the Second Indulgence, announced by the Privy Council in September. In some ways it was a lazy measure by a government tiring of the whole time-consuming business of conciliation, and attempting to deal in a blanket fashion with an immediate problem: some eighty ministers were simply ordered to take up vacancies, sometimes doubling up with existing incumbents; it resembled more a policy of confinement than indulgence. The assumption was that all those who returned accepted the royal supremacy, and would at least pay lip service to the bishops. No attempt was made to obtain the views of those affected, and some simply refused to obey; it also had the effect of angering men like Robert Douglas, who had accepted the First Indulgence. In the end, though the two Indulgences had reconciled some 150 former Resolutioner ministers, almost half of the total outed in 1662–3, the old Protestors were more troublesome, and obdurate, than ever.[38]

Leighton, despairing of accommodation, and tiring of his burden, asked in May 1673 that he be allowed to resign the Glasgow appointment; he was induced to stay on for another year, though he was little more than an exhausted volcano. His sense of disappointment and despair was conveyed in a letter to Lauderdale:

> I can give as yet as little further account of our distempered church affairs then formerly, onely that I am informed that ye last act [the Second Indulgence] relating to our divided brethren had divided them more among themselves then anything yt hath yet befallen them; for though they generally think it girds them too straite into a corner, yet ye soberer of them incline to bee doing with it till better come, wch they are still gasping for, and let them doe, for it keeps them from despair; but others of them have some scruple concerning it, but what kind of scruple that can bee, I think passes the skille of any man in his right wits to imagine. However, there is good in it, that it amuses them, and keeps their heads and tounges busy, wch otherwise would possibly not be so innocently employed. And truly I beleev yt ye vtmost yt is to be expected from ye best councils relating to this affair, is ye preventing of mischief, and keeping things from running to extreme confusion; but for church order and cordial agreement I confesse I have given over to look for it in those parts for our time; but had this change bin either a little lower modelled at first [the reintroduction of Episcopacy], or at least, as it was, a little more calmly managed, it might likely have attained a much better reception and settlement long ere this time; but it was vnhappily, and I fear irrecoverably lost, at first setting out, by too high and too hot and hasty counsels. And I looke on it at present as a forlorn aftergame, and nothing remains but to make ye best that may bee of it as it is.[39]

As an assessment of church politics since 1661 it was remarkably insightful, and might easily have been written by Lauderdale himself.

But he was now committed to a course that could not be altered, a course that was to weaken him politically without bringing any lasting peace or credit to the church. A new instability was also entering into British politics as a whole, again with profound consequences for Lauderdale, uniting undercurrents of opposition against him in both England and Scotland.

When the English Parliament met in February 1673 it almost immediately began to demonstrate intense hostility towards the king's Declaration of Indulgence, more in fear of the growth of Catholic influence at court than of the Protestant dissent that had preoccupied it in the past. Lauderdale, angered by the challenge to the prerogative, urged Charles to stand firm, even promising, in Burnet's account, to bring an army from Scotland and seize Newcastle 'and pressed this with as much vehemence, as if he had been able to have executed it'.[40] If this statement was ever made it was likely to be just another piece of Lauderdale exaggeration; there was no army in Scotland ready to march, and the militia could not leave the country undefended and unsecured. Burnet's allegation, however, is just as likely to be an outright lie. But as his story-telling was soon to have a seriously damaging effect on Lauderdale's reputation it might be as well at this point to consider the relationship between the two men in a little more detail.

The Burnets had a long-standing association with the Maitlands, Gilbert's father being a particular friend of the first Earl of Lauderdale. Unlike his father, Gilbert Burnet's religious views were orthodox, allowing him to become the minister of Saltoun after the Restoration. He was also a particular friend and protégé of Robert Leighton, and was strongly influenced by his notions of a modified Episcopacy. Despite his support for Episcopacy as a form of church government, his views on James Sharp and his more worldly colleagues were almost as critical as those being expressed by the ministers who had been ejected in the early 1660s. He first met Lauderdale in 1663. Soon 'the coldest friend' he ever knew was taking a close interest in the career of the talented young cleric, doubtless amused by his self-importance and his somewhat pompous critique of his superiors in the church. In the new liberal climate ushered in by Lauderdale in 1669 Burnet left Saltoun to become Professor of Divinity at Glasgow University. Lauderdale continued to take a close interest in his career, particularly in his research for *The Lives of the Dukes of Hamilton*, and not just for disinterested intellectual reasons: this was a sensitive subject, touching on aspects of his own past. He liked and trusted Burnet well enough to introduce him to both Charles and James, Duke of York. It was also through

Lauderdale's influence that Burnet was appointed as one of the royal chaplains. More than this, he gave him his trust. Lauderdale always admired clever men, regardless of their status in life, and extended to them a confidence and familiarity unique amongst his peers.

Burnet was destined to become the first and the greatest of the Whig historians, whose *History of My Own Time* provides a valuable insight into the personalities and the politics of the age; it is also a work that has to be handled with a considerable amount of care, reflecting all of the strengths and the defects of Burnet's character, particularly his sense of self-righteous importance. Above all, far from being a detached work of scholarship it is a kind of extended party manifesto, one that also sets out to settle a number of personal scores. His insight, cool and detached at one moment, descends into hypocrisy and exaggeration at the next: Charles II, whom he once described as 'a prince of extra-ordinary virtue' was eventually to be likened to Tiberius![41] In many ways Burnet, literal-minded and humourless, was the worst kind of man to have as a personal confidant. Lauderdale's remark that Charles thought that Presbyterianism was 'not a religion for gentlemen' looks and sounds like a joke; but it is still reported through Burnet as the literal truth. Burnet reports all of Lauderdale's remarks, whether made in humour or temper, in the same deadpan spirit. In the long perspective of history this simply created inaccuracy; but in the context of the times it was to cause Lauderdale some serious political embarrassment.

Burnet came to London in September 1673 to obtain a licence for his book on the Hamiltons. Lauderdale was pleased to see him, having first read his manuscript some time before, clearly seeing nothing that put him at any personal risk. In a private conversation with the professor he touched upon aspects of the political situation, allegedly asking Burnet if he thought a Scots army could be used against the king's opponents in England.[42] Burnet demurred; Lauderdale then responded by saying that the spoil of England would draw them in. Some time before this Burnet reports him as saying that the 'king's edicts were to be considered and obeyed as laws, and more than any other laws'. On another occasion Lauderdale is reported to have expressed the wish that his severity against conventicles would drive the dissidents into rebellion 'so I might bring over an army of Irish papists to cut all their throats'.[43] Lauderdale by this was at once embracing the destruction of Wentworth and the dishonour of Montrose. Set against Burnet's observations we might consider the later observation by Rothes, a political enemy, but one who never entirely lost affection for the Secretary: 'I know he is very high, and often shaggarin, and angry; but not of an evil nature.'[44] Lauderdale's off-the-cuff remarks, if they were ever made in the form Burnet reports, were soon circulating among the parliamentary opposition in London, darkening a reputation already made sinister by his participation in the Cabal and by reports from Scotland. From Lauderdale's own perspective it was soon to look as if some political conspiracy was in operation; and the link between his enemies in both England and Scotland was Gilbert Burnet.

The year 1673 was one of the most crucial of the reign. Parliament's rejection of the Indulgence was bad; worse was to follow. To ensure supply for the prosecution of the war Charles was obliged to accept the passing of a Test Act, requiring all office holders to denounce aspects of the Catholic faith. At a stroke the Cabal was ended. Sir Thomas Clifford, sincere in his Catholic sympathies, resigned rather than take the Test, to be succeeded as Lord Treasurer by Sir Thomas Osborne. A far more serious resignation followed by a man who had always been a member of the Cabal, though not in name. Towards the end of March, soon after the passing of the Test Act, John Evelyn, the diarist, went to the Chapel Royal: '. . . to see whither (according to custome) the Duke of York did receive the communion, with the King, but he did not, to the amazement of everybody; this being the second year he had foreborn to put it off, and this being within the day of the Parliament's sitting, who had lately made so severe an Act against the increase of Poperie, gave exceeding griefe and scandal to the whole nation: that the heyre of it . . . should apostatise; What the consequences of this will be God only knows and wise men dread'.[45]

Evelyn was reporting what was to become the central fact of the late Stewart age: James was a Catholic, a truth that many had long suspected. As the only living brother of the king this was bad enough; what made it infinitely worse was that he was also the heir to the throne; Queen Catherine, it was clear to all by now, would never have a child, and Charles, despite repeated urging, would not divorce her. The constitutional implications of a Catholic succession were not yet clear, though James, unable to take the Test, had to resign as Lord High Admiral.

England was undergoing a political earthquake that eventually left two old friends on the opposite side of the chasm. Lauderdale had advised Charles to stand firm to Parliament over the Indulgence; Shaftesbury went in the opposite direction. He had been disappointed by the rejection of the Indulgence, at least so far as it affected Protestant dissenters; but if it came to a contest he would take the side of Parliament, not the king. He was now set on a course that was to turn him into the champion of both Protestantism and the English Constitution, an enemy in equal measure of Catholicism and Absolutism.

It was probably at this time that he began to give credence to the rumours that Lauderdale intended to use a Scottish army to interfere in English affairs in support of the king. In the most recent version of the story, soon to be augmented by the tales being spread by Burnet, it was said that he had raised 25,000 troops, and an advanced guard had already been stationed on the borders.[46] By March 1673 Moray was reporting to Tweeddale, now an associate of Hamilton, that 'JR [John Red] and Shaftesbury are not now as they were'.[47] In July their differences were so advanced that it came to an open breach in Council: '. . . a bout between the L. Chancellor [Shaftesbury] and J.R. in the Junto, about a clause in the new commission for supplying the Admirals [James] place that hath made the breach yet wider . . . J.R. was talking how the clause was agreeable to the laws of England (on which it seems he had enlarged) and the Chancellor told the King that he hoped his Commissioner for Scotland would not be allowed to teach the Chancellor of England the laws of England and so the debate ended'.[48]

It seems certain that Lauderdale had no intelligence of the conspiracy that was beginning to take shape against him. He had, along with the other members of the Cabal, obtained a royal pardon for any crimes alleged to have been committed prior to 29 September 1673, as a kind of blanket political insurance policy; but beyond that he took no other precautions.[49] Lauderdale was not just another member of the Cabal; he was widely disliked, for no very understandable reason, other than rumour and innuendo. One informant telling Sir Joseph Williamson that Lauderdale has returned to Ham House goes on to say that 'many wish him hamstrung there, that he never come further'.[50] A pamphlet circulating at this time indicates that the Westminster Parliament was intent on attacking both the Dutch war and the whole foreign policy of the Cabal: 'Our grandees were afraid, if so many clear sighted men came together; some one or other would spy out the snake in the grass, and if their mind had once taken vent, the whole design had miscarried.'[51] When the Lords and Commons began to gather at Westminster the ground had already been prepared: one of the biggest snakes was to be the Secretary for Scotland, as it was reported to Williamson that October:

At this great baiting, one of the bears intended to be brought to the stake is his Grace of Lauderdaill, and there are shrewd mines ready to spring soe soone as the members sitt, he having let fall . . . some words which have provoked some . . . this part of the story lyes among the Commons, where some have engaged to break the ice, and very many to follow the blow; but among the Lords his principal antagonist is the little one [Shaftesbury] once his great confidant, who (though his Grace said hee would crush the little worme with his great toe) most believe will wriggle from under him and trip up his heeles; but to be out of reach his Grace goes the 8th instant for Scotland, where the discontents against him are, I believe, more just and weighty than those here, and I am assured that if once they begin here, will breake like thunder from thence, so wee shall be sure to heare of them.[52]

Lauderdale left for Scotland, not aware what he had left behind, and not aware what lay ahead. The argument that the ensuing troubles were more to do with the personality of Lauderdale, his gradual slide into an arrogant abuse of power, can be overstated.[53] Hamilton had been shaping up as a political enemy for some time, an enmity dictated by frustrated ambition rather than a surfeit of principle. Letters passed between Hamilton and the Secretary show that Hamilton was full of private grudges and anxious for money and public recognition; he wanted his debts repaid, he wanted the Garter and he wanted command of Dumbarton Castle.[54] But when he was given the chance of public employment earlier in the year, he retreated in alarm. On the suggestion of Leighton he was to be put in charge of a small commission of Privy Councillors to enforce the laws against dissent in the south-west. This was his territory, so he could hardly have been kept out; but he believed such an impossible task to be part of a plan to ruin him, refusing to serve, even though he incurred the displeasure of the king. Lauderdale continued to treat Hamilton with personal kindness, even lobbying to have him admitted to the Garter; he expressed his gratitude and sharpened his knife.

The third Dutch war, like the second, had caused some real economic difficulties: incomes were low and public revenues lower still. Parliament had been summoned to grant a supply, leading to fresh anxieties and renewed concern about the operation of public supported monopolies in the trade of salt, tobacco and brandy. Hatton's administration of the Mint was another – fully justifiable – source of discontent. He was, Mackenzie says, a person 'more obliged to fortune than to fame, being as much injured by the one, as raised by the other'.[55] People were more than ready to believe the reports that he had adulterated and lessened the coinage. Apart from these economic considerations there were other matters of concern, most notably the adulteration of the law itself by the advancement of men untrained and unsuited to the profession. These were all genuine grievances that could have formed the basis for an effective manifesto. Hamilton's allies, soon to be known as 'the Party', were only partly motivated by empirical issues; the real glue binding their association together was spite and envy. The Party was made up of men who, in times past, would have governed Scotland through the Privy Council; now this ancient body was little more than a rubber stamp for Lauderdale. The abolition of the Scots Council may have ended English interference in the affairs of the northern kingdom; it only did so by concentrating ever more power in the hands of the Secretary. The Hamiltonians were not natural allies: Tweeddale, bewildered and angry, had been in government long enough to obtain sufficient insight into the character of his new associate; old Middeltonians, like the earls of Morton and Dumfries, were representative of more ancient grudges; and William Douglas, Earl of Queensberry, a talented opportunist, looking to advance his own career. Rothes, as always, stood on the fringes, careful to avoid compromising himself by any direct association. Parliament was due to meet on 12 November. In the days beforehand Hamilton and his colleagues prepared their plans with a reasonable expectation of success. Lauderdale was not to be attacked in isolation; this was part of a far grander strategy involving Shaftesbury and the English opposition.[56] Gilbert Burnet arrived back in Edinburgh the night before Parliament met, learning of the plans in Hamilton's lodgings.[57] He was later to claim that Lauderdale's enmity towards him began because he was enjoying too close an association with the King and the Duke of York; as it was the Secretary himself who introduced him to these men this does not seem very plausible. Burnet, rather, gave all the appearance of a 'grey eminence', compromised by his timing, his lack of discretion and his bad judgement rather than by any weight he was able to place on the levers of power.

Almost as soon as he crossed the Border Lauderdale became aware of the general undercurrent of discontent, induced by yet another unpopular war with the Netherlands, though this did nothing to weaken his confidence. In early October he wrote to Charles from the old family home of Lethington:

> Yor commands are onely to quiet the mindes and secure the peace of this yr kingdome, and I find already there was a great need of sending some body hither to that purpose, for tamperings of several hands have been from that place [Holland] with divers hier, and the disaffected heir have divers sorts of correspondents at London, wch much hardens them and they industriously spread such news as yor small friends at London wold have them. Yet I trust in God, I shall disappoint them and give you a good account of yor commands by letting the world see that this kingdome is quiet, and both the parliament and the kingdome ready to serve yow against your enemies.[58]

Lauderdale delivered his speech before Parliament with the same blind assurance, detailing the king's request for funds for the prosecution of the war. When he stopped he received what was arguably the greatest shock of his whole career: the mouse roared. In responding, Hamilton stood up and said that before the house replied to the king's letter attention should be given to various grievances, in imitation of a practice long established at Westminster, though unknown in Scotland. One by one the members of the Party rose to support this demand: the three monopolies were attacked, as was the administration of justice and the adulteration of the coin.[59] One can imagine the shock with which the Commissioner received this verbal onslaught, a ' strange torrent of opposition' that both surprised and amazed him.[60] Burnet was well aware of the dangers this new parliamentary assertiveness represented for the political system that Lauderdale had done so much to create: 'With this the duke of Lauderdale was struck as one almost dead; for he had raised his credit at court by the opinion of having all Scotland in his hand, and in a dependence on him: so a discovery of his want of credit with us must sink him there [in London]'.[61]

No sooner had he recovered his composure than he wrote to his brother Charles, indicating where he believed the real source of trouble to be: 'Yesterday I went up to the house and opened the parliament, where I met with such a spirit as I thought never to have seen heir, wch makes me wth more assurance repeat what I hinted before at my first coming into this kingdome, that there have been industrious tamperings from London heir.'[62]

Though supported by John Murray, Earl of Atholl, an increasingly close political ally, and by Argyll and Kincardine, he had enough sense to accept that the mood was against him, adjourning the session, intending to discuss the specific grievances in a less damaging public fashion. As always, Lauderdale played the game in a masterly fashion, showing himself to be far less vulnerable than Burnet and Mackenzie and all the supporters of the Party had assumed. Sir Frances Scott and Sir Patrick Hume, two of the lesser members of the Party, had attempted to widen the issues by criticising the war and the constitution of the Articles: Lauderdale resisted this, focusing only on the rather limited economic issues on which Hamilton and the Party grandees had made a stand: 'I, considering that the removing those pretended grievances might probably take off such as were not ingaged in worse designs . . .'[63]

The worst design, of course, was his own removal from office, a project in which Shaftesbury was deeply involved, as Lauderdale was quick to tell the king. Charles needed no warning about a man he increasingly distrusted, believing him to be in secret contact with the opponents of the court. At Westminster royal demands for war funds had also run into trouble: Parliament refused to restrict its discussions, opening an attack on the king's ministers. Lauderdale was an early target, his support for the English Declaration of Indulgence being signalled out. On November 13, the same day that Hamilton announced his opposition in Edinburgh, the Secretary was denounced for the first time as 'an evil councillor'.[64] To allow tempers to cool off, Charles prorogued the sitting until January. Just before this a pamphlet was circulated saying that 'the alliance with France was a grievance; that the King's evill counsel was a grievance, and that the Duke of Lauderdaill was a grievance'.[65] To believe that what was happening in both Edinburgh and London was a simple coincidence was too much: soon after Parliament prorogued Shaftesbury was dismissed from the government.

In Edinburgh Lauderdale continued to step carefully. Shaftesbury was a dangerous opponent but Hamilton was a man whose intellect was in inverse proportion to the size of his conceit. The discussions over the monopolies revealed something of his general deportment: 'D. Hamilton intimated his desire to have it brought into Parliament and no more meeting, but I said so faire to all the 3 pretended grievances that all seemed satisfied except the Duke, who desires brouillerie and to mak himself popular, wch he seems to take for the way to be a great man, and I am sure he brays what great friends he hath in London, I much doubt Mr Burnet hath contributed much to puffing him up.'[66]

With the king's permission Lauderdale announced an end to the monopolies; any further opposition would then be revealed for what it was. As the session proceeded the Commissioner continued to refuse all concession over the composition of the Articles, which he defended as the basis of monarchical government in Scotland. He could do nothing to save Sir Andrew Ramsay, his old ally in the burghs, who, threatened with impeachment, resigned both as the Lord Provost of Edinburgh and as a Lord of Session.[67] It is one of those peculiar ironies of the whole political situation that Lauderdale, while being criticised for supporting one set of monopolies, had lost support because he had previously taken action to end another. From London the beleaguered Commissioner received letters of support and encouragement from the King, the Duke of York and Sir Thomas Osborne, fast emerging as a new political ally. In the end Parliament could not be managed. Lauderdale conveyed something of his frustration and disappointment to Charles:

> . . . I have beat doune . . . all extravagant motions and all manners of vote except to those acts which I moved and caryed on my self. This cannot be contradicted but with impudent lying, so that none but gross lyers can

say that there is the least difference betwixt yor parliament and yor Commissioner. This hath been the care of all my labor, and yow may thinke it was no easie taske seeing it was advised and fomented in London, yow know by whom [Shaftesbury], resolved heir before we sat doune and hath been openly consulted and carried on by those I have before mentioned to yow, who meet day and night publickly where E. Tweeddale is the head and heart, with whom their 2 or 3 lawyers meet, and the Duke Hamilton is content to appear as the leader and dryver . . .[68]

Parliament was adjourned until June 1674; but it was never to meet again. Lauderdale had survived a challenge that, in some ways, was as potentially damaging as the billeting affair, with considerably augmented personal credit. Though in his reports to Charles he had likened developments in Scotland to the onset of the Covenanter Revolution, the Party conspiracy failed for much the same reasons as the billeting scheme: it was never more than a petty intrigue conceived in the minds of second-class politicians. Hamilton was far too limited in both imagination and energy to harness popular discontent in the same way that was later to turn Shaftesbury into one of the most effective, and dangerous, party leaders in British political history. With none of the restless intellect of Shaftesbury, or the native cunning of Middleton, Hamilton was in many ways the ideal enemy – transparent and patently shallow. When he and some of his Party colleagues came to see the king in December he told them quite bluntly that he would not have his chief supporter brought down either by billeting or by cabals among those who simply wished to take his place.[69] Charles had the measure of the opposition: '. . . the King knew men beyond any sovereign prince, although people imagined that his pleasures were his only thoughts; and by that great knowledge he easily perceived that Duke Hamilton's representations were only grounded out of self-interest, and that he blasted his adversary with the hopes of governing all himself – he and his creatures – and that did my lord Lauderdale more good than can be imagined'.[70]

The year after the attack of the Party a pamphlet appeared with the title *An Accompt of Scotland's Grievances by Reason of the D. of Lauderdales Ministry*. It was addressed to the king, though clearly intended for a much wider audience, in England as much as Scotland. It begins by attacking the Militia Act, though the writer must have been well aware that this had been formulated well before Lauderdale became Commissioner. . Interestingly the fall of Clarendon is highlighted as removing the only restraint on Lauderdale's exercise of absolute power, though few at the time regretted the departure of the Scottish-hating busybody.[71] The monopolies on brandy, salt and tobacco are all identified; but the real grievance is Lauderdale's 'excessive greatness' and, more particularly, his 'arrogant undervaluing of Parliaments'.[72] By way of example his treatment of William Moor in the 1672 session is mentioned. When the hapless Moor happened to slip in his address from the singular to the plural, Lauderdale is said to have pounced on him 'What, Sir, are there mice in your arse?'[73] Lauderdale's political strategy is carefully unravelled: '. . . he looked upon the Supremacy [Act] and the Militia, so settled, and in a manner, both in his own hands, as two brave leading cards, wherewith such a court gamester as he, in the many chances and changes that do there happen, might sometime or other come to do mighty feats'.[74]

It's a clever polemic, finely calculated and well balanced, hitting several significant targets, including Lauderdale's capacity to embrace and discard allies with alarming ease. It was clearly intended to stimulate the continuing onslaught on Lauderdale at Westminster, now that he could not be subject to a similar critique in Edinburgh. It was an indication, moreover, that the opposition, despite the deficiencies of Hamilton as a leader, had at last found a voice; it was a voice that not only refused to go away but grew ever louder, ever more persistent as the years passed. It was a sign that the great days of Lauderdale were over.

12

LORD OF HOSTS

As expected, Parliament gathered at Westminster, thirsty for blood, stimulated by the presence in London of Hamilton and his allies. Now that Clifford was gone, and Shaftesbury safe with his new associates, the remaining members of the Cabal were all targeted, Arlington and Buckingham, as well as Lauderdale. Of the three, Lauderdale was in the weakest position, with no faction to support him in the Lords or the Commons; even among adherents of the court party he was a suspect figure.[1] Confident of the support of Charles, the Secretary, now himself in London, was dismissive of the threat taking shape to the point of outright contempt. When told that he might be subject to an impeach- ment he is alleged to have said that he 'had a dog in his arse which would outbark all those curs'.[2] About the same time a caricature was circulating, showing Lauderdale on a dog's lead, barking at Parliament, though it is impossible to say if this can be directly attributed to his remarks.[3]

As the debate opened he was linked with Arlington and Buckingham in a 'great triumvirate of iniquity'. In the Commons Sir Robert Thomas was the first to raise the name of Lauderdale as a 'person that has contributed as much to our misfortune as any man'.[4] The house was particularly concerned by the implications of the Militia Act, which gave him 'great forces in readiness and pay, and for no other end, he believes, than to awe us'.[5] Sir Nicholas Carew took the baton from Thomas, arguing that the duke was at the head of a great army in Scotland, and suggesting that the king be asked to send him back there, never to allow him to return to England.[6] Sir Thomas Littleton followed on, saying that a cloud hung over England that had to be scattered. Once again a picture was painted of the grand old Duke of Lauderdale, marching his men up and down the hills of Scotland: '. . . his power is great, and the army under his power . . . Pray God! This be not elsewhere, a man so principled and arbitrary! . . . there are 20,000 foot and 2,000 horse, ready in Scotland, and no colour for it: a man of such principle is not to be trusted with such an army, nor with our counsels . . .[7]

Parliament next got its teeth into the assertion that the king's edicts were 'superior to law', indicating that some such story had already been spread by Gilbert Burnet. One member suggested that Lauderdale be sent 'where edicts are in fashion'. Even more damaging charges were raised, including the old slander that he had been active in the murder of the late king, and was intent on completing his malevolent design by destroying his successor by giving him ill advice. Colonel Sandys increased the temperature several degrees by suggesting that a Bill of Attainder be raised, the very device that had destroyed Strafford all those years before, though the suggestion was not supported.[8] The house returned to safer ground with the Militia Act, another member neatly combining it with Parliament's other great obsession: this measure put 'the king in power plainly to alter any thing in Church or State, and so, by this army, Popery may be set up'.[9] The debate concluded with a motion to the king, asking him to remove Lauderdale from his presence forever 'as a person obnoxious and dangerous to the government'.

This is a good point to consider Burnet's contention that Lauderdale said that the king's edicts were equal or superior to law. Beyond Burnet there is no way of proving that this politically damaging assertion was ever made. Even Osmond Airy, a kind of latter-day Whig, and no friend of Lauderdale's, says that there must be considerable doubt whether the phrase was really used, or, if it was, if it was really intended to carry the meaning attached to it.[10] Lauderdale was certainly given to extravagant statements, especially in his correspondence with Charles, but in this he was little different from any other politician, past or future, seduced by an overblown phrase, especially where his own performance was amplified. In December 1673 he told Charles that 'for as I have often said the whole course of my life shall be to obey yow in yor owne way'.[11] For Lauderdale, in a personal sense only, the king's edicts might indeed be said to be the equal of laws, a subtlety that clearly escaped the humourless and literal-minded Burnet.

Burnet tells another story that finds no supporting evidence. When Hamilton and Tweeddale came to see Charles in the December before the parliamentary sitting he received them with some kindness.[12] Clearly worried that the Commons would prove obstinate over a grant of supply, he told them he would be happy to drop Lauderdale if this put them in a more accommodating frame of mind. It was further hinted that the Party would benefit from his fall: 'He gave them so good a hearing, that they thought they had fully convinced him; and he blamed them for not complaining to himself of those grievances. But as soon as he saw it was to no purpose to look for money from the house of commons . . . he sent them down with full assurance that all things should be left to the judgement of the parliament [of Scotland]'.[13]

Charles could be duplicitous and two-faced, often saying different things to different men; but he never gave any indication at this time that he was prepared to abandon Lauderdale. There was no negotiation over the parliamentary address against him: it was simply ignored. It would seem fairly clear that if these remarks were ever made, assuming that Burnet didn't just make them up, they were intended to seduce the opposition, with the intention, perhaps, of inducing Hamilton and Tweeddale into some indiscreet revelation of their own personal ambitions. Lauderdale was openly lauded when he came back from Scotland, ostentatiously and publicly greeted by both Charles and James. In May the English Privy Council declared that he was innocent of the charges raised against him in the Commons. Charles followed this up in June by raising him to the English peerage as Earl of Guilford and Baron Petersham, in theory giving him legal immunity from further attacks by the Commons.[14]

Not long before this he had taken his Scottish opponents by complete surprise. Hamilton and Tweeddale had returned north in March, full of expectations for the new session of Parliament, only to witness Lauderdale announce a further prorogation, followed in May by a full dissolution; no other was to meet until the summer of 1681. As a mark of his political success the Scottish Privy Council was remodelled to exclude Tweeddale and all the supporters of the Party. Hamilton alone remained in splendid isolation, which only served to emphasise his political impotence. Lauderdale's first round with the Party had come close to a knock-out: 'But the Duke of Lauderdale soon gott many for him, so that a great heat grew betwixt the two parties; but Lauderdale having the King's ear, and being, indeed, the King's great favourite in all the three nations, he easily mastered his contrar partie'.[15]

In England Lauderdale attached himself firmly to a new political star. Buckingham fell from power and Arlington was fading from the scene; in their place came Thomas Osborne, Viscount Latimer, who was created Earl of Danby in the same month that his Scottish colleague acquired the Guilford title. This was to have an important bearing on Lauderdale's political outlook, with particular reference to the question of religious dissent. Though he had met the attacks of the English Parliament with arrogant confidence, he was now fully aware just how isolated he was in England from any significant party. Parliament had been prorogued until the summer of 1675, but when it reassembled it was likely to renew its attacks on Lauderdale, now the last significant member of the Cabal. A link with Danby, a committed Anglican, who admired the Scot's political methods, also offered a link to Sheldon and the English bishops, a significant power bloc in the Lords. An alliance with Sheldon, of course, involved a fresh appraisal of the role of James Sharp and the hardliners in the Scottish episcopate.

In October 1674 Lauderdale joined with Danby in a series of conferences with the English bishops with a view to securing a new consensus in the drive against dissent. John Locke, the philosopher and scientist, a close associate of Shaftesbury, was clearly amused by the historical irony involved here: 'that old Covenanter Lauderdale is become a patron of the church, and his coach and table filled with bishops'.[16] In early 1675 the Venetian ambassador noted that: 'Lauderdale and the Treasurer [Danby], now the confidential ministers of the court, are seen constantly with the bishops and will postpone the meeting of parliament so much desired by the country for the sake of pleasing them and for their own personal interests; Lauderdale least his impeachment of the last session be revived and the treasurer for fear that his enemies may draw up a new one against him.'[17]

Their association, of course, was a target for the satirists, circulating a doggerel verse based on an exchange between the two men, in which Lauderdale admits that they are brothers in infamy:

> Right, Tom; and, by my soul, I'll never fear
> Before the insulting Commons to appear,
> And let them best affront me if they dare.
> For all their lumming noise, I'll make them know,
> I'll sit above them when they sha'nt sit below.[18]

The Duchess of Lauderdale also continued to attract adverse attention, noticed in the kind of way Anne Home had always managed to avoid. Mackenzie holds her responsible for the ejection of the Earl of Kincardine, the last of Lauderdale's most capable allies, who had performed invaluable service as his deputy while he was attending the Parliament of 1673.[19] She is said to have conspired with Atholl in arranging his downfall in the course of 1674, convincing her husband that he was a serious risk to his own position, 'caballing' with Hamilton in the hope of succeeding Lauderdale to the Secretaryship. Burnet takes a contrary view, saying that Kincardine was dismissed because he had opposed the new authoritarian direction in the Secretary's policy.[20] It is certainly possible to overestimate Dysart's political influence with her husband, strong though it was. When the Laird of Glenorchy tried to enlist her help in his campaign to secure the earldom of Caithness, she told him that all she could do was to remind the duke of his interest: 'this is the real truth, so I hope ye doe believe it; if ye doe not, I am sorry for itt but cant helpe it'.[21] Nevertheless, her reputation for interference was well established, also attracting the attention of the satirists:

> Methinks this poor land has been troubled too long
> With Hatton and Dysart and old Lidington;
> Those fools, who at once makes us love and despair,
> And preclude all the way to his Majesty's ear,
> While justice provokes me in rhyme to express
> The only truth which I know of my bonnie old Bess.
>
> She is the Bess of old Noll [Cromwell]
> She was once Fleetwood's Bess, now she's Bess of Atholle;
> She plots with her tail, her lord with his pate.
> With a head on one side, and a hand lifted hie,
> She kills us with frowning, and makes us to die.
>
> The nobles and Barons, the Burrows and Clownes,
> She threatened at home, e'en the principall townes,
> But now she usurps both the sceptre and crown
> And thinks to destroy with a flap of her gown.
> All hearts feel excited whenever she comes,
> And beat day and night, lyke Gilmour his drums.[22]

Now that Kincardine was gone Lauderdale had lost the last of his liberal allies, entering into a period of personal dictatorship, which defines the character of the remainder of his rule in Scotland. It is to this time – 1674 onwards – that most of the stories of oppression and arbitrary rule can be traced, though as always there is a large measure of exaggeration and outright lies in the stories of wholesale torture and terror. Lauderdale was at once arrogant in his exercise of power, and deeply concerned by his continuing inability to master the intractable problem of public order. His more extravagant measures seem dictated by a combination of concern and bad temper, rather than malevolence and cold calculation. To those anonymous propagandists who were to describe his government as a tyranny beyond that of the Inquisition, or who likened him to Cesare Borgia or Nero, we can do no better than quote James Kirkton, a man who had no particular reason to love Lauderdale. Kirkton repeats some of the prejudices and misconceptions of the day, but in general he presents a far more measured assessment: 'At this time Lauderdale governed Scotland at his pleasure. Whatever he desired of the King was granted; whatever he required of the council was obeyed more readily than a hundred of our other Kings; and truly whatever the man was, he was neither judged a cruel persecutor nor ane avaritious exactor (excepting his brother and wife's solicitations) all the times of his government . . .'[23]

Gilbert Burnet considered the political temperature too high to remain in Scotland, abandoning his divinity post in 1674, moving to permanent exile in England, though Lauderdale never made any serious attempt to take any personal revenge on the loose-tongued and interfering clergyman, who had caused him so much political trouble. In general those who opposed him, or crossed his will, could expect an unrestricted onslaught. Some of the political struggles of the time have an almost baroque character, bearing a close resemblance to old-fashioned naval battles, broadside exchanged for broadside. Nowhere is this clearer than in Lauderdale's contest with two of the most significant interest groups: the burghs and the lawyers.

The old royal burghs had never reconciled themselves to the loss of their trading monopoly, hoping to raise the matter once again in the 1674 parliamentary session. When this opportunity was denied the Convention of Royal Burghs decided to take the unusual, and dangerous, step of writing directly to the king in August, complaining of: '. . . the acts in favours of burghs of regalities, and the act of adjudications, both past in the third session of the last parliament, by the first of which our priviledges wer communicated to many thousands who boore not burden with us . . .'[24]

In defending their sectional interests, the burghers, probably unknown to them, were asking for a complete reversal in the direction of government policy. Charles was asked to agree to a new session of Parliament, and to issue instructions to the Commissioner to arrange to have the offensive legislation repealed. It was amusingly audacious, causing a certain amount of aristocratic outrage. In writing to the Duchess of Lauderdale, Atholl expresses his indignation at this 'saucy letter' written by 'vermin' and 'machanick fellows'.[25] It was an act of sedition, causing Lauderdale to take immediate action. In Burnet's account he was 'lifted up out of all measure and resolved to crush all that stood in his way'.[26] Burnet, of course, was not party to Lauderdale's thoughts at the time, nor was he acquainted with his intentions. Some were fined and imprisoned, hardly crushed, while others were commended for their greater sense of discretion in distancing themselves from the 'impertinent' letter, notably the burghers of Dundee, Aberdeen and St Andrews.

The dispute with the lawyers was potentially far more serious, because it gave all the appearance of being a calculated – and revolutionary – challenge to the sources of authority; more particularly it offered a way, for some at least, of reversing Lauderdale's recent successes against the Party. It began simply enough: Sir George Lockhart, acting for the Earl of Callendar, urged him to appeal to Parliament, challenging a decision of the Court of Session in favour of the Earl of Dunfermline: '. . . hoping thereby to bring the President of the Session and his friends in question, knowing that Dunfermline, as Lauderdale's uncle, would want in Parliament that favor which Callendar might expect, as having married the Duke of Hamilton's daughter; and that the parliament would be glad to draw to itself the last and supreme decision of all causes'.[27]

Such appeals were unprecedented, and would have weakened the power of the judges, all royal appointees, while magnifying that of Parliament. Above all, it would ensure that Parliament was no longer an occasional assembly but a permanent part of the political scene, thus making long-term prorogation impossible: the law did not stop, so neither could Parliament. Many of the advocates lined up behind Lockhart, hoping to enlist the support of the burghs, in what was a clear declaration of war against both the judges and the government. Lauderdale was not blind to the political implications of this manoeuvre, nor to the encouragement the advocates received from the Hamiltonians, ordering them to disavow appeals on oath; those who did not were forbidden to practise. In the summer of 1675 the mutineers were told that unless they submitted the ban would be made permanent: the ministers had been outed, so too had the advocates. All were to be ejected from Edinburgh, where the Court of Session was based, deprived of all prospect of making a living. In Burnet's account of the affair the town council was unco-operative, so Lauderdale obtained a letter from the king, ejecting twelve of the chief magistrates, declaring them incapable of public trust, an uncomfortable echo of billeting, 'so entirely had he forgot his complaints formerly made against incapacity . . . '[28] Once again the Secretary emerged as the clear winner in an unequal struggle; the sources of royal power continued to be safe. The affair also resulted in a small but significant realignment of loyalties: Sir George Mackenzie, a talented lawyer, broke ranks with his brother advocates because of his hostility to Lockhart. A long-standing enemy of Lauderdale, right back to the time of Middleton, he now changed sides, and was quickly received into favour. He now embarked on a career that was to give him a fearsome – and unfair – reputation, emerging, in the course of time, as 'Bloody Mackenzie', a kind of Scottish version of Judge Jeffries.

Lauderdale's troubles this season came in threes. In July 1674 he received a letter from Kincardine, not yet ejected, noting how strange it was that 'all sorts of people should grow mutinous together. I pray God avert what it threatens'.[29] Kincardine was referring to the growing demand for a National Synod of the Church, a General Assembly by any other name, supported by Archbishop Leighton against the wishes of his fellow primate.

For Lauderdale, whose attitude towards dissent was undergoing a significant change, Leighton was now probably more of an embarrassment than an asset: his 'accommodation' scheme had been hopelessly lost, sinking deep into a bog of mistrust and incomprehension. Lauderdale wrote him an interesting and revealing letter in June 1674 regarding Leighton's support for a synod to discuss and resolve the problems within the church:

> . . . I well remember what such effects flowed from the petition of the ministers in the year 1638, and for a General Assembly too. I doe also remember how the tumult in Edenburgh begun by woemen, and now I find woemen more tumultuously petitioning. I wish some may not be intending on the same play ower again, but a burned child dreads the fire, and upon all these considerations I dare not, I can not concurre in the desire for a Synod at this time from which I may fear evill and expect no maner of good. If the late mad pranks so evidently threatening rebellion, had not fallen out, I was much inclined to any maner of moderation that could have been proposed for quieting the soberest of the disaffected party, and I was for granting an Indulgence to the peaceable of them wch might have consisted with the maintenance of the present church government established by law, and wch would not probably have perpetuated the schism; but the late mad practices have much cooled me until I shall see some more hopes of peace by the Councell's vigorous quelling this spirit; yet I shall not discourage any motions for quieting the spirits of such as wilbe peaceable . . . I can not disguise my own melancholy thowghts that until the desperate party see that their violent courses can not prevaile, I have but little hope of moderation and Indulgence.[30]

Was Lauderdale giving serious thought to a third Indulgence? The evidence suggests not. In the instructions he had received as Commissioner for the opening of the parliamentary session in November 1673 it was to be made perfectly clear that the existing Indulgences had been 'much abused', and that no further concessions were to be offered.[31] Any further Indulgence would also have weakened his new understanding with Sheldon and the English bishops. Moreover, as Hamilton was closely associated with the whole campaign for a National Synod, the letter to Leighton was a way of letting him know indirectly that the failure of the movement, and the failure of indulgence, could be directly attributed to his own scheming.

Lauderdale's refusal to countenance a synod was backed up by fresh attacks on conventicles: 'The Deuk of Lauderdaill,' the Earl of Linlithgow reported, 'is very ernest that resolute courses may be takin vith that krou [crew].'[32] Leighton, with nothing more to offer, was eventually allowed to stand down, retiring to England. That same year he wrote what might stand as the best epitaph for church policy of the Restoration monarchy:

> The errors in the management of these whole church affaires have been so great and so many, all along from the first setting out that it looks like a judicial stroke from heaven either on the business itself or on ws that we were intrusted with it, for we have been still tossed betwixt the opposite extreams of too great rigour and too great relaxation and indulgences, well made lawes too severe to be exacted and for a counterpoise have executed almost none of them, except by exorbitant fitts and starts that by their extreamitie made all men sure of their short continuance.[33]

Who was to replace Leighton in such a sensitive posting? It had to be someone in tune with the Secretary's new thinking on dissent as an issue not of liberty of conscience but political sedition. His problem was that the choices were fairly limited, few men of the first rank occupying the Scottish episcopate. His dilemma led to one of the great reversals of his life. Only three years before he had written with annoyance to a suggestion by Tweeddale that he might bring Alexander Burnet back to Glasgow: 'As for the late Archbishop Burnet, I wonder how yow can so much as let it enter your mind that I will so much as thinke of readmitting him. That wold quite ruine all. No, I shall never never so much as consent to it'.[34]

No sooner was Leighton out than Burnet was in, announcing to all those in the west what they could expect from the government from now on. By the beginning of 1675 all of the elements were in place: Lauderdale was allied with Danby and the High Anglicans; Burnet was back and Sharp had acquired a new authority: accommodation, and all hopes of a 'primitive episcopacy', was dead. Lauderdale's perception of opposition acquired a fresh significance: between the Hamiltonians and the Protestors lay only the briefest of margins. Hamilton, who had been a leading persecutor when Rothes was Commissioner, and a supporter of the military party, had embraced the cause of dissent out of simple opportunism: any concession by Lauderdale to the disaffected would now look like political weakness.

Of necessity Sharp and Burnet formed an important element in the new Privy Council, virtually by default. Not only could they be relied upon to give uncritical support to the Secretary, but also there was really no one else of sufficient stature to stand alongside them. Lauderdale's ability to create and discard allies had forced him on to a dangerously narrow ground amongst his own class: by the mid 1670s most of the aristocracy supported the opposition. Atholl and Argyll were useful, though lacking in the abilities and energy that had motivated Tweeddale and Kincardine, but their activities were largely confined to the Highlands, where Argyll was bogged down in his endless struggle with the Macleans. Besides, each of the two men nurtured a deep personal resentment against the other, and could hardly be expected to co-operate in offering advice. Nevertheless, the suggestion that Sharp and Burnet determined policy is based on a serious mis-reading of political reality: to the end they were Lauderdale's creatures.[35] He was still very much the great wheel by which all the little wheels moved.[36]

The support of the archbishops was made all the more necessary by further desertions amongst the aristocracy. The cruellest blow came in September 1674, when Rothes was revealed as a supporter of the Party. Although Lauderdale had considered him as a friend, the Chancellor had always played a deep game, and had probably never forgiven the Secretary for the humiliation he had felt over the loss of the Treasury and Commissionership in 1667. Now his treachery was apparent, revealed to Sharp in a letter from the Duchess of Lauderdale: 'I am really sory hee has so dishonoured him selfe as to dissert his best frinds to adhere to his greates enimyes. I have long known how my Lord's heart has stood to him, and the deepe impressions I found in my Lord's mynd att the time of the Chancellours' desertion did not a little aggravate the greefe of mynd wch lay upon my spirit . . .'[37]

Earlier that season, a ghost from the past reappeared in Scotland, ready to haunt the dreams of Archbishop Sharp. James Mitchell, the failed assassin, clearly believing himself safely forgotten, returned to Edinburgh. He had the singular misfortune to come too close to Sharp, and was promptly recognised and arrested. He was examined before the Privy Council on 12 March, making a free and voluntary confession of his part in the Pentland Rising, but denying that he had attempted to kill the Archbishop.[38] Only after he was given a promise that his life would be spared, apparently by Rothes, though the records do not say, did he make a full confession. When he subsequently appeared before the Justiciary Court he had thought the better of this, refusing to repeat his confession, though he was offered the same promise as before. The assurance was then declared void. It seems that the Council had no clear idea of what to do with him: he and his friends assumed that a trial was imminent; instead he was sent to prison, and seemingly forgotten. There he is likely to have remained but for a failed escape attempt in December 1675, which brought him once again to the attention of the authorities. Still uncertain what to do with him, and perhaps fearful of the implications of a public trial, the Council ordered that he be tortured to extract the former confession, though there is no evidence that this was ever carried out.[39] Mitchell was then sent to the Bass Rock in the Firth of Forth, the Devil's Island of the Covenanters, where some of the more prominent dissenters were kept. His fate was now dependent on political circumstances.

Mitchell was not the only man under examination in those years. Parliament reassembled in April 1675, in no better mood than it had been in the previous year. The Commons in particular were set on a fresh onslaught against Lauderdale, regardless of his English peerage. In Scotland the opposition took fresh heart from this, believing that his position was 'desperate and despicable'.[40] Within twenty-four hours of meeting the Commons had appointed a committee to formulate a demand for his dismissal. This time they were determined to ensure that their efforts did not miscarry, summoning Gilbert Burnet to appear before the House, as the source of the most damaging rumours against the Secretary.[41] It was only now that the clergyman realised that he had placed himself in an invidious position, a consequence of his gossiping and rumour-mongering. He did his best to squirm out of a profoundly uncomfortable situation, only making himself look treacherous and untrustworthy in the process. He was examined on two points: Lauderdale's supposed intention to use a Scottish army in England, and his declaration that he was prepared to bring Irish Catholics to Scotland to cut the throats of the dissenters. No one seemed to pick up on the simple point that the two charges were contradictory: if he had sufficient forces available to invade England he would hardly need to bring in outsiders, Irish or otherwise, to crush dissent. Examined first in committee Burnet 'begged pardon if he did not inform the committee about what passed in private conversation; there having been some difference between him and the duke, it might be thought done in revenge'.[42] In his own account he says: 'I desired to be excused, as to what had passed in private discourse, which I thought I was not bound to answer to, unless it were high treason'.[43] If the threat to invade the realm with an alien army could not be construed as high treason it would be difficult to know what could. Burnet was warned of the consequences of his obduracy and ordered to appear before the bar of the Commons.

Once again he tried to escape the moral dilemma his lack of discretion had placed him in, saying that the Duke was liable to say things in a temper that he did not really mean. Parliament was not having this. Under pressure he caved in, saying that he had never heard Lauderdale say that he intended to bring a Scottish army into England. What it amounted to was that Lauderdale had asked him in September 1673 if he thought Scotland would support the king in upholding the 1672 English Declaration of Indulgence: Burnet said it would not, Lauderdale said that it would. The whole thing was patently absurd: an off-the-cuff remark given the force of policy that was never in fact to be implemented. It was another of those statements of exaggerated loyalty to which the Secretary was prone, which Burnet confirmed in further testimony, reporting that Lauderdale believed that only he and Lord Clifford had stood firm to Charles over the Indulgence, while he was abandoned by all others. On this unsatisfactory note the session was adjourned.

Lauderdale seized the opportunity, ordering the immediate printing of a thousand copies of the dedication to him in A Vindication, written after the conversation of 1673, and which the clergyman subsequently tried to suppress. This document, with its effusive references to Lauderdale's 'nobility', 'illustrious quality', 'deep judgement' and the 'vast endowments' of his mind, had an immediate affect: no further use was to be made of so tainted a source.[44] Mackenzie notes the effect of Burnet's actions, without doubt the worst episode in his whole career: '. . . in an epistle dedicatory posterior thereto, magnified the Duke of Lauderdale as the chief pillar of the protestant religion, the odium designed against the Duke of Lauderdale returned to the author; whom the best of his friends acknowledged to have betrayed friendship, and all indifferent men concluded to have wronged truth'.[45]

Richard Baxter, Lauderdale's old friend, made his own observations: 'because Mr Burnet had lately magnified the said Duke in an epistle before a public book, many thought his witness now to be most unsavoury and revengeful'.[46] Years later Burnet attempted to defend his conduct, in a disingenuous way that still has the power to disarm and amuse:

> I have told the matter as it was, and must leave my self to the censure of the reader. My love to my country, and my private friendships carried me perhaps too far; especially since I had declared much against clergymen's meddling in secular affairs, and yet had run myself so deep in them. The truth is, I had been for above a year in a perpetual agitation, and was not calm nor cool enough to reflect on my conduct, as I ought to have done. I had lost much of a spirit of devotion and recollection and so it was no wonder if I committed grave errors.[47]

Parliament continued in its drive against Lauderdale, although the case against him lost much of its force. Some of the addresses against him were reduced to angry generalities, alleging that he intended to introduce popery and arbitrary power and that he had spoken with disdain against the Commons, saying, 'Let them address against him, and he would fart against them'.[48] In the formal request for his removal from government, Parliament mentioned the allegation that he had said that the king's edicts were equal to laws, and that he had intended to use a Scots army in England, though neither charge had been conclusively proved. Sir Joseph Williamson delivered Charles' response to the petition on 7 May, telling them that the Militia Act, the basis of their chief complaint, had been passed before Lauderdale became Commissioner, and that any other alleged misdemeanours had been wiped out by the last act of grace 'to wch ye Duke had as good title as anybody else'.[49] Thereafter the king took Lauderdale riding around Hyde Park in his own coach, in full public view, to the fury of the Commons 'they looking upon it as an indignitie put upon ym for ye king to honour yt person so signally whom they now complain of'.[50] Earlier, while the parliamentary session was in full swing, Prince Rupert had advised Lauderdale, perhaps recalling the case of Strafford, that it might be better to leave the court. He refused, confident in the support of the king, and confident also, it would seem, that between the England of the 1640s and the England of the 1670s there was a universe of difference: 'Indeed, the king did very much adhere to Lauderdaill, and put honour upon him above others of his nobility; and Lauderdaill well understood, that there was a great difference betwixt this parliament and that, these tymes and yonder tymes'.[51]

As so often in the past, once again manoeuvres against the Secretary rebounded to his advantage. In October Burnet told Hamilton that the Secretary was still in absolute favour with the king, an outcome to which he himself had made an important contribution: '. . . and thinks he has got over all his difficulties and is confidently given out that the party against him is almost quite broken and a few more vigorous proceedings will save all after which he will study a great mildness'.[52]

It would do no harm to let it be known that a milder policy would follow from the defeat of politically hostile cabals, as a way of separating moderate dissenters from Hamilton and the Party; but there is very little sign now of any degree of real restraint in the pursuit of official policy. In March 1676 a further proclamation was issued for the suppression of conventicles and requiring the indulged ministers to keep to the terms of their agreement, implying some at least had been slipping.[53] Action against non-conformity became quite as severe as anything pursued by Rothes prior to 1666. As so often in these cases the more severe the repression the more pronounced the dissent. Lauderdale's political credit was still high at court; but the gap between performance and achievement was to grow dangerously wide: Lauderdale's continuing success, in other words, was increasingly dependent on solving a problem that was steadily slipping out of control.

It was no longer, if indeed it ever was, a question of liberty of conscience; those who officiated at conventicles, Lauderdale believed, were political incendiaries rather than spiritual guides.[54] Dissenters were all the more dangerous because he also believed, with some justification, that some of them at least had links with Hamilton and the opposition, as Robert Law explains:

> Lauderdale, supposing that the Presbyterians in Scotland did more favour Duke Hamilton and his way than himself and his way, conceives prejudice against them, and marrs the extent of the indulgence which was intended. That was a great mistake, for nothing can be more certainly affirmed than that the indulged breathren did love the peace of the nation, and the peace of those two noble families, wishing peace to both. Howbeit, it cannot be denied but that there were some not indulged, who sought to fish in muddie waters.[55]

Non-conformity, when linked with effective political leadership, could conceivably give shape to the same kind of movement that created the 1648 Whiggamore Raid. In Lauderdale's mind political resistance was clearly linked with religious dissent. His attempt to deliver a hammer blow to both at once led in time to the most controversial move of his entire career.

Having won such a significant victory over the impeachment issue, it might have been possible – and advisable – to open some kind of overture to his Scottish opponents. A deep sense of mutual distrust seems to have precluded such a move. In December 1675 Hamilton was back at court, complaining of the activities of the Secretary, pleading for an extension of the indulgence, enough in itself to condemn such a concession: '. . . the truth is, the Duke of Lauderdaill being so great a favourite of the King, and haven taken such a dislyk at Duke Hamilton for the opposition he and his party made him in the last parliament, that there is nothing Duke Hamilton will be for but he will be against'.[56]

In a very real sense Scotland was being turned into a 'one-man' state. There were, however, definite weaknesses in the whole structure. From London the Secretary was hardly in a position to control the day-to-day operation of government. His standing with many of his fellow peers was undermined by the deep resentment caused by the corruption of Hatton. Lauderdale's brother was the Achilles Heel of his government, causing much trouble and bringing little benefit. He had no very high opinion of Hatton and his abilities, only making use of him in the absence of any acceptable alternative. In January 1676 Queensberry was moved to wish that the Duke and Duchess of Lauderdale were informed of his 'injustices and brutalities'. Queensberry goes on to complain to Hamilton that Hatton's 'rude way of business' had occasioned the Lauderdales more trouble and enemies than 'he and all the Maitlands on earth ar worth'.[57] He was also accused of entering into a partnership with the duchess, the two of them allegedly receiving bribes for granting legal and commercial favours. While the accusations against Elizabeth Murray were often based on rumour and innuendo, those against Hatton were real enough: he was eventually to be convicted of perjury and embezzlement.[58] It was by one of those odd historical paradoxes that in the two brothers the Maitland family reached its greatest height and descended to its worst depths; that the greatness of one was paralleled by the venality of the other.

Accusations of corruption also attached themselves to Lauderdale, although the evidence is not quite so definite. The business over the sale of the Leith fort to Edinburgh, his obvious self-interest in ending the trading privileges of the burghs, the awarding of monopolies to personal allies, and his arrangement for the crown to buy the Bass Rock from one of his friends are actions that would hardly conform to contemporary standards of good public service, though they were not all that unusual for the times; Lauderdale and his fellow ministers would all expect to make profits from public service. Yet Macaulay's later accusation that Ham House was built out of the 'plunder of Scotland and the bribes of France' is groundless.[59] In the late 1670s an official enquiry into Lauderdale's emoluments concluded that he had an annual income of £2,700, hardly excessive for such a key public figure.[60] Much of this was to be spent on improvements to Ham House and other Lauderdale properties, and to turning Thirlestane Castle into one of the most impressive buildings of Restoration Scotland.[61]

While at the height of his power and earthly glory Lauderdale received an Ecclesiastes-style warning from Richard Baxter, who retained a strong affection for his old intellectual companion, presuming to take on the mantle once worn by Robert Baillie:

> . . . God forbid that you should lose that in prosperity which you gained in adversity and that God who was near you in prison, should be put farre from you in a court. O my Lord, do I need to tell you that the

fashion of this world doth passe (and hastily passe) away, and that it is only God that must shortly be your peace and comfort, or you will be swallowed up in sorrow and despaire! Do I need tell you that all this glory will quickly set in the shadows of death and that all this sweetness will turn soure! And how little it will comfort a despairing soule to look back on prosperity, and how terrible it will be to look back on a life of covenant breaking and unfaithfulness to God![62]

Baxter details some of the wilder accusations against Lauderdale, including the assertion that he had pimped for Charles, but immediately describes them as 'base and odious slanders' to which 'I never gave the least beliefe myself'. In his fatherly advice Baxter tells him not just to look to the welfare of his soul, but also to beware, in essence, of the malice of his enemies. He had the courage, moreover, to defend his friend in private conversation and, more dangerously, by public gesture, dedicating a work published in 1673 to the duke at a time when his personal standing in England was weak and weakening.[63] It is interesting that even at the height of his alleged depravity Lauderdale was still able to attract the good reports of moderate dissenters like Baxter, Law and Kirkton.

In May 1677, a few weeks before Lauderdale set out on another visit to Scotland, Sir John Reresby attended a reception at Ham House, leaving an interesting account of his experience in his memoirs. He had a particularly revealing conversation with the Duchess of Lauderdale:

> I went to visit the Duke and Duchess of Lauderdale at their fine house at Ham. After dinner the duchess in her chamber entertained me with a long discourse on matters of state. She had been a beautiful woman and the supposed mistress of Oliver Cromwell, and was a woman of great parts. She and her duke, that was much governed by her, were entirely in my Lord Treasurer's [Danby] interest. She complained of the Duke's [James] adhering to Papists and fanatics . . . and she gave also the whole scheme of the state of Scotland at that day, which, her husband being Lord Commissioner, she had good reason to understand. But the Scots, being a mercenary people, when the Duke was sent afterwards into that kingdom, whatever was there before was then changed into another thing.[64]

Lauderdale came to Scotland in July, seemingly with the view that the time had come to moderate some of the more severe attacks on the non-conformists. There were to be some interesting developments that summer, perhaps indicative of his desire to increase his room for manoeuvre. The previous year his clerical allies on the Council had caused him some political embarrassment. James Kirkton had been recognised in Edinburgh by one Captain William Carstares, an unsavoury individual not beyond using his official commission as a basis for blackmail and extortion. He tried the same with Kirkton, who promptly shouted for help and escaped with the assistance of some local people. Carstares reported these men to the Council, and they were duly fined and ordered to produce the outlawed Kirkton.[65] Hamilton and his adherents were not slow to see an opportunity. Carstares was well known, having been reprimanded by the Council in 1675 for his thuggish behaviour. His behaviour now was an ideal occasion to attack the arbitrary and illegal nature of an administration that allowed such men to operate. Sharp, far keener to prosecute dissidents than address injustice, protested to Lauderdale. Hamilton, Kincardine and some others were duly purged from the Council. Quite apart from his personal hostility to Hamilton, Lauderdale had no choice but to condone the actions of Sharp. But with Hamilton now free of all association with official policy, he was in a far better position to pursue outright opposition. Action against dissent, moreover, was now dangerously close to free enterprise banditry. The time had come to offer some further concession as a way out of an uncomfortable deadlock.

No sooner was Lauderdale in Scotland than he opened fresh negotiations with the non-conformists, a strategy that endangered both the bishops and Hamilton: the bishops were fearful of a loss of power that a further indulgence would bring, and Hamilton was faced with a loss of influence. Sir John Lauder of Fountainhall tells an interesting story:

> It was politique of my Lord Lauderdale and his Duchess to render himselfe gracious and acceptable in the hearts of the people and regain his lost credit; which undoubtedly was likewayes a course that made him listen and give ear to ane indulgence and accommodation with the Presbyterians; for he was serious in it, and did it not merely to cajoll or guile them. The carrier of it was the President, Argyll, Melville, and Arniston, with James Stewart [a lawyer] and the ministers of that party, who were allowed freely to come to Edinburgh. They offered to raise 15,000 lib sterling presently for my Lord Lauderdale's service, and to contrive the elections, so that in a Parliament he should carry a subsidy, and the President got a ratification of what he pleased providing their indulgence was secured to them by an Act of Parliament, so that it might not be the nixt day recalled: all thir propositions my Lord Lauderdale greedily embraced; but when they came to explain the way they would effectuate all this, he could not comprehend it so weel, wheirupon it stood.[66]

Hamilton was kept informed of these negotiations, clearly believing that yet another rupture in policy was imminent; by September, however, it was evident that Lauderdale was acting entirely on his own, without any backing from the bishops. Unable to make headway with the Presbyterians, and temporarily alienated from the Episcopalians, he was soon forced to backtrack; by October Dr George Hickes, Lauderdale's Anglican chaplain, was reporting that the whole initiative had been no more than a malicious rumour intended to discredit his patron.[67] In October Lauderdale openly declared before the Council that no new indulgence had ever been intended.[68] The aim behind this initiative was in all probability quite sincere, and may have done much to strengthen the Secretary's position as the man who had solved the most intractable of Scotland's problems; its failure left him more isolated and with less freedom to manoeuvre than before. Hickes had not been fully aware of Lauderdale's thoughts in this matter. Now, most likely on his prompting, he wrote to a friend in England later that same month, clearly intending to limit any damage the rumoured indulgence had caused with the High Church party. He also revealed that policy in Scotland was now about to enter the politics of the last resort:

> . . . I formerly wrote you word how my Lord's enemies had reported all about this country, yt he intended an Indulgence for ye Whigs . . . The report was so general, yt I question not but it hath reached London, and here . . . [it was] blown about with so much confidence, yt ye clergy were universally discouraged about it, and ye Whigs themselves made so confident of it before ye last Counsell . . . that they boasted of it . . . This rumour was disseminated wth a designe to render my Lord suspect to ye Bishops and odious to ye clergy, and to encourage those bloody malcontent fanaticks to insolence and rebellion; and indeed since they see themselves disappointed in their expectations, they have threatened to make an insurrection (and are encouraged to it) insomuch as yt ye Counsell hath made provisional orders to have forces in readiness in case they should be so mad as to rise. I suppose you know yt ye country where these people most abound is in ye West about Glascow, Eyre [Ayr] etc. and upon their first motion several thousand Highlanders will be brought down upon them to cut ym off and quarter in their country.[69]

Lauderdale's failure with the dissenters was Hamilton's opportunity. Though he himself had been behind a campaign for a third indulgence, religious peace was far less important to Hamilton than discrediting his enemy: 'I am very glad that it is not in Lauderdale's power to medle with the Chancellor [Rothes], and I wish he may fixe his interests with such as former friends principles and friends be not deserted. However

I think iff right managed, ther is a fair oportunetie to try what can be done against Lauderdale for I suppose the bishops will not befriend him so much as formerly, els they ar strange kind of men'.[70]

Hamilton did not come to Lauderdale's door; Lauderdale came to his. Conventicling was increasing, the Party troublesome, and the bishops uneasy. In August legislation requiring all landlords to ensure that their tenants attended the authorised church was renewed. Ignored by the very people who were meant to enforce it, the law was ineffective, as had so often been the case. Lauderdale was now the absolute master of the Privy Council, the king having indicated that all state appointments were no longer for life but during the royal pleasure, which, in practice, meant the pleasure of the Secretary. In a position of unparalleled authority he decided on an extraordinary measure: the disaffected shires of the west would be treated as if they were already in a state of rebellion, or indeed as if the area were a foreign country, to be invaded and occupied. It was the beginning of what was to be known as the Highland Host. It was to be a double-edged sword, cutting first one way and then the other; decapitating dissent and political opposition with equal ruthlessness. Hamilton had hoped for Lauderdale's political embarrassment; Lauderdale now set out to show his enemy's incapacity.

All landlords, great and small, would be forced to face up to their obligation under the law in the clearest possible way. The best way of achieving this was to oblige them to sign bonds, promising to ensure that their immediate families, their dependants and all their tenants would neither attend conventicles nor harbour 'vagrant preachers'. The gentry of Ayrshire, headed by the Earl of Loudon, the son of the old Covenanter Chancellor, objected to this unusual way of proceeding, in effect saying that it was beyond their capacity to suppress disorder.[71] Instead they suggested an extension of the indulgence. It was all that Lauderdale needed. In Burnet's account he is said in the presence of his fellow Councillors to have bared his arm above the elbow and sworn by Jehovah that he would make them all enter into the bonds.[72] Charles was told that the conventicling movement threatened to erupt into a full-scale rebellion, with only 1,500 men in the regular forces to face perhaps as many as 10,000 Whigs – 'nor could his Majesty probably expect great assistance from the militia, which consists of commons much inclined to the opinion of the heritors [landlords] also inclined to the Party'.[73] This was a remarkable admission, confirming that the Acts of 1663 and 1669, which had caused Lauderdale so much political trouble in England, had completely failed in their intention of providing the king with an uncritically loyal force. Instead he was given the authority to supplement the small number of reliable militia units with

Highland auxiliaries. Permission was also given for forces to be mobilised in Ireland and northern England in case of need.[74]

By the autumn of 1677 a cloud of fear and apprehension lay over much of southern Scotland: in the west fear of the approaching Host, in the east fear of a Whig rising. Hamilton was told of the worrying stories the Earl of Nithsdale was spreading in the capital:

> Ther wes a great alarm att Edinburgh that the West was about rising in arms. The bishops bleu the coil, and Earl Nithsdale wes cheaff informer, for he said ther wer conventickels keapt consisting off over 3000, whereof 1000 als weall mounted and armed as any in the nation to his certain knouledge. Some others told that some gentlemens houses wer provyded with arms far abov the condition off pryvett fameleis; that in some wer 20 pair of pistols, 20 carbyns, besyd musquetts and fyerlocks. Bott the principall point wes moir considerable, which is, that within this year or thirby 7000 horses ar transported from Ireland: hitherto none can geit account of them bott that they ar in the hands off disaffected persons in the western and southern shyres.[75]

All of this suited Lauderdale, allowing him to justify militant action. It is not entirely clear if he believed himself that the west was really about to rebel – though he certainly conveyed this impression to George Hickes – or if he hoped to provoke such a rising, with the intention of crushing it all the more effectively, a view taken by Hamilton and his allies.[76] It was certainly the case that the Party had hoped to use Lauderdale's apparent inability to control religious dissent to demonstrate his incapacity to the king 'that his Majesty might have recourse to them as abler physicians of the state'.[77] The Host was a way of showing that he, and not the Party, was in control of events. In November he wrote explaining his actions to Danby, emphasising the danger of political sedition over that of religious dissent:

> How soon they may take armes no man can tell; for, as I have often said, they are perfectly fifth monarchye men [radical republicans], and no judgement can be made upon the grounds of reason what they may attempt; and therefore all preparations possible are to be made in case they rise, for this game is not to be played by halfes, we must take this opportunity to crush them, so as they may not trouble us any more in hast, or else we are to expect to be thus threatened by them nixt year.[78]

In December Charles gave permission for the Host to move to the west. The Marquis of Atholl, together with the earls of Perth, Caithness and Airlie were ordered to raise their tenants and rendezvous with militia units and regular forces at Stirling by mid-January 1678. In all under 8,000 troops were mustered, 750 horse and 7,224 foot, the largest force ever raised in Restoration Scotland, but far short of the grand army promised by the Militia Acts. Most of the men were Highlanders, drawn from the more settled parts of central and northern Perthshire, rather than from the wilder clans of Lochaber and the Isles; but they were still fearsome enough, if indifferently armed. Though some were Catholic and others Episcopalian, most had very little interest in the religious differences between them and their southern neighbours. Politically they hated the Whigs and Covenanters, who had become ancestral enemies to men whose fathers and grandfathers had served with Montrose; but by far the greatest motivation was the prospect the Host offered for wholesale – and licensed – plunder.

From conception to execution the Highland Host was Lauderdale's idea; the assumption that such an important – and dangerous – tactic was the work of the bishops is unsupported by any evidence; and the suggestion that the Secretary was the 'humble servant' of Sharp and Alexander Burnet and that he was being 'driven' by them is patently ludicrous.[79] It was a grand demonstration that would emphasise his superiority over the opposition, confirm his loyalty to the church and his control of Scotland. George Hickes was a close companion throughout these days, doing his best to counter the damaging rumours being spread against Lauderdale by Hamilton and Gilbert Burnet, telling his friends in England that if it was ever in his power he would introduce the Book of Common Prayer into Scotland, though this is almost certainly a wild exaggeration. With the Host about to march Hickes wrote to one of his Anglican friends, indicating Lauderdale's intentions and his advanced recognition of the uses the Party would make of his actions: 'There is no other way left to correct their [the dissenters] insolence, and bring them to a sober sense of their duty; and now they must be chastised for their impudence, they are much against the patriots of the faction, who made them believe they could protect them; and they on the other side know not what to say, but to cry out against arbitrary government and tell the people they will go to the King and remonstrate with his Majesty . . .'[80]

Anticipating such a move the Privy Council issued an order on 3 January, preventing anyone leaving Scotland without official permission. All was ready: in late January the Host marched, advancing through Glasgow onwards to Ayr like a great swarm of locusts, with orders to seize all weapons, and live free at the expense of the unfortunate Whigs. Landlords were required to sign the bond, promising to ensure that their tenants would keep the peace; otherwise they risked a visit from the Host. But it was the ordinary people of Ayrshire,

Lanarkshire and Galloway who suffered most from its attentions. Everything was taken, from livestock to pots and pans. Although the Highlanders stayed only a few weeks, leaving only the militia units and regular forces in place, they left the west as if they had been at the sack of a besieged city, weighed down with plunder.[81] The following year, when the Whigs finally did rise in rebellion, a *Declaration* was published protesting that 'all manner of outrages have been most arbitrarily exercised upon us through the tract of several years past; particularly in the year 1678 by sending among us an armed host of barbarous savages contrary to all law and humanity'.[82]

Apart from the wholesale looting, the Host caused much terror but little real harm; there were reports of beatings but none of murder and rape. Even so Lauderdale was clearly concerned that matters had got so far out of hand, which explains why the Highlanders were withdrawn at such an early stage. In a letter to Hamilton he had previously emphasised that all things would be done 'regularlie and legallie'.[83] In practice the conduct of the Host was neither regular nor legal. The fear that Highlanders might be used against dissent was a far greater political weapon than the reality; in firing this gun Lauderdale had lost all the psychological advantage. Any benefit gained was purely temporary, more than offset by the long-term political disturbance caused by the Host.

As a tactic the Highland Host was a failure. No sooner had it left then the people of the western shires began to re-arm, and field conventicles continued as vigorously as before. Lauderdale had reached for what proved to be just another short-term solution to a long-term problem, that did little more than demonstrate the military incapacity of the government: while the Highlanders looted the militia deserted, including men from Lauderdale's own Maitland Regiment. William Cleland, a 17-year-old student from St Andrews University, and an ardent Whig, later wrote a lengthy satire on the Host, part of which focuses on the conduct of Lauderdale:

> . . . Tho in patience he exceed
> Socrates, and all we read:
> If the King's credit be at stake
> Some course effectual he must take.
> It's like ye'll say, there's something lurking,
> That there is some other thing a working:
> Some Powder Plot, a strange contriving,
> Within his Grace's brain is hiving:
> But I declare, I know nothing
> Of his intentions or design;

Whatever some may vainly boast,
They know not what mov'd him to call this Host:
Yet doth his Grace it so conceal,
That he'll to no man it reveal . . .[84]

The Host was the one episode that was to define the nature of
Lauderdale's rule for his enemies in England, allowing Sir John
Oldmixon, the eighteenth-century Whig, to be carried away in a flood
of invective and hatred:

> These Russians and Robbers are all the while pretending zeal for
> Episcopacy, that they will extirpate the Presbyterians, if they cannot
> extirpate Presbytery. Can a sett of villans without morals, without
> principles sacred or civil, have any regard to religion? The brutality of
> the persecuting pagans equals not that of *Lauderdale*. The arbitrary
> acts of the governments of Morocco, or Moscow came not up to those
> in Scotland in the reign of Charles II, and in the ministry of that loathed
> and wretched *Lauderdale*, who is using all the damnable arts, to drive
> the Scotch protestants into rebellion, that he might afterwards murder
> and plunder them.[85]

In the circumstances Lauderdale's actions had been perfectly rational:
yet another attempt at accommodation had failed, dissenters were
becoming bolder, and the landlords and magistrates of the west were
effectively saying that they had lost control. Nevertheless, he had handed
his enemies an additional weapon that might be used against him: it's
almost as if he had deliberately given substance to some of the
accusations laid before the Commons in 1675, though the picture was
somewhat blurred, as if viewed through badly focused glasses, reality
and expectation not quite managing to meet. Most worryingly for him,
all the accusations of arbitrary power were soon to acquire a new
urgency by political developments in England. A stone had been thrown
into the pond; it would never be calm again.

13

SHADOWS

Hamilton and his allies did the one thing Lauderdale did not expect: in April 1678, in defiance of the Privy Council, they crossed the Border, making for London and the presence of the king.[1] The Party had been augmented by the defection of Atholl and Perth, supposedly disturbed by the irregularities they had witnessed in the west; but as both men had exercised on-the-spot command, any injustices or excesses were attributable directly to them, or to their inability to control their troops, rather than to Lauderdale. The truth would appear to be that they had expected far greater political benefits to flow from the exercise than proved to be the case, turning against their mentor out of frustrated ambition rather than principle.[2] By mid-April over sixty members of the Scots' nobility and gentry followed Hamilton to London, including the young Earl of Cassillis, the son of Lauderdale's old friend.[3] Charles would not receive any of them, but assigned some of the Council to receive their complaints in writing, which would, of course, have opened them to a charge of leasing-making. Lauderdale could continue to rely, at least for the time being, on the outward support of the king. Just the month before he had given his own views on the affair in an interview with the Earl of Arran:

> . . . he said it was a strange thing, that he had been tormented for several weeks, with horrible complaints of the cruelty and outrages done in the west of Scotland, yet he had done them faire play, for he had cause send down to Scotland as many complaints as he could gett; and that he had now received a full account of the whle proceedings in the west, and that it was from persons he wold trust, that he found it all to be false as hell, and that there was nothing done there but was done by law, and that things were not pushed so farr as the law allowed; that as he was a Christain he did not see what els could be done, to prevent open rebellion: that he approved of what was done . . . his majesty said he knew Scotland as well as any body, that he had been in it at the worst if times, that he was sure it was so farr from being unjust and severe to make gentlemen

answere for their tenants, that he knew it was the easiest thing in the world for them to doe it, that there was no nation or kingdome in the world, where his tenants had so great a dependance upon the gentlemen, as in Scotland, and he was glad it was so, and that therefore they must be answerable for their tenants . . .[4]

In a further interview with Richard Maitland, Lauderdale's nephew, he said that the dissidents in the west only used religion as a cover for political sedition, and that as the Indulgences had been rejected, only severity would do. It made no sense for the Scottish nobility to complain of this, or to create problems, for if there were a rebellion in Scotland it would soon spread to England 'and that England should turn common wealth, Scotland would be a province next summer after'.[5] Even so he did not send Hamilton and Cassillis back to Scotland for trial, as the Council had requested. This was particularly dangerous because the Cavalier Parliament was about to reassemble, with all the opportunities this would offer for mischief-making. Something grand was intended, as an anonymous letter from Amsterdam makes abundantly clear: 'The sum is: get out the great loon in Scotland, and perhaps none else can saddle or mount 'em for the King's service. If he cannot be impeached in Scotland you may do it at Westminster. The pitcher has two ears; if you cannot long hold on one side, take him by the other and dash him to the ground. Remember he is not only Lauderdale but Guilford too.'[6]

To compensate for the presence of the Party at Westminster, Lauderdale, preoccupied by business in Scotland, sent his own agents to London to manoeuvre on his behalf: Sir George Mackenzie of Roseheaugh, now Lord Advocate, Alexander Burnet and Alexander Stewart, Earl of Moray. They were well favoured by Charles, James and Danby, but the Hamiltonians had secured an important connection in James Scott, Duke of Monmouth, the king's much-loved bastard son. Monmouth was linked with Shaftesbury, which inevitably meant further trouble for the Secretary, especially with the coming of a new session of Parliament. A great many were prepared to believe the alarming rumours that what was happening in Scotland represented a new style of government that would soon extend to England.[7] In early April the Earl of Moray, almost as bad a speller as Rothes, alerted Lauderdale to the intrigues against him: 'As I am urytinge this my Lord Maenrd and Lord Arlingetoune caem to me and after compareing nots uee ffynd all the paerty hear very basic tamperinge uithe and misinforminge the members of the House of Commons, all shall be done that possibly can be to undeseave them of thos malicious aspersions forged and spread abroad by them.[8]

Things did not always go the way Hamilton wished for. In the royal council, Heneage Finch, the Earl of Nottingham, challenged some of his assumptions about the alleged injustice of the bond. Nottingham had enough understanding of Scottish politics and history to point out that Highland chiefs had long been subject to a similar procedure, obliged to sign pledges for the good behaviour of their tenants and dependants.[9] The opposition responded by saying that the circumstances were quite different, and that bonds in the Highlands were intended as a measure against depredation and murder, and that it was unheard of to oblige any man to stand bond for others in matters of religion and conscience. This was revealing: not only was the Party seemingly criticising the whole basis of Restoration policy in the matter of church government, but it also showed its failure to understand the simple truth behind Lauderdale's bond: they were not being asked to police the conscience of others, merely to ensure their good behaviour.

For some weeks this cat-and-mouse game was played around Whitehall, sometimes one side gaining the advantage, sometimes the other. Clearly getting nowhere with the king, who continued to give his open support to the policies that led to the Highland Host, Hamilton eventually descended from the heights of principle to the depths of personal dissatisfaction, moaning that he had lost some horses and that he had been forbidden to wear a sword, causing James, Duke of York, to call to mind an old Scottish proverb: 'Meikill dine and littill dirdume' – lots of noise and little substance.[10] Elizabeth Murray, who had been unsettled by the continuing attacks upon her husband, had the comfort of a letter of personal support from Margaret Leslie, Countess of Wemyss, Rothes' sister:

I am very curious to know your grace thoughts of what may be the importance of this strange motion that many of our grandees are in, I doe represent it to myself as a contrivance wher in I doe not know whither ther be mor of malice and ill nature, or follie and precipitance; ther appears much of ill nature in it, that to act their hatred and furie, they have laid hold of a season wherin his majestie is incumbered with multitude and perplexity of great affairs, which they think to profite by, in bringing his majestie under ane apprehension of the great confusion and disorder that is in Scotland and so of a necessitie to grant ther desire, and that this may appear the more probable they have set up, without leave, and contrair to his majesties order, a great number of ther partie all of them persons of little or no experience in the world and of violent and boisterous passions to mak the greater noyce and clamour, which will mak itt the greater that they are all for the most part persons of qualitie in this nation. This I doe think is the venome of ther desyn bot in my poor judgement it is so foolishlie contrived and managed that it is impossible it can tak any affect, becaws ther is not any thing that can give so much as the least shadow or pretext to hyd ther wreth and discontent which so palpalle shews itself throw ther whole affair (which yet above all things they should have kept hid) that it is open to every eye, and will I am confident crush all ther projects.[11]

Parliament offered the Party one last hope. Soon after the session opened on 29 April Lauderdale was yet again identified as a suitable case for treatment. One assault followed hard upon another: he 'grew fat upon the displeasure of the House of Commons', was 'a man of no morality', a man whose crimes 'exceed others as much as the bigness of his person'.[12] Sir John Hotham reached quickly into the heart of the debate, touching on the fears of the House in a wonderfully exaggerated fashion: 'Is any man desirous to have these counsels here. In Scotland, if any man looks but discontented, they kill him, shoot him, eat him up! Will you have him do the same thing here?'[13] In the face of this rhetoric some were bold enough to rise to the Secretary's defence, reminding the House, still deeply conservative in its religious views, of its own actions against conventicles in England. It was not proper, Sir John Ernele said, for the House to involve itself in the affairs of Scotland:

> . . . but on the contray they ought to applaud what was done lately there, it having been to suppress the insolencies of the conventiclers, whose irregular courses are equally condemned by the law of England as by that of Scotland, and that if they would insist in those enquiries the reports there of goeing into Scotland, would so blow up the opinions of the phanaticks that, as they would easily be persuaded to beeleive that the parliament sits for no other purpose than to promote their interests (which would soon procure an open rebellion) . . .[14]

At the conclusion of the debate the motion against Lauderdale was lost by a single vote.[15] Charles, furious at the whole proceeding, lost his composure, a thing he almost never did: 'the Kinge hes not at any tyme bene observed in such a passion; his countinans became paell and he shouke uithe eagerness'.[16] Moray could not let such an occasion pass away: Charles was reminded of the unsettling effect of the Party in London, and of the incendiary activities of Gilbert Burnet, acting more as a political agent than a clergyman. Hamilton and his friends were badly discomfited by yet another failure. They had a frosty audience with the king towards the end of May, where he said that he would not countenance any of their complaints unless they were put in writing and signed, which of course they would not do: 'since they refused to signe hee lookt upon those stories as spok at randome'.[17] In a previous conversation with Danby, Hamilton had apparently told him that he would never return to Scotland to live in such slavery 'bot wold as lief goe to Turkey'.[18] By the early summer he had clearly thought the better of this, deciding to return home after all; for another opportunity had arisen.

To pay for the expenses of the Highland Host in particular, and national security in general, Lauderdale had obtained permission to summon a Convention. It was a clever move: strictly speaking the Convention, though a Parliament in all but name, could only vote on money issues; but it was an occasion Hamilton could not ignore, clearly believing that it offered a fresh occasion to attack the Lauderdale administration.[19] In June he was drawn away from the dangerous hothouse of London politics back to Edinburgh; Lauderdale had made sure that the ground was prepared for his reception, setting the scene for what was to be his last political triumph. The Duchess of Lauderdale was glad to see Hamilton go, celebrating his departure from England and warning of his coming to Scotland in a letter to the Earl of Linlithgow, raising questions about his loyalty to his native land:

> D[uke] H[amilton] tooke leave of their majesties yesterday [23 June]. He hes had no reason to boast of his usage. Hee maks many complaints to all sorts of people, and by divers hee is better liked, by reason that from him, and that party, they are made to believe, that they are ready to bring Scotland under the subjection of England. The truth is, their carriage is most detestable to all honest and sober men, but the longing desire of such a conquest as would be the cantonising of Scotland, maks them respected by only thos, who will be the most ready for them so soon as they shall have no more use of them. Iff ye but hear how unworthily they doo lay open the poverty of their owne nation, what contemptable caracters they give of all the persons of quality who are not of their party, both as to their several interests, and as to their abilitys, ye would admire att their impudence above all things; and yet that is not so dangerous as the confident reports they cause to be spread, both by themselves, and all their emisaryes of a rebellion, and the impossibility of hindering itt by reason of the tirany all Scotland does lye under. Yr Lordship will conclude, that as it is the concern of all men, so it is of the greatest importance to thos upon whom ye King hes now cast the weighty management of his affaires, not to lett it fall in their hands, nor leave any honest cours untried that may defeat the common enimy, secure to his majesty that peace which this unworthy party have, and done so much endeavour to obstruct.[20]

Dysart, as always, with too high a public and political profile to escape her husband's enemies, continued to be a target for satirists, a particularly scurrilous example of their art making an appearance in Scotland sometime in the course of 1678, under the title *A Litany*:

> From a King without money, and a court full of
>   Whores
> From an injured Parliament turned out of doors,
> From the Highlands set lowse on our countrie boors.
> *Libera nos, Dominae.*
>
> From this huffing Hector [Lauderdale] and his Queen of Love,
> From all his blank letters sent from above,
> From a Parliamentarie Council that doth rage and
>   Rave
> *Libera nos, Dominae.*
>
> From old Noll's whore [Dysart] to govern our land,
> From her bastards innumerable as the sea-sand,
> From her pyking our pockets by way of a band
> *Libera nos, Dominae.*[21]

The Highland Host is the one great event that will forever define the politics of 1678; the other is the trial of James Mitchell, where personal tragedy acquired national significance. In October 1677 the decision was finally taken to bring Mitchell to trial the following January. The timing of this is fairly significant: it was decided on in the same month as the Highland Host, suggesting a closer connection than mere chance. It is almost certain that Lauderdale was seeking to use the trial as part of the wider game of psychological warfare, intending to terrorise the dissidents into submission.[22] As a tactic it was to prove to be especially inept, turning the wretched Mitchell into a kind of proto-martyr. Sir George Mackenzie, in his role as Lord Advocate, conducted the prosecution, appearing before Sir Archibald Primrose, the Lord Justice General. Mitchell was defended by Sir George Lockhart, Mackenzie's old enemy, which presumably helped to give the whole proceeding an added bitterness. When asked to explain his attempt on the life of the Archbishop Mitchell said, 'I looked upon him to be the main instigator of all the oppression and bloodshed of my brethren . . . and the continued pursuing after my own'.[23] As a trial the Mitchell affair is unique in Scottish, or indeed the whole of British criminal law: for the panel of witnesses was the greatest ever cited in such a case.[24] Alongside Lauderdale was Rothes, the Lord Chancellor, the Archbishop of St Andrews and Charles Maitland, Depute Treasurer. The only evidence against Mitchell was the confession of 1674, which had only been made, as the defence argued, on the promise that his life would be spared. Lauderdale and the other witnesses all denied that such an assurance had ever been given.[25] Lockhart asked that the relevant council register be brought into court, which immediately brought Lauderdale to his feet, in defiance of all convention: 'Duke Lauderdale, who was in court only as a witness, and so had no right to speak, stood up, and said, he hoped that he and those other noble persons were not brought thither to be accused of perjury; and added that the books of the council were the king's secrets, and that no court should have the perusing of them. The court was terrified of this, and divided in opinion'.[26]

Mitchell was duly found guilty of a capital crime by his own confession, and as no satisfactory proof was produced that he had ever received a promise of life, he was condemned to die. In Burnet's account, based on a conversation he had with Primrose, Lauderdale is said to have discovered, after sentence had been passed, that Mitchell had in fact been told that his life would be spared, and therefore proposed to ask the king to grant a reprieve. Sharp, fearing that such a move would mean an open season on the lives of archbishops, objected, whereupon Lauderdale conceded, saying that Mitchell should 'glorify God in the Grassmarket', the traditional place for the execution of ordinary criminals, just outside the Edinburgh city walls.[27] We have to treat this story with some care: Burnet is uniformly hostile to Sharp, consistently depicting him as a supine and cowardly figure, recording absolutely nothing in his favour. Moreover, if Mitchell were suddenly reprieved it would have been a serious embarrassment to the government at a time when the Highland Host was making ready to march. Nevertheless, both Burnet and Primrose were prominent among Lauderdale's political opponents, unlikely to wish to put a favourable interpretation on any of his actions, so the story is worth some qualified acceptance. For Lauderdale Mitchell's death was probably little more than an act of political necessity, regardless of the wider moral issues involved. It was a mistake: Mitchell was a pathetic figure, a murderous fanatic best forgotten, whose execution on 18 January made him, in Burnet's words, 'more pitied than could be imagined'. Sir John Lauder of Fountainhall wrote the best epitaph of the whole affair: 'And thus they hunted this poor man to his death; a prey not worthy of so much pains, troubles and oblique as they incurred by it; and some of their own friends and well wishers desired they had never dipt in it, but only keipt him in perpetual imprisonment; for it made a wonderful noice in the country, who generally believed the law was stretched to get his neck stretched . . .'[28]

Hatton was later tried for perjury, though this was less out of a desire for justice than part of a general attack upon him by his many political enemies, at a time when he was particularly vulnerable, no longer able to rely on the support of his brother. No action was ever contemplated against Lauderdale or against Rothes, who, of all the men involved, was seemingly the most culpable, allegedly being the first to promise Mitchell that he would not be executed if he confessed to the assassination attempt.

The Edinburgh Convention opened in late June with a high sense of expectation. Hamilton and the Party were all there ready to make as much trouble as possible. The population of Edinburgh swelled rapidly; people came from all parts of the country with a sense of excitement and anticipation: 'Many people expected some tumult and blushing att this convention: wherefore on purpose they flock in to Edinburgh fra all quarters and airts of the Kingdom, with their arms and weapons about them, expecting either to do or to see some thing done.'[29]

For Lauderdale, who had done his best to manage the whole occasion, public order was now a serious worry. Having once promised Charles a loyal citizen army, and having suffered such trouble for making this promise, he was now confronted by a simple irony: 'There is not one regiment of all the militia of Scotland that the Commissioner puts trust in, for, to tell the truth, he has no reason.'[30] He requested that the magistrates allow regular forces into Edinburgh, meeting with a courageous refusal 'it not being their custom to suffer any soldiers within the city'.[31] He was assured that the city militia would be enough to guarantee order, a promise that was faithfully kept. Just before the Convention opened Lauderdale tried to reach an understanding with Hamilton, with no success. Hamilton was out to cause trouble; Lauderdale made sure that he had almost no opportunity. The elections had been well managed, ensuring an overwhelming support for the government; even Sir George Mackenzie of Tarbet, on the threshold of rehabilitation after so many years in the political wilderness, came to support the Commissioner. Unable to challenge the main business of the Convention, and thus appear disloyal to the king, Hamilton and his few supporters were reduced to technicalities, raising objections over disputed elections and other procedural issues. It made little difference: the Convention was a political and personal triumph for Lauderdale, voting £150,000 in a land tax, to be spread over five years. All the heightened expectations of the opposition were drowned in a sense of anti-climax.

In July the Convention concluded business by sending a formal report to the king, commending Lauderdale and making oblique references to contemporary political disputes in both Scotland and England. Charles was assured that 'though factious and humorous persons may seduce some in this Nation to depart from their dutie, yet there is generallie so much innate national and unalterable kindness and duty in the hearts of the subjects'.[32] The members then took a clear swipe at their English cousins, saying that supply had been voted 'without prying into forreigne misteries (qch are the proper impolyment of Princes).' Matters could not have been concluded more effectively: it's almost as if the whole body were seeing with Lauderdale's eyes and speaking with his tongue. He received early congratulations from James, Duke of York: '. . . the ill people here had great hops of sturs where you are, and I believe some of our neighbours did build upon it also, and I hope it will also have this other good effect, that it will strengthen his Majestie in the resolution he has taken of sticking to himself and those that he employs in his service, especially such as have served him so well as you have done'.[33]

While proceedings were underway the English authorities had been kept advised by one Matthew Mackaile, who had a particularly good understanding of some of the main political issues. In a report of 19 June he identifies three parties in Scotland: first the Episcopal and Court interest, represented by Lauderdale; second the party of Liberty and Privilege, represented by Hamilton, third the party of Religion and Presbytery, still waiting for an effective political lead.[34] Mackaile contends that the line between the second and third parties was very thin, that they are divided in appearance only, the one only too ready to join with the other in rebellion. The bond had been designed to oblige all those who pretend for Liberty and Privilege to persecute all those who pretend for Religion and Presbytery, thus reducing the possibility of a common association, which was almost certainly the intention of Lauderdale and the Court.

The potential for political upheaval in Scotland that summer was very great. Nothing happened, precisely because the line between the second and third parties was far greater than Mackaile – and Lauderdale – allowed. Hamilton was a place-seeker not a revolutionary; he was never to be the kind of man who could reach from conventions and parliaments into the street; Scotland was not England and Hamilton was not Shaftesbury. His dispute with Lauderdale came in the end to one simple truth: 'they striving only who should be most in power'.[35] Mackaile's reports proceed with an unconscious humour, or a finely balanced sense of irony; it is not always clear which. He writes to Sir John Frederick that Lauderdale is 'much wearied of the trouble in this Kingdom', going on to observe that 'no doubt among other undutiful lies, some will write to London that this nation is all wearied of his trouble and with much more reason'.[36] As for the relationship between the two dukes, they were so anxious to avoid one another that they gave the appearance of being two buckets in a well: 'When one goes, the other comes.'

Not many weeks after the Convention ended a huge conventicle took place near Maybole in Ayrshire, giving added force to the need for additional security. More than 10,000 people are reported to have gathered to hear John Welsh and other outed ministers preach up 'the Solemn League and Covenant, and the lawfulness, conveniency, and necessity, of defensive arms . . . '[37] Oddly enough, although there were plenty prepared to denounce Lauderdale, some of the dissidents persisted in the illusion that he secretly favoured their cause, at least according to a report lodged by Mackaile in late October:

> . . . and so he weakens that party by a sub-division of his own making. He extended, when he was here, an act of indulgence to one of the Presbyterian ministers, Anthony Murray, by installing him in a public congregation. This he did in the face of the clergy, who durst not gainsay him, and the policy he follows is the point of absolute supremacy in his Majesty's person and he values the presbytery, when it comes in competition with that point, and, I believe, will live and die in this opinion.[38]

Two things were clear: the Highland Host had completely failed in its intention of crushing dissent by intimidation alone, and Lauderdale was now committed to a course of militant repression, likely to be no more successful in the end than that previously followed by Rothes and Sharp. Worst of all, and despite his success at the Convention, he was beginning to lose his political grip. Earlier in June Charles had written to him, beginning with the usual bland assurances and commendations, but then going on to suspend the taking of bonds and telling the Secretary to treat Hamilton with greater consideration in future. For a man who had things going his way for so long, it had a shocking and unsettling impact; it marks the beginning of the end of the whole Lauderdale system. In a mood of deep depression he gave orders, subsequently carried out, that the letter be hung around his neck and buried with him after death.[39] In August he finally left for London, never to return to his native country in life.

Back at Ham House Lauderdale was still in power, but no longer quite as unassailable as he had been. It was an open question now how long he could expect to enjoy the king's uncritical support, or if he would survive another attack by Parliament. He was now sixty-two years old and visibly failing in health. The strain of so many years in public life was having a telling effect, especially on his temperament. Elizabeth Murray was even moved to confide in Rothes about her husband's huffing and ranting, and 'cries when she speaks of my Lord's infirmity of falling into passions'.[40] The problem got steadily worse: 'he flies out often into such indecent fits of rage some think his head is affected'.[41] For the time being, however, he was able to enjoy a temporary rest between storms in the security of Ham House. That same August he received a visit from John Evelyn, who left a charming description of Ham in the days of the Lauderdales in his *Diary*: 'After dinner I walked to Ham to see the house and garden of the Duke of Lauderdale, which is indeed inferior to few of the best villas in Italy itself; the house furnished like a great Prince's; the parterres, flower-gardens, orangeries, grove avenues, courts, statues, perspectives, of fountains, aviaries and all this at the banks of the sweetest river in the world, must seek to be admirable'.[42]

The sun shone for all too brief a time. Also in August Charles met a half-mad clergyman by the name of Israel Tongue, who told him that the Jesuits were planning to assassinate both him and Ormonde, prior to raising a rebellion in all three kingdoms with the support of the French. The whole idea was patently ludicrous, and the king was inclined to treat it as such, though he referred the matter to Danby and the Privy Council for investigation. Tongue subsequently introduced his chief informant to the Council, a man by the name of Titus Oates, possibly one of the most unsavoury characters in the whole of English history. Oates, far more persuasive than Tongue, was able to give the weight of apparent substance to speculation and rumour. A fire took hold, spreading rapidly across the country: it was the beginning of a great moral panic that in time was to be known as 'the Popish Plot'. Charles lost control; Parliament seized the initiative. Moving through fine degrees the Plot eventually settled on its central theme: the Catholics planned to kill Charles and replace him with James. It was the chance that many had been waiting for, especially Shaftesbury, who loathed James both as a recusant and as a man. Soon he and his supporters were arguing that James should be excluded altogether from the succession. But the Plot offered something more than an opportunity to get rid of James: it gave renewed focus to years of mistrust over royal policy, at home and abroad. The Restoration government was about to be dissected, limb-by-limb. Danby, though a committed Protestant, was to be one of the early targets, attacked because of his secret treaty negotiations with the French. In the spring of 1679, threatened with impeachment, he was sent to the Tower. Now, of the great ministers of state, only Lauderdale remained.

When lifted clear of the hysteria of the streets, the Popish Plot was far more than yet another onslaught on a vulnerable minority. Shaftesbury and his principal associates' dislike of Catholicism extended well beyond simple confessional differences: in their minds it was associated with political absolutism, best represented by the France of Louis XIV, and thus a threat to basic English liberties. This attitude was best summed up by Sir Henry Capel in the Commons debate of 27 April 1679: 'From popery came the notion of a standing army and arbitrary power . . . Formerly the crown of Spain, and now France supports this root of popery among us; but lay popery flat, and there's an end of arbitrary government and power. It is a mere chimera or notion without popery.'[43] This association of popery and arbitrary government called a far more immediate figure than Louis XIV to mind. If the major target of the Popish Plot was James and Catholicism, the minor target was Lauderdale and Arbitrary Government. Briefed by Hamilton, Shaftesbury rose to his feet in March 1679, mounting a direct offensive:

> Popery and slavery, like two sisters go hand in hand; sometimes one goes first, and sometimes the other, in a door; but the other is always following close at hand. In England popery was to have brought in slavery; in Scotland, slavery before, and popery to follow . . . Scotland has outdone all the eastern and southern countries, in having their lives liberties and estates sequestered to the will and pleasure of those that govern. They have lately plundered and harassed the richest and wealthiest counties of that kingdom, and brought down barbarous Highlanders to devour them . . .[44]

Shaftesbury was in a uniquely powerful position. Earlier that year the king had dissolved the Cavalier Parliament, which had sat for so many years; but its going brought him little relief. Many in the new House of Commons backed Shaftesbury, both in his demands for exclusion and his attack on Lauderdale. In time Shaftesbury and his allies, loosely known as the 'country party', to distinguish them from the 'court party', were to be given a new name by their enemies – the Whigs – after the extreme Covenanters. There was, of course, not the slightest connection between the two, but the name persisted, becoming one of the first great political badges of British history. Something of the character of the restless little nobleman, one of the greatest politicians of his day, was later captured in John Dryden's brilliant satire *Absolom and Achitophel*:

> Of these false Achitophel was first:
> A name to all succeeding ages curst.

For close designs, and counsels fit;
Sagacious, bold, turbulent of wit:
Restless, unfixt in principles and place;
In power unpleased, impatient in disgrace.
A fiery sole, which working out its way,
Fretted the pigmy-body to decay:
And o'r informed the tenement of clay.
A daring pilot in extremity;
Pleased with danger, when the waves went high
He sought the storms; but for calm unfit,
Would steer to nigh the sands, to boast his wit.
Great wits are sure to madness near allied:
And thin partitions do their bonds divide:
Ere, why should he, with wealth and honour blest,
Refuse his age the needful hour of rest?
Punish a body which he could not please;
Bankrupt of life, yet prodigal of ease? . . .
In friendship false, implacable in hate:
Resolved to ruin or to rule the state.[45]

The Scottish opposition now knew whom to approach, even sending the English nobleman a list of names of those who would take office in the political purge that would follow from the anticipated fall of Lauderdale.[46] The hysteria spread beyond Parliament, as Evelyn noted: 'Now were those papers, speeches, and libels, publicly cried in the streets against the Dukes of York and Lauderdale, etc., obnoxious to the Parliament, with too much, indeed too shameful a liberty: but the people and parliament had gotten head by reason of the vices of the great ones.'[47]

Lauderdale seems to have remained remarkably calm throughout this whole crisis, remaining in London, while York was sent to Brussels both for his own safety and to get him out of the public eye. Charles continued to stand by the beleaguered minister, who, unlike Danby, had a power beyond the ken and the competence of the English Parliament. He could not be protected, however, from the poets, who included Andrew Marvell, the MP for Hull:

This haughty Monster with his ugly claws
First tempered poison to destroy our lawes,
Declares the Councel Edicts are beyond
The most authentic Statutes of the Land,
Sets up in Scotland alamode de France,
Taxes, Excise and Armyes dos advance.

> This Saracen his Countrey's freedom broke
> To bring upon our Necks the heavier yoke:
> This is the Savage Pimp without dispute
> First brought his mother for a Prostitute:
> Of all the Miscreants ever went to hell
> This Villin Rampant bares away the bell.[48]

Lauderdale's enemies tried hard to associate him with Catholicism.[49] As a strategy this was never able to make very much progress, as there was no proof that he had ever shown any sympathy for Catholics, and the laws against them in Scotland were just as severe as those in the rest of the United Kingdom. Parliament was more convinced when it came towards his alleged contempt for the English constitution, outlined in a pamphlet of 1679: 'He hath upon all occasions spoken of the House of Commons and their Magna Carta with the greatest contempt calling the latter magna farta . . . and usually said if they would address against him he would fart against them . . . '[50] Despite all, Charles continued to ignore the motions against the Secretary, able to defend him far more effectively than he had defended York or Danby: 'but as things grew worse and necessities increase this last point must change'.[51] In early May things grew worse: Archbishop Sharp was pulled from his coach and murdered on his way back to St Andrews. In the intense, sultry heat of Scottish politics it was like a sudden flash of lightning.

Since the beginning of 1679 the attitude of the Covenanter underground was becoming ever more threatening. In one particularly notorious case a group of twenty armed men attacked Major Johnston of the Edinburgh city guard, threatening to kill him if he took any further action against conventicles. He refused and was badly wounded. But by far the most serious incident to date took place at Lesmahagow in Clydesdale on Sunday 30 March, when a company of dragoons under one Lieutenant Dalzell intercepted a large body of armed Whigs. The Earl of Livingston, the commander-in-chief in Scotland, reported the outcome to Lauderdale: 'When they perceived the dragoons (who were but fourteen with their officer) the whiggs formally drew up in a party of eighty foot and advanced. The rest designed to surround the dragoons, whereupon the officer of the dragoons required ym in the King's name to dissipate; whereupon the commander of the whiggs horse answered disdainfully, Farts in the King's teeth, the Counsels and all that hes sent you, for wee appear here for the king of Heaven . . .'[52] In the scuffle that followed Dalzell was wounded and seven of his men captured, while the rest made off. This incident was followed by the murder of some soldiers at Newmilns in Ayrshire on 20 April.

John Graham of Claverhouse, a dragoon commander, wrote to Linlithgow after this, warning that an armed rebellion was being planned. There is very little evidence for this assertion. The situation, rather, was very much like that of 1666. Discontent was once again reaching a peak and government forces were badly overstretched. To patrol the whole of the south-west Claverhouse and his colleague, Lord Ross, had only 500 troopers between them. Any small incident was likely to grow quickly out of control.

By the time news of Sharp's murder reached Edinburgh some of the assassins were making their way to the west. The Privy Council at once issued a Hue and Cry, with the names of the assassins printed in red. A reward of 10,000 merks was offered for their capture, and the deed was associated with conventiclers, on the basis of prejudice rather than evidence. It is certainly true, though, that a mood of political fanaticism was growing among some of the lay Covenanters, though it had little support from the ministry. Sir Robert Hamilton, a nephew of Gilbert Burnet, was the most prominent among the zealots, believing, amongst other things, that the assassination of apostates like Sharp was justified. Burnet had little time for his nephew, whom he described as 'a crack brained enthusiast' and 'an ignominious coward'. But the union of Hamilton with David Hackston and John Balfour of Burleigh, two of Sharp's murderers, was the signal for a new rebellion.

All three men came to Glasgow to meet Donald Cargill, one of the more extreme ministers, to agree a manifesto. On 29 May, the king's birthday and the anniversary of the Restoration, a party of men rode into Rutherglen near Glasgow and promptly extinguished the celebratory bonfires. They then forced the magistrates to accompany them to the market cross, where Hamilton read out the manifesto, denouncing episcopacy, the rejection of the Covenants, the outing of the ministers, the imposition of Restoration Day, royal supremacy and the Indulgences, just about everything associated with the government since 1660. The document was then fixed to the cross, and all copies of the official statutes burned.

For the Council, still hunting for the murderers of Sharp, the Rutherglen Manifesto was a declaration of war. Claverhouse was ordered to join Lord Ross in Glasgow. Yet, despite all the warnings, the threat was still seriously underestimated. On the last day of May Claverhouse rode out of Glasgow in pursuit of Hamilton and the others with only 150 troopers, the rest staying behind with Ross. Early on the morning of 1 June he came across a large body of conventiclers, many armed, at a place called Drumclog close to Loudon Hill in Ayrshire. Not bothering to wait for reinforcements, and misjudging the whole situation, Claverhouse attacked, only to see his unit badly cut up by the rebels, protected by a bog. Drumclog was a skirmish, and not a particularly large one, rather than a serious battle; but it had an effect well beyond its proportions. Here was the sign of divine favour that many had waited on for so long. Soon hundreds were on the march from all over the region to join the victorious rebels, far more than had come out in 1666. Glasgow had to be abandoned in the face of the Whig army, now 7,000-strong. As Claverhouse and Ross retreated to Stirling, the rebels made camp at Bothwell on the west bank of the Clyde.

By early June reports of the rising had reached London, accompanied by the usual rumours and exaggerations, helping to stimulate a sense of panic: there were, it was said, 18– to 20,000 rebels in arms; the militia had gone over to them and the regular forces were considering retreating to Leith for safety.[53] That sense of panic seems to have echoed down the ages, with one twentieth-century historian claiming that the events in Scotland were 'ominously reminiscent' of the time of the Bishops' Wars.[54] They were not. The rebels had no aristocratic support; none of the opponents of Lauderdale made any attempt to speak for or assist the rebels in any way. It was not 1639; larger and more significant it may have been, but it was still only a reprise of 1666. Lauderdale had an early appreciation of this, countering the panicky rumours with sober intelligence that the rebel numbers were fluctuating, and that they were ill disciplined.[55]

For Lauderdale the political situation in London was far more dangerous than the military situation in Scotland. His enemies argued that the rising was evidence of his incapacity. It was an ideal opportunity for Hamilton, who had been at court for some weeks, in pursuit of his unrelenting campaign against his enemy. The rebellion seemed to give added credence to his complaints of misgovernment. It was all the more dangerous as Charles had admitted Shaftesbury to the Privy Council, in a vain attempt to head off some of the excesses of the Popish Plot; Shafterbury simply used the appointment to advance his own position. Lauderdale was openly attacked in Council, and his removal urged on the king.[56] Hamilton, in contact with Shaftesbury and Monmouth, his close protégé, was preening himself as a kind of Scottish Achilles, deprived of his just rewards, as he told Henry Sidney: '. . . that he would be hanged if he had not suppressed it [the rebellion] with two or three troops of horse; but he had been kept under for so long, and so ill used, that he begun to be out of heart, he having been put out of all employment, and never receiving a shilling of the King's money; whilst my Lord Lauderdale hath £12,000 from the King'.[57]

Charles refused to surrender to the pressure, maintaining Lauderdale in face of all. It is almost certain, though, that he was beginning to see his once formidable Secretary as a political embarrassment, especially as his personal faculties were no longer quite so acute, and Scotland was so obviously no longer under his complete control; but it is equally true that he was not giving in to Shaftesbury and risking an overhaul of Scottish government at such a sensitive time. As far as he was concerned the complaints of Hamilton and the Party were expressive only of generalities, lacking in substantive detail: 'They [the opposition] propose the new modelling of the whole council there, upon whom and their ill conduct they seem to lay blame of this insurrection, and though they aim at my Lord Lauderdale, yet they neither name nor describe him. His Majesty's answer was that to comply with their proposition was to overthrow the government of that kingdom, and though they complain of exorbitant grievances, yet they make out none.'[58]

Charles looked for government by results, and if anyone but the ambitious, shallow and self-seeking Hamilton had been ready to take his place, it is quite possible that Lauderdale would have been removed at an early stage. But having survived the Council debates the Secretary was immediately faced with a new threat: Charles decided to send Monmouth, his son, to deal with the crisis, with powers akin to a plenipotentiary, allowing him to deal with the military and political situations as he saw fit. It was an unwelcome development for the Secretary, whose powers, however temporarily, had been completely eclipsed for the first time in many years. Intellectually Monmouth was a lightweight; but his association with Shaftesbury, with whom he tended to side in Council, was well known: he was the Absolom to Shaftesbury's Achitophel.

Both Hamilton and Shaftesbury hoped to spin out the crisis in Scotland as long as possible, to complete the discredit of Lauderdale.[59] But Monmouth fulfilled his commission too well, less because of his own innate abilities as a soldier and far more because of the total incapacity of his enemies. On 22 June their rag-tag army was easily defeated at the Battle of Bothwell Brig. Ironically Lauderdale himself might have been said to have prepared the foundations for this victory years before. His earlier policies of indulgence had been intended to drive a wedge between moderates and extremists, to revive the old conflict between the Protestors and Resolutioners. Rather than prepare for the expected counter-attack the Whig camp had degenerated into a kind of mad General Assembly in the brief weeks before the battle, with debates between the indulged and the non-indulged taking the place of serious military defence.

The events of May and June destroyed some of the illusions long nurtured about the nature of Lauderdale's Scotland: it even looked at one
point as though it might be necessary to bring English soldiers north of
the Border, an interesting reversal of the promise of 1669. Scotland was
the weakest, not the strongest link in the royal chain. No sooner was the
crisis over than the vultures began to settle, waiting to pick the flesh of a
fallen giant. His demise was eagerly anticipated, as George Saville, Viscount
Halifax, was told in early July: 'I am very glad your Scotland business is in
so fair a way towards its conclusion. Surely these accidents will at last
cure my master of his infinite passion for his beautiful paramour of
Lauderdale, who must certainly deal with the devil if after this he can
keep his station much longer either in our nation or his own.'[60]

Favoured by both the devil and the king, Lauderdale did indeed
keep his station despite all. Charles openly commended him in a letter
to the Scottish Privy Council.[61] Yet the presence of Monmouth in
Scotland had gone part of the way towards implementing the aims of
the opposition, completely reversing the Secretary's own policy. The
rebels were treated with great leniency and a Third Indulgence
announced, allowing a partial concession to the holding of house
conventicles. More than this, Charles was treating the opposition with
a courtesy unthinkable in the past, taking on the role of a neutral
referee. Hamilton and his colleagues were allowed to put their case at
a conference in July. Once again the rumours spread that the departure
of Lauderdale was imminent; as a special irony it was even suggested
that he was likely to be replaced by Charles, Earl of Middleton, the
son of his old adversary, and George Mackenzie of Tarbet, acting as
joint secretaries.[62] All of Charles' energies were being directed against
the continuing attempts to have his brother James excluded from the
succession; he had little left over to shore up an administration that
was so obviously crumbling away. At a special meeting of the Privy
Council in August a letter from the king was read out. Charles
announced that he had been favourably impressed by the Party's
representations, and that an indemnity would be issued pardoning all
past offences against ecclesiastical law, though this was partially offset
by the appointment of the hardliner, Alexander Burnet, to the vacant
see of St Andrews.[63] In October the decision was taken to send James
to Scotland, where he was to replace Lauderdale as High Commissioner,
announcing a new and decisive presence on the stage of Scottish politics.
Once again power was divided, as it had been in the days of Middleton.
But as the brother and heir of the king, James had far greater weight
than the ailing Secretary, quickly building up a party of his own, which
included some of the Hamiltonians. The end was beginning.

Lauderdale's exit was neither tragic nor dramatic, like that of Clarendon and Danby; like the old soldier he simply faded away, a sad finale to a magnificent career. In the early months of 1680 those who met him remarked on the rapid onset of old age, and the decay in both his physical capacity and mental acuity.[64] Amongst other things he had long suffered from kidney stones, a source of acute pain that probably does much to explain the deterioration in his temper. Spending increasing amounts of time taking the waters at Tunbridge Wells and Bath, in a futile attempt to recover his lost health, his influence over Scottish affairs was in sharp decline, even before his resignation as Secretary of State in October 1680. Monmouth had reversed his policies in religion; James now did the same in administration. The long partiality shown to the Argyll family was at an end. James, convinced that there might be an armed struggle over the succession, was determined to encourage all loyal forces, including the Macleans of Duart, who had been the chief victims of Campbell imperialism during the days of Lauderdale. In rescuing the Macleans, James set about reducing the power of Argyll, setting in motion a process that was to end in the Campbell chief's political destruction at the close of 1681. Lauderdale's efforts on his behalf had a limited effect, if we read between the lines of one of his last letters to Argyll, written in July 1680: 'My lord, I know not whether you will be pleased with what I have done in this matter, but I doe assure your lordship ther was nothing in my power wanting to have it settled in the most advantageous method for your service. However, if you shall have no other esteem of my best indeavours to have served your lordship these two or three years past, I have reason to look on myselfe as very unlucky.'[65]

Soon after Lauderdale resigned as Secretary he received a letter from the Scottish bishops, expressing their 'great concernment' at his departure, and offering prayers 'for his honor, interest and glorie in both worlds'.[66] Soon after his resignation he voted with most of his fellow peers in the House of Lords for the execution of the Catholic Earl of Stafford, one of the chief victims of the ongoing Popish Plot. This is said to have earned him the permanent enmity of James, who did his best to reduce his remaining influence with Charles, though the evidence for this is very thin.[67] If he was hated by the Catholics, he was just as hated by the extreme dissidents: in September 1680 he was among those formally excommunicated by Donald Cargill, preaching at a conventicle at Torwood in Stirlingshire.[68] In one of the last political acts of his career he intervened actively on behalf of Argyll, who was put on trial for leasing-making in December 1681: 'but he was sinking in both body and mind and was like to be cast off in his old age'.[69]

The end came suddenly, and unexpectedly. Once again he travelled away from home to take the waters at Tunbridge Wells. On 22 August 1682 he suddenly took ill, 'so that phsitianes are sent for to him, and that he is in danger'.[70] Two days later he was dead, the news of which was the occasion for some philosophical – and gloomy – reflection by the Laird of Brodie: 'The wyse man dyes, and so does the fool; they who have bein a terror in the land of the living, how easily ar they brought doun to the grave in a moment'.[71] Sir Andrew Forrester sent news of the event in a letter to the Earl of Aberdeen, striking a more personal note: 'At my coming through Kensington, in my last night from Windsor, I received the (to me) sad news of the Duke of Lauderdale's having last Thursday, about halfe and hour past 8 at night, departed this life at his lodging near Tunbridge Wells.'[72]

Forrester goes on to speak of his confusion 'in which I am at present for the losse of an old and kind master'. The Duchess of Lauderdale was likewise reported to be greatly afflicted by the 'loss of her lord'.[73] The reaction of Charles to the news is not recorded, but he would appear to have long discarded his old servant and friend: '. . . Lauderdale, some weeks before he dyed, was heard to regrait, in Cardinal Wolsees words, that if he had been as faithful to his God as he had been to his King, he would not have shaken him off in his old age, as his master, and his brother, the Duke of York, had done'.[74]

As a final irony Hamilton took his place on the Garter. Charles Maitland succeeded as third Earl of Lauderdale, though the dukedom was permanently lost. Lauderdale's remains were brought back to Scotland for burial, and finally interred beside his father and amongst his ancestors at St Mary's Church, Haddington, on 5 April 1683. As the greatest Scot of his day the funeral was attended by a great many of the nobility and gentry, their horses filling the highway, it was reported, for four miles – 'so wele was he beloved', Charles Maitland wrote to Elizabeth Murray, 'that the whole countrie keindly gave ther presence to the assisting in this last dewtie'.[75] Tweeddale and Lord Yester were invited but did not come; neither did Mary Maitland. The burial of Lauderdale was the one occasion when it seems appropriate to use a cliché: it really was the end of an era.

EPILOGUE

THE MAN AND THE SEASON

At the journey's end we are in a better position to judge the true significance of the life of John Maitland. He was neither Nero nor Caliban, but a man and a politician true to the sense and spirit of his age, representing all that was best and all that was worst. In a sense he continues to be one of the last hostages to the Whig view of history; many things have been attributed to him, it was once correctly observed, 'in the bitterness of party spirit, of which he was guiltless'.[1] For K. H. D. Haley, the biographer of Shaftesbury, Lauderdale, as we said at the outset, was one of the most 'repellent' politicians of the age, though he was not responsible for hounding innocent men to their deaths for party advantage, in the way that his own hero was. Other assessments persist, less biased perhaps, but just as inaccurate. Consider the following by Professor J. R. Jones:

> A second model of absolutism existed, cruder and less systematic, but far nearer to home, in Scotland. During the 1670s the northern kingdom was controlled by Lauderdale . . . A formidable army formed the basis of a rough and repressive regime. Parliament was managed and subordinated. The power of the crown was substantially increased, and the unpopular Episcopal church imposed on a largely antagonistic people. Of course conditions were far more favourable for the establishment of absolutism in a poorer country, where many of the nobility were dependant on royal patronage, and the tribal Highlanders could be easily mobilized. The single-chamber Scottish parliament had no tradition of independence, and never gained the initiative in legislation, and the support of the Scottish Episcopal church was always completely dependent on royal support.[2]

Here we have it: all the main elements of the Lauderdale regime are summed up: secure in the possession of a powerful army, the government imposed its will on Parliament, church and civil society. There is only one problem: it's about as far from real historical truth as it is possible to get. The army was a fiction; the attempt to manage Parliament failed; the nobility showed themselves to be far from dependent, many of them, under the guidance of Middleton and then Hamilton, relentlessly pursuing their own agenda. The people of southern Scotland, especially the south-west, were indeed hostile to the imposition of episcopacy, but the problems their resistance caused obscure the simple truth that it was accepted by much of the rest of the country: while in 1661–2 one-third of Scottish ministers either voluntarily left their charges, or were forcibly ejected, two-thirds remained in place. The Highlanders, or at least a small part of them, were only ever mobilised on one occasion, and proved so problematic that they were quickly sent back home. Furthermore it would seem to be an odd, rather topsy-turvy kind of absolutism that disbands professional troops and substitutes a citizen army that was never to be entirely trusted by the very man who conjured it into being. Jones' misconceptions over the true nature of the militia are shared by at least one Scottish historian, who quite happily tells us that Lauderdale's model of absolutism – less sophisticated but cheaper than that of France – was based on the raising of these 22,000 troops 'which was eventually implemented in 1668'.[3]

It is the stuff of Whig nightmares, an unquestioningly loyal army ready to cross the Border and destroy the liberties of England. Few scholars would now accept the once popular view that the 1670 Treaty of Dover was a serious plan to deliver Britain into the hands of Catholic absolutism, though the view that a different form of absolutism threatened to descend from the north clearly still has its defenders. But an army in excess of 20,000 soldiers, even humble militiamen, needs to be equipped and fed. Could Lauderdale seriously have mounted an effective invasion of England in support of the royal prerogative, as the Westminster Parliament clearly feared he might? The answer is no. Scotland had neither the will, nor the capacity nor the resources to impose an alien political system on England, even if Lauderdale had ever considered such a proposal. After the imposition of the cess or land tax of 1678 the total revenue of the country amounted to approximately £90,000 per annum. Compare this with the tax revenues of England, which came to well over £1,700,000 in 1678–9 alone.[4] Even the revenues of Ireland were significantly higher than those of Scotland. In 1644 and 1645 the Scots were only able to campaign in England because of the financial support they received from Westminster; once payments stopped their army ceased to operate as an effective fighting force. Scottish revenues in the 1670s were almost completely absorbed by Scottish problems, including the problem of internal security. In other words, the Militia Acts, which caused such fear in England, and such intellectual confusion to the present, were simply a way of providing security at the least possible cost.

In 1682, the year Lauderdale died, Alexander Mudie published a book under the title *Scotiae Indiculum*, which provided an outline of the Scottish model of absolutism: 'The King is an absolute and unaccountable Monarch, and (as the law calls him) a free Prince of a sovereign people, having as great liberty and prerogative by the laws of his realm, and the privileges of his crown and diadem, as any other King or potentate whatsoever . . .'[5]

It was certainly the image Lauderdale chose to promote, telling Charles in 1669 that never was a king so absolute as he was in 'poor old Scotland'. But Lauderdale was magnifying the prerogative, rather than establishing an untrammelled absolutism in the sense that Mudie understands. He was a politician, acting like a politician and exaggerating like a politician. Charles' word in Scotland may have been more complete than his rule in England, but it was a bare whisper when compared with the voice of Louis XIV, even when all the allowances are made for the disparities in relative wealth. The Act of Supremacy, the occasion for this claim of absolutism, was really little more than a measure to regulate what had in fact become a branch of the civil service. The bishops were intimidated because the whole basis of Restoration church politics in Scotland, in clear contrast to England, was based in part on the co-option and part on the bullying of churchmen. After James VII and II was toppled from power in the revolution of 1688, John Paterson, Archbishop of Glasgow, was forced to make a rather shamefaced defence of the failure of the Scottish church to take a more active role against the late king in a letter to the Archbishop of Canterbury:

> The King's supremacie, by the first Act of Parliament, 1669, is so asserted and establisht, that by the words of that law, it is in the King's power not onlie to dispose of the persons and places of all Bishops at his pleasure, by removing them from their offices and benefices . . . but even to change Episcopacie it self into anie other form of government. Now this cannot be legally done in England, your lordships' offices and benefices being secured by right of freehold; and when your rights are invaded, the nobilitie and gentrie of England are readie and zealous to owne and support you in them; but here, if the court chance to frowne on us, it is farr otherwise, to say no worse, so that the bishops here lay open to farr greater temptations to yield to the importunities of court than yours doe.[6]

In other words, the Act of Supremacy, the centrepiece of Lauderdale's legislative system, was only possible because the nobility and gentry, determined to prevent a recurrence of the Covenanter days, were willing participants in a strategy designed to keep churchmen in their place. It magnified the prerogative because Parliament was keen to see the prerogative magnified; if this was absolutism it was based on agreement and participation, not coercion of the politically significant classes. It was when such coercion was attempted that the model began to fail.

Lauderdale's dissolution of the Scottish Parliament in 1674 might be likened to Charles' dissolution of the Oxford Parliament of 1681: in both cases it was an admission that the state was no longer able to co-exist alongside national assembles, when these assemblies took a different view from that of the government. The nobility was indeed dependent on court patronage; but there was only a limited amount to give. Hamilton, Tweeddale and all the other outsiders may have only been frustrated place-seekers, or disappointed politicians, but they were well able to use the Scottish Parliament to undermine the executive, fully demonstrating that the body had acquired an assertiveness quite unthinkable in the days before the Revolution. Lauderdale attempted to mollify the emergent opposition by private agreement, which he was not able to achieve, forcing him to work without Parliament for the remainder of his 'reign'. The 1678 Convention was a partial success, in that the government was able to raise some much-needed cash with a minimum of political fuss; but it was also an open admission that Lauderdale was no longer confident of his ability to manage a full Parliament. If any new legislation were required, particularly over the question of religious conformity, it is quite possible that the government would have run into serious trouble. Scottish absolutism was little different from the English absolutism of 1681 onwards: in both cases it was limited in time and scope.

There was no ideology, no philosophy of untrammelled royalism, behind Lauderdale's political project. Essentially he was a pragmatist, fully aware of how far the tree could be bent without breaking. His views on the Treaty of Dover are unrecorded, but, contrary to Burnet's view, he was quite aware of the dangers of political Catholicism for the future of the monarchy, as he made clear in a conversation with George Hickes: '. . . in speaking to him once of ye D. of York he gave him his free character. This good Prince, sayed he, has all ye weakness of his father without his strength. He loves, as he saith, to be served in his own way and he is a very papist as ye Pope himself, wch will be his ruine. And when ye Dr. [Hickes] replyed, my Lord will he venture the loss of 3 Kingdoms for his religion? The Duke answered, yes, if he had ye empire of ye whole world, he would venture ye loss of it . . .'[7]

For Lauderdale, extremism was a threat to the equilibrium of the nation, and was thus a danger to the interests of the ruling class. The prerogative was magnified as the best way of defending those interests, a way of preventing the upheaval and anarchy that flowed from the Civil Wars, not as a way of ensuring uncritical absolutism. Lauderdale never at any point in his career mounted a defence of the Divine Right of Kings, though he was to create a far stronger model of monarchical government in Scotland than had existed for many years. It is not stretching the point to say that the events of 1688 provided a posthumous measure of his success. Scotland played very little part in the Glorious Revolution, played out largely in England, an interesting reversal of the situation only fifty years before.

It seems to me that there was always an element of experimentation in Lauderdale's approach to policy, especially over the church question. The moderate approach, implemented in 1669, was based on an attempt to see how far concessions could be made which did not break the system. The intention was to divide the recusants in such a way that the less compromising among them would be shown to be more interested in political revolution than religious liberty. In the end, most of the dissidents were happy to accept concessions from the state, so much so that by 1680 the second generation of the Protestor party was reduced to a small core of irreconcilable fanatics, lead by the Revd Richard Cameron. Early in that year, Lauderdale received from Bishop Paterson confirmation that the seeds planted all those years before had finally germinated: '. . . and if the feat were done, it's easie to see that the indulged presbyterian partie and even welsh etc. [John Welsh, a leading field preacher] should be more obliged thereby, then the King or the Church; since Cameron divides the former people, and cryes out against them as betrayers of the Crowne of Christ, by erastianisme, more then against the others by prelacie . . .'[8]

This willingness to compromise on fundamental beliefs was to continue after Lauderdale's death, so that by then almost all Presbyterians were happy to accept a further indulgence, offered by the Catholic James VII in the summer of 1687, the purist form of Erastianism imaginable.

Lauderdale', problem was that, like all politicians, he could not afford to wait to reap the benefits of time: his reputation, he realised, would stand, or fall, in the short term. The emergence of a well-organised political opposition in 1674 emphasised the vulnerability of his position, and explains, in part, the increasing harshness towards non-conformity. This harshness was also born of disappointment and anger, and, perhaps, bewilderment over the obduracy of men who had once been his allies. He was also the captive, in a sense, of his own past, causing many to believe that he had no deep attachment to the Episcopalian order, and that further concessions – perhaps even the end of that church – were only a matter of time. Under attack in both Scotland and England, he was forced into a new alliance with the most conservative elements in church and state, which, by the mid 1670s, reduced his room to manoeuvre to the minimum extent. It was his tragedy that he was obliged to defend a church policy of which he had never approved, forcing him into ever more oppressive measures in an elusive search for order.

Lauderdale was such a dominant figure in Scottish politics that there is a tendency to attribute almost every initiative directly to him. It is certainly true that he acquired an almost total domination of the Privy Council. Even so, considering that he spent most of his time in London, and considering that even the fastest communication took some days to travel from the south to the north, the Council as an executive authority was inevitably left with a considerable degree of latitude. There is no convincing evidence, for example, that it was Lauderdale who made the running in the Mitchell case, which all along seems to have been the responsibility of the Privy Council. This is not offered by way of excuse: there were serious issues of justice and legality attached to the whole affair, of which he was perfectly well aware. But once the decision had been taken to pursue the matter to a conclusion, especially in the circumstances of the day, he could not be seen to take a contrary view to Sharp and the others.

There are other cases, most notably the enhancement of Argyll, which can indeed be attributed directly to his power and influence. Lauderdale, almost completely absorbed by Lowland problems, and the wider issues of foreign and domestic policy, never really understood the Highlands. His encouragement of Argyll in his attempt to dispossess the Macleans, which resulted in a kind of intermittent civil war in the west central Highlands, created the very problems of disorder that he was so anxiously trying to prevent in the south. The problems in the north also emphasise, if any further emphasis is needed, how far the Lauderdale regime was removed from a true model of absolutism: no other part of the United Kingdom was troubled by the political problems that beset the Highlands during the Restoration. Yet perhaps it is wrong to attribute this too closely to the policy, and alliances, of the Secretary. For him the 'Argyll solution' was the only answer to a power vacuum left by the disappearance of the oppressive military order imposed by Cromwell; few of his contemporaries could suggest a realistic – and cheap – political alternative, other than to substitute Argyll by some other powerful and self-interested individual. When the Campbell chief, robbed of the protection offered by his great friend, finally slipped from power he was replaced by the Duke of Gordon, who lorded over Lochaber in no better manner than his rival.

In the end it has to be said that Lauderdale outlived his reputation and his authority, a sad conclusion to a brilliant career. It was indeed a brilliant career that little deserves the mistaken judgements passed in the succeeding ages after his style of politics, along with the Stewart monarchy itself, had gone out of fashion. The kind of arbitrary power that he exercised might indeed have been a 'bad thing', but it answered a clear need at a time when no acceptable alternative existed. He may have failed in his project to turn Scotland into a 'model state', but is it true to say that he 'left behind him a nation with its horizons clouded by misery, and its temper seething with sedition'?[9] Even Robert Wodrow, the great doyen of Presbyterian historians, attributes little in the way of oppression to Lauderdale, preferring to magnify the bishops and lesser figures like John Graham of Claverhouse, the future Viscount Dundee. By 1680, moreover, the war against sedition, as Bishop Paterson suggests, had largely been won, though neither Lauderdale nor the subsequent authorities recognised it at the time.

Lauderdale, in his later career, did much to redress a dangerous imbalance in the structure of the Stewart state. The crisis that began in 1637 showed how weak the Union of the Crowns really was. After 1603, executive authority in Scotland was vested in the Privy Council; but these men could not make policy, which remained the prerogative of the distant king. In the late 1630s the Privy Councillors, divided in their own political loyalties, and lacking a clear sense of direction, simply lost control. After 1660 Lauderdale, in responding to this, recreated a form of direct and proactive government that had long been absent before the Civil Wars. More than any other man he defined the character of Restoration Scotland, ruling the country in his royal master's interests in the same way that Lord Deputy Wentworth had once ruled Ireland for Charles I. It has to be said in his favour that he enjoyed some notable successes, and was to be the longest lasting of Charles II's ministers, outlasting men as variously talented as Clarendon, Arlington and Danby. But in the end the Lauderdale system simply created a new problem of imbalance: Scotland was bent to the prerogative power; England was not. The only real solution to the problem of security and order in the United Kingdom was, as Lauderdale had recognised in his youth, a far closer political union, which finally came in 1707.

NOTES

Introduction

1. Mackenzie, Sir George, of Roseheaugh, *The Laws and Customs of Scotland*, 1678, Dedication.
2. Points made in turn by Macaulay, T. B., *Critical and Historical Essays*, vol. 1, 1850, p. 184; Clarendon, Edward Hyde, Earl of, *The History of the Rebellion*, vol. IV, 1992 reprint of 1888 edn pp. 320–1; Macaulay, T. B., *The History of England*, 1913–15 edn, vol. 1, p. 198; Kirkton, James, *A History of the Church of Scotland*, R, Stewart ed., 1992, p. 92; Ailesbury, Thomas Bruce, Earl of, *Memoirs*, 1890, p. 14; Mathieson, W. C., *Politics and Religion*, vol. 2, 1920, p. 203.
3. Oldmixon, J., *The History of England During the Reign of the Royal House of Stewart*, 1730, p. 538.
4. Roundell, C., *Ham House: its History and Architecture*, vol. 1, 1904, p. 14; Mathieson, W. C., op. cit., p. 203.
5. Lang, A., *History of Scotland*, vol. 3, 1904, p. 42n.
6. Scott, Sir Walter, 'Wandering Willie's Tale', in *Redgauntlet*, 1997 Penguin edn, p. 96.
7. Hewison, J. K., *The Covenanters*, vol. 2, 1913, p. 117; Barbour, V., *Henry Bennett, Earl of Arlington*, 1914, p. 79.
8. Macpherson, J., ed., *Original Papers*, 1775, p. 67; Law, R., *Memorials*, 1819, p. 65.
9. Burnet, G., *History of My Own Time*, ed. O. Airy and H. C. Foxcroft, vol. 2, 1900, pp. 184–5.
10. Airy, O., 'Lauderdale, 1670–1682', in *The English Historical Review*, 1886, p. 445.
11. Airy, O., ed. *The Lauderdale Papers* (hereinafter LP.), vol. 2, p. XXI.
12. Macaulay, 1913–5, op. cit., pp. 98–9.
13. Macaulay, 1850, op. cit., p. 184.
14. North, R., *Examen*, 1740, p. 79.
15. Hewison, J. K., 1913, op. cit., vol. 1., p. 385.
16. Butler, D., *Life and Letters of Robert Leighton*, 1903, p. 441.
17. Willcock, J., *A Scots Earl of Covenanting Times*, 1907, p. 2.
18. Carlyle, T., *Oliver Cromwell's Letters and Speeches*, 1892 edn, p. 459.

19. Napier, M., *Memorials and Letters Illustrative of the Life and Tomes of John Graham, Viscount Dundee*, vol. 1, 1859–62, p. 228.
20. Haley, K. D., *The First Earl of Shaftesbury*, 1968, p. 170. Despite Haley's impressive scholarship his understanding of Scottish politics and politicians is not especially well informed. He describes the 9th Earl of Argyll as a 'stiff Presbyterian', which he most assuredly never was. See R. C. Paterson, *No Tragic Story: the Fall of the House of Campbell*, 2001.
21. Hutton, R., *Charles the Second, King of England, Scotland and Ireland*, 1989, p. 161. A similar misjudgement was made at the time by the Earl of Clarendon and the Earl of Middleton.

Chapter 1

1. Pinkerton, J., ed., *Ancient Scottish Poems*, vol. 2, 1786, p. 258. The poem is not by Sir Richard himself, as W. C. Mackenzie asserts.
2. Balfour-Paul, Sir James, *The Scots Peerage*, vol. 5, 1908. p. 276.
3. Ibid., p. 278.
4. Scott, Sir Walter, *Minstrelsy of the Scottish Border*, ed. T. F. Henderson, vol. 1, 1902, p. 253. The poem is thought to be of much more modern origin than that accorded by Scott.
5. Balfour-Paul, op. cit., pp. 280, 291. Sir Robert Maitland at the Battle of Neville's Cross in 1346; William Maitland at Flodden in 1513.
6. *Correspondence of the Earl of Ancrum and the Earl of Lothian*, vol. 1, 1875 p. 27.
7. Sir Richard spent some years at St Andrews studying philosophy and literature. See *The Poems of Sir Richard Maitland of Lethington*, 1830, p. xx. Although it cannot be proved, it is possible that he may have been the first of the family to attend an institution of higher learning. The connection with Haddington is more tenuous, though it is not unreasonable to suppose that Sir Richard's sons received their early education there. See M. Lee, *John Maitland of Thirlestane*, 1959a, p. 28.
8. *Memorials of George Bannatyne*, 1829, p. 46. Sir Richard also performed good service as a collector of ancient Scottish poetry, and was well enough thought of to have a nineteenth century literary society named after him.
9. Sadler, Sir Ralph, *State Papers and Letters*, vol. 1, p. 448; *Register of the Privy Council of Scotland*, (hereinafter RPCS) vol. 5, p. 311, Item 1172.
10. Beattie, C. M., *The Early Political Career of John Maitland, Duke of Lauderdale, 1637–1651*, Masters Thesis, 1977, pp. 11–12. A commendable piece of research, which successfully incorporates all the main sources for Lauderdale's early career. Its main weakness is its brevity.
11. See his entry in the *Dictionary of National Biography*, vol. 12, 1909.
12. *The Laird of Lethington's Counsel to his Son*, in The Maitland Quarto Manuscripts, ed. W. A. Craigie, 1920, pp. 176–8.
13. Bannatyne, Richard, *Memorials*, 1836, p. 52.
14. Calderwood, D., *History of the Kirk of Scotland*, vol. 3, p. 231.

15. Laing, D., ed., *The Works of John Knox*, vol. 2, 1848, pp. 418–9.
16. Lee, M., 1959a, op. cit., p. 26.
17. His name figures on the student rolls for 1555. See *Early Records of the University of St Andrews*, ed. J. M. Anderson, 1926, p. 261.
18. Lee, M., 1959a, op. cit., p. 28; Russell, E., *Maitland of Lethington*, 1912, pp. 3–4.
19. See William Maitland's entry in the *Dictionary of National Biography*.
20. Lee, M., 1959a, op. cit., p. 37.
21. These men were infamous in Scottish history as the Tulchan Bishops. A 'tulchan' is a stuffed calf intended to induce the cow to produce milk.
22. Calderwood, D., op. cit., vol. 5, p. 121.
23. Ibid., vol. IV, pp. 349–50.
24. *Calendar of State Papers Scotland*, vol. 9, pp. 623–4.
25. *Acts of the Parliament of Scotland* (hereinafter APS), vol. 3, pp. 454, 489–91; *Privy Seal Register*, vol. 55, pp. 110–12; M. Lee., 1959, op. cit., p. 154.
26. Calderwood, D., op. cit., vol., 4, p. 429; RPCS, vol. 4, 427–9.
27. *Calendar of State Papers Scotland*, vol. 10, pp. 300–1.
28. Calderwood, D., op. cit., vol. 5, pp. 150–6.
29. Cobbett, W., *A Parliamentary History of England*, 1806, vol. 1, p. 1110.
30. Lee. M., 1959a, op. cit., p. 4.

Chapter 2

1. Balfour, Sir James, *Historical Works*, vol. 4, p. 358.
2. Balfour-Paul, Sir James, op. cit., vol. 5, pp. 301–2; *The Complete Peerage*, vol. 8, 1929, pp. 487–90; *The Peerage of Scotland*, ed. J. P. Wood, 1813, p. 70.
3. He does not even merit a separate entry in the *Dictionary of National Biography*.
4. Historical Manuscripts Commission (hereinafter HMC) *Mar and Kellie*, 1904, p. 137; *Scottish Historical Society Miscellany*, vol. 2, 1904, p. 263.
5. *Hardwicke State Papers*, 1778, vol. 2, p. 116.
6. APS, vol. 7, pp. 134–5; C. Beattie, 1977, op. cit., p. 14.
7. Row, J., History of the Kirk of Scotland, vol. 1, 1842, p. 174.
8. APS, vol. 4, p. 645.
9. Mackenzie, W. C., *The Life and Times of John Maitland, Duke of Lauderdale*, 1923, p. 15n; 'Genealogy of the Macraes', in *Highland Papers*, vol. 1, 1914, p. 229.
10. Burnet, G., 1897–1900, op. cit., vol. 1, pp. 184–5. Secretary Lethington, Lauderdale's grandfather, also had some knowledge of Greek, the teaching of which did not make an appearance in Scotland until 1545. See E. Russell, 1912, op. cit., p. 4n1.
11. If such an assumption can be made on the basis of his book collection,

which contained a number of Spanish and Italian works. See *Biblioteque de fea Monseigneur la Duc du Lauderdale*, 1690.

12. North, R., *The Lives of the Norths*, ed. A Jessop, vol. 2, 1890, p. 303.

13. Lindsay, Alexander Leslie, Lord, *Lives of the Lindsays*, vol. 2, 1875, pp. 175–6.

14. *Correspondence of the Earl of Ancrum and the Earl of Lothian*, op. cit., vol. 1, 175–6.

15. 'Eleven Letters of John, second Earl (and first Duke) of Lauderdale to the Reverend Richard Baxter', in *Bulletin of the John Ryland's Library*, (hereinafter BJRL), ed. J. Powicke, 1922–3, pp. 73–105.

16. Burnet, G., 1897–1900, op. cit., pp. 184–5; LP, vol. 1, op. cit., p. 159.

17. *The English part of the Library of the Duke of Lauderdale*, 1690. Apart from works on divinity and history, his collection also included works on geography, medicine, mathematics, architecture and philology.

18. Aliesbury, *Memoirs*, op. cit., vol. 2, p. 14; Fountainhall, Sir John Lauder of, *Historical Observes*, 1840, p. 74; Ranke, Leopold von, *A History of England*, vol. 3, 1875, p. 520.

19. LP, vol. 2, op. cit., p. 203.

20. The contracts are dated August and September 1632, when Lord John was sixteen years old. Anne would have been even younger. *Register of the Great Seal of Scotland*, vol. 8, pp. 711–2.

21. Anne, and her sister Margaret, stood to inherit the lucrative Home estates after their elder brother James, second Earl of Home, died childless a few weeks after Anne's marriage to Lord Maitland. It was his wish that the estate be divided equally between his sisters; but the lands – and the title – eventually went to Sir James Home of Cowdenknows after a lengthy legal battle. See *The Scots Peerage*, vol. 4, p. 407; Sir John Scott of Scotstarvet, *The Staggering State of Scottish Statesmen*, 1872, p. 45.

22. National Library of Scotland (hereinafter NLS) MSS 7023 f287. She was buried in Paris. Lauderdale did not attend the funeral.

23. The only reference to this child is in a letter by Robert Baillie. See Robert Baillie, *Letters and Papers*, 1841, vol. 2, p. 295.

24. *Scots Peerage*, vol. 8, op. cit., p. 413; Burnet, G., 1897–1900, op. cit., p. 187. It has been suggested that Mary may have been deformed in some way. See C. Beattie, 1977, op. cit., p. 16.

25. RPCS., second series, vol. 3, pp. 604, 608.

26. Chambers, R., *Domestic Annals of Scotland*, vol. 2, 1859, pp. 43–4.

27. Law, Robert, *Memorials*, intro., cxiii–cxiv. Another story he related while a prisoner at Windsor in 1659. Lauderdale's laugh caries across the centuries.

28. Ibid., cxiv. Lauderdale was later to discourage some of the witch-burning excesses of the judiciary. See Sir John Lauder of Fountainhall, *Historical Notices of Scottish Affairs*, 1848, vol. 1, p. 189.

29. BJRL, 19?, op. cit., p. 89n.

30. Burnet, G., 1897–1900, op. cit., p. 81.

31. Quoted in R. C. Paterson, *A Land Afflicted: Scotland and the Covenanter*

Wars, 1638–1690, 1998, p. 2. Most of what follows is drawn from this work.

32. Ibid., p. 1.
33. Burnet, G., 1897–1900, op. cit., p. 81.
34. Lynch, M., *A New History of Scotland*, 1991, p. 267.
35. Lee, M, *The Road to Revolution*, 1985, p. 160.
36. Scottish Record Office, Hamilton Papers, TD75/100/26/8310; Row, J., op. cit., vol. 4, p. 384.
37. Burnet, G., 1897–1900, op. cit., p. 38.
38. Quoted in R. C. Paterson, op. cit., pp. 9–10.
39. Baillie, R., *Letters and Papers*, op. cit., vol. 1, p. 23.
40. Ibid., p. 49.
41. *Hardwicke State Papers*, op. cit., vol. 2, pp. 96–7.
42. Rothes, John Leslie, Earl of, *A Relation of the Proceedings Concerning the Kirk of Scotland . . .* , 1830, pp. 39, 42, 56.
43. Clarendon, *History*, op. cit., vol. 4, p. 508.
44. *Hardwicke State Papers*, op. cit., vol. 2, p. 115.

Chapter 3

1. Guthry, H., Memoirs, 1747, p. 110; Beattie, C., 1977, op. cit., p. 26.
2. Guthry, loc. cit., p. 110.
3. Foxcroft, H. C., An Early Recension of Burnet's Memoirs of the Dukes of Hamilton, in the *English Historical Review*, vol. 24, 1909, p. 520; Lindsay, Lord, op. cit., vol. 2, pp. 36, 47.
4. Burnet, G., *Lives of the Dukes of Hamilton*, 1852 edn, p. 204; Rushworth, J *Historical Collections*, vol. 2, p. 596; HMC Traquair, pp. 253–5; Spalding, J., *History of the Troubles*, vol. 1, 1828, p. 266; See also E. J. Cowan, *Montrose*, 1977, p. 89. Lord Maitland is wrongly identified here as the Earl of Lauderdale. There is a repeated tendency to confuse the son with the father, who did not die until early 1645. See C. V. Wedgewood, *The King's War*, 1997 edn, p. 350, where the confusion over identities leads to a major error of interpretation.
5. Quoted in R. C. Paterson, 1998, op. cit., p. 28.
6. Burnet, G., 1852, op. cit., p. 188.
7. Burnet, G., 1897–1900, op. cit., vol. 1, p. 48.
8. Orr, R. L., *Alexander Henderson, Churchman and Statesman*, 1919, pp. 255–6.
9. Beattie, C, 1977, op. cit., p. 28.
10. *Analecta Scotia*, second series, ed. J. Maidment, 1837, pp. 256–7.
11. *Correspondence of the Earl of Ancrum* etc., op. cit., p. 127.
12. RPCS, 1638–43, second ser., pp. 143, 480. C. V. Wedgewood once again substitutes the son for the father, suggesting that it was Lord Maitland who was appointed to the Privy Council. He could not for as long as his father was alive. She also numbers him among the King's enemies, though it is not clear if Lord Maitland or the Earl of Lauderdale is meant. In any

case neither man deserved this description. See *The King's Peace*, 1997 ed., p. 475. The error is also repeated in H. Rubinstein, *Captain Luckless: James, first Duke of Hamilton*, 1975, p. 138. Lord Maitland was not admitted to the Privy Council until 1647, by which time he had inherited his father's title.

13. There is no evidence to support D. Stevenson's contention that he was a Covenanter as early as 1639. See *The Scottish Revolution, 1637–44*, 1973, p. 171.
14. APS, vol. 5, p. 375; APS, vol. 6 part one, pp. 97, 285–6; Baillie, R., 1841, vol. 2, op. cit., vol. 2, p. 263.
15. Lang, A., 1904, op. cit., vol. 3, pp. 105, 111, 293.
16. APS, 5, pp. 334, 625, 645; Balfour, Sir James, 1824, op. cit., p. 27; Baillie, R., loc. cit., vol. 1, pp. 378–9, 389; Beattie, C., 'The Political Disqualification of Noble's Heirs in Seventeenth Century Scotland', in the *Scottish Historical Review*, vol. 60, 1980, pp. 174–77.
17. Ibid., p. 174.
18. Balfour, Sir James, op. cit., vol. 3, p. 48.
19. Hamilton, C. C., *The Covenanters and Parliament*, unpublished PhD thesis 1959, p. 93.
20. Baillie, R., op. cit., vol. 2, p. 34.
21. HMC Hamilton MS Supplementary Report, p. 68.
22. Baillie, R., op. cit, vol. 2, pp. 45–54; Peterkin, A., *Records of the Kirk of Scotland*, 1838, p. 330; Spalding, J., op. cit., pp. 172–3.
23. Baillie, R., loc. cit., vol. 2, p. 43.
24. Peterkin, A., op. cit., p. 330; Spalding, J., op. cit., vol. 2, p. 91; HMC Fifth Report, p. 645; Hewison, J. K., 1913, op. cit., vol. 1, p. 380; Guthry, H., op. cit., p. 119–20; *A True Copy of the Whole Private Acts of the General Assembly*, etc. 1682.
25. Peterkin, A., op. cit., pp. 324–6; Hamilton, C. C., op. cit., pp. 94–5.
26. In writing to Charles to notify him of the decisions of The Assembly, the Earl of Dunfermline, the Royal Commissioner, only identifies Lord Maitland. HMC Fifth Report, op. cit., p. 645; Baillie. R., op. cit., vol. 2, p. 43.
27. RPCS, vol. 7, pp. 317–8.
28. Guthry, H., op. cit., p. 122.
29. Baillie, R., op. cit., vol. 3, p. 406.
30. Burnet, G., 1897–1900, op. cit., vol. 1, p. 61.
31. Baillie, R., op. cit., vol. 2, pp. 88–90.
32. Ibid.
33. Ibid, p. 96; *Correspondence of the Scottish Commissioners in London, 1644–1646*, ed. H. W. Meikle, 1917, p. xiii.
34. Guthry, H., op. cit., p. 138.
35. Hope, Sir Thomas, *A Diary of Public Transactions, 1633–1645*, 1843, p. 195; Spalding. J., op. cit., vol. 2, pp. 148, 161; Burnet, G, 1852 op. cit., p. 307; Meikle, H. W. op. cit., p. xiii.
36. APS, vol. 6, part one, p. 59.

37. Beattie, C', 1977, op. cit., p. 41.
38. *Journal of the House of Lords*, vol. 6, pp. 288–90.
39. Baillie, R., vol. 2, op. cit., p. 485.
40. Ibid., p. 107.
41. APS, vol. 6 part one, pp. 70–1, 159.

Chapter 4

1. Calendar of Venetian State Papers, vol. 27, p. 71.
2. Ibid., p. 77.
3. Mulligan, L., 'The Scottish Alliance and the Committee of Both Kingdoms', in *Historical Studies*, 1970, pp. 174–5.
4. Mackenzie, Sir George, of Roseheaugh, *Memoirs of the Affairs of Scotland*, 1821, p. 9. This does not stop W. C. Mackenzie repeatedly describing Maitland as president.
5. Baillie, R., vol. 2, op. cit., pp. 145–6, 237.
6. Ibid. p. 483.
7. Ibid. p. 117.
8. Ibid. p. 111.
9. *Correspondence of the Earl of Ancrum* etc, op. cit., vol. 1, pp. 175–6.
10. The Scottish people have short memories. Montrose's excesses tended to be overlooked in the hagiography that descended on his career in the nineteenth century.
11. Baillie, R. vol. 2, op. cit., pp. 245, 246.
12. Crawford, P., 'The Saville Affair', in the *English Historical Review*, vol. 90, 1975. pp. 76–93.
13. Whitelocke, Bulstrode, *Diary*, 1990, p. 155–6.
14. Baillie, R., vol. 2, op. cit., p 246.
15. Whitelocke, Bulstrode, *Memorials*, vol. 5, pp. 343–7; *The Quarrel between the Earl of Manchester and Oliver Cromwell*, ed. J. Bruce and D. Masson, 1875. p. 78.
16. Balfour, Sir James, vol. 3, op. cit., pp. 255–6. Henry Guthry says that he died of a broken heart – no longer a fashionable condition – after he received news of Montrose's victory at the Battle of Inverlochy. The actual date of his death was 18 January; Inverlochy was not fought until 2 February. See Guthry, op. cit., p. 182.
17. Gardiner, S. R., *History of the Great Civil War*, vol. 2, 1893 p. 121; Clarendon, *History*, op. cit., vol. 3 p. 478.
18. There were twenty parliamentary commissioners in all, four of whom were Scots. See C. Carlton, *Charles I, the Personal Monarch*, 1995 edn p. 276.
19. Montereul, Jean de, *Diplomatic Correspondence*, trans. J. G. Fotheringham, 1898–9, vol. 1, p. 22.
20. Gardiner, S. R., 1893, op. cit., vol. 2, p. 122.
21. Wedgewood, C. V., *The King's War*, op. cit., p. 402.
22. Clarendon, History, op. cit., vol. 3, p. 478.
23. Beattie, C., 1977, op. cit., p. 49.

24. Meikle, H. W., op. cit., p. 60.
25. Carleton, C., *Charles I, The Personal Monarch,* 1995 edit. p. 277.
26. In this regard it is worth noting that the eventual restoration of the monarchy in 1660 was the work of the parliamentary moderates, not the royalists. Charles II, in other words, was brought to power by men who had once been his enemies, not his friends.
27. Meikle, H. W., op. cit., p. 76.
28. Baillie, R., op. cit., vol. 2, pp. 295–6.
29. APS vol. 6 part one, pp. 439–61 passim; *Journal of the House of Lords,* vol. 7, pp. 522, 566.
30. Meikle, H. W., op. cit., p. 110.
31. *Records of the Commission of the General Assembly,* ed. A. F. Mitchell and J. Christie, 1892 vol. 1, pp. xxii, xxix. The editor suggests that, because they were present at the battle, Lauderdale and Argyll may have witnessed the terrible massacre of the Irish civilians that followed. There is no evidence either way. It does not seem likely, though, that Lauderdale would have been in a position to accuse Montrose of war crimes if he himself had been compromised in this fashion.
32. Meikle, H. W., op. cit., pp. 134–5; CSPD, 1645–7. p. 276.
33. Beattie, C., 1977, op. cit., p. 52.
34. Montereul, J., op. cit., vol. 1, pp. 89–90.
35. *Journal of the House of Lords,* vol. 6, pp. 192–3, 231–2.
36. Baillie, R., op. cit., vol. 2, p. 367; CSPD, 1645–7 pp. 329–30; *Designs and Correspondence of the Present Committee of Estates,* 1648, pp. 10–11.
37. Burnet, G., 1852 op. cit., p. 351.
38. Rushworth, J., op. cit., vol. 4 pp 268–9.
39. *The Hamilton Papers,* ed. S. R. Gardiner, 1880, p. 110.
40. Correspondence of the Earl of Ancrum etc., op. cit., vol. 1, p. 182.
41. HMC Hamilton MSS. P. 107.
42. APS, vol. 6 part one, p. 836. His appointment was approved in March 1647.
43. Carlile, C., op. cit., p. 307.
44. Burnet, G., 1852 op. cit., p. 371.
45. Rubinstein, H., op. cit., p. 171.
46. Burnet, loc. cit., p. 307.
47. Montereul, J., op. cit., vol. 1 p. 438.
48. Burnet, loc. cit., p. 376–7.
49. Mackenzie, Sir George, op. cit., p. 49; LP op. cit., vol. 1, pp 125, 128. In 1674, while at the height of his power, the charge was still current, causing him to write a remarkable memorandum, which outlines his movements and actions in the late 1640s, a document subscribed with the title 'Concerning the late King'. NLS MSS, f. 263.
50. Lauderdale to Hamilton, 26 Oct. 1646 SRO GD/406/1/2041.
51. Montereul, J., op. cit., vol. 1, pp. 439–40; Thurloe, J., *State Papers,* vol. 1, 1742, p. 87.

52. Foxcroft, H. C. 1909, op. cit., p. 521.
53. Montereul, J, vol. 1, op. cit., p. 210.

Chapter 5

1.   Hobbes, Thomas, *Behemoth*, ed. Ferdinand Tonnies, 1969 p. 135.
2.   Carte, T., *A History of the Life of James Duke of Ormonde*, vol. 2, 1736. p. 14.
3.   *Records of the Commission of the General Assembly*, op. cit., p. 186; *Calendar of Clarendon State Papers* (hereinafter CCSP), vol. 1, ed. O. Ogle and W. H. Bliss, 1872, p. 363.
4.   APS, vol. 6, part one, p. 731.
5.   Ibid., pp. 764–5.
6.   Whitelocke, B., *Memorials* op. cit., p. 344.
7.   Beattie, C., 1977, op. cit., p. 75.
8.   Lauderdale to Hamilton 27 April 1647, SRO GD/406/1/2239.
9.   *Journal of the House of Lords*, vol. 9 p. 246; Calendar of Venetian State Papers vol. 28, 1927 p. 2; *The Declaration of the Commissioners of Scotland Concerning the Removal of His Majesty from Holdenby*, 1647.
10. Montereul, J., op. cit., vol. 2, p. 182.
11. Baillie, R., op. cit., vol. 3, p. 22.
12. *Records of the Commission of the General Assembly*, op. cit., p. 326.
13. Gardiner, S. R., 1893, op. cit., vol. 3, p. 334.
14. Montereul, J., op. cit., vol. 2, p. 254–5; Carte, T., 1736 op. cit., pp. 14–5.
15. Burnet, G., 1852 op. cit., p. 405; Clarendon, History op. cit., vol. 4 p. 260; Records of the Commission etc., op. cit., pp. 4666, 493; A Letter from the Commissioners of Scotland, 1647, pp. 1–2; Menteith, R., *The History of the Troubles of Great Britain*, 1735 p. 280.
16. 'The Narrative of Sir John Berkely', in *Memorials of a Martyr King*, ed. A. Fea, 1905, pp. 173, 190.
17. Lang, A., op. cit., vol. 1, p. 357.
18. Carte, T., *A Collection of Original Letters and Papers*, vol. 1, 1739 p. 244. Implied also by Clarendon: *History*, vol. 4, p. 320–1.
19. Gardiner, S. R., *Oliver Cromwell*, 1900 p. 129.
20. Clarendon, *History* vol. 4, p. 292; Burnet, G., 1852, op. cit., p. 411.
21. Clarendon, loc. cit., p. 347.
22. Burnet, G., loc. cit., p. 411.
23. HMC Ormonde MSS, vol. 2, 1903 pp. 353–5.
24. Burnet, G., loc. cit., p. 411.
25. Ibid. p. 412.
26. Burnet, G., *Lives* etc., 1677 edn, p. 327. It is so blunt that it was removed, without acknowledgment, from the 1852 edition.
27. Ibid., p. 415.
28. *Memoirs of Edmund Ludlow*, 1751, p. 89.
29. Ibid., p. 90.

30. The terms of the Treaty are reproduced in full in H. Rubenstein, op. cit., Appendix one, pp. 246–55.
31. Clarendon, History, op. cit., vol. 4, pp. 301–2.
32. Bishop Burnet also claims that Charles promised to cede the northern counties of Northumberland, Cumberland and Westmoreland to Scotland. See 1897–1900 op. cit., vol. 1, p. 59. He was apparently told of this by Lauderdale in person, though it does not feature in any other source. It does not seem very likely and is thus best disregarded.
33. *Narrative of Sir John Berkely*, op. cit., p. 194.
34. Lee, M., *The Cabal*, 1959, p. 31.
35. Burnet, G. 1852, op. cit., pp. 337–8: *Records of the Commission of the General Assembly*, op. cit., vol. 1, p. 326–7.
36. Baillie, R., vol. 3, op. cit., p. 35.
37. Ibid.
38. Donaldson, G., *Scotland from James V to James VII*, 1965, p. 337.
39. A position he took at the Restoration.
40. Burnet, G., 1852 op. cit., p. 426.
41. Montereul, J., op. cit., vol. 1 pp392–3; Baillie, R., vol. 3 op. cit., pp. 32–3.
42. Guthry, H., op. cit., p. 256.
43. Baillie, R., loc. cit.
44. Montereul, J., vol. 1, op. cit., p. 207.
45. Baillie, R., loc. cit., p. 33.
46. Foxcroft, H. C., 1909 op. cit., p. 522. In this they anticipated Dryden's similar comparison of the Duke of Monmouth and the Earl of Shaftesbury.
47. *Records of the Kirk of Scotland*, op. cit., p. 501; *A Declaration of the Commissioners of the General Assembly*, 1648 p. 3. J. K. Hewison, 1913, op. cit., vol. 1, p. 446 says that Hamilton and Lauderdale were denounced as 'treacherous Episcopalians' by the Assembly. There is no evidence of this in the records of the time, and no other source is cited.
48. *Records of the Commission of the General Assembly*, op. cit., vol. 2, p. 4.
49. Montereul, J., vol. 2, op. cit., p. 407–8.
50. Cowan, I, B., 'The Covenanters: A Revision Article', in the *Scottish Historical Review*, vol. 47, 1968, pp. 41–2; Mitchison, R., *Lordship and Patronage: Scotland, 1603–1745*, 1983, p. 58.
51. Clarendon, History, vol. 4 op. cit., p. 320–1.
52. HMC Lang, MSS, vol. 1, 1914, p. 237.
53. 'Narratives Illustrative of the Duke of Hamilton's Expedition', in *Miscellany of the Scottish History Society*, vol. 2, 1904, pp. 296, 302.
54. Baillie, R., op. cit., vol. 3, p. 64.
55. Burnet, G., 1852, op. cit., p. 447.
56. Ibid.
57. Stevenson, D., *Revolution and Counter Revolution in Scotland*, 1977, p. 112.
58. Leslie to Glenorchy, 1 August 1648. SRO Breadalbane Papers GD/112/39/93/8.

59. *The Designs and Correspondence,* etc, op. cit., p. 5.
60. APS vol. 6, part two, pp. 137, 175; CCSP, vol. 1 op. cit., pp. 433–4; *The Hamilton Papers,* 1880, op. cit., pp. 233–4.
61. 'Wigton Papers', in *Miscellany of the Maitland Club,* vol. 2, 1840, pp. 465–6.
62. A date he gives himself. NLS, MSS 597. Other accounts give it as a day later. Burnet, G., 1852, op. cit., p. 282; Guthry, H., op. cit., p. 282; *Hamilton Papers,* op. cit., p. 237. He appears to have left Lethington on 4 August, boarding ship at Elie in Fife, finally setting sail the following day.
63. Guthry, H., op. cit., pp. 282–3.
64. *Hamilton Papers,* op. cit., p, 237.
65. Ibid., p. 247.
66. CCSP, vol. 1, op. cit., p. 433–4.
67. Montereul, J., vol. 2, op. cit., p. 529; Lauderdale to Hamilton, 20 August 1648 SRO, GD/406/1/1950/2479.
68. Hutton, R., op. cit., p. 28; Stevenson, D., 1977, op. cit., p. 113; Burnet, 1852 op. cit., p. 465.
69. Burnet, G. 1897–1900, op. cit., vol. 1, p. 73; Turner, Sir James, *Memoirs,* 1829, p. 68.
70. *Oliver Cromwell's Letters and Speeches,* ed. T. Carlyle, op. cit., vol. 1, p. 102.
71. APS, vol. 6, part two, pp. 147–8.

Chapter 6

1. Clarendon, *History,* vol. 4 op. cit., pp. 377–8; Scott, E., *The King in Exile,* 1905 p. 62.
2. Clarendon, loc. cit., p. 378.
3. Burnet, G., 1852 op. cit., p. 480. Lauderdale himself refers to such instructions but does not reveal what they were. See NLS, 597 op. cit.
4. Carte, T., 1739, vol. 1, p. 238.
5. NLS 597; Balfour, Sir James, vol. 3, op. cit., p. 386; Carte, T., loc. cit., p. 200.
6. NLS, 597.
7. Beattie, C., 1977, op. cit., pp. 127–9.
8. Ibid., p. 127.
9. Carte, T., 1739, vol. 1, pp. 244, 279.
10. HMC, Fourth Report, p. 538.
11. CCSP, vol. 1, op. cit., pp. 400, 461.
12. *A Perfect Diurnal of Some Passages of Parliament, 25 January–5 February 1648* (i.e. 1649).
13. Foxcroft, H. C., 1909, op. cit., p. 522.
14. NLS, 597.
15. Ibid., Balfour, Sir James, vol. 3 op. cit., p. 386; Burnet 1852 op. cit., p. 480.

16. Balfour loc. cit., Turner, Sir James, op. cit., p. 69.
17. Carte, T., vol. 1, 1739 op. cit., p. 244.
18. Quoted in E. Scott, op. cit., p. 87.
19. Baillie vol. 3 op. cit., pp. 72–3.
20. Ibid.
21. Clarendon, *History*, vol. 5, pp. 19–22.
22. Carte, T., vol. 1, op. cit., p. 244.
23. Clarendon, loc. cit., p. 18.
24. Beattie, C. 1977 op. cit., p. 135.
25. Scott, E., op. cit., p. 96.
26. *The Nicholas Papers*, vol. 1, 1886 pp. 126–7.
27. HMC Fourth Report, p. 538.
28. McCoy, F. N., *Robert Baillie and the Second Scots Reformation*, 1974, p. 129.
29. Baillie vol. 3, op. cit., pp. 95–6.
30. 'Letters Relating to Scotland', ed. F. B. Bickly, in the *English Historical Review*, vol. 11, 1896, p. 117; *Memorials of Montrose and his Times*, vol. 2, 1850, pp. 406–7.
31. *Charles II in Scotland in 1650*, ed. S. R. Gardiner, 1894, p. 41.
32. 'Life of John Livingstone', in *Select Biographies*, ed. W. K. Tweedie, vol. 1, 1845 p. 175; *Diaries of the Lairds of Brodie*, 1863, p. 144.
33. *Charles II in Scotland*, op. cit., p. 49.
34. Balfour, Sir James, op. cit., vol. 4, pp 14, 42; APS, vol. 6, part two, p. 594; Nicoll, John, *A Diary of Public Transactions, 1650–1667*, 1836, p. 14.
35. Balfour, loc. cit., 63–5; *Life of Robert Blair*, ed T. McCrie, 1848, p. 228; *Diary of John Lamont, 1649–1671*, 1830, p. 67: Whitelocke, B., *Memorials*, op. cit., vol. 3, p. 200.
36. Quoted in R. C. Paterson, 1998, p. 184.
37. Burnet, 1897–1900, op. cit., pp. 90–1.
38. *Correspondence of the Earl of Ancrum* etc, vol. 2, op. cit., p. 276. He was signalled out along with George Villars, second Duke of Buckingham, one of Charles' leading English advisors.
39. Balfour, vol. 4, op. cit., pp. 63–5, 75–6.
40. *Selections from the Minutes of the Presbytery of St Andrews and Cupar, 1641–1698*, 1837, pp. 60–1; HMC, Laing MS, op. cit., vol. 1, p. 251.
41. *Diary of John Lamont*, op. cit., p. 25.
42. The Nicholas Papers, vol. 1, op. cit., pp. 193–4.
43. Nicoll, John, op. cit., p. 17.
44. Baillie vol. 3 op. cit., p.117; *Charles II in Scotland* op. cit., p. 150; *Life of Robert Blair*, op. cit., p. 243.
45. Quoted in R. C. Paterson, 1998, p. 206.
46. *Life of Robert Blair*, op. cit., p. 269; D. Stevenson, ed., *The Government of Scotland under the Covenanters*, 1982, pp. 111, 115. 144.
47. *Diary of Sir Archibald Johnston of Warriston*, vol. 2, ed. D. Hay Fleming, 1919, p. 319n. Beattie, 1977, argues that Lauderdale was now acting as

the effective head of government, though one rather slender reference is hardly sufficient weight for such a sweeping assertion.

48. Carey, H, *Memorials of the Great Civil War*, vol. 2, 1842 p. 305.
49. Ibid.
50. Fea, F., *After Worcester Fight*, 1904, pp. 6, 77; CCSP, op. cit., vol. 2, p. 107.
51. CSPD, 1651, p. 459.
52. *Oliver Cromwell's Letters and Speeches*, vol. 2, op. cit., p. 330.
53. Fea, A., op. cit., p. 77: Cripps, D., *Elizabeth of the Sealed Knot*, 1975, p. 40.
54. CSPD, 1651 pp. 432, 478–9; Whitelocke, B., *Memorials,* op. cit., p. 354; HMC Lang, MS, vol. 1, p. 312.
55. Lauderdale to Dickson, 16 October 1651, NLS, MS 3922, f37.
56. NLS, MS 578, f100.
57. Fraser, A., *Cromwell, our Chief of Men*, 1973, pp. 488–9.
58. Cripps, D., op. cit., p. 41.
59. 'One More Lauderdale Letter', ed. L. F. Browne, in BJRL, vol. 12, 1928, pp. 134–6.

Chapter 7

1. Stephen, W., ed., *Consultations of the Ministers of Edinburgh*, vol. 2, 1930, p. 37.
2. Mackenzie, W. C., op. cit., p. 192 n1.
3. APS, vol. 7 pp. 817–8; Nicoll, John, op. cit., p. 125; Whitelocke, B., *Memorials*, vol. 4, op. cit., p. 190.
4. Clarendon, Edward Hyde, Earl of, *The Life of Edward Earl of Clarendon* [Also known as The Continuation], vol. 1, 1760, p. 290.
5. CSPD, 1655, pp. 274–5.
6. Lindsay, Lord, op. cit., vol. 2, pp. 101, 102 and n.
7. CCSP, op. cit., vol. 3, p. 118.
8. Ibid., p. 55.
9. Stephen, W., op. cit., p. 37.
10. Ibid. Earlier in his career Baillie had been the minister of Kilwinning in Ayrshire.
11. Baillie, vol. 3, op. cit., p. 230.
12. BJRL, 1922–3, op. cit., pp 73–105.
13. Baxter, Richard, *Reliquiae Baxteranae*, 1696, part 4, p. 12.
14. Carey, H., vol. 2, op. cit., pp. 306–7; *Journal of the House of Lords*, vol. 10, pp. 542–36.
15. NLS, MS 3423, f23.
16. CSPD, 1655–6, p. 362; Scotstarvit, Sir John Scott of, op. cit., p. 45.
17. NLS, MS 3423, f12.
18. CSPD, 1654, pp. 30–1.
19. Coke, R., op. cit., pp. 441–2; HMC, Fifth Report, p. 649.
20. BJRL, 1922–3, op. cit., p. 91; CSPD, 1658–9, pp. 130, 171.

21. BJRL, *One More Lauderdale Letter*, ed. L. F. Browne, vol. 12, 1928 pp. 134–6.
22. Burghclerc, W., op. cit., pp. 97–8.
23. Burnet, *History* etc., vol. 1, op. cit., p. 187.
24. Letters of John, second Earl of Tweeddale to John, second Earl of Lauderdale, Paton, H. M. ed., in *Miscellany of the Scottish History Society*, vol. 6, 1939, pp. 114, 121–2.
25. NLS, MS 3136, f1.
26. BJRL, 1928, op. cit., pp. 5–8.
27. CCSP, vol. 4 p. 591; John Lamont, op. cit., p. 121; John Nicoll op. cit., p. 277; Bulstrode Whitelocke, *Diary*, op. cit., p. 524.
28. NLS, MS 3423, f29.
29. LP, vol. 1, p. 13.
30. Thurloe, J., op. cit., vol. 7, p. 98.
31. BJRL, 1928, op. cit., p. 134–6.
32. Baxter, R., 1696, op. cit., p. 215.
33. Stephen, W., op. cit., p. xxix.
34. Buckroyd, J., *The Life of James Sharp*, 1987, p. 56. There is nothing to suggest that he supported such a scheme for Scotland at this stage. He most likely shared Lauderdale's view that moderate Episcopalianism in England might happily coexist with a moderate Presbyterianism in Scotland, the 1690 solution.
35. LP, vol. 1, p. 23.
36. CCSP, vol. 4, p. 686.
37. Lee, M., 1959, op. cit., p. 34.
38. Ibid.
39. Clarendon, 1760, vol. 1, op. cit., p. 290.
40. Burnet, *History*, vol. 1, op. cit., p. 192.
41. Ibid., p. 195.
42. British Museum, MS 23114, f126.
43. HMC, Fifth Report, part 1, pp 610–11. Swinton enjoyed possession of the Lauderdale estates without troubling himself over the fate of the former incumbents. Lauderdale, in contrast, once he had recovered his property, paid for the education of Swinton's son, and gave allowances to other members of his family. Those who emphasise his corruption and greed overlook – or ignore – these inconvenient facts. See HMC, Finch MS, vol. 2, 1922, pp. 63–4.
44. Mackenzie, Sir George op. cit., pp 8–9.
45. Patrick, J., 'A Union Broken? Restoration Politics in Scotland', in J. Wormald ed., *Scotland Revisited*, 1991, p. 121.
46. Clarendon, 1760, vol. 1, op. cit., p. 291.
47. Mackenzie, Sir George, op. cit., p. 8.
48. LP, vol. 1, p. 59.
49. Baillie, vol. 3, pp. 421–2.
50. Burnet, *History*, vol. 1, pp. 194–5; Mackenzie, op. cit., p. 24. Lauderdale also benefited financially from the move, acquiring as his personal property

the old Cromwellian fort at Leith. He later sold the land to the city of Edinburgh for £5,000, after the burghers had been panicked by reports that he was intending to set up a new burgh in competition to them.

51. Ibid., p. 25.
52. Burnet, *History*, vol. 1, p. 195.

Chapter 8

1. Displayed in Linlithgow on Restoration Day, 29 May 1662. Quoted in R. C. Paterson 1998 op. cit., p. 232.
2. Patrick, J., 1991, op. cit., p. 122; Hutton, R., op. cit., p. 160; Mackenzie, op. cit., pp 6–7; LP 1, 61–2; John Nicoll, op. cit., p. 311.
3. Ferguson, W., *Scotland's Relations with England: A Survey to 1707*, 1977, p. 151.
4. CSPD, 1660–1, p. 260.
5. Stephen, W., op. cit., p. 221; Mackenzie, op. cit., p. 16.
6. Davies, G., and Hardcastle, P., 'The Restoration of Scottish Episcopacy', in *Journal of British Studies*, vol. 1, 1961–2, p. 39.
7. Ibid., p. 40.
8. Clarendon, 1760, op. cit., vol. 1, p. 294.
9. Ibid.
10. Burnet, *History*, 1, p. 235.
11. Clarendon, loc. cit., p. 296.
12. Ibid. p. 298. His first official visit back to his native land was not until 1663. There is some evidence, though, that he came home on private business in 1661. See Balfour-Paul, op. cit., p, 304. It would be very surprising if he had not.
13. CCSP, 5, p. 88.
14. Hutton, R., op. cit., p. 161.
15. Ferguson, W., op. cit., p. 147; Buckroyd, J., *Church and State in Scotland, 1660–1681*, 1980, p. 24.
16. Quoted in R. W. Lennox, *Lauderdale and Scotland: A Study in Restoration Politics and Administration*, unpublished PhD thesis, 1977, p. 28.
17. LP 1, p. 42.
18. Ibid., pp. 44, 57.
19. Cunningham, A., *The Loyal Clans*, 1932, pp. 330–1.
20. APS, vol. 8, pp. 6–7.
21. Ibid., pp. 10, 16, 18, 30–1.
22. LP 1, p. 63.
23. Davies, G., etc., 1961–2, op. cit., p. 43.
24. Baillie, vol. 3, p. 448.
25. APS, vol. 7, p. 86–7.
26. Burnet, *History*, vol. 1, p. 214.
27. Davies, G., etc. op. cit., p. 44–5.
28. APS, vol. 7, p. 162–3.
29. Baillie, vol. 3, pp. 458–60.

30. Burnet, *History*, vol. 1, p. 216.
31. Buckroyd, J., 1980, op. cit., p. 35; APS, vol. 7, p. 193.
32. Baillie, vol. 3. p. 459.
33. *Scottish Review*, vol. 5, 1884–5, p. 24.
34. In April 1656 he married Ann, the eldest daughter of the first Duke of Hamilton, who carried the title in her own right. By her special pleading Selkirk was allowed to assume the Hamilton title for life.
35. Mackenzie, p. 56.
36. Ibid., pp. 57–9.
37. Ibid., p. 60; RPCS, 1661–4, p. 37.
38. Buckroyd, J., 'Anti-Clericalism in Scotland during the Restoration', in N. MacDougall, ed. *Church, Politics and Society*, 1983 pp. 170–1.
39. *A Brief and True Account of the Sufferings of the Church of Scotland* etc., 1690 p. 12.
40. NLS, MS 3922, f17.
41. Burnet, *History*, vol. 1, p. 217.
42. Ibid., pp. 219–20.
43. *Scottish History Miscellany*, vol. 1, 1893, p. 250.
44. Mackenzie, p. 62.
45. LP, vol. 1 p. 98.
46. Burnet, *History*, p. 223.
47. For the fate of the Argyll family at this time see Paterson, R. C., *No Tragic Story: The Fall of the House of Campbell*, 2001.
48. Mackenzie, p. 38.
49. His wife was the eldest daughter of Lady Margaret Home, Countess of Moray, Countess Anne's younger sister.
50. Kirkton, James, op. cit., p. 97; also Wodrow, R., *The Sufferings of the Church of Scotland from the Restoration to the Revolution*, 1828–30, vol. 1, p. 297.
51. Mackenzie, pp. 71–2.
52. Ibid.
53. Ibid., p. 82.
54. APS, vol. 7, pp. 372–6.
55. Ibid., pp. 410–11.
56. Baillie, vol. 3, pp. 482–5.
57. McCoy, F. N., op. cit., p. 219.
58. Mackenzie, Sir George., *A Vindication of the Government of Scotland During the Reign of King Charles II*, 1691, p. 9.
59. *Diaries of the Lairds of Brodie*, op. cit., p. 241; McCrie, T., op. cit., p. 417.
60. LP, vol. 1, p. 105.
61. Mackenzie, 1821, p. 64–5.

Chapter 9

1. APS, vol. 7, pp. 415–6; Mackenzie, 1821 p. 65.

2. Ibid., p. 66.
3. Ibid., p. 11.
4. Ibid., p. 68.
5. Ibid.
6. Buckroyd, J., 1980 op. cit., suggests that Clarendon, who drafted the English Act, was behind the scheme. There is absolutely no evidence for this assumption. Clarendon hated Lauderdale, but he was not politically inept. He knew that Charles resented being put under any kind of pressure, and reacted angrily over any move to reduce the prerogative. Clarendon, using this understanding, had already warned the Middeltonians against a proposal that Lauderdale might be charged with leasing-making.
7. Mackenzie 1821, p. 73.
8. Ibid.
9. Burnet, *History*, vol. 1, p. 260.
10. LP, vol. 1, pp. 106–8.
11. Ibid., pp. 108–10.
12. Ibid.
13. Mackenzie, 1821, p. 76.
14. Foxcroft, H. C., 1902, op. cit., p. 25.
15. Burnet, *History*, vol. 1, p. 265. Burnet's statement (p. 264) that Lauderdale was warned in time by Lord Lorne is clearly untrue. Lorne, a close prisoner, would have had no access to the kind of detailed information clearly available to William Sharp through his brother.
16. *Scottish History Society Miscellany*, vol. 5, 1933, p. 140.
17. LP, vol. 1, p. 136.
18. Burnet, *History*, vol. 1, p. 266.
19. LP, vol. 1, p. 125.
20. Ibid., p. 114.
21. Mackenzie, 1821, p. 49.
22. Brown, T., ed., *Miscellanea Aulica*, 1702, p. 3; Mackenzie, 1821, p.86; Burnet, *History*, vol. 1, p. 359; CCSP, vol. 5, pp. 299–300; Lairds of Brodie, pp. 289–90, 308.
23. Mackenzie, 1821, pp. 112–3.
24. *Scottish History Society Miscellany*, vol. 5, p. 158.
25. HMC, Ormonde, vol. 3, p. 52.
26. LP, vol. 1, pp. 136, 146–7, 151, 158, 160; Lee, R., 'Retreat from Revolution: the Scottish Parliament and the Restored Monarchy', 1661–2, in J, R. Young ed., *Celtic Dimensions of the British Civil Wars*, 1997; Hutton, R., op. cit., pp. 202–3.
27. Burnet, *History*, vol. 1, p. 363; Mackenzie, 1821, p. 114.
28. Ibid., pp. 114–5.
29. Ibid., p. 116.
30. NLS, MS 3423, f. 15.
31. NLS, MS 3423, f. 37.
32. LP, vol. 1, p. 162.

33. Ibid., p. 136.
34. Mackenzie, 1821, p. 132–3; Burnet, *History,* vol. 1, p. 117.
35. LP, vol. 1, pp. 169–174.
36. Burnet, *History*, vol. 1, p. 368.
37. APS, vol. 7, pp. 450–1, 471–2.
38. LP, vol. 1, p. 168.
39. Nicoll, John, op. cit., p. 407; Hutton, R., op. cit., p. 205.
40. CSPD, 1663–4, p. 29.
41. LP, vol. 1, pp. 144–5.
42. Burnet, *History*, vol. 1, p. 365.
43. LP, vol. 1, pp. 153, 159.
44. *Letters of Archibald Campbell, Earl of Argyll, to John Duke of Lauderdale*, 1829, p. 26; Law, Robert, op. cit., p. 12.
45. NLS, MS 3423, f12.
46. Hopkins, P., *Glencoe and the End of the Highland War*, 1986 p. 39.
47. *Letters of Archibald Campbell* etc, op. cit., p. 14.
48. LP, vol. 1, pp. 148–9.
49. HMC, Laing MS, p. 342; NLS, MS 2512, f29, 33.
50. Mackenzie, 1821, p. 8.
51. LP, vol. 1, p. 172.
52. Quoted in Barbour, V., op. cit., p. 80, n. 27.
53. CCSP, vol. 5, p. 364.
54. *Diary of Samuel Pepys*, ed. R. C. Latham and W. Matthews, 1970–83, vol. 5, p. 57.
55. Ibid., p.34.
56. Brown, L. F., *The First Earl of Shaftesbury*, 1933, pp. 124, 140.
57. Christie, W. D., *A Life of Anthony Ashley Cooper, First Earl of Shaftesbury*, 1871, vol. 1, p. 273.
58. Ibid.
59. LP, vol. 1, p. 204.
60. Ibid., p. 234.
61. Ibid., pp. 211, 215; APS, vol. 7, p. 529.
62. *Letters of Lady Margaret Kennedy to John Duke of Lauderdale*, 1828, pp. 36–7.
63. Kirkton, op. cit., p. 152.
64. Forster, W. R., *Bishops and Presbytery: The Church of Scotland, 1661–1688,* 1958.
65. Burnet, History, vol. 1, p. 370.
66. LP, vol. 1, pp. 219, 242–4.
67. Ibid., p. 241.

Chapter 10
1. Buckroyd, J., 1980, op. cit., p. 67.
2. LP, vol. 1, p. 260.
3. *Pepys Diaries*, vol. 7, op. cit., p. 260.
4. LP, vol. 2, pp. 28–30.

5. Ibid., vol. 1, pp. 258–60.
6. HMC, Laing MS, vol. 1, p. 356.
7. LP, vol. 1, addendum, p. 255.
8. *Letters of Lady Margaret Burnet* etc., op. cit., p. 59.
9. Kirkton, p. 152.
10. Ibid.
11. LP, vol. 2, p. 1.
12. Ibid., p. 2.
13. Ibid., vol. 1, p. 283.
14. Ibid., vol. 2, p. 15.
15. Kirkton, p. 153.
16. LP, vol. 2, p. 31.
17. *Miscellany of the Scottish History Society*, vol. 1, op. cit., p. 263.
18. This, according to the legend, was the occasion for Lauderdale's petticoat dance, intended to lift the King out of his depression. Kirkton, p. 92.
19. *Memoirs of the Reverend John Blackadder*, compiled by A. Crichton, 1826, p. 134.
20. LP, vol. 2, p. 39.
21. Ibid., pp. 69–71.
22. NLS, MS 3136, f23.
23. Burnet, *History*, vol. 1, p. 427.
24. NLS, MS 7023, f100.
25. Abbot, W. C., 'The Long Parliament of Charles II', in the *English Historical Review*, 1906, pp. 46–7.
26. Sutch, V. D., *Gilbert Sheldon, Architect of Anglican Survival, 1640–1675*, 1973 p. 106.
27. *The Rawden Papers,* ed. E. Berwick, 1879, p. 230; LP, vol. 2, pp. 48, 72–5.
28. Hughes, E., 'The Negotiations for a Commercial Treaty between England and Scotland in 1668', in the *Scottish Historical Review*, 1927, pp. 33–4.
29. Bruce, J., *Report on the Circumstances which Produced the Union of England and Scotland,* 1799 p. 214.
30. LP, vol. 2, p. 90.
31. Ibid., p. 101–2.
32. Burnet, *History,* vol. 1, p. 188.
33. Lamb, J. A., 'Archbishop Alexander Burnet', in *Records of the Church History Society,* vol. 11, 1955, p. 136.
34. LP, vol. 2, p. 90.
35. Ibid., p. 105.
36. Hickes, George, *Ravillac Redivivus*, 1682, p. 2.
37. NLS, MS 7024, f102.
38. *Miscellany of the Scottish History Society*, vol. 6, op. cit., p. 263.
39. LP, vol. 2, p. 125.
40. *Miscellany of the Scottish History Society*, loc. cit., p. 215.
41. Ibid., p. 216.
42. RPCS, 1669–1672, pp. 38–40; Burnet, *History*, vol. 1, pp. 507–8.

43. *An Inflammatory Vindication*, 1707; *A Hind Let Loose*, 1744, p. 128. Italics in the original.
44. Brown, J., *A History of the Indulgence*, 1678, pp. 26, 27, 92; Burnet, *History*, vol. 1, p. 509.
45. LP, vol. 2, p. 137–8.
46. RPCS, 1669–1672, p. 80.
47. Law, Robert, op. cit., p. 20.
48. CSPD, 1667–1668, pp. 527–8.
49. *The Speech of His Grace the Duke of Lauderdale* etc., 1669, p. 1; *Life of Robert Blair*, op. cit., p. 527; CSPD, 1669, p. 538.
50. HMC, Laing MS, vol. 1, p. 372.
51. NLS, MS 3136, f160. Differs slightly from the version given in LP, vol. 2, pp. 163–4.
52. Burnet, *History*, vol. 1, p. 504.
53. Lee, M., 1959b, p. 51.
54. Cowan, I. B., *The Scottish Covenanters, 1660–1688*, 1976 p. 74.
55. *Life of Robert Blair*, op. cit., p. 398.
56. Dalrymple, Sir James, *An Apology*, 1690, p. 5.
57. LP, vol. 2, p. 200.
58. Lee, 1959b, wrongly says that all attenders were threatened with the death penalty, probably imitating a similar error in W. C. Mackenzie, 1923, op. cit., pp. 322–3.
59. Kirkton, p. 178.
60. NLS, MS 3136, f128.
61. Mackenzie, 1821, p. 140; Burnet, *History*, vol. 1, p. 505.
62. LP, vol. 2, p. 154.
63. Lee, M., 1959b, op. cit., p. 51.
64. Bruce, J., 1799, op. cit., p. 230.
65. Ferguson, W., 1977, op. cit., pp. 155–6.
66. NLS, MS 7023, f240.
67. A view put forward by D. Ogg, *England in the Reign of Charles II*, vol. 2, 1955 p. 413.
68. Mackenzie, 1821, p. 177.
69. Ibid., p. 181.
70. NLS, MS 7023, f240.

Chapter 11

1. *Miscellany of the Scottish History Society*, vol. 6, op. cit., p. 118; Mackenzie, 1821, p. 165; *Life of Robert Blair*, op. cit., p. 527.
2. CSPD, 1670, pp. 129, 156.
3. Burnet, *History*, vol. 1, p. 437.
4. NLS, MS 14406, f231. Dated September 13 but no year is mentioned. It has been catalogued to 1671, but 1670 seems more likely.
5. *Twenty-Four Letters* etc., op. cit., p. 265.
6. LP, vol. 2, p. 213–4.

7. NLS, MS 7023, f259.
8. HMC, Laing MS, vol. 1, p. 381.
9. LP, vol. 2, p. 216.
10. Burnet, *History*, vol. 1, p. 439; Mackenzie, 1821, p. 217.
11. Robertson, A., *The Life of Sir Robert Moray*, 1922, p. 142.
12. LP, vol. 2, p. 211.
13. SRO, GD 406/1/6129.
14. Fountainhall, Sir John Lauder of, *Journals*, ed. D. Crawford, 1900, p. 319.
15. Aubrey, John, *Brief Lives*, vol. 2, ed. A. Clark, 1898, pp. 81–2.
16. *Register of the Great Seal of Scotland,* vol. 11, pp 366, 548–50.
17. Burnet, *History*, vol. 1, p. 534.
18. Mackenzie, 1821, p. 212.
19. *Miscellany of the Scottish History Society*, vol. pp. 238–9.
20. Kirkton, p. 183.
21. NLS, MS 3234, f626.
22. Quoted in J. Willcock, op. cit., p. 157.
23. *Memoirs of Lady Anna Mackenzie,* op. cit., p. 98.
24. Mackenzie, 1821, p. 217.
25. SRO, GD/112/39/117/17.
26. Mackenzie, loc. cit.
27. CSPD, 1671, p. 585.
28. Ibid., 1671–2, pp. 344, 437, 609.
29. Ibid., pp. 8–9.
30. Ibid; Feilding, F., *History of the Tory Party, 1640–1714*, 1924, p. 137.
31. Burnet, *History*, vol. 1, p. 601.
32. Mackenzie, 1821 pp 219–20; also Law op. cit., p. 48.
33. APS, vol. 8, p. 63; Rait, R., *The Parliaments of Scotland*, 1924, p. 260.
34. Ibid., p. 81: Mackenzie, 1821, pp. 226–7.
35. Mathieson, W. L., 'The Scottish Parliament, 1560–1707', in the *Scottish Historical Review,* 1907, p. 59.
36. Mackenzie, 1821, p. 230.
37. LP, vol. 2, p. 217.
38. Buckroyd, J., 1977, op. cit., p. 96.
39. *Bannantyne Miscellany*, vol. 3, 1855 pp. 231–2. The letter is undated but probably written sometime in 1673.
40. Burnet, *History,* vol. 2 p. 25.
41. Ibid., vol. 1, p. 470.
42. Ibid., vol. 2, p. 26.
43. Ibid., vol. 1, pp, 604, 605.
44. Napier, M., op. cit., vol. 2, p. 367.
45. *Diary of John Evelyn*, 1996 reprint of the 1906 edition, vol. 2, p. 356.
46. CSPD, 1672–3, p. 153.
47. NLS, Yester MS, 7006 f18.
48. Ibid., f32.
49. CSPD, 1673, p. 567.

50. Ibid., p. 475.
51. *England's Appeal for the Private Cabal at Whitehall*, 1673.
52. *Letters to Sir Joseph Williamson*, ed. W. D. Christie, vol. 2, 1874, p. 29; *The Political Diary of Sir Edward Dearing*, ed. B. D. Henning, 1940, p. 158.
53. Hutton, R., op. cit., pp. 309–10.
54. Lang, A., *Sir George Mackenzie . . . His Life and Times*, 1909, p. 107.
55. Mackenzie, 1821, pp. 239–40.
56. Dalrymple, Sir John, *Memoirs of Great Britain and Ireland*, 1777, pp. 50–1; Jones, J. R., 'The Scottish Constitutional Opposition in 1673', in the *Scottish Historical Review*, vol. 37, 1958 p. 35.
57. Burnet, *History*, vol. 2, p. 38.
58. LP, vol. 2, p. 237.
59. Mackenzie, 1821, p. 256; Burnet, loc. cit., p 39; Law op. cit., p. 4; Kirkton op. cit., p. 200; *An Accompt of Scotland's Grievances by Reason of the D. of Lauderdale's Ministry* etc., 1675, p. 6; Baxter, R., op. cit., part 3, p. 147.
60. Kirkton, op. cit., p. 200.
61. Burnet, *History*, vol. 2, p.39.
62. LP, vol. 2, p. 241.
63. Ibid., p. 243.
64. *Letters to Sir Joseph Williamson*, op. cit., pp. 59, 70.
65. Ibid., p. 82.
66. LP, vol. 2, pp. 244–5.
67. Mackenzie, 1821, pp260–2.
68. LP, vol. 3, p. 3.
69. Mackenzie, 1821, p. 264; Law, op. cit., p. 56.
70. Ailesbury, *Memoirs*, op. cit., p. 16.
71. An Accompt etc., op. cit., p. 8.
72. Ibid., pp. 23, 30.
73. Ibid., p. 30.
74. Ibid., p. 32.

Chapter 12

1. Whitecombe, D., *Charles II and the Cavalier House of Commons, 1663–1674*, 1966, p. 152 and note.
2. CSPD, 1673–75, p. 131.
3. Ibid., p. 108.
4. Grey, A., *Debates in the House of Commons*, vol. 2, 1763, p. 236; Cobbett, W., *The Parliamentary History of England*, vol. 4, 1808, pp. 626–30.
5. Grey, A., loc. cit., p. 237.
6. Ibid., p. 238.
7. Ibid.
8. Cobbett, W., op. cit., pp 626–30.

9. Grey, A., loc. cit., p. 242.
10. LP, vol. 3, intro. p. ii.
11. Ibid., p. 3.
12. Burnet, *History,* vol. 3 p. 52.
13. Ibid., p. 53.
14. CSPD, 1673–75, p. 272.
15. Law, op. cit., p. 65.
16. Oldmixon, J., op. cit., p. 583.
17. *Calendar of State Papers Venetian,* vol. 38, 1940, p. 350.
18. *Roxburgh Ballads,* vol. 4, 1883, pp. 91–3. An undated poem consigned by the editor to *c.*1679–80 but possibly written as early as 1675.
19. Mackenzie, 1821, pp. 314–5.
20. Burnet, *History,* vol. 2, pp 66–7.
21. SRO, GD/112/39/119/9.
22. 'On the Duchess of Lauderdale', in *A Book of Scottish Pasquils, 1568–1715,* ed. J. Maidment, 1868, pp. 241–2.
23. *A History of the Affairs of Scotland from the Restoration of King Charles the Second,* anon. 1690 p. 10; *A letter to D. L.* [Duke Lauderdale], anon., *c.*1679, pp. 1, 3; Kirkton, op. cit., p. 211.
24. *Records of the Convention of Royal Burghs, 1615–1676,* 1878, pp. 640–1.
25. LP, vol. 3, pp. 65–6.
26. Burnet, *History,* vol. 2, p. 57.
27. Mackenzie, 1821, pp. 267–8.
28. Burnet, *History,* vol. 2, pp. 56–7.
29. LP, vol. 3, p. 75.
30. Ibid., p. 54.
31. Ibid., vol. 2, p. 235.
32. HMC, Twelfth Report, part 8, manuscripts of the Duke of Atholl and the Earl of Home, 1891, pp. 32–3.
33. HMC, Eleventh Report, appendix part 6, manuscripts of the Duke of Hamilton, 1887, pp. 148–9.
34. NLS, MS 7023, f259.
35. Bishops 'calling the shots' is a view supported by J. Buckroyd, 1980, op. cit., pp. 113–6. Lauderdale was always the architect; the bishops were never more than masons.
36. Wodrow, R., op. cit., vol. 2, p. 298.
37. Scottish History Society Miscellany, vol. 5, 1893, p. 281.
38. RPCS, 1673–76, p. 152; Burnet, *History,* vol. 2, p. 136.
39. RPCS, 1676–78, p. 198.
40. SRO, GD 406/1/2920.
41. Grey, A., op. cit., vol. 3, p. 30; Cobbett, W., op. cit., vol. 4, p. 686; Burnet, *History,* vol. 2, p. 73.
42. Cobbett, W., loc. cit., p. 686.
43. Burnet, *History,* vol. 2, p. 73.
44. Ibid., p. 74 and n3; HMC, Fifth Report, part one, p. 317; Marvell, Andrew, *Works,* vol. 2, 1776, pp. 221–3, 229; Bulstrode, Sir Richard,

The Bulstrode Papers, 1667–1675 ed. Morrice, A., 1897, pp. 285, 286, 287; *Miscellany of the Maitland Club* vol. 4, 1847, pp. 176–7; Clarke, T. E. S., and Foxcroft, H. C., *A Life of Gilbert Burnet*, 1907, pp. 136–7.

45. Mackenzie, 1821, p. 315.
46. Baxter, R., op. cit., part 3, p. 167.
47. Burnet, *History*, vol. 2, p. 75.
48. *Miscellany of the Maitland Club*, vol. 4, op. cit., p. 179.
49. Bulstrode, Sir Richard, op. cit., p. 291. The reference is to the pardon of October 1673.
50. Ibid., p. 291.
51. Law, op. cit., p. 78.
52. HMC, Supplementary Report, the Duke of Hamilton MSS, 1932, p. 89.
53. RPCS, 1676–78, p. 547.
54. Elder, J. R., *The Highland Host of 1678*, 1914, p. 9.
55. Law, op. cit., p. 72.
56. Ibid., p. 88.
57. HMC, Eleventh Report, p. 151.
58. LP, vol. 3, p. 229.
59. Macaulay, 1850, op. cit., vol. 3, p. 127.
60. HMC, Finch MS, vol. 2, pp. 62–3.
61. See Dunbar, J. G., 'The Building Activities of the Duke and Duchess of Lauderdale, 1670–1682', in *The Archaeological Journal*, vol. 132, 1975, pp. 202–30.
62. LP, vol. 3, pp. 235–9. Letter undated, but consigned by Airy to 1672 for no very clear reason; it could have been written at any time from the early 1670s onwards.
63. Mackenzie, W. C., op. cit., p. 501, n1.
64. Reresby, Sir John, *Memoirs*, ed. J. J. Cartwright, 1875, p. 116.
65. RPCS, 1676–78, pp. 2, 10, 18, 21, 34, 72.
66. Fountainhall, Sir John Lauder of, 1848, op. cit., vol. 1, pp. 177–8.
67. HMC, Fifteenth Report, part 8, MSS Duke of Buccleuch and Queensberry, 1897, pp. 221, 225, 226; HMC Portland MS, Report 13, part 2, 1893, pp. 37–9.
68. Fountainhall, loc. cit., p. 227.
69. HMC Portland loc. cit.
70. HMC Buccleuch etc., loc. cit., p. 227.
71. RPCS, 1676–78, pp. 279–80; Law, op. cit., pp. 135–7; Burnet, *History*, vol. 2, p. 144.
72. Ibid., p. 145.
73. Mackenzie, 1821, p. 329.
74. HMC, Ormonde MS, vol. 4, pp. 61, 63, 72–3; LP vol. 3 p. 91.
75. HMC, Buccleuch etc., p. 230.
76. Ibid., p. 229; HMC, Portland, op. cit., pp. 37–9.
77. Ibid.
78. LP, vol. 3, p. 89.
79. Ibid., p. 93n. This view is shared by J. R. Elder, op. cit. The terms 'humble

servant' and 'driven' are used by W. C. Mackenzie, op. cit., pp. 402, 403.

80. HMC, Portland, op. cit., p. 222.
81. Kirkton, op. cit., p. 44.
82. *The Declaration of the Rebels Now in Arms*, etc., 1679, p. 2.
83. NLS, Wodrow, Folio xxviii, f37.
84. Cleland, William, *A collection of Several Poems and Verses*, 1697, p. 24. Later commanding the Cameronian Regiment, Cleland was killed in battle with the Jacobite Highlanders at Dunkeld in 1689.
85. Oldmixon, J., op. cit., p. 637.

Chapter 13

1. Law, op. cit., p. 136.
2. Crawford, G., *The Lives and Characters of the Officers of the Crown and State of Scotland*, 1736, p. 233: CSPD, 1677–8, pp. 35–6; Kirkton, op. cit., p. 233.
3. HMC, Ormonde, vol. 3, p. 423.
4. LP, vol. 3, pp. 99–102.
5. SRO, G/112/39/124/15.
6. CSPD, 1678, p. 122.
7. Burnet, *History*, vol. 2, p. 148.
8. LP, vol. 3, pp. 107–9.
9. Burnet, loc. cit., p. 148.
10. LP, loc. cit., p. 126.
11. Ibid., pp. 109–110.
12. Grey, A., op. cit., vol. 5 pp. 358, 359, 360.
13. Ibid., p. 359.
14. LP, vol. 3, pp. 13–14.
15. Ibid., p. 147; Reresby, Sir John, *Memoirs*, op. cit., p. 137.
16. LP, loc. cit., p. 131.
17. Ibid., p. 149.
18. Ibid., pp. 132–3.
19. HMC, Fifteenth Report, op. cit., p. 237.
20. *Letters to Lady Margaret Burnet*, op. cit., p. 108.
21. *A Book of Scottish Pasquails*, op. cit., p. 251. This poem has been assigned, for unexplained reasons, to the year 1671. The reference to the Highlanders makes it clear that it was written some time after early 1678.
22. Buckroyd, J., 1977, op. cit., p. 101.
23. Cobbett, W., *Complete Collection of State Trials*, vol. 6, 1810, p. 1216.
24. Fountainhall, 1848, op. cit., vol. 2, pp. 183–5.
25. Ibid., pp. 183–4; Mackenzie 1821, pp. 327–8; Hickes, G., op. cit., p. 14; Cobbett, W., 1810, op. cit., p. 1257.
26. Burnet, *History*, vol. 2, p. 139.
27. Ibid., p. 141.

28. Fountainhall, 1848, vol. 2, op. cit., p. 185.
29. Law, op. cit., p. 138.
30. CSPD, 1678, p. 234.
31. Law, loc. cit.
32. APS, vol. 8, p. 230.
33. LP, vol. 3, p. 160.
34. CSPD, 1678, p. 232.
35. Balcarres, Colin, Earl of, *Memoirs, 1841, p. 2.*
36. CSPD, loc. cit., p. 292.
37. Ibid., p. 353.
38. Ibid., p. 477.
39. Hutton, R., op. cit., p. 354.
40. Napier, M., op. cit., vol. 1 p. 367.
41. Some Unpublished Letters by Gilbert Burnet, ed. H. C. Foxcroft, *Camden Miscellany,* vol. 11, 1907, pp. 18–9.
42. Evelyn, J., op. cit., vol. 3, p. 18.
43. Quoted in R. C. Paterson, 2001, op. cit., p. 41.
44. *Somers Tracts,* vol. 8, ed. Sir Walter Scott, 1812.
45. Dryden, John, *Absolom and Achitophel,* 1682 4th edn, p. 5.
46. Jones, J. R., 1958, op. cit., p. 38.
47. Evelyn, John, vol. 3, op. cit., p. 31.
48. Marvell, Andrew, *Letters and Poems,* vol. 1, 1971, p. 221.
49. HMC Seventh Report, 1879, p. 408.
50. Quoted in R. W. Wallace, 1977 op. cit., p. 375.
51. HMC, Ormonde, vol. 4, p. 523.
52. LP, vol. 3, pp. 162–3.
53. HMC, Ormonde, loc. cit.
54. Jones, J. R., *The First Whigs: the Politics of the Exclusion Crisis, 1678–1683,* 1961, p. 79.
55. HMC, Ormonde, loc. cit., p. 523.
56. Sidney, Henry, *Diary of the Times of King Charles II,* 1843, vol. 2, pp. 1, 43; CSPD, 1679–80, p. 169.
57. Ibid., p. 7.
58. HMC, Ormonde, vol. 5, p. 133.
59. Temple, Sir William, *Works,* vol. 1, 1754, p. 427; *Memoirs of William Veitch and George Bryson,* ed. T. McCrie, 1825, p. 111.
60. *Saville Correspondence,* ed. W. D. Cooper, 1858, p. 105.
61. RPCS, 1678–80, pp. 280–1.
62. *Saville Correspondence,* loc. cit., p. 119; HMC, Ormonde, vol. 5, p. 135: Law, op. cit., p. 163; Cripps, D., 1975, op. cit., p. 221.
63. RPCS, loc. cit., pp. 301–4.
64. *Camden Miscellany,* vol. 6, op. cit., pp. 18–9; Sidney, Henry, op. cit., pp. 14, 17.
65. HMC, Sixth Report, p. 621.
66. LP, vol. 3, pp. 211–2.
67. Fountainhall, *Observes,* op. cit., p. 75.

68. LP, loc. cit., p. 209.
69. Burnet, *History*, vol. 2, p. 231.
70. HMC, Drumlanrig, vol. 2, p. 109.
71. *Diaries of the Lairds of Brodie*, op. cit., p. 473.
72. *Letters to the Earl of Aberdeen*, 1851, p. 516.
73. HMC, Twelfth Report, vol. 2, 1889, p. 77.
74. Fountainhall, *Observes,* op. cit., p. 74.
75. LP, vol. 3, p. 230.

Epilogue

1. Clarke, W. N., 1852.
2. Jones, J. R., Main Trends in Restoration England, in *The Restoration Monarchy, 1660–1688*, ed. J. R, Jones, 1979, p. 16.
3. Macinnes, A. I., *Clanship, Commerce and the House of Stuart*, 1996, p. 130.
4. Wallace, R. W., 1977, op. cit., p. 382.
5. Mudie, A., *Scotiae Indiculum*, 1682.
6. Clarke, W. N., ed., *A Collection of Letters . . . to Sancroft, Archbishop of Canterbury*, 1858 p. 2.
7. Gardiner, W. B., 'The Later Years of John Maitland, Second Earl and First Duke of Lauderdale', in the *Journal of Modern History, vol. 20, 1948*, pp. *121–2*.
8. LP, vol. 3, p. 188.
9. Mackenzie, W. C., op. cit., p. 508.

SELECT BIBLIOGRAPHY

⚜

Unpublished Primary Sources

National Library of Scotland (NLS)
Lauderdale Letters
Yester Papers
Wodrow Folios, all as cited in notes

Scottish Record Office (SRO)
Breadalbane Papers
Hamilton Papers, all as cited in notes

Published Documentary and Narrative Sources

Acts of the Parliament of Scotland, vols., 4, 6 part one

An Accompt of Scotland's Grievances by Reason of the D. of Lauderdales Ministry, 1675

Ailesbury, Thomas Bruce, Earl of, *Memoirs*, 1890

Aubrey, John, *Brief Lives*, vol. 2, 1898

Baillie, Robert, *The Letters and Journals of Robert Baillie*, 3 vols. 1841–2

Balfour, Sir James, *Historical Works*, vol. 3, 4, 1824–5

Balcarres, Colin, Earl of, *Memoirs*, 1841

Bannatyne, George, *Memorials*, 1829

Bannatyne, Richard, *Memorials*, 1836

The Bannantyne Miscellany, vol. 3, 1855

Baxter, Richard, *Reliquiae Baxterinanae*, 1696

Berkeley, Sir John, 'The Narrative of Sir John Berkeley', in *Memoirs of a Martyr King*, ed. A. Fea, 1905

Biblioteque de fea Monseigneur le Duc de Lauderdale, 1690

Bickley, F. B, 'Letters Relating to Scotland in 1650', in *English Historical Review*, vol. 11, 1896 pp. 112–7

A Brief and True Account of the Sufferings of the Church of Scotland, etc. 1690

Brown, J., *A History of the Indulgence*, 1678

Browne, L. F. ed. 'One More Lauderdale Letter', in *Bulletin of the John Ryland's Library*, vol. 12, 1928, pp. 134–6

Bulstrode, Sir Richard, *The Bulstrode Papers, 1667–1675*, ed. A. Morrice, 1897

Burnet, Gilbert, *A Vindication of the Authority, Constitution and Laws of the Church of Scotland*, 1673

Burnet, Gilbert, *History of My Own Time*, ed. O. Airy, 1900

Burnet, Gilbert, *The Memoirs of the Lifes and Actions of James and William, Dukes of Hamilton*,1677 and 1852 editions

Calendar of State Papers Domestic (CSPD), variously edited

Calderwood, D., *History of the Kirk of Scotland*, vol. 4, 1843

Calendar of Clarendon State Papers, vols. 1–5, eds O. Ogle and W. H. Bliss, 1872

Calendar of State Papers Venetian, vol. 26, 27, 38, ed. A. B. Hinds

Camden Miscellany vol. 6, H. C. Foxcroft ed. *Some Unpublished Letters of Gilbert Burnet*, 1907

Carlyle, T., ed., *Oliver Cromwell's Letters and Speeches*, vol. 2 1897

Carstares, W., *State Papers and Letters*, 1754

Carte, T. ed., *A Collection of Original Letters and Papers*, vol. 1, 1739

Cary, H., ed., *Memorials of the Great Civil War*,1842

Clarendon, Edward Hyde, Earl of, *The History of the Rebellion*, vols. 3–5, 1992 reprint of 1885 edn

Clarendon, Edward Hyde, Earl of, *The Life of Edward Earl of Clarendon*, 2 vols,. 1760

Cleland, William, *A Collection of Several Poems and Verses*, 1697

Cobbett, W., *Parliamentary History of England*, vol. 4, 1808

Cobbett, W., *Complete Collection of State Trials*, vol. 6, 1810

Coke, R., *A Detection of the Court and State of England*, 1697

A Collection of Letters . . . to Sancroft Archbishop of Canterbury, ed. W, N. Clarke, 1852

Correspondence of the Earl of Ancrum and the Earl of Lothian, 2 vols., 1875

'Correspondence of Sir Robert Moray with Alexander Bruce, second Earl of Kincardine, 1657–1660', in *Scottish Review*, vol. 5, 1884–5, pp. 22–43

Dalrymple, Sir John, *An Apology*, 1690

Dalrymple, Sir John, *Memoirs of Great Britain and Ireland*, 1771

A Declaration of the Commissioners of the General Assembly, 1648

The Declaration of the Commissioners of Scotland Concerning the Removal of His Majesty from Holdenby, 1647

A Declaration of the Committee of Estates of the Parliament of Scotland, 1648

The Declaration of the Rebels now in Arms etc., 1679

The Designs and Correspondencies of the Present Committee of Estates, 1648

The Diaries of the Lairds of Brodie, 1863

Dryden, John, *Absolom and Achitophel*, 1682, 4th edn

Englands Appeal for the Private Cabal at Whitehall, 1673

Essex Papers, ed. O. Airy, 1890

Evelyn, John, *Diary*, vols. 2 and 3, 1996

The Hamilton Papers, ed. S. R. Gardiner, 1880

Fountainhall, Sir John Lauder of, *Historical Observes*, 1840

Fountainhall, Sir John Lauder of, *Historical Notices of Scottish Affairs*, 2 vols., 1848

Fountainhall, Sir John Lauder of, *Journals*, ed. D. Crawford, 1900

Foxcroft, H. C., ed. *A Supplement to Burnet's History,* 1902

Foxcroft, H. C., 'An Early Recension of Burnet's Memoirs of the Dukes of Hamilton', in *English Historical Review,* vol. 24, 1909 pp. 510–40

Gardiner, S. R., ed., *Charles II in Scotland in 1650,* 1894

Grey, A., *Debates in the House of Commons from the year 1667 to the Year 1694,* vols. 2–5, 1763

Guthry, Henry, *Memoirs,* 1747

Hickes, George, *Ravillac Redivivus,* 1682

The History of the Affairs of Scotland from the Restoration of King Charles II, Anon., 1690

HMC Fourth Report, 1874

HMC Fifth Report 1876

HMC Sixth Report, 1877

HMC Seventh Report, 1879

HMC Ninth Report, 1884

HMC Eleventh Report, Appendix, part 6, MSS, Duke of Hamilton, 1887

HMC Twelvth Report, Rutland MSS, vol. 2, 1889

HMC Thirteenth Report, Portland MSS, 1893

HMC Fifteenth Report, 1897

HMC Finch MSS, vol. 2, 1922

HMC Laing MSS, vol. 1, 1914

HMC Mar and Kellie, MSS, 1904

HMC Ormonde MSS, vols. 2–5, 1903–8

HMC Portland MSS, 1893

HMC Supplementary Report to the Duke of Hamilton's Manuscripts. 1932

Hope, Sir Thomas, *A Diary of Public Transactions, 1633–1645,* 1843

Hardwicke, Philip Yorke, Earl of, *Miscellaneous State Papers,* vol. 2, 1778

Journals of the House of Lords, vols. 6, 8

Kirkton, James, *A History of the Church of Scotland, 1660–1679,* ed., R. Stewart, 1992

Lamont, John, *The Diary of John Lamont, 1649–1671,* 1830

The Lauderdale Papers, 3 vols, ed. O. Airy, 1884–5

Law, Robert, *Memorials, 1819*

Letters from Archibald, Earl of Argyll to John Duke of Lauderdale, 1829

A Letter from the Commissioners of Scotland etc, 1647

A Letter Sent to DL [Duke Lauderdale], c1679

Letters to the Earl of Aberdeen, 1681–1684, 1851

Letters to Sir Joseph Williamson, vol. 2, ed. W. D. Christie, 1874

Letters from Lady Margaret Burnet to John Duke of Lauderdale, 1828

The Life of Robert Blair, ed. T. McCrie

Ludlow, Edmund, *Memoirs,* 1751

Mackenzie, Sir George, of Roseheugh, *The Laws and Customes of Scotland,* 1678

Mackenzie, Sir George, of Roseheugh, *A Vindication of the Government of Scotland during the Reign of King Charles II,* 1691

Mackenzie, Sir George, of Roseheaugh, *Memoirs of the Affairs of Scotland from the Restoration of King Charles II,* 1821

Macpherson, J., ed., *Original Papers*, 1775

Maidment, J., ed., *Analecta Scotia*, 1837

Maidment, J., ed., *A Book of Scottish Pasquils, 1568–1715*, 1868

Marvell, Andrew, *Works*, vol. 2, 1776

Marvell, Andrew, *Letters and Papers*, ed. H. M. Margoliouth, revised by P. Legouis and E. E. Duncan-Jones, 1971

Meikle, H. W., *Correspondence of the Scots Commissioners in London, 1644–1646*, 1917

Memoirs of William Veitch and George Bryson, ed. T. McCrie, 1825

Memoirs of Sir John Reresby, ed. J. J. Cartwright, 1875

Memoirs of the Reverend John Blackadder, compiled by A. Crichton, 1826

Memorials of Montrose and his Times, vol. 2, 1850

Miscellanea Aulica, ed. T. Brown, 1702

Miscellany of the Maitland Club, vol. 2, 1840, vol. 4, 1847

Miscellany of the Scottish History Society, vol. 1, 1893

Miscellany of the Scottish History Society, vol., 2, 1904

Miscellany of the Scottish History Society, vol. 5, 1893

Miscellany of the Scottish History Society, vol. 6. 1939

Montereul Correspondence, 2 vols., 1898–99

Mudie, A., *Scotiae Indiculum,*1682

Napier, M., ed., *Memorials and Letters Illustrative of the Life and Times of John Graham, Viscount Dundee*, 1859–62

The Nicholas Papers, vol. 1, ed. G. F. Warner, 1886

Nicoll, John, *A Diary of Public Transactions, 1650–1667*, 1836

North, Roger, *Examen*, 1740

North, Roger, *The Lives of the Norths*, vol. 2, ed., A. Jessop, 1972

Oldmixon, J., *The History of England during the Reign of the Royal House of Stuart*, 1730

The Parliamentary Diary of Sir Edward Dearing, 1670–1673, ed. B. D. Henning, 1940

A Perfect Diurnall of Some Passages in Parliament, No. 288, 1649

Pepys, Samuel, *Diary*, ed. R. C. Latham and W. Matthews, vols. 5 and 7, 1970–83

Peterkin, A., ed., *Records of the Kirk of Scotland*, 1838

Pinkerton, J., ed., *Ancient Scottish Poems*, vol. 2, 1786

The Poems of Sir Richard Maitland of Lethington, 1830

Powicke, F. J., 'Eleven Letters of John second Earl, (and first Duke) of Lauderdale . . . to the Reverend Richard Baxter', in *Bulletin of the John Ryland's Library*, vol. 7, 1922–3 pp. 73–105

Powicke, F. J. ed., 'Another Lauderdale Letter', in *Bulletin of the John Ryland's Library*, 1926

The Quarrel between the Earl of Manchester and Oliver Cromwell, ed. J. Bruce , 1875

The Rawden Papers, ed. E. Berwick, 1819

The Records of the Commission of the General Assemblies of the Church of Scotland, ed. A.. F. Mitchell and J. Christie, 1892

Register of the Consultations of the Ministers of Edinburgh, 1657–1660, vol. 2, ed. W. Stephens, 1930

Records of the Convention of Royal Burghs, 1615–1676, 1878

Register of the Privy Council of Scotland (RPCS) second and third series, variously edited

Register of the Great Seal of Scotland

Rothes, John Leslie, Earl of, *A Relation of the Proceedings Concerning the Affairs of the Church of Scotland,* 1830

Row, J., *History of the Kirk of Scotland,* 1842

The Roxburgh Ballads, vol. 4, 1883

Rushworth, J., ed., *Historical Collections,* vol. 2, 1701

Sadler, Sir Ralph, *State Papers,* vol. 1, 1809

Saville Correspondence, ed. W. D. Cooper, 1858

Selections from the Minutes of the Presbyteries of St Andrews and Cupar, 1641–1698, 1837

Scott, Sir John, of Scotstarvet, *The Staggering State of Scottish Statesmen,* 1872

Sidney, Sir Henry, *Diary of the Time of Charles II,* 2 vols. 1843

Some Particular Matters of Fact Relating to the Administration of Scotland under the Duke of Lauderdale, 1679

Somers Tracts, ed. Sir Walter Scott, vol. 8, 1812

Spalding, J., *History of the Troubles,* vol. 2, 1829

The Speech of His Grace the Duke of Lauderdale..1669

Stevenson, D., ed., *Government of Scotland under the Covenanters, 1637–1651,* 1982

Temple, Sir William, *Works,* vol. 1, 1754

Thurloe, J., *State Papers,* vols. 1 and 7, 1742

A True Copy of the Whole Printed Acts of the General Assemblies of the Church of Scotland, 1682

Turner, Sir James, *Memoirs of his own Life and Times,* 1829

Warriston, Sir Archibald Johnston of, *Diary 1650–1654,* ed. D. Hay Fleming

Whitelocke, Bulstrode, *Memorials of English Affairs,* vols. 3–4, 1853

Whitelocke, Bulstrode, *Diary,* ed., R. Spalding, 1990

Secondary Works

Abernethy, G. R., 'The English Presbyterians and the Stuart Restoration', 1648–16663, in *Transactions of the American Philosophical Society,* vol. 55 part 2, 1965

Balfour-Paul, Sir James, *The Scots Peerage,* vol. 5, 1908

Barbour, V., *Henry Bennet, Earl of Arlington,* 1914

Beattie, C., 'The Political Disqualification of Noblemen's Heirs in Seventeenth Century Scotland', in *Scottish Historical Review,* vol. 60, 1980, pp. 174–7

Brown, L. F., *The First Earl of Shaftesbury,* 1933

Bruce, J., *Report on the Circumstances which Produced a Union of England and Scotland,* 1799

Buckroyd, J., 'The Dismissal of Archbishop Alexander Burnet, 1669', in *Records of the Scottish Church History Society*, vol. 18, 1972–4, pp. 149–55

Buckroyd, J., *Church and State in Scotland, 1660–1681*, 1980

Buckroyd, J., 'Anti-Clericalism in Scotland during the Restoration', in N Macdougall ed., *Church, Politics and Society: Scotland, 1408–1929*, 1983

Buckroyd, J., 'Bridging the Gap: Scotland, 1659–60', in *Scottish Historical Review*, vol. 66, 1987, pp. 1–25

Buckroyd, J., *The Life of James Sharp, Archbishop of St Andrews, 1618–1679*, 1987

Burghclere, W., *George Villars, Second Duke of Buckingham, 1628–1687*, 1903

Butler, D., *The Life and Letters of Robert Leighton*, 1903

Carleton, C., *Charles I – the Personal Monarch*, 1995 edn

Carte, T., *A History of the Life of James Duke of Ormonde*, vol. 2, 1736

Chambers, R., *Domestic Annals of Scotland*, vol. 2 1859

Christie, W. D., *A Life of Anthony Ashley Cooper, First Earl of Shaftesbury*, 1871

Clarke, T. E. S., and Foxcroft, H. C., *A Life of Gilbert Burnet*, 1907

The Complete Peerage, vol. 7, 1929

Cowan, E. J., *Montrose*, 1977

Cowan, I. B., 'The Covenanters – a *Revision* Article', in *Scottish Historical Review*, vol. 47, 1968, pp. 35–52

Cowan, I. B., *The Scottish Covenanters, 1660–1688*, 1976

Cripps, D., *Elizabeth of the Sealed Knot*, 1975

Cunningham, A., *The Loyal Clans*, 1932

Davies, G., and Hardacre, P. H., 'The Restoration of the Scottish Episcopacy', in *Journal of British Studies*, vol. 1, 1961–2, pp. 32–53

Dewar, R., 'Burnet on the Scottish Troubles', in *Scottish Historical Review*, vol. 4, 1907 pp. 384–8

The Dictionary of National Biography

Donaldson, G., *Scotland – James V to James VII*, 1965

Dunbar, J. G., 'The Building Activities of the Duke and Duchess of Lauderdale, 1670–1682', in *The Archaeological Journal*, vol. 132, 1975 pp. 202–30

Elder, J. R., *The Highland Host of 1678*, 1914

Fea, A., *After Worcester Fight*, 1904

Feilding, K., *A History of the Tory Party, 1640–1714*, 1924

Ferguson, W., *Scotland's Relations with England: a Survey to 1707*, 1977

Foster, W. R., *Bishop and Presbytery. The Church of Scotland, 1661–1688*, 1958

Fraser, A., *Cromwell Our Chief of Men*, 1973

Gardiner, S. R., *History of the Great Civil War*, vols. 2–4, 1893

Gardiner, S. R., *Oliver Cromwell*, 1901

Gardiner, W. B., 'The Later Years of John Maitland, Second Earl and First Duke of Lauderdale', in *Journal of Modern History*, vol. 20, 1948, pp. 113–22

Haley, K. H. D., *The First Earl of Shaftesbury*, 1968

Hartmann, C. H., *Clifford of the Cabal*, 1937

Henderson, G. D., *Religious Life in Seventeenth Century Scotland*, 1937

Hewison, J. K., *The Covenanters*, 2 vols., 1913

Hopkins, P., *Glencoe and the End of the Highland War*, 1986

Hughes, E., 'The Negotiations for a Commercial Treaty between England and Scotland in 1668', in *Scottish Historical Review*, vol. 24, 1927, pp. 30–47

Hutton, R., *Charles the Second, King of England, Scotland and Ireland*, 1989

Jones, J. R., The Scottish Constitutional Opposition in 1673, in *Scottish Historical Review*, vol. 37, 1958, pp. 37–41

Jones, J. R., *The First Whigs – The Politics of the Exclusion Crisis, 1678–1683*, 1961

Jones, J. R., 'Main Trends in Restoration England', in J. R. Jones ed., *The Restored Monarchy, 1660–1688*, 1979

Kaplan, L., *Politics and Religion during the English Revolution – the Scots and the Long Parliament, 1643–1645*, 1976

Laing, M., *History of Scotland*, 1800

Lamb, J. A., 'Archbishop Alexander Burnet, 1614–1684', in *Records of the Scottish Church History Society*, vol. 11, 1955, pp. 133–148

Lang, A., *History of Scotland*, vol. 3, 1904

Lang, A., *Sir George Mackenzie*, 1909

'Lauderdale MSS in the British Museum,' in *Quarterly Review*, vol. 157, 1984, pp. 407–39

Lee, M., *The Cabal*, 1959a

Lee, M., *John Maitland of Thirlestane and the Foundation of Stewart Despotism in Scotland*, 1959b

Lee, M., *The Road to Revolution: Scotland under Charles I*, 1985

Lee, M., 'Retreat from Revolution: the Scottish Parliament and the Restoration Monarchy', in J. R. Young, ed., *Celtic Dimensions of the British Civil Wars*, 1997, pp. 185–204

Lindsay, Alexander William, Lord, *Lives of the Lindsays*, vol. 2, 1849

Lindsay, Alexander William, Lord, *A Memoir of Lady Anna Mackenzie*, 1868

Macaulay, T. B., *Critical and Historical Essays*, vol. 1, 1850

Macaulay, T. B., *History of England*, ed. C. H. Firth, vol. 2, 1913–5

McCoy, F. N., *Robert Baillie and the Second Scots Reformation*, 1974

Macinnes, A., *Clanship, Commerce and the House of Stuart, 1603–1788*, 1996

Macphail, J. R. N., ed., *Highland Papers*, vol. 1, 1914

Mackenzie, W. C., *The Life and Times of John Maitland, Duke of Lauderdale*, 1923

Mitchison, R., *Lordship to Patronage – Scotland, 1603–1745*, 1983

Mathieson, W. L., *Politics and Religion: a Study in Scottish History from the Reformation to the Revolution*, 2 vols., 1902

Mathieson, W.L. 'The Scottish Parliament, 1560–1707', in *Scottish Historical Review*, vol. 4, 1907, pp. 49–62

Mentieth, R., *The History of the Troubles of Great Britain*, 1735

Mulligan, L., 'Peace Negotiations, Politics and the Committee of Both Kingdoms', in *History Journal*, vol. 12, 1969, pp. 3–22

Mulligan, L., 'The Scottish Alliance and the Committee of Both Kingdoms", in *Historical Studies,* vol. 14, 1970, pp. 173–88

Ogg, D., *England in the Reign of Charles II,* 1955

Orr, R. L., *Alexander Henderson – Churchman and Statesman,* 1919

Paterson, R. C., *A Land Afflicted. Scotland and the Covenanter Wars, 1638–1690,* 1998

Paterson, R. C., *No Tragic Story. The Fall of the House of Campbell,* 2001

Paterson, R. C., 'King of Scotland: Lauderdale and the Restoration North of the Border', in *History Today,* January 2003, pp.21–7

Patrick, J., 'The Origins of the Opposition to Lauderdale in the Scottish Parliament of 1673', in *Scottish Historical Review,* vol. 53, 1974, pp. 1–21

Patrick, J., 'A Union Broken? Restoration Politics in Scotland', in J. Wormald, ed., *Scotland Revisited,* 1991

Rait, R. S., *The Parliaments of Scotland,* 1924

Ranke, Leopold von, *A History of England,* vol. 3, 1875

Roundell, C., *Ham House, its History and Architecture,* vol. 1, 1904

Rubenstein, H. L., *Captain Luckless – James, First Duke of Hamilton,* 1975

Russell, E., *Maitland of Lethington,* 1912

Sadler, Sir Ralph, *State Papers and Letters,* vol. 1, 1809

The Scots Peerage, vols. 5 and 8

Scott, E., *The King in Exile,* 1905

Stevenson, D., *The Scottish Revolution ?*

Stevenson, D., *Revolution and Counter – Revolution in Scotland,* 1977

Terry, C. S., *The Scottish Parliament – Its Constitution and Procedures, 1603–1707,* 1905

Thomson, A., *Lauder and Lauderdale,* 1902

Robertson, A., *The Life of Sir Robert Moray,* 1922

Wedgewood, C. V., *The King's Peace,* 1997

Wedgewwod, C, V., *The King's War, 1997*

Willcock, J., *A Scots Earl in Covenanting Times,* 1907

Wodrow, R., *History of the Sufferings of the Church of Scotland from the Restoration to the Revolution,* 4 vols., 1829–30

Wood, J. P., *The Peerage of Scotland,* 1813

Unpublished Academic Theses

Beattie, C. M., *The Early Political Career of John Maitland, Duke of Lauderdale, 1637–1651,* McGill University MA Thesis, 1977

Hamilton, C. C., *The Covenanters and Parliament,* Cornell University PhD Thesis, 1959

Lennox, R. W., *Lauderdale and Scotland: A Study in Restoration Politics and Administration,* Columbia University PhD Thesis, 1977

Pocus, P. P. *Gilbert Burnet: A Case Study in the Genesis and Development of Revolutionary Consciousness and Activism in Late Stuart England,* University of Chicago PhD Thesis, 1988.

INDEX